THIS BOOK is for Ntsiki, Mamphela, Thenjiwe, Nohle, Malusi, Thami, Mxolisi, Hlaku, Percy, Aelred, Beyers, Theo, David, Cedric, Peter, and all our friends now banned, exiled, detained or dead.

BIKO

DONALD WOODS

PADDINGTON
PRESS LTD
NEW YORK & LONDON

Library of Congress Cataloging in Publication Data
Woods, Donald, 1933–
   Biko

   Includes index.
   1. Biko, B. S.   2. Political Prisoners – South
   Africa – Biography.   3. Woods, Donald, 1933–
   4. Journalists – South Africa – Biography.
   5. South Africa – Race Relations.   I. Title
   DT779.8.B48W66   322.4'4'0924 (B)   78–1882
   ISBN 0 448 23169 7

Filmset in England by SX Composing Ltd., Rayleigh,
Essex
Printed and Bound in the United States
Designed by Colin Lewis

In The United States
PADDINGTON PRESS
Distributed by
GROSSET & DUNLAP

In The United Kingdom
PADDINGTON PRESS

In Canada
Distributed by
RANDOM HOUSE OF CANADA LTD.

79-79

CONTENTS

IN MEMORIAM

The following South Africans are known to have died in detention in the hands of the Nationalist government's Security Police. All were imprisoned without trial, charge, prosecution or evidence. All were denied legal representation and access to friends or relatives. The causes of death alleged by the Security Police are given in brackets.

L. NGUDLE died in Pretoria on September 5, 1963 (suicide by hanging)

B. MERHOPE died in Worcester on September 19, 1963 (causes undisclosed)

J. TYITYA died in Port Elizabeth on January 24, 1964 (suicide by hanging)

S. SALOOJIE died in Johannesburg on September 9, 1964 (fell seven floors during interrogation)

N. GAGA died in Transkei on May 7, 1965 (natural causes)

P. HOYE died in Transkei on May 8, 1965 (natural causes)

J. HAMAKWAYO died in Pretoria in 1966 (suicide by hanging)

H. SHONYEKA died in Pretoria on October 9, 1966 (suicide)

L. LEONG PIN died in Pretoria on November 19, 1966 (suicide by hanging)

A. AH YAN died in Pretoria on January 5, 1967 (suicide by hanging)

A. MADIBA died in an undisclosed prison on September 9, 1967 (suicide by hanging)

J. TUBAKWE died in Pretoria on September 11, 1967 (suicide by hanging)

AN UNNAMED PERSON died on an unknown day in 1968 (death disclosed under questioning in Parliament on January 28, 1969)

N. KGOATHE died in Pretoria on February 4, 1969 (slipped in shower)

S. MODIPANE died in prison on February 28, 1969 (slipped in shower)

J. LENKOE died in Pretoria on March 10, 1969 (suicide by hanging)

C. MAYEKISO died in Port Elizabeth on June 17, 1969 (suicide)

J. MONAKGOTLA died in Pretoria on September 10, 1969 (thrombosis)

IMAM A. HARON died in Cape Town on September 27, 1969 (fell down stairs)

M. CUTHSELA died in undisclosed prison on January 21, 1971 (natural causes)

A. TIMOL died in Johannesburg on October 27, 1971 (leapt from tenth-floor window during interrogation)

J. MDLULI died in Durban on March 19, 1976 (fell against chair during scuffle)

M. MOHAPI died in Kei Road on August 5, 1976 (suicide by hanging)

L. MAZWEMBE died in Cape Town on September 2, 1976 (suicide by hanging)

D. MBATHA died in undisclosed prison on September 25, 1976 (suicide by hanging)

E. MZOLO died in Johannesburg on October 1, 1976 (no details given)

W. TSHWANE died on October 14, 1976 (no details given)

E. MAMASILA died on November 18, 1976 (no details given)

T. MOSALA died in Butterworth on November 26, 1976 (no details given)

W. TSHAZIBANE died on December 11, 1976 (no details given)

G. BOTHA died in Port Elizabeth on December 14, 1976 (fell down stairwell)

DR. N. NTSHUNTSHA died on January 9, 1977 (no details given)

L. NDZAGA died on January 9, 1977 (no details given)

E. MALEL died on January 20, 1977 (no details given)

M. MABELANE died on February 15, 1977 (no details given)

T. JOYI died on February 15, 1977 (no details given)

S. MALINGA died in Maritzburg on February 22, 1977 (natural causes)

R. KHOZA died in Maritzburg on March 26, 1977 (suicide by hanging)

J. MASHABANE died on June 5, 1977 (suicide)

P. MABIJA died in Kimberley on July 7, 1977 (fell six floors during interrogation)

E. LOZA died in Cape Town on August 1, 1977 (no details given)

DR. H. HAFFEJEE died in Durban on August 3, 1977 (no details given)

B. EMZIZI died on August 5, 1977 (no details given)

F. MOGATUSI died on August 28, 1977 (suffocation in epileptic fit)

S. BIKO died in Pretoria on September 12, 1977 (injured in scuffle)

AFRICAN ANTHEM

Nkosi Sikelel' i Afrika
God bless Africa
Malupakam' upondo lwayo
Raise up her spirit
Yiva imitandazo yetu
Hear our prayers
Usi – sikelele
And bless us

Sikelel' amadol' asizwe
Bless the leaders
Sikelela kwa nomlisela
Bless also the young
Ulitwal' ilizwe ngomonde
That they may carry the land with patience
Uwusikilele
And that you may bless them

Sikelel' amalinga etu
Bless our efforts
Awonanyana nokuzaka
To unite and lift ourselves up
Awemfundo nemvisiswano
Through learning and understanding
Uwasikelele
And bless them

Yihla Moya! Yihla Moya!
Descend Spirit! Descend Spirit!
Yihla Moya Oyingcwele
Descend, Holy Spirit!

INTRODUCTION

On Tuesday, September 6, 1977, a close friend of mine named Bantu Stephen Biko was taken by South African political police to Room 619 of the Sanlam Building in Strand Street, Port Elizabeth, Cape Province, where he was handcuffed, put into leg irons, chained to a grille and subjected to twenty-two hours of interrogation in the course of which he was tortured and beaten, sustaining several blows to the head which damaged his brain fatally, causing him to lapse into a coma and die six days later.

The fatal blows were struck by one or more of the following members of the South African Security Police: Colonel P. Goosen; Major H. Snyman; Warrant Officers J. Beneke, R. Marx, B. Coetzee, J. Fouche; Captain D. Siebert; Lieutenant W. Wilken; Sergeant S. Nieuwoudt and Major T. Fischer. Most, if not all, of these men were members of two interrogation "teams" – one operating by day and one by night. Detainees with personal experience of Security Police methods say the day interrogation teams specialize in coordinated questioning, psychological tactics and verbal abuse, but that the night teams are the assaulters, beating up detainees to "soften them up" for the day teams. If this procedure was followed against Steve Biko, the fatal blows were struck by one or more of the "night team" – Wilken, Coetzee and Fouche.

However, these men were simply agents. The man ultimately responsible for the death of Steve Biko was James Thomas Kruger, Minister of Police, because it was his indulgent attitude toward the homicidal tendencies of his Security Police that created the atmosphere within which the torturers were given scope to act. Kruger cannot validly claim to have known nothing of these matters, because two years previously I had warned him that there were criminal elements in his Security Police.

On the same occasion I told him of the importance of Steve Biko and later published a warning that if any harm came to him in detention, the consequences would be disastrous for the entire nation, and in particular for the Nationalist government. Mr. Kruger and his colleagues ignored this warning. Not only was Steve Biko detained several times, but he was increasingly persecuted, harrassed, put into solitary confinement and ultimately tortured and killed.

Kruger immediately implied that Steve had starved himself to death, but I knew this was nonsense. Steve and I had had a pact that if he should be detained, if he should die in detention, and if it should be claimed that he had taken his own life, I would know this to be untrue. Clearly, he had been killed by Security Police under the powers granted to them by the Nationalist government.

Therefore, in addition to being a personal testimony to Steve Biko, this book is an indictment of the Nationalist government and of the policy and the system it represents.

Steve Biko's death echoed around the world. He was only thirty years old when he died, and he had lived in obscurity, silenced from public utterance by banning orders and restricted to a small town remote from the metropolitan areas. He was forbidden to make speeches; forbidden to speak with more than one person at a time; forbidden to be quoted; forbidden to function fully as a political personality. Yet in his short lifetime he influenced the lives and ideals of millions of his countrymen, and his death convulsed our nation and reverberated far beyond its boundaries.

What made him so remarkable? What was so special about his life and his death? This book is an attempt to answer these questions from at least one perspective. It is an inadequate account, and others are better qualified to render it. One of them will surely write the definitive biography of Steve Biko. Many others who knew Steve closely could contribute to the fleshing out of this striking personality, and many books will be written about him in the course of the next few years as appreciation of his historical importance grows. Some will concentrate on his official writings and speeches, while others will be more chronologically biographical. The more books written about Steve Biko the better, because the more that is known about him the more the significance of the man will be acknowledged. This book is, above all else, intended as a personal tribute by one who was privileged to be his friend.

It was written in difficult circumstances. The manuscript was begun on November 1, 1977, ten days after I myself had been banned for helping to raise a public outcry throughout South Africa over Steve's death. I was placed under surveillance in my home and ordered to write nothing for five years under threat of imprisonment. The manuscript had, therefore, to be written in secret, subject to frequent interruptions and alarms, since every knock at the door and every approaching footfall could mean the arrival of Security Police. They had warned me that they would come at any time of day or night to ensure that I was not breaking the ban by writing or by being with more than one person in a room other than members of my immediate family.

Looking back over a diary note I made at the time of beginning the manuscript, I find that I wrote: "This account is set down in haste, while the tragedy of Steve's death is still painfully fresh in my mind, and it is done under threat of possible Security Police intrusion at any time. Given these strange circumstances, I will try to render as faithful a testimony to the greatness of Steve Biko as is possible at this abnormal time in this abnormal society."

Only my wife and eldest child, fourteen-year-old Jane, knew what I was doing, apart from a friend in London to whom sections of the manuscript were sent for conveyance to my publishers, Paddington Press. Parts of the manuscript were smuggled in personal baggage by friends flying to London and others were sent by ordinary air freight at risk of security police spot-checks on all outgoing mail.

Within two months the manuscript was complete and safely received in London. But by that time the nature of it was such that there was no device by which its authorship could be disguised, so it became one of the reasons why I and my family had to go into exile on New Year's Eve of 1977. Initially I had had the unrealistic hope that the manuscript might be published under the guise of a collection of memoirs of Steve used "against my will" from material allegedly written before my ban, in the hope that such a fictional device might lessen the penalties imposed on me for its publication abroad. But as the work progressed it became increasingly obvious that I could withhold nothing of my own involvement from the book to the extent necessary for such legalistic deception.

At the same time, events were increasingly compelling me to consider going into exile for several other reasons. The banning orders served on me on October 19, 1977, were identical to those which had been served on Steve Biko some years before. I could no longer edit my newspaper, the *Daily Dispatch*, because the ban prevented me from writing for any publication and from entering all printing establishments, factories, schools, and educational premises, from leaving the magisterial district of East London, Cape Province, from being quoted and from all social or other gatherings involving more than two persons.

Up until October 19, we editors in South Africa had clear lines established within which we could criticize apartheid. There were more than twenty statutes governing what we could publish and we had to be careful at all times to stay within these limits. But on October 19, Police Minister Kruger tore up all these rules when he banned me, detained my fellow editor and friend Percy Qoboza, and closed down Percy's paper, *The World*, without even a pretense at legal process of any kind.

I had always vowed that if the Nationalist government ever made it impossible for me to function as a critic of apartheid, I would seek the next best method of opposing the regime without violence. By the time the ban had entered its third month it was clear that this would involve self-exile.

My wife and I felt that by going into exile we could add our voices and witness in the international forum to those of others seeking a peaceful end to apartheid through external pressure, and we decided that when the book was ready for publication we would leave South Africa, knowing we could return only after the downfall of the existing regime.

But again events compelled us to accelerate our plans. Our youngest child, five-year-old Mary, was sent an acid-impregnated T-shirt through the post by right-wing terrorists. Although we had lived for more than ten years under threat of attack by such people, the Vorster government's November election gains appeared to encourage the right-wing extremists to further excesses. Other banned people were attacked by them. There was a shotgun blast through the front door of the Meer family in Durban. We ourselves had had five revolver shots fired into the front of our house. But such attacks appeared to increase as the year drew to a close, and there was every indication that these attacks came from members of the Security Police. Clear evidence existed that the two men involved in the shootings into our house were Security Police officers G. Cilliers and J. Jooste and that the men responsible for the T-shirt incident were Security Police officers L. Van Schalkwyk and J. Marais. Such evidence was handed to the regular police but it was soon clear that they would take no action against their colleagues in the political sector of the force.

It was, therefore, for a number of reasons, not least among them the prospect of the consequences which would follow the publication of this book, that we decided to flee into exile.

It was a painful decision. It meant leaving friends and relatives without bidding them farewell, since preknowledge might have implicated them in our escape; leaving our beautiful home, which we had designed ourselves, and leaving our country (which our forebears had settled several generations ago) in the sad knowledge that we could not return until the long fight against apartheid was over.

My wife and I made our decision on the morning of Wednesday,

December 28. The following evening, as it began to grow dark, I crouched on the floor of the car inside our garage. My wife opened the garage door and reversed out, driving past where the security police "observer" was usually posted, creating the impression that she was alone in the car. Beyond the city limits I got out and hitch-hiked (in disguise and with my hair dyed) to near the Lesotho border, where with the help of black sympathizers I was guided to the Telle River and crossed to gain political asylum in the Lesotho capital of Maseru. The rest of my family crossed the border through the passport control point by car several hours later, having left in the early hours of the following morning with their departure timed to coincide with my crossing of the river. We were all in Lesotho before my absence from home was discovered by the Security Police.

Unfortunately the full story of our escape cannot be told at this time, because the Security Police would thereby be enabled to trace my helpers. It is a story of such courage and self-sacrifice by the latter, and a story of such remarkable chance and coincidence in a number of respects, that I hope one day it can safely be recounted in tribute to those who rendered brotherhood and aid when it was most needed. What can be said now is this: for me that journey to the border was the most frightening experience of my life, involving eight hours of unbroken tension, dread of roadblocks around every bend and constant concern over whether my wife and children could join me safely in refuge.

From Lesotho we flew by charter aircraft to Gaberone, Botswana, from there to Lusaka, Zambia, and from there to London. The welcome we received in Lesotho, Botswana and Zambia was heartwarming to us as white Africans, and on the eve of our departure from Lusaka for London, President Kaunda gave a dinner for us in State House.

On arrival in London, I settled down to edit the manuscript, and this book is the result. It is a portrait of Steve Biko as I knew him and as I saw his significance as a leader of our people. It is arranged in six parts. The first seeks to explain the background of South African history which produced his philosophy. The second deals with his personality, thoughts and human qualities. The third is a record of what he advocated. The fourth recounts the circumstances in which he died. The fifth records the inquest which followed and the sixth is an indictment of his killers.

This book is written as objectively as grief and anger in bereavement permits, because Steve Biko's significance to Africa and to the cause of freedom everywhere is more important for the reader to understand than his loss to me as a friend. But for whatever lack of objectivity it contains in consequence of the sense of outrage which motivates it, no apology is offered to anyone.

1: THE BACKGROUND
THE WHITE SETTLERS

BECAUSE STEVE BIKO was uniquely a product of South Africa and its history it is necessary to give a short synopsis of that history, with particular emphasis on those elements of it which influenced his stance and philosophy.

Recorded history in South Africa begins with the arrival of white settlers in 1652, when the Dutch established a sailing base where the city of Cape Town is now situated. But the country's history of human habitation extends far back in time, and archaeologists have found traces here of some of the earliest human habitation on this planet. When the Dutch settlers arrived they found the Cape area and hinterland inhabited by sallow-skinned hunters and herders, the Khoisan. Much of the interior of the country was inhabited by Negroid Bantu-speaking tribesmen. School-children in South Africa are taught that the arrival of the white settlers coincided with the arrival of these "Bantu" tribesmen, but radiocarbon dating provides evidence of Negroid communities in the Transvaal as early as the fifth century A.D. The southward migration of the Bantu-speakers to the shores of the country was considerable in the fourteenth century, and they were certainly established as far as the Gamtoos River in the Cape Province by the fifteenth century.

White settlements at the Cape Peninsula were augmented by parties of German and French settlers, the latter being Huguenots fleeing from religious persecution in Europe. These groups fused, in time, into a single white cultural group which evolved its own language, Afrikaans, and whose descendants came to be known as Afrikaners. The Afrikaans language derived from Dutch, with some German influences, and was a simplification of these European languages. It grew more distinctively practical as these whites settled further inland away from the Table Bay harbor and the European influences brought there by the sailing ships which called en route to the East.

In 1814 the British annexed the entire colony as part of a post-Napoleonic deal involving Britain, Holland and Sweden. The British brought in four thousand British settlers (including my great-great-grandfather) in 1820, to settle the Eastern Cape area as a buffer zone between the mutually hostile Afrikaner farmers and black tribesmen. The British also abolished slavery and gave in to the demands of two settler journalists, Thomas Pringle and John Fairbairn, for press freedom. For a number of reasons, including the abolition of slavery and what the Afrikaners regarded as too liberal a policy toward blacks by the British colonial government, many of the Afrikaners migrated from the colony into the hinterland in what became known as the Great Trek. They established two independent republics, one in the north (Transvaal) and one in the central area of the country (Orange Free State), the latter named for the Netherlands royal family, the House of Orange.

By the dawn of the twentieth century, the British had control of the two coastal provinces, Cape Province and Natal, and the Afrikaners had control of the two northern republics. The discovery in the Transvaal of the world's richest reef of gold brought prospectors and miners from all ends of the earth, mostly from English-speaking countries – Britain, the United States, Canada, Australia and New Zealand. This posed a new problem for the Afrikaner leader Paul Kruger, president of the Transvaal republic, because these newcomers now constituted a majority outnumbering the Afrikaners in this area. These people, referred to by Kruger as the Uitlanders (foreigners), clamored for civil rights and particularly the vote, claiming that they provided most of the Transvaal's revenue and were entitled to full citizenship. Their demands were backed up by the British colonial government, whose zeal for the civil rights of their kith and kin was influenced considerably by the prospect of gold revenues for Queen Victoria.

In a tragic foreshadowing of what a future Afrikaner leader, Vorster, would do, Kruger refused all significant negotiations with the clamoring majority, persistently offering too little too late in the way of concessions. Eventually the situation exploded into violence – the Anglo-Boer War – which exacted a ghastly toll of life. More than twenty thousand Afrikaner women and children died of disease and neglect in wretched concentration camps where they were quartered after the British burned down their farmsteads to prevent their feeding and harboring of the Afrikaner guerrillas who were harassing the imperial forces.

Shortly after the end of the war the British handed all of South Africa back to what it regarded as a united white nation under Afrikaner leaders Louis Botha and Jan Smuts. The two former Afrikaner republics and the two former British colonies were united in the Act of Union and given full independence in 1910 as one sovereign state, the Union of South Africa, in which Afrikaners now constituted a majority of whites. Given the historic background of the two white groups that were to share control of the country, the Afrikaners and the English-speakers (roughly 60 and 40 percent respectively), this was a simplistic and superficial formula for the future. And given the historical and political background of the vast black majority whose own aspirations were virtually ignored in this dispensation, the formula was one for future racial disaster.

Black politics up until 1910 was hardly an issue in white political thinking in South Africa. At the time of union only the Cape Province insisted on retaining voting rights for blacks on a basis of qualified franchise as introduced by the British colonial regime. The two Afrikaner republics had granted no political rights to blacks, and Natal was scarcely less conservative. Yet what minimal rights for blacks were provided for in the 1910 formula were not only destined not to be developed, but were actually whittled away.

In 1913 legislation pegged black land ownership rights to specific areas totaling barely 10 percent of the entire national territory, and successive onslaughts on black rights intensified with the birth of Afrikaner nationalism as articulated by the founder of the Nationalist party, former Boer General James Hertzog. Hertzog realized that Afrikaners formed a 60 percent majority within the white community and that by exploiting their racial conservatism he could oust Botha and Smuts and achieve control of the country. He therefore founded the Nationalist party in 1914 in opposition to the more moderate policies of Botha and Smuts. The twin formula of Afrikaner chauvinism and antiblack bigotry was so successful in electoral terms that his party came to power in the election of 1924 in coalition with a racist white Labor party largely representative of white miners.

Legislatively this signaled the start of a program of apartheid, or racial discrimination enshrined in statute, although the most extreme forms of this were to be enacted by Hertzog's political successors in 1948. Hertzog had certain inhibitions his successors did not have, including reservations about tearing up clauses of the 1910 constitution dealing with the voting rights of "Coloureds" (mulattoes) in the Cape Province. Besides, Hertzog's plans were set back when Smuts capitalized on anti-Hitler feeling in the South African Parliament in 1939 and forced a vote which toppled Hertzog from power. By the end of the Hitler war, Hertzog was dead and his political heir as leader of the Nationalist party, Daniel Malan, used the old Hertzog formula of Afrikaner chauvinism and antiblack bigotry to win power in the election of 1948.

The Nationalist party has been in power ever since, and for thirty years has systematically and ruthlessly implemented the racial policy of apartheid which has earned the regime the revulsion of the world and the hatred of the black masses within the apartheid State.

THE BLACK RESPONSE

MEANWHILE, WHAT OF BLACK POLITICS in South Africa? What of the black response, first to white settlement and later to the legislative tightening of the apartheid screws? The first major black reaction to white expansionism from the Cape settlement was war. Over a period of a hundred years, from 1779, no fewer than nine wars were fought between Xhosa tribesmen and frontier farmers. Although the blacks were vastly superior in numbers, the spear was no match for the musket, and Xhosa military power was broken by the end of the nineteenth century. The other major black group, the Zulus, waged fierce war in Natal before going down to British weaponry in 1879.

For the next hundred years the black political response to white power was generally conciliatory, the overall aim of successive black political organizations being to bring the white rulers to the negotiating table for a fair dispensation in a shared society. From the beginning, the Eastern Cape was the fountainhead of black politics, partly because it was the home of black education in South Africa. Educational institutions such as Fort Hare University, Lovedale Institute and Healdtown College produced black leaders not only for South Africa but for countries as far afield as Kenya, Tanzania, Malawi and Zambia. This educational foundry cast all the leaders of the first black liberation movements, Dr. T. Jabavu, Dr. A. B. Xuma, P. Mzimba, E. Makiwane, W. Rubusana, A. K. Soga, J. Dube, M. Pelemi, J. Gumede and P. Seme, and in the stormy era since the Nationalist party's accession to power in 1948, all the three most important black leaders to emerge were Eastern Cape men – Nelson Mandela, Robert Sobukwe and Steve Biko.

Ironically, the first manifestation of black political activity was when a substantial body of black voters qualified for the Cape franchise in 1869 to assist a white candidate, George Wood, to gain election to the legislative assembly. In at least one constituency in the Cape, black voters helped a white candidate to victory over a black candidate, and first indications were that the black vote would not be cast racially. However, this nonracial attitude did not persist in the face of white moves to raise the voting qualifications as black voters grew more numerous, and blacks turned increasingly to all-black associations and organizations functioning as pressure groups. For a long time these black pressure groups tried to lobby the white politicians in power to permit black participation in national affairs, but failure to make satisfactory headway spurred black leaders to seek aid abroad for their cause. After a conference in King William's Town in 1887, Dr. T. Jabavu founded the Cape Native Convention, as whose delegate he was to travel to London in 1909 to contest the racial formula through which Britain intended to grant full independence to the Union of South Africa.

His mission a failure, Jabavu returned to a climate of considerable black anger within the country over the terms of the proposed Act of Union. A black lawyer named Seme drew away a number of Jabavu's followers into a more militant black organization called the South African Native National Congress. Supporting Seme were influential black leaders such as Rubusana, Pelemi, Mapikela, Makgatho, Mangena, Msimang and Dr. J. L. Dube, an American-trained disciple of Booker T. Washington. Jabavu stayed out of the new body, and set up his own South African Races Congress as a separate organization, pinning his hopes on the good faith of white liberals in the Cape power hierarchy. Both Botha and Smuts were already feeling the force of Hertzog's appeal on the race issue, and introduced the 1913 Land Bill designating racial land zones (the birth of territorial apartheid).

Jabavu, believing the land segregation plan would be of benefit to blacks, backed the bill. The Native National Congress split over the issue, its members dividing behind Dube, who had no objection to segregation in principle, and Makgatho, who rejected it and gained the support of the majority, succeeding to the presidency in 1917. This development foreshadowed a future era in which some black leaders would accept the "homeland" policy of territorial segregation and be criticized as "sellouts" for settling for less than full black rights throughout South Africa.

The first tragic effect of the land segregation policy was the Bulhoek Massacre of 1921, when a group of blacks refused to budge from land they had squatted on at Bulhoek, near Queenstown, and charged a police patrol sent to evict them. The police patrol opened fire and cut them down –

another foreshadowing, this time of the charge on the police station at Sharpeville, Transvaal, in 1960, which ended in the same sort of massacre.

From time to time in South Africa's Nationalist era, black anger and frustration was to break out in similar manifestations, the most recent on a large scale being the Soweto riots of 1976, but the end results were the same as in the frontier wars. Stones, like spears, are no match for guns.

The Native National Congress became more aggressive between 1917 and 1924, turning to passive resistance and strikes – methods later to be tried by the African National Congress and the Pan-Africanist Congress – but strikes require financial resources to sustain the strikers for any significant length of time, and sheer grinding poverty caused the collapse of every black strike attempt. One of the more successful strike leaders was Clements Kadalie, an expatriate Malawian, and the main inspiration for passive resistance was a Natal lawyer, Mohandas Gandhi, later to achieve fame as the Mahatma who rid India of British rule through the passive resistance methods he had evolved in South Africa.

By this time, in addition to all the other complex problems occasioned by politically encouraged awareness of racial differences among black and white, Afrikaner and English-descended, and so-called "Coloureds" (mixed-blood descendants of union between black and white), South Africa now had in addition what was called an "Indian problem," as well as a "Chinese problem." Indians had been brought to South Africa as cheap labor for the sugarcane fields of Natal, and Chinese to work the goldmines. After objections from white miners many of the latter were repatriated, but some numbers remained. Efforts to repatriate Indians were less successful, so that today there are almost a million South Africans of Indian descent, mostly in Natal. Gandhi first came to prominence in the fight against discriminatory measures by Jan Smuts against Indians, and it was due to his zealous groundwork that the vigorous South African Indian Congress came into being in 1923.

The following year, 1924, brought a new urgency to the black and "Indian" political movements, because 1924 saw the first coming to power of Afrikaner nationalism. Hertzog's government in its fifteen years (the last six in coalition with the former Botha-Smuts party, the South African party, after economic misgovernment in the depression years had cost Hertzog a governing margin of support) laid the legislative foundation for the massive structure of apartheid laws the 1948 Nationalists would erect. The Hertzog government not only put a stop to all prospects of black political advancement in a common society, but put such prospects into reverse. Indirect black representation in the central Parliament was limited to a small handful of seats – occupied by whites.

By this time the African National Congress had been constituted from the pioneering efforts of the Native National Congress, and it was to spearhead the black cause for the next forty years as the undisputed articulator of black political aspirations. Under Chief Albert Luthuli and later Nelson Mandela, two towering giants of the black liberation movement in the stormy years of the post-1948 Nationalist administration, the ANC gained massive support throughout the country.

STEVE BIKO'S PREDECESSORS

IT WAS ONLY WHEN Mandela's patience in appealing to whites for compromise was exhausted that a split occurred in the popular movement. Mandela decided that future appeals to reason were a waste of time and that only violence could jolt Afrikaner nationalism out of its refusal to negotiate. The violence campaign was to start with selective sabotage of electricity pylons and power stations. If the Nationalist government remained obdurate, police stations and military installations would be the next targets. If this made no significant impression, the violence would escalate if necessary into full civil war. To launch this program, Mandela toured Africa in search of aid and declared he would accept it from any source.

Communist powers needed no second invitation. It had long been part of Russian communist strategy to exploit black discontent anywhere in Africa, and particularly in the south, with its fabulous mineral treasury. Mandela's decision therefore suited the communists admirably. An alliance with the black liberation movement for their own special purposes was something they needed, because communists in South Africa initially had a bad name among blacks on account of the readiness of communist organizers in 1922 to promote white racism in fomenting a strike of miners. With tortuous logic they had tried to justify a strike slogan of "Workers of the world unite, and fight for a white South Africa" by saying that it was necessary to build an alliance between white townsmen and countrymen so that the mining tycoons could be broken – paving the way for later reforms.

The result had been violence between white strikers and black workers, in which thirty of the latter were killed.

The Russian-oriented South African communists saw in Mandela's appeal a chance to gain black favor and further exploit the growing resentment among blacks toward the Western powers, whom blacks felt were more interested in protecting their investment contacts with the apartheid regime than in championing black rights. This trend, too, was a foreshadowing of a similar attitude among blacks in the late 1970s, who felt the Western vetoes against sanctions were based primarily on self-interest in protecting trade and investment.

The communist bloc had long sought black favor by harping on the fact that unlike the West they had no investments in South Africa and no military or business alliances with Nationalism. Mandela's readiness to accept communist help was therefore acted on with alacrity. Firearms, explosives and money were provided. In accepting such aid, Mandela did not adopt communist ideology. He remained a noncommunist and did not commit the ANC to the communist line. However, the alliance between the ANC and the Communist party led to an increasing blurring of policy lines, aided by the socialistic elements in ANC economic policy, to an extent that began to perturb younger members of the movement such as Robert Sobukwe. Sobukwe was worried not only about the growing communist influence over ANC policy but also about the apparently growing influence of whites as such in the alliance – a trend which he saw as diluting the essentially black nature of the struggle. Another foreshadowing, this time of the future Black Consciousness movement which Steve Biko helped to launch.

The break between Sobukwe and Mandela came in 1959, Sobukwe forming the Pan-Africanist Congress and taking with him a substantial number of the young supporters of the ANC. By 1961 both movements had vast followings among the black masses, and in that year both the ANC and PAC were banned. Sobukwe, Mandela and their chief lieutenants were jailed, Mandela for planning the violent overthrow of the Nationalist government. Both were imprisoned on Robben Island in Table Bay. Sobukwe was banned on completion of his sentence and restricted to the remote Kimberley area. Mandela is still on Robben Island, in his fifteenth year of imprisonment, and the Vorster government has stated it will never commute his sentence.

By present South African law Mandela may not be quoted and nobody within the country may repeat his words. Therefore his own countrymen may not debate or discuss his views. That he is a remarkable man, however, can be seen from various speeches by Mandela, excerpts of which are

reproduced here because in my opinion his intellectual readiness to seize
the initiative against his oppressors was typical of the later Biko style.

In his first trial, Mandela was charged on two counts: inciting African
workers to strike (the March 1961 stay-at-home); and leaving South
Africa without a valid travel document. He turned the trial into a scathing
indictment of white domination, and challenged the moral jurisdiction of
the court:

I want to apply for Your Worship's recusal from this case. I challenge the right
of this court to try me. Firstly, I challenge it because I fear that I will not be given
a fair and proper trial. Secondly, I consider myself neither legally nor morally
bound to obey laws made by a Parliament in which I have no representation.
What sort of justice enables the aggrieved to sit in judgment over those against
whom they have laid a charge?

The white man makes all the laws, he drags us before his courts and accuses
us, and he sits in judgment over us. In this courtroom I face a white magistrate,
I am confronted by a white prosecutor, and I am escorted into the dock by a
white orderly. The atmosphere of white domination lurks all around in this
courtroom. It reminds me that I am voteless because there is a Parliament in
this country that is white-controlled. I am without land because the white
minority has taken a lion's share of my country and forced my people to occupy
poverty-stricken reserves, overpopulated and overstocked, in which we are
ravaged by starvation and disease. These courts are not impartial tribunals
dispensing justice but instruments used by the white man to punish those
among us who clamor for deliverance from white rule.

I became a member of the African National Congress in 1944 and I have
followed its aims for eighteen years. It sought the unity of all Africans, overriding tribal differences. It sought the acquisition of political power for Africans
in the land of their birth. The African National Congress further believed that
all people, irrespective of the national groups to which they may belong, and
irrespective of the color of their skins, all people whose home is South Africa
and who believe in the principles of democracy and of the equality of men,
should be treated as Africans; that all South Africans are entitled to live a free
life on the basis of fullest equality of the rights and opportunities in every field,
of full democratic rights, with a direct say in the affairs of the government.

Any thinking African in this country is driven continuously to a conflict
between his conscience and the law. Throughout its fifty years of existence the
African National Congress has done everything possible to bring its demands
to the attention of successive South African governments. But this government
has *set the scene for violence by relying exclusively on violence with which to answer
our people and their demands.* We have been conditioned to our attitudes by
history which is not of our making. We have been conditioned by the history
of white governments in this country to accept the fact that Africans, when they

make their demands powerfully enough to have some chance of success, are met with force and terror from the government.

Government violence can only breed counterviolence. Ultimately, if there is no dawning of sanity on the part of the government the dispute between the government and my people will be settled by force.

I hate all race discrimination, and in my hatred I am sustained by the fact that the overwhelming majority of people, here and abroad, hate it equally. I hate the systematic inculcation in children of color prejudice and I am sustained in that hatred by the fact that the overwhelming majority of people, here and abroad, are with me in that. I hate the racial arrogance which decrees that the good things of life shall be retained as the exclusive right of a minority of the population, which reduces the majority of the population to a position of subservience and inferiority, and maintains them as voteless chattels to work where they are told and behave as they are told by the ruling minority. I am sustained in that hatred by the fact that the overwhelming majority of people both in this country and abroad are with me.

I have done my duty to my people and to South Africa. I have no doubt that posterity will pronounce that I was innocent and that the criminals who should have been brought before this court are the members of this government.

Mandela was sentenced to three years' imprisonment for incitement to strike, and two years' imprisonment on a second charge of leaving South Africa without a valid permit or passport. He began to serve his five-year sentence in Pretoria Central Prison. There he spent twenty-three out of twenty-four hours in solitary confinement in his cell.

On June 11, 1963, the police raided the underground ANC headquarters in Rivonia, a Johannesburg suburb, and arrested Walter Sisulu, Govan Mbeki, Raymond Mhlaba, Ahmed Kathrada, Dennis Goldberg, Lionel Bernstein and others. The Rivonia trial began in October 1963 and Mandela was taken from his cell to join those in the dock facing trial for sabotage and a conspiracy to overthrow the government by revolution and by assisting an armed invasion of South Africa by foreign troops. The leaders were joined by Elias Motsoaledi and Andrew Mlangeni, making nine accused men in all. The prosecution's key witnesses had nearly all been held for long periods in solitary detention. Mandela opened the defense case, and in his statement to court on April 20, 1964, he said he had been one of the founders of Umkonto we Sizwe (Spear of the Nation), the sabotage wing of the ANC:

I am the First Accused. I hold a Bachelor's Degree in Arts and practiced as an attorney in Johannesburg for a number of years in partnership with Oliver Tambo. I am a convicted prisoner serving five years for leaving the country without a permit and for inciting people to go on strike at the end of May 1961.

At the outset, I want to say that the suggestion made by the State in its opening that the struggle in South Africa is under the influence of foreigners or communists is wholly incorrect. I have done whatever I did, both as an individual and as a leader of my people, because of my experience in South Africa and my own African background, not because of what any outsider might have said. In my youth in the Transkei I listened to the elders of my tribe telling stories of the old days. Among the tales they related to me were those of wars fought by our ancestors in defense of the fatherland. I hoped then that life might offer me the opportunity to serve my people and make my own contribution to their freedom struggle. This is what has motivated me in all that I have done in relation to the charges made against me in this case.

Having said this, I must deal with the question of violence. Some of the things so far told to the court are true and some are untrue. I do not, however, deny that I planned sabotage. I did not plan it in a spirit of recklessness, nor because I have any love of violence. I planned it as a result of a calm and sober assessment of the political situation that had arisen after many years of tyranny, exploitation, and oppression of my people by the whites.

I admit immediately that I was one of the persons who helped to form Umkonto we Sizwe, and that I played a prominent role in its affairs until I was arrested in August 1962. I, and the others who started the organization, did so for two reasons. Firstly, we believed that as a result of government policy, violence by the African people had become inevitable, and that unless responsible leadership was given to channel and control the feelings of our people, there would be outbreaks of terrorism which would produce an intensity of bitterness and hostility between the various races of this country which is not produced even by war. Secondly, we felt that without violence there would be no way open to the African people to succeed in their struggle against the principle of white supremacy. All lawful methods of expressing opposition to this principle had been closed by legislation, and we were placed in a position in which we had either to accept a permanent state of inferiority, or to defy the government. We chose to defy the law. We first broke the law in a way which avoided any recourse to violence; when this form was legislated against, and the government resorted to a show of force to crush opposition to its policies, only then did we decide to answer violence with violence.

But the violence which we chose to adopt was not terrorism. We who formed Umkonto were all members of the African National Congress, and had behind us the ANC tradition of nonviolence and negotiation as a means of solving political disputes. We believed that South Africa belonged to all the people who lived in it, and not to one group, be it black or white. We did not want an interracial war, and tried to avoid it to the last. But the hard facts were that fifty years of nonviolence had brought the African people nothing but more and more repressive legislation, and fewer and fewer rights. Four forms of violence were considered – sabotage, guerrilla warfare, terrorism and open revolution. We chose to adopt the first method and to exhaust it before taking any other decision.

The initial plan was based on a careful analysis of the political and economic situation of our country. We believed that South Africa depended to a large extent on foreign capital and foreign trade. We felt that planned destruction of power plants, and interference with rail and telephone communications, would tend to scare away capital from the country, make it more difficult for goods from the industrial areas to reach the seaports on schedule, and would in the long run be a heavy drain on the economic life of the country, thus compelling the voters of the country to reconsider their position.

Attacks on the economic lifelines of the country were to be linked with sabotage on government buildings and other symbols of apartheid. These attacks would serve as a source of inspiration to our people. In addition, they would provide an outlet for those people who were urging the adoption of violent methods and would enable us to give concrete proof to our followers that we had adopted a stronger line and were fighting back against government violence. In addition, if mass action was successfully organized, and mass reprisals taken, we felt that sympathy for our cause would be roused in other countries, and that greater pressure would be brought to bear on the South African government.

This then was the plan. Umkonto was to perform sabotage, and strict instructions were given to its members that on no account were they to injure or kill people in planning or carrying out operations.

Experience convinced us that rebellion would offer the government limitless opportunities for the indiscriminate slaughter of our people, but it was precisely because the soil of South Africa was already drenched with the blood of innocent Africans that we felt it our duty to make preparations as a long-term undertaking to use force in order to defend ourselves against force. If war was inevitable, we wanted the fight to be conducted on terms most favorable to our people. The fight which held out prospects best for us and the least risk of life to both sides was guerrilla warfare. We decided, therefore, in our preparations for the future, to make provision for the possibility of guerrilla warfare. All whites undergo compulsory military training, but no such training was given to Africans. It was in our view essential to build up a nucleus of trained men who would be able to provide the leadership which would be required if guerrilla warfare started.

Another of the allegations made by the State is that the aims and objects of the ANC and the Communist party are the same. I wish to deal with this and with my own political position, because I must assume that the State may try to argue that I tried to introduce Marxism into the ANC. The allegation is false. The ideological creed of the ANC is, and always has been, the creed of African Nationalism. It is not the concept expressed in the cry, "Drive the white man into the sea." The African Nationalism for which the ANC stands is the concept of freedom and fulfillment for all as enshrined in our Freedom Charter, which is by no means a blueprint for a socialist state. It calls for redistribution, but not nationalization, of land; it provides for nationalization of mines, banks and monopoly industry, because big monopolies are owned by one race only, and without such nationalization racial domination would be perpetuated despite the spread of political power.

As far as the Communist party is concerned, and if I understand its policy correctly, it stands for the establishment of a state based on the principles of Marxism. Although it is prepared to work for the Freedom Charter, as a short-term solution to the problems created by white supremacy, it regards the Freedom Charter as the beginning, and not the end, of its program. The ANC's chief goal was for the African people to win unity and full political rights. The Communist party's main aim, on the other hand, was to remove the capitalists and to replace them with a working-class government. The Communist party sought to emphasize class distinctions while the ANC sought to harmonize them. This is a vital distinction.

It is true that there has often been close cooperation between the ANC and the Communist party. But cooperation is merely proof of a common goal – in this case the removal of white supremacy – and is not proof of a complete community of interests. The history of the world is full of similar examples. Perhaps the most striking illustration is to be found in the cooperation between Great Britain, the United States of America and the Soviet Union in the fight against Hitler. Nobody but Hitler would have dared to suggest that such cooperation turned Churchill or Roosevelt into communists or communist tools, or that Britain and America were working to bring about a communist world.

, Another instance of such cooperation is to be found precisely in Umkonto. Shortly after Umkonto was constituted, I was informed by some of its members that the Communist party would support Umkonto, and this then occurred. At a later stage the support was made openly.

I believe that communists have always played an active role in the fight by colonial countries for their freedom, because the short-term objects of communism would always correspond with the long-term objects of freedom movements. Thus communists have played an important role in the freedom struggles fought in countries such as Malaya, Algeria and Indonesia, yet none of these states today are communist countries. Similarly in the underground resistance movements which sprung up in Europe during the last world war, communists played an important role. Even General Chiang Kai-shek, today one of the bitterest enemies of communism, fought together with the communists against the ruling class in the struggle which led to his assumption of power in China in the 1930s. This pattern of cooperation between communists and noncommunists has been repeated in the National Liberation Movement of South Africa. Prior to the banning of the Communist party, joint campaigns involving the Communist party and the Congress movements were accepted practice. African communists could, and did, become members of the ANC, and some served on the national, provincial and local committees. Among those who served on the National Executive are Albert Nzula, a former secretary of the Communist party, Moses Kotane, another former secretary, and J. B. Marks, a former member of the central committee.

I joined the ANC in 1944, and in my younger days I held the view that the policy of admitting communists to the ANC, and the close cooperation which existed at times on specific issues between the ANC and the Communist party, would lead to a watering down of the concept of African Nationalism. At that stage I was a member of the African National Congress Youth League, and was one of a group which moved for the expulsion of communists from the ANC. This proposal was heavily defeated. Among those who voted against the proposal were some of the most conservative sections of African political opinion. They defended the policy on the ground that from its inception the ANC was formed and built up not as a political party with one school of political thought but as a parliament of the African people, accommodating people of various political convictions, all united by the common goal of national liberation. I was eventually won over to this point of view and I have upheld it ever since.

It is perhaps difficult for white South Africans, with an ingrained prejudice against communism, to understand why experienced African politicians so readily accept communists as their friends. But to us the reason is obvious. Theoretical differences among those fighting against oppression is a luxury we cannot afford at this stage. What is more, for many decades communists were the only political group in South Africa who were prepared to treat Africans as human beings and their equals; who were prepared to eat with us, talk with us, live with us and work with us. They were the only political group which was prepared to work with Africans for the attainment of political rights and a stake in society. Because of this, there are many Africans who, today, tend to equate freedom with communism. They are supported in this belief by a legislature which brands all exponents of democratic government and African freedom as communists and bans many of them (who are not communists) under the Suppression of Communism Act.

It is not only in internal politics that we count communists as among those who support our cause. In the international field, communist countries have always come to our aid. In the United Nations and other councils of the world the communist bloc has supported the Afro-Asian struggle against colonialism and often seems to be more sympathetic to our plight than some of the Western powers. Although there is a universal condemnation of apartheid, the communist bloc speaks out against it with a louder voice than most of the white world. In these circumstances, it would take a brash young politician, such as I was in 1949, to proclaim that the communists are our enemies.

I turn now to my own position. I have denied that I am a communist, and I think that in the circumstances I am obliged to state exactly what my political beliefs are. I have always regarded myself, in the first place, as an African patriot. I am attracted by the idea of a classless society, an attraction which springs partly from Marxist reading and partly from my admiration of the structure and organization of early African societies in this country. The land, then the main means of production, belonged to the tribe. There were no rich or poor and there was no exploitation.

Yes, I have been influenced by Marxist thought, but so have other leaders such as Gandhi, Nehru, Nkrumah and Nasser. We all accept the need for some form of socialism to enable our people to catch up with the advanced countries of this world and to overcome their legacy of extreme poverty. But this does not mean we are communists, or even Marxists. Indeed, for my own part, I believe that it is open to debate whether the Communist party has any specific role to play at this particular stage of our political struggle. The basic task at the present moment is the removal of race discrimination and the attainment of democratic rights on the basis of the Freedom Charter. In so far as that party furthers this task, I welcome its assistance. I realize that it is one of the means by which people of all races can be drawn into our struggle.

From my reading of Marxist literature and from conversations with Marxists, I have gained the impression that communists regard the parliamentary system of the West as undemocratic and reactionary. But, on the contrary, I am an admirer of such a system. The Magna Carta, the Petition of Rights and the Bill of Rights are documents which are held in veneration by democrats throughout the world. I have great respect for British political institutions, and for the country's system of justice. I regard the British Parliament as the most democratic institution in the world, and the independence and impartiality of its judiciary never fail to arouse my admiration. The American Congress, that country's doctrine of separation of powers, as well as the independence of its judiciary, arouses in me similar sentiments.

I have been influenced in my thinking by both West and East. All this has led me to feel that in my search for a political formula I should be absolutely impartial and objective. I should tie myself to no particular system of society other than socialism. I must leave myself free to borrow the best from the West and from the East. As to the suggestion that we received financial support from abroad, I wish to state that our political struggle has always been financed from internal sources – from funds raised by our own people and by our own supporters. Whenever we had a special campaign or an important political case – for example, the Treason Trial – we received financial assistance from sympathetic individuals and organizations in the Western countries. We had never felt it necessary to go beyond these sources.

But when in 1961 the Umkonto was formed, and a new phase of the struggle introduced, we realized that these events would make a heavy call on our slender resources, and that the scale of our activities would be hampered by the lack of funds. One of my instructions, as I went abroad in January 1962, was to raise funds from the African states. I must add that, while abroad, I had discussions with leaders of political movements in Africa and discovered that almost every single one of them, in areas which had still not attained independence, had received all forms of assistance from the socialist countries, as well as from the West, including that of financial support. I also discovered that some well-known African states, all of them noncommunist, and even anticommunist, had received similar assistance.

The government often answers its critics by saying that Africans in South Africa are economically better off than the inhabitants of the other countries in Africa. I do not know whether this statement is true and doubt whether any comparison can be made without having regard to the cost-of-living index in such countries. But even if it is true, as far as the African people are concerned it is irrelevant. Our complaint is not that we are poor by comparison with people in other countries, but that we are poor by comparison with the white people in our own country, and that we are prevented by legislation from altering this imbalance. The lack of human dignity experienced by Africans is the direct result of the policy of white supremacy. White supremacy implies black inferiority. Legislation designed to preserve white supremacy entrenches this notion.

Africans want a just share in the whole of South Africa, we want security and a stake in society. Above all, we want equal political rights, because without them our disabilities will be permanent. I know this sounds revolutionary to the whites in this country, because the majority of voters will be Africans. This makes the white man fear democracy. But his fear cannot be allowed to stand in the way of the only solution which will guarantee racial harmony and freedom for all. It is not true that the enfranchisement of all will result in racial domination. Political division based on color is entirely artificial, and when it disappears so will the domination of one color group by another. The ANC has spent half a century fighting against racism. When it triumphs it will not change that policy.

This then is what the ANC is fighting. Our struggle is a truly national one. It is a struggle of the African people, inspired by our own suffering and our own experience. It is a struggle for the right to live. During my lifetime I have dedicated myself to this struggle of the African people. I have fought against white domination, and I have fought against black domination. I have cherished the ideal of a democratic and free society in which all persons live together in harmony and with equal opportunities. It is an ideal which I hope to live for and to achieve. But if needs be, it is an ideal for which I am prepared to die.

Those were the last words South Africans were to hear from Mandela before he was put behind bars to serve out the rest of his natural life in captivity on Robben Island. They are recorded here because they seem to me appropriate to this account of Steve Biko, and because in much of his life style, personality and intellectual power Mandela was in the authentic line of major black South African leaders culminating in Biko himself.

South African history will one day accord full and due honor to the distinguished roll of courageous leaders who devoted their energies to the cause of their people. The contributions of black spokesmen of varying shades of moderation and activism will be recorded, including the earliest and the latest, from Jabavu and Soga, Mzimba, Makiwane, Rubusana, Pelemi, Seme, Gumede, Bokwe, Xuma, Makgatho, Mapikela, Mangena, Msimang and Dube, to Luthuli, Mandela, Sobukwe and Biko. I believe, though, that Steve Biko will be accorded a special place in our national history, not only because of his own remarkable qualities, but because he was to become the first of these major leaders to die at the hands of the State.

THE RISE OF
BLACK CONSCIOUSNESS

WITH MANDELA IMPRISONED and Sobukwe banned, there was for some years a leadership vacuum in South African black politics. It was filled toward the close of the 1960s by Bantu Stephen Biko.

Biko's was a new style of leadership. It was not an obvious style. He never ever proclaimed himself as leader, and in fact he generally discouraged the cult of personality and often tried to play a backroom role. He preferred to think that the struggle for black liberation was led by many rather than few, and that Black Consciousness was a mass movement of which he was only one of many articulators. But in this he deceived himself. From early youth he was so obviously a leader and was perceived by so many of his contemporaries as such, that he was inevitably deferred to in any gathering of which he was a part.

He was, in fact, the main guiding founder and inspiration of Black Consciousness, which addressed itself to black youth to prepare it for a new phase of the struggle for freedom.

The idea behind Black Consciousness was to break away almost entirely from past black attitudes to the liberation struggle and to set a new style of self-reliance and dignity for blacks as a psychological attitude leading to new initiatives. From this philosophy came many black organizations which sprang from the Black Consciousness movement, mainly the Black People's Convention (BPC) and the all-black South African Students' Organization (SASO). Biko and his associates used almost brutal language to initiate these bodies, because they felt they first had to get blacks to break away from the whites in multiracial organizations such as the National Union of South African Students.

It was the height of irony that the first major manifestation of Black Consciousness sprang from a black breach with one of the most courageously pro-black white youth organizations, the National Union of South African Students. NUSAS consisted mainly of white English-speaking students of the liberal universities of Cape Town, Witwatersrand (Johannesburg), Natal (Durban and Pietermaritzburg), and Rhodes (Grahamstown). Its leaders and office bearers had repeatedly been jailed, banned and prosecuted for protesting against racial injustice, and although NUSAS tried valiantly to build up and maintain a multiracial membership, the dice were loaded against its efforts in this regard because of the national environment. There happened to be more white students than black students in the land, and this fact, and the general set of legislative obstacles which militate against socio-political integration in South Africa, meant that its leadership was white-oriented – the very fact which provided the black students with their launching pad for the all-black South African Students' Organization.

The formation of SASO, a traumatic event for white liberal youth committed to the NUSAS ideals (and traumatic also for at least one liberal newspaper editor, proud to be a NUSAS honorary vice-president!), was inspired by Steve Biko. But the gestation process was initially best publicly described by two spokesmen on opposite sides of the dispute. One, a NUSAS leader named Clive Nettleton, gave a strikingly perceptive analysis which is excerpted here:

The formation of SASO has disrupted the traditional alignment of the South African student world. The old alignment consisted of, on the one side, the Afrikaanse Studentebond, representing the Afrikaans-language universities supporting apartheid, and on the other hand NUSAS, representing the English-speaking campuses, including the black university colleges. The formation of SASO has introduced a new force into the situation and has underlined the inability of NUSAS to represent adequately the views of black students. SASO also has importance because it reflects a new movement in society at large – Black Consciousness.

The major problem facing NUSAS as a nonracial organization existing in a society based on racism is that, while preaching the ideal of nonracism, the members of the organization are unable to live out their ideals. While it is still possible for white and black students to hold joint congresses and seminars, and to meet occasionally at social events, they live in different worlds.

The white English-speaking students are unable to find an identity outside the student framework, while the black students feel a strong identification with the aspirations of the black people as a whole and feel in a forum such as a NUSAS congress that they represent not only black students but all black people.

Legality and multiracialism do not yoke together easily in South Africa. A NUSAS commission examined laws that infringed the rights of the individual, an issue white students felt had great importance. However, for the first time there was a new response from the black students. "What," asked one delegate, "is the use of a black man talking about the erosion of freedom in South Africa? We have no freedom and one or two laws more or less make no difference to our situation."

The NUSAS Congress of 1967 had been the turning point. The conditions under which the black delegates were (separately) accommodated at Rhodes University were appalling and NUSAS was unable to do anything about it.

The black student community now stands united in the belief that in their unity lies the strength to overcome so many problems they face, first as students and then as members of the oppressed community. Briefly these sentiments are expressed in the following:

(i) Black students owe their first allegiance to the black community with whom they share the burdens and injustices of apartheid. Student unity, where this involves consolidating ranks encompassing people of variable aspirations, is not to be encouraged. It has been shown in the past that black-white student co-operation often leads to a divergence of expectations with the resultant frustrations.

(ii) The student population is already divided and black students feel it is more effective to go it alone instead of standing piously on ineffective platforms, issuing impotent fulminations against "the System."

(iii) It is essential for the black students to elevate the level of consciousness of the black community by promoting black awareness, pride, achievement and capabilities. In the long run this will prove far more valuable than the sentimental and idealistic attitude of perpetually trying to "bridge the gap" between races.

The confusion which the formation of SASO has caused among liberal whites is considerable and needs to be looked at carefully. The problem is that believing in nonracism seems to be contradicted by an acceptance of a black-only organization. But the essence of the matter is that NUSAS was founded on white initiative, is financed by white money and reflects the opinions of the majority of its members who are white. SASO, on the other hand, also faces considerable problems. The purpose of SASO would seem in the first instance to be to build up among black students a Black Consciousness, and within this framework to confront the white power structures. Initially the confrontation is with the liberal structures, which are both the most accessible and the easiest to attack on the grounds of their middle-of-the-road nature. Any group seeking confrontation needs also to establish clear polarities, and the middle-of-the-road section needs to be eliminated in order to bring about the confrontation. So it should not be surprising that the first attack by SASO should be directed against NUSAS rather than the more extreme right-wing organizations.

SASO have realized that in South Africa today it is impossible to live the nonracial ideal and that it is therefore better to withdraw in order to achieve congruence between program and reality.

Nettleton's exposition admirably summed up the issue, and an equally admirable exposition of Black Consciousness came also from Barney Pityana, Steve Biko's chief lieutenant in the SASO movement. Typically Biko took a back seat at this early stage, feeling that if he kept a low public profile initially, this would boost second-echelon leadership – which indeed it did. This is Pityana's account:

To ask the right questions, to encourage a new consciousness, and to suggest new forms which express it, are the basic purposes of our new direction.

It is true that the question of race is one which we often find embarrassing. It should rather not be discussed, like the problem of sex during the Victorian era. "Oh, you see, I love you as a person and it never occurs to me that you are black!" – this is the sort of gesture we receive from our sympathetic friends. Many would prefer to be color-blind; to them skin pigmentation is merely an accident of creation. To us it is something much more fundamental. It is a synonym for subjection, an identification for the disinherited. Hans Morganthau's Realist school of thought suggests that by power we mean man's control over the minds and actions of other men. Political power refers to the mutual relations of control between the holders of public authority and the people. The holders of public authority exercise their power by the consent of their subjects. The subjects have an ultimate right to revoke this authority in the event of its abuse, or corruptive employment. Power, therefore, is an essential element of politics.

The South African population consists of more than 25 million people. Of these only about 5 million are white. Yet all political and economic power is in the hands of this white minority. They have a right to vote for, and to be voted on to, all effective legislative bodies. They monopolize all key positions and centers of power and preferred occupations. Whites are protected by legislation from competition with blacks in spheres of employment, sport and politics. They appropriate far more than their fair share in educational, welfare and other social services, and they maintain a wide gap between themselves and other races in terms of technical skills, and consequently the wealth of the land. The so-called nonwhite people are kept in total subjection by the white authority. It is government policy to keep the different racial groups in complete separation from one another. The obvious result is that they have developed prejudices, complexes and suspicions about one another. They are competing for favors from the powers that be. There is differentiation in living conditions, social amenities and salary scales.

The bulk of the black people, moreover, have accepted their degenerate status. The pride of peoplehood in them has been shattered. They have more than just accepted their lot, for some even help to destroy their worth as human beings. They are being resettled in droves; and 13 per cent of the land, and that the most uneconomic, is allocated for their use.

South Africa uniquely demonstrates that a powerful minority will perpetuate social indignities even on the labor force of a vigorously expanding economy. Civic status is determined at birth and for life by color. Whether he is a wage earner, a businessman, an intellectual or a chief, no black can be admitted to the national Parliament.

The black person has been "uprooted, pursued, baffled, doomed to watch the dissolution of the truths that he has always treasured." As a result of this antinomy that coexists with us blacks, we can draw two conclusions – that white men consider themselves superior to black men, and that black men want to prove to white men at all costs the equal value of their intellect. This is to be regretted. It is a negative way of expressing one's values. It creates the unfortunate impression that all values are white-oriented and all standards are white-determined. This I cannot accept. I believe that we have values and standards which are bound to be different from those of the whites simply because the whites enjoy the privileges of which blacks are robbed. There cannot be much in common between the two peoples in that situation of imbalance. I am not aspiring to be equal to a white man but I am determined to establish my worth as a God-created being. I have to assert my *being* as a person.

I realize that all this may be very theoretical. One has to take account of the years of indoctrination starting from the first encounter of the white colonists with black tribesmen, when whites were set up as a standard. From their capitalistic tendencies one has come to measure status by the amount of money one has. In this way the class situation was introduced as a value even for blacks. The urgency of the moment is that we have to liberate the mind of the black man.

Black Consciousness can therefore be seen as a stage preceding any invasion, any abolition of the ego by desire: The first step, therefore, is to make the black man see himself, to pump life into his empty shell; to infuse him with pride and dignity, to remind him of his complicity in the crime of allowing himself to be misused and therefore letting evil reign supreme in the country of his birth. This is what we mean by an inward-looking process. This makes consciousness, Black Consciousness, imminent in our own eyes. "I am not a potentiality of something," writes Fanon. "I am wholly what I am. I do not have to look for the universal. No probability has any place inside me. My negro consciousness does not hold itself out as black. It IS. It is its own follower. This is all that we blacks are after. TO BE. We believe that we are quite efficient in handling our BEness and for this purpose we are self-sufficient. We shall never find our goals and aspirations as a people centered anywhere else but in US. This, therefore, necessitates a self-examination and a rediscovery of ourselves. Blacks can no longer afford to be led and dominated by nonblacks."

I do not believe that there was nothing of value in the way of life of the indigenous black peoples. The tribe was seen as an extension of the family and all collective enterprise was geared to the general good. The chief was merely a custodian of the property of the tribe. There cannot be a better collective system of government. Blacks must reject the exploitative nature of white society. The norms of Western society are, by definition, norms required by the capitalist for its survival. Thus exploitation, which is natural in Western culture, will never willingly be renounced by whites. Culture is largely a social product which is imposed on each individual by the socializing process to which he is subjected in his particular society. Culture is a living tradition, a collection of ideas and beliefs which represent a people's collective way of life. The culture orientation of the black people is influenced by their life style in the black ghettos! They have had to generate a "soul force" which would enable them to remain human beings in these camps. I view the government's attempts at developing the cultures of the various ethnic groups as an "arrested image of culture." Government policy aims at breaking down the life thread; and Black Consciousness is determined to build a new culture and value-orientation which, though influenced by other forces, will articulate the priorities and needs of the black people and act in terms of these needs.

The fact that a concerted delving into our roots and a rewriting of our history is considered necessary to ignite a consciousness should not be stretched to absurd proportions. I would not like to exalt the past at the expense of the present and the future. It may, however, be necessary for both the present and the future because a correct interpretation of events, that is of history, will be obtained by understanding both the opposing tendencies and the result of their conflict. This is our theory of history: past events can shape the present and the future.

To hope that change might come through the existing political parties in South Africa is a pipedream, because a political party that appeals to white voters alone invariably makes their claims the touchstone of policy, plays on their racial antagonisms and consolidates them into a hegemonic block in opposition to the voteless majority. This means that black people must build themselves into a position of nondependence upon whites. They must work towards a self-sufficient political, social and economic unit. In this manner they will help themselves towards a deeper realization of their potential and worth as self-respecting people. The confidence thus generated will give them a sense of pride and awareness. This is what we need in South Africa for a meaningful change to the status quo. The way to the future is not through a directionless multiracialism but through a positive unilateral approach. Black man, you are on your own.

The ultimate irony had occurred. Apartheid, designed to suppress a unified black response, had created precisely such a response. In denying validity to any claim by blacks to even the slightest share in a common multiracial society, the racists had driven the most articulate young blacks into claiming not merely a share but the dominant share in such a society – on their own terms.

The young Steve Biko and his colleagues had seized the shoulder of the sleeping giant of black awareness in South Africa to shake him from his slumber. And more than that: to raise him to his feet, to stretch him to his full height and to place him for the first time into the attitudes of total challenge toward all who had sought to keep him prone. Black Consciousness was born, a new totality of black response to white power, and with it a new era in the racial struggle in South Africa.

And with it was born the increasingly perceptible leadership of Steve Biko. Despite all his efforts to keep in the background, to generate collective leadership on a broad front so that the movement would be one of all the people rather than a movement tied to one personality, his own modesty was no proof against the inexorable processes whereby even the most able group of men will turn to one among them in some form of acknowledgment that he, more than any other, is their recognized guide. Though the Black Consciousness movement from the beginning produced a wide array of gifted leaders and spokesmen, it was the name of Biko that increasingly worked its way to the fore out of this large group in the months and years ahead, and by the dawn of the decade of the 1970s there were already signs that the young Steve Biko was the personification of an immense new force at the forefront of black politics in South Africa.

In the process of mobilizing blacks against the white racists, the Black Consciousness advocates felt they first had to wean their fellow blacks away from the white antiracists, the white liberals, by attacking liberalism itself. As a liberal, I was therefore one of those whose first awareness of Black Consciousness was through attacks by people like Biko on all that I personally believed in, in the South African political context. I, after all, was one of these white liberals whose "paternalism" and "negative influence" were under attack, along with my liberal heroes like Alan Paton. We liberals believed in a common nonracial society in South Africa, in an end to all apartheid and in a brotherhood among all South Africans of every race, creed and color. We could not see that, for young blacks in our repressed society, such concepts were utterly impractical, and that our unavailing efforts to achieve these ideals were no longer adequate.

There were few enough of us, in all conscience. Few white South Africans shared our anti-apartheid views, and even for many of us who described ourselves as liberal, a long political road had had to be traveled away from racism.

This was certainly so in my case.

MY OWN WHITE WORLD

To ESTABLISH from what vantage point I observed and evaluated the significance and philosophy of Steve Biko, I should explain my own background and the influences which shaped my own thinking. I was born on December 15, 1933, in the Transkei territory of Eastern Cape Province, a territory later to become the first "Bantustan" or "homeland." Like most white South Africans, I was born into a home highly conservative on the racial issue. My father was a trader and so was my mother's father. A trader is a rural shopkeeper in a tribal reserve, who sells blankets, beads, buckets, hoes, spades and a variety of basic goods to the tribesmen, buying from them grain, hides, skins, wool and coarse tobacco. A trader's child therefore has an unusual environment, early learning a tribal language (in our case Xhosa), and living close to extremely primitive people far from the amenities of the towns.

My early view of blacks was therefore of backward people, few of whom could read or write, most of whom wore loinclothes and blankets, not "European clothes," and people in the grip of extreme superstition dominated by sorcery and witchcraft, one of whose effects appeared to be an alarming degree of callousness and cruelty. Limitlessly kind and courteous in their dealings in most circumstances, the tribespeople appeared to be savage in certain specific aspects of their society such as faction fighting and ritual murder. The faction fighting was done with axes, the combatants literally chopping each other open, and the toll of deaths every weekend from such clashes was heavy. For some reason the axe fights always took place on Sundays, and on Monday mornings the death toll in our district alone ran into dozens. In addition to this, domestic chastisement assumed almost homicidal dimensions, wife beating and child beating sometimes being fatal – this was accepted in the tribal society as quite normal given what was regarded as provocation.

A white child brought up in these circumstances, being taught at an early age to read and write while noting that even adult tribesmen could not form a single letter of the alphabet, understandably regarded blacks as inferior and easily accepted the general white attitude that color and race were the determinants of the chasm in cultures. I had two distinctly separate early childhoods. One was in the Xhosa world, where my playmates were Twalidcobo and Bhatuni and other contemporaries whose interests were totally in the physical world of making tiny clay oxen and toy spears, running and stick fighting. The other was my white world of English school stories and American comic books – a world my black playmates simply could not comprehend. In vain I tried to tell them of Dick Tracy, Batman, Superman, Li'l Abner, the Lone Ranger, Hopalong Cassidy and Captain Marvel – it was a world, a language, and an entire culture apart. At my bedside was the *Greyfriars Annual* with its stories of Harry Wharton, Bob Cherry and Bunter, the owl of the Remove. But in my playground were boys in loinclothes, some of them doomed to die by battle axe before reaching their middle teens.

Mine was not a typical childhood for a white South African boy. On the contrary, most white children in South Africa live outside tribal areas and learn no tribal language. In fact, when I went to boarding school far away in Kimberley I was regarded as something of a curiosity by many of my schoolmates. They spoke of the Transkei as if it were on the other side of the moon, and all its inhabitants primitive beyond disdain, as, I suppose, in some ways we were.

My contact with other white children reinforced the generally accepted white version of the black stereotype – that blacks could never be the same as us; that they did not want to be the same as us; that they were created black because the Almighty clearly intended that they be set apart and should stay different, with a different color, different smell, different language, different attitudes (all naturally inferior to ours). The priests told us occasionally that this was not the Christian version of things, and that racist thinking was un-Christian – but somehow this never seemed convincing to us. It was all academic theory, contradicted by what we thought we could see for ourselves.

The year I matriculated and enrolled for law studies in Cape Town, 1952, saw the start of one of the intermittent periods of urban black violence, under Nationalist rule, and I recall profoundly shocking my Roman Law lecturer, one Harold Levy, with my reply to his question as to whether I had an answer to the country's race problem. I echoed the cliche that the best blacks were the blacks in the reserves, kept in their simple tribal state, untainted by education: "Yes, shoot the niggers or send them back to the reserves." His expression of revulsion had a deep effect on me. He was a man I admired tremendously, and the fact that he could be shocked by my reply jolted my confidence that mine was the right and commonsense view, or that such "toughness" was necessarily smart. My confident bigotry was jolted further by the increasingly obvious chasm between it and the principles of justice which ran consistently through the Roman and Roman-Dutch Law, in particular much of the Christian-based legal principles enunciated in the Institutes of Justinian.

A further jolt came with the brief participation in one of the university law classes of a visiting student from America who was black (the Nationalists had not yet passed the statute segregating universities). This black American youth spoke, to my amazement, in an American accent! Just like on the movie screen . . .

Which meant that blacks did not automatically talk in a different accent from whites . . .

Which meant that accent had nothing to do with race . . .

Which meant that a Japanese or Indian, or for that matter a Xhosa, brought up from childhood in Buckingham Palace, would speak exactly like the King of England . . .

Which meant a whole lot of other things besides . . .

Including the thought that culture is a matter of environment, not race or color.

This really set off a chain reaction of conclusions, culminating in the conclusion that if all these things were determined by environment, we white South Africans might by virtue of the same principle of environmental conditioning be victims of inherited thinking wrongly based in fact and therefore false. I sought further answers in books, many books, by or about the likes of Abraham Lincoln, William Wilberforce and the British Liberals, and at about this time there burst into print Alan Paton's novel *Cry, the Beloved Country*, followed by works of other great South African writers like Nadine Gordimer. These tore into final shreds for me any of apartheid's claims to validity, and for the next twenty years I believed my education out of racism was complete – until I met Steve Biko.

But to explain the extent to which Steve opened my eyes on this issue, I must first explain the extent to which they had been closed. When I concluded in my twentieth year that apartheid was the Great Obscene Lie, I concluded also that it had to be fought. Accordingly I dropped my law studies and went into politics. As apartheid was a creature of the Nationalist party government, I went first to join the United party – the major white opposition party. But on reading over its policy papers I concluded that it was not totally opposed to apartheid. In fact, its own policy was simply a watered-down version of the Nationalist brand of racial discrimination. The United party wanted apartheid without its rougher edges. It wanted segregation – but along more "humane" lines. This was not for me; I could see no sense in opposing an evil merely to settle for a slightly lesser degree of that evil.

The only other political party then on the scene was the recently formed

Federal party, which advocated a nonracial franchise based on educational qualification and a decentralization of governmental powers to the provinces in a federal system similar to that of the United States. These ideas appealed to me – the first because it implied abolition of all racial segregation without opening the voting floodgates overnight, and the second because federalization of South Africa could lead to federal union with Swaziland, Lesotho, Botswana, Namibia, Zimbabwe and Zambia in a rational and greater Federation of Southern Africa.

The Federal party nominated me two years later for election in a parliamentary constituency, but the white electorate was horrified at the idea of a nonracial franchise which would lead in time to black majority rule, and I lost the election utterly, polling fewer than a thousand votes. Being twenty-three years old and resilient, I was undismayed. Concluding that it would be a long time before white voters could be persuaded to scrap apartheid, I quit the white political party scene and went into journalism. If I couldn't convert my fellow whites with oratory I would try to do so with the pen! That, at least, was the intention . . . Today, twenty years later, and having written an estimated million words or more against apartheid, I acknowledge that the effort has not been crowned with success. People are reluctant to abandon their prejudices, especially a minority of whites fearful of an overwhelming majority of blacks, and although there has been an increase in the number of whites rejecting apartheid, the majority of South African whites remain committed to it.

Having decided finally in 1958 on a career in journalism, I realized that I had to compress a great deal of journalistic experience into a short space of time to catch up with the earning capacities of journalists of my age who had five years of training while I was unsuccessfully attempting careers first in the law and second in politics. Accordingly I went overseas and worked as a journalist in Britain and Canada for two years, the highlight of my assignments being one for the London *Daily Herald* – to travel through America's Deep South comparing Dixie segregation with South African apartheid. Barely an hour after I arrived in Little Rock, Arkansas, Ku Klux Klansmen dynamited the house of a Negro, Mr. Cartelyou Walls, who readily granted me an interview which was the first of many interesting discussions with Southerners – white as well as black.

Although there were obvious similarities in the Deep South and South African manifestations of racism, I found some interesting differences both in fact and style. The major difference was of course that Southern racism was strongly disapproved of by the federal government in Washington, whereas in South Africa it was actually promoted and legislatively implemented by national government. There has never been a pattern of lynching in South Africa, or any open equivalent of the Klan. Nationalists prefer to exercise their racial prejudices through statutory enactments framed in decorous parliamentary surroundings after hours of pious oratorical attempts to justify such measures to their allegedly Calvinist consciences.

I returned to South Africa in 1960, the year of Sharpeville, and joined the *Daily Dispatch* in East London as a reporter. I applied to the *Dispatch* because I admired the paper's general political stance and because it circulated in my home area of the Eastern Cape Province. The *Daily Dispatch* has maintained its independence for more than a hundred years. It belongs to no chain of papers and is owned by a charitable foundation, the Crewe Trust, which donates two-thirds of all dividends to charities every year. The trust is administrated by *Dispatch* executives and the board of directors is drawn from staff members, including the editor, who is given full mandate to ordain policy.

I found a happy team of some forty journalists deeply committed to the paper and what it stood for, and had a succession of interesting jobs there, including political correspondent, columnist and leader writer. I was appointed editor in 1965, and although most of the staff were considerably senior to me in years and professional experience there was no resentment at a thirty-one-year-old being appointed over them by the board of directors. Indeed, from that time they never wavered in their loyal support, although I immediately embarked on a more forceful editorial policy of literally daily condemnation of apartheid, which many must at times have felt jeopardized their livelihoods through laying the paper open to frequent government threats to ban it.

I seldom shared such apprehensions, because after studying the Nationalist mentality for two years in the parliamentary press gallery as a political correspondent I knew the Nationalist style would be to go for me as an individual rather than go for the paper, and as a general strategy I tried to act as a lightning conductor for the paper by signing the more "dangerous" editorials personally.

First reactions to the harder line were howls of rage from the white community, and a number of advertising contracts were canceled and subscriptions terminated, but in time the growth in both circulation and advertising revenue was marked and was to show a steady increase with each succeeding year. This was due to sheer good fortune, in that there was an unforeseen boom in black readership at a time when national advertisers were seeking black customers in a growing consumer market.

When I took over the editorship of the *Dispatch* I prayed for three years of immunity from arrest, detention or banning. I was to have twelve, and to be deeply grateful for the credit balance of nine years! During these past twelve years political developments in South Africa had been fast and furious. In the realm of white politics the Progressive party had been formed in 1958, a more substantial body than my old Federal party but with virtually the same policies and principles, the fledgling Federal movement having foundered the year before. The Liberal party had also been formed, but its policy of one-man-one-vote stood utterly no chance of electoral support among whites, and the party, gallantly led for some years by author Alan Paton, disbanded after the Nationalists banned many of its key office bearers and legislatively prohibited multiracial-membership political parties. Even the Progressive party, with its more cautious policy of qualified franchise, was regarded as too dangerously radical by the white electorate, and more than a decade was to elapse before the Progressives could win more than one seat in Parliament – that of the gallant Helen Suzman, who earned the love and admiration of the voteless masses of South Africa for her lone parliamentary championship of the antiracist cause.

In the years immediately preceding my first meeting with Steve Biko, the general political situation was therefore as follows: the Nationalists were in firm control of the white Parliament and had entrenched themselves even more firmly in power since winning the apartheid election of 1948. Because of the loaded vote favoring rural (Nationalist) over urban (anti-Nationalist) areas, with each Nationalist vote gerrymandered to count as equivalent to almost two opposition votes, the Nationalists held two-thirds of the seats in Parliament. Up until 1974, the remaining seats, except that of Helen Suzman, were all held by the neo-Nationalist party once led by Jan Smuts, the United party. But following Progressive successes in the 1974 general election, the United party was whittled down, later split, and ultimately disbanded in 1977. The position after the general election of November 30, 1977, was:

NATIONALISTS	135 seats
PFP *(Progressives)*	17 seats
NRP *(ex-United Party)*	10 seats
SAP *(South African Party)*	3 seats

Clearly, in November 1977 most of the white electorate in South Africa voted to confront and resist the black liberation movements by all available means, including fullscale civil war if it came to that.

But such a public endorsement by white voters for racist policies backed by force was a culmination of a pattern of increasing legislative racism begun many years before. For three decades the Nationalists had been adding constantly to the massive burden of oppressive race laws, evolving literally hundreds of apartheid rules and regulations forbidding blacks to vote, to do certain categories of work, to associate with whites politically or socially or in sport, to have sexual relations with whites, to live in the cities, to move from area to area to seek work, to campaign effectively against apartheid, to form trade unions, to use the same elevators, entrances to buildings or public toilets as whites, or indeed to compete with whites on any fair basis in any significant sector of life. Blacks had to carry pass books, special documents of identity of a remarkable complexity, and could be jailed for not being able to produce a pass correctly endorsed under all circumstances. Not since Hitler's Nuremberg laws has any regime anywhere in the world inflicted so monstrous a burden of racial regulations on any community as the Nationalist minority government of South Africa has inflicted on the vast majority of its own citizens.

All Nationalist policy is based on arithmetic, and on the aim of retaining all power in the hands of 3 million of South Africa's 4½ million whites, to rule over 16 million blacks, 1 million "Coloureds," 1 million "Indians" and the non-Afrikaner and anti-Nationalist whites. So that 3 million may divide and rule over more than 20 million, the "homeland" policy has been evolved. Less than 15 percent of the nation's territory has been set aside for the creation of "homelands," the idea being that if the 16 million blacks are divided into citizenship of some nine "independent homelands" they will cease to be citizens of greater South Africa, leaving the 4½ million whites the largest racial group in the main land area of South Africa. Thus the 4 million Zulus are designated as citizens of the small homeland of Kwa Zulu, the 4 million Xhosas are designated as citizens of two Xhosa "homelands," Transkei and Ciskei, and with these two major "ethnic" groups of blacks thus disposed of, the rest are designated as citizens of the other six "homelands."

The word "homelands" is used to imply that these areas are the natural home areas of these "ethnic groups" – although many of these so-called homeland citizens have never set eyes on their alleged homeland, their families having lived in some cases for generations in the major urban areas far from the homelands. The pious claim of the Nationalists is that their policy is aimed at benefiting the blacks concerned by preserving their separate ethnic identities in that Zulus, Xhosas, Swazis, Vendas, Tswanas and Sotho groups each have their own culture, language and "national pride." But this is hypocritical nonsense. The Nguni language (Zulu, Xhosa, Swazi) is common to most South African blacks – Zulu and Xhosa are almost identical, having more words and expressions in common than

English and Afrikaans have – yet there is no concern to place English-speaking and Afrikaner whites in separate "homelands." Their whiteness transcends ethnicity – the blackness of blacks does not!

At no time have blacks been allowed to indicate for themselves in a fair poll whether they want such ethnic separation into homeland territories. That has been decided for them by the Nationalist regime, because of its own arithmetical requirements for purposes of divide and rule. All the evidence indicates that, if given a chance, an overwhelming majority of blacks would reject the "homelands" policy along with all other manifestations of apartheid. Yet some blacks have accepted the homelands dispensation, making it plain that it is not their first choice (which would be equal rights in an undivided South Africa), but that they prefer to have at least some portion of South Africa they can live normally in and call their own, free of the scourge of apartheid. One such is Paramount Chief Kaiser Matanzima, who has accepted independence for the Denmark-sized territory of Transkei as a homeland for some 2 million Xhosas. But most of Transkei's budget is donated by the Nationalist government, and many blacks point out that this is a dubious independence tied to the pursetrings of Pretoria.

After a year of independence, Transkeians seem happy enough, and have abolished all apartheid within the territory, yet the political heirs of Albert Luthuli, Nelson Mandela, Robert Sobukwe and Steve Biko condemn Matanzima and other homeland leaders such as Kwa Zulu's Chief Gatsha Buthelezi, Bophutatswana's Chief Lucas Mangope, Gazankulu's Professor Hudson Ntsanwisi, Ciskei's Chief Lennox Sebe and Lebowa's Dr. Cedric Phatudi as "sellouts" who collaborate with tribal and ethnic apartheid by accepting balkanization of the black territorial heritage and thereby lend some degree of credibility and respectability to the homelands dispensation. Although all these homelands leaders without exception – and particularly Chief Buthelezi, who has a large following – condemn apartheid strongly and unequivocally, they are deeply resented by the more militant black leaders, and particularly by the black youth now in revolt in the large urban areas, who believe they should dissociate themselves totally from what they regard as a compromise stance that lets down the total cause of liberation of all blacks throughout all of the nation. Similar resentment is expressed by young "Coloured" and "Indian" activists toward members of the State-recognized Colored Persons' Representative Council and South African Indian Council respectively.

After the banning of the African National Congress and the Pan-Africanist Congress there had been a public vacuum in black resistance politics. Although remnants of these groups went underground, the cream of the leadership had been jailed, and public ANC and PAC influence was minimal. It was during this period that most of the homelands leaders decided it made pragmatic sense to settle for a portion of the loaf instead of striving futilely for the whole loaf. But ANC and PAC followers remained utterly opposed to such pragmatism, even if they could not publicly articulate such opposition because of strict security laws and because of the leadership vacuum.

Into this vacuum stepped this unusually gifted man, Bantu Stephen Biko, and he filled it to articulate the aims and philosophy of the black struggle as no black leader had quite been able to do before. He assumed the mantle of leadership unpretentiously and unobtrusively. That was his style. In fact, so reserved and unegotistical was he that a considerable time was to elapse before the realization began to spread among blacks that he had done so. And the fact that he had done so at barely twenty-one years of age was in itself as remarkable as the man himself.

It was several years later that I first met Steve Biko, and I did so only after more than a year of urging by mutual friends. The fact is that in spite of such urging I didn't want to meet him because I had an idea of what he stood for and I didn't like it. For five years he had been founder and chief promoter of the Black Consciousness movement, which I regarded as a manifestation of black racism, and after doing my best to oppose white racism I did not feel disposed to tolerate any suggestion of black racism. There seemed no point in replacing one type of racism with another, and all that I had heard and read about the Biko movement led me to regard it as racial exclusivism in reverse.

My education was about to begin! But before I introduce its beginnings through my first meeting with Steve Biko, I must make one final personal introduction – to my wife Wendy, who shared the Biko experience with me, grasped all its implications sooner than I did, and with a natural gift of political perception helped Steve to lead an often puzzled orthodox liberal through depths of black political profundity I never knew existed. Although she, also born in the Transkei, had a similar background to mine and had had similar racial prejudices, she worked her own way out of those far quicker than I had managed to do, and left me lagging behind in the race away from rigid conservatism. I had needed lectures, books and enlightening experiences. She worked most of it out on her own. Her fleetness of perception occasionally led Steve in later years to say to me, "Wendy sees it, so why can't you?"

Before we became friendly with Steve, Wendy and I had shared orthodox white South African liberal views, and our joint approach was reflected in my editorials and syndicated columns which appeared in six daily newspapers once a week. My stance was one of total opposition to apartheid in all its aspects, and as long ago as 1972 Prime Minister Vorster once confronted me angrily with the words, "The stuff you are writing is stirring the blacks to revolution!" My response was that his apartheid laws were doing that, but thanks to Steve Biko I later came to see that the black struggle had to do with more than the apartheid laws; that his Black Consciousness movement was aimed at psychic oppression as well as legislative oppression, at economic exploitation as well as at the apartheid statutes which made such exploitation possible; and that the entire terms of the struggle generally went well beyond the limits envisaged and bounded within the white party political processes. In getting to know Steve Biko, I came to realize that his special genius was for the breaking of chains – the psychological chains which had trapped the black man as securely as the legislative chains of statutory apartheid.

2: THE MAN
MY INTRODUCTION
TO STEVE BIKO

IT WAS A BLACK BOMBSHELL of a girl who bullied me into my first meeting with Steve Biko. My secretary rang through to tell me that a Dr. Ramphele was in the office and wished to see me. I knew from the name that Dr. Ramphele was black, and pictured an elderly gray-haired medico with an Uncle Tom diffidence. No image could have been further from the actuality.

She burst through the door, a slight figure in blue jeans and a white sweater, and stood challengingly in front of my desk with her hands on her hips, declaiming in a near-shout: "Why do you give all the headlines to sellouts like Buthelezi and Mantanzima? Why don't you get to know the real black leaders? When are you coming to talk to Steve Biko? You know he is banned and can't come to you, so why don't you go to him? What's the matter with you?"

This was really something. There are few black doctors in South Africa, and very few black female doctors, and though I had met black women in Zambia, London and elsewhere with the poise and confidence to stride into a journalist's office to deliver such a tirade, I had never thought such people existed in my own country. Black women in South Africa, in fact most blacks, male or female, are highly diffident in the presence of whites.

This was a new breed of black South African – the Black Consciousness breed – and I knew immediately that a movement which produced the sort of personality now confronting me had qualities which blacks had been needing in South Africa for three hundred years. It was an exciting moment – a moment of discovery in my own country that added a new element to the whole national equation.

Something of this realization must have shown in my face, in fact I seem to recall that my response to the tirade was a broad grin of sheer delight, because this astonishing Dr. Ramphele calmed down immediately, drew up a chair and began a patient and quite amiable explanation of black political reality and Black Consciousness philosophy with the confident (and quite correct) assumption that all my other appointments had suddenly paled into insignificance.

As previously explained, I had had up to then a negative attitude to Black Consciousness. As one of a tiny band of white South African liberals, I was totally opposed to race as a factor in political thinking, and totally committed to nonracist policies and philosophies. From the little I knew at that time of Biko and the Black Consciousness philosophy and organizations he had founded, he and they represented a repudiation of the liberal position, a fact illustrated by the way in which this man Biko had led a breakaway from NUSAS to found the blacks-only South African Students Organization, arguing that black students could only develop political self-reliance by "doing their own thing" as blacks. His argument that black students had to develop their own black identity appeared to me to be racist reasoning, and I regarded the foundation of SASO as an act of betrayal of the white liberal commitment. And I felt the same way about the other Black Consciousness groups Biko had founded, such as the Black Community Programs and all-black sports bodies and trust funds for maintenance of families of political prisoners. They seemed to me to be inversions of the apartheid mentality – racism in reverse.

Dr. Ramphele heard me out patiently, then burst out in another near-shout: "You've got the whole thing wrong, man! We're not racist. We're just insisting on being ourselves. You must come and talk to Steve, he'll explain the whole thing."

The meeting was arranged, and on the day as I drove from East London to King William's Town, an hour away by car, I reviewed in my mind what I had heard and read of Biko.

From what I knew he was an unusually intelligent and charismatic personality who had won a dedicated following at an early age. I had been intrigued by the attitude of white NUSAS leaders toward him. I was an honorary vice-president of NUSAS, and had expected the white NUSAS leaders to resent Biko's breakaway move with all its implications of repudiation of their ideals. But they were strangely noncritical of his stance, much though they regretted it. I had been somewhat impatient with their apparent condonation of it all, regarding it as a rather weak-kneed compliance borne of white liberal reluctance to criticize blacks generally. In fact, I had adopted a strongly critical attitude, attacking SASO bitterly in editorials and speeches and accusing them of being as racist in their way as the Nationalists were on the other side of the spectrum. I was impatient with all this talk of black pride and "black is beautiful," maintaining that black was no more beautiful, or ugly, than white, and that there was no more merit or demerit in being born black than there was merit or demerit in being born white. All solid, straight-down-the-line liberal stuff, and valid enough.

But, as I was to learn, you simply have to be black in South Africa to perceive comprehensively every single nuance of the fact of blackness, and it is impossible to understand the totality of this experience through academic or theoretical idealism. This was what Biko had managed to convey to the young white NUSAS leaders and this fact, together with his personal charisma, was what had impressed them and made them so reluctant to condemn Black Consciousness.

I had looked up the basic details of Steve Biko's short and stormy career. Born in King William's Town on December 18, 1946, he had begun his schooling at Brownlee Primary for two years, continued at Charles Morgan Higher Primary for four years, then moved on to Lovedale Institute to prepare for his matriculation. He was at Lovedale for only three months when the school was closed down as a result of strikes by senior pupils. He then moved to Marianhill in Natal, a Catholic institute, where he did very well. In 1966 he enrolled as a student at the University of Natal to study medicine, but after initial academic success became so involved in politics that his grades suffered and he was barred from further study. By this time, however, he was an acknowledged leader in several bodies he had founded or had helped to found, including the South African Students Organization (SASO) and the Black Community Programs, and became a fulltime organizer for these bodies, spreading the creed of the Black Consciousness movement he had launched, which had been the motivating philosophy behind the formation of these associations. Shortly thereafter, he had been banned and restricted to the King William's Town area.

As I drove toward that first meeting, I pondered with mounting anger an article Biko had written as a fiery young founder of SASO. It had appeared in 1972 in a volume, later banned, called *Student Perspectives on South Africa* edited by H. W. van der Merwe and David Welsh in association with the Bailey Institute of Interracial Studies, and contained such statements as the following:

"No race possesses the monopoly of beauty, intelligence and force, and there is room for all of us at the rendezvous of victory." I do not think Aimé Césaire was thinking about South Africa when he said these words. The whites in this country have placed themselves on a path of no return. So blatantly exploitative in terms of the mind and body is the practice of white racism that one wonders if the interests of blacks and whites in this country have not become so mutually exclusive as to remove the possibility of there being "room for all of us at the rendezvous of victory."

It will not be long before the blacks relate their poverty to their blackness in concrete terms. Because of the tradition forced onto the country, the poor people shall always be black people. It is not surprising, therefore, that the blacks should wish to rid themselves of a system that locks up the wealth of the country in the hands of a few. No doubt Rick Turner was thinking of this when he declared that "any black government is likely to be socialist." [Author's note: Rick Turner was shot dead in his home by an unknown killer in January 1978.]

We now come to the group that has longest enjoyed confidence from the black world – the liberal establishment, including radical and leftish groups. The biggest mistake the black world ever made was to assume that whoever opposed apartheid was an ally. For a long time the black world has been looking only at the governing party and not so much at the whole power structure as the object of their rage. In a sense the very political vocabulary that the blacks have used has been inherited from the liberals. For a long time, in fact, it became the occupation of black leadership to "calm the masses down," while they engaged in fruitless negotiation with the status quo . . .

Of course this situation could not last. A new breed of black leaders was beginning to suspect the involvement of liberals in a struggle they regarded as essentially theirs, when the political movements of the blacks were either banned or harassed into nonexistence. This left the stage open once more for the liberals to continue with their work of "fighting for the rights of the blacks." It never occurred to the liberals that the integration they insisted upon as an effective way of opposing apartheid was impossible to achieve in South Africa. One has to overhaul the whole system in South Africa before hoping to get black and white walking hand in hand to oppose a common enemy. As it is, both black and white walk into a hastily organized integrated circle carrying with them the seeds of destruction of that circle – their inferiority and superiority complexes. The myth of integration as propounded under the banner of the liberal ideology must be cracked because it makes people believe that something is being achieved when in reality the artificially integrated circles are a soporific to the blacks while salving the consciences of the few guilt-stricken whites. It works from the false premise that, because it is difficult to bring people of different races together in this country, achievement of this is in itself a step toward the total liberation of the blacks.

The essence of politics is to direct oneself to the group which wields power. Most white dissident groups are aware of the power wielded by the white power structure. They are quick to quote statistics on how big the military defense budget is. They know exactly how effectively the police and the army can control protesting black hordes – peaceful or otherwise. They know to what degree the

black world is infiltrated by the Security Police. Hence they are completely convinced of the impotence of the black people. Why then do they persist in talking
to the blacks? Since they are aware that the problem in this country is white
racism, why do they not address themselves to the white world? In an effort to
answer these questions one has to come to the painful conclusion that the liberal
is in fact appeasing his own conscience, or at best is eager to demonstrate his
identification with the black people only insofar as it does not sever all his ties
with his relatives on his side of the color line. Being white, he possesses the
natural passport to the exclusive pool of white privilege from which he does not
hesitate to extract whatever suits him. Yet, since he identifies with the blacks,
he moves around his white circles, whites-only beaches, restaurants and cinemas
with a lighter load, feeling that he is not like the rest. However, at the back of his
mind is a constant reminder that he is quite comfortable as things stand and
therefore should not bother about change. Although he does not vote for the
Nationalists (now that they are in the majority anyway), he feels secure under the
protection offered by the Nationalists and subconsciously shuns the idea of
change.

I am not sneering at the liberals and their involvement. Neither am I suggesting that they are the most to blame for the black man's plight. Rather I am illus-
trating the fundamental fact that total identification with an oppressed group in a
system that forces one group to enjoy privilege and to live on the sweat of
another is impossible. White society collectively owes the blacks so huge a debt
that no one member should automatically expect to escape from the blanket
condemnation that needs must come from the black world. It is not as if whites
are allowed to enjoy privilege only when they declare their solidarity with the
ruling party. They are born into privilege and are nourished by and nurtured in
the system of ruthless exploitation of black energy. The liberals must fight on
their own and for themselves. If they are true liberals they must realize that they
themselves are oppressed, and that they must fight for their own freedom and
not that of the blacks with whom they can hardly claim identification. . . . What
I have tried to show is that in South Africa political power has always rested
with white society. Not only have the whites been guilty of being on the offensive
but, by skillful maneuvers, they have managed to control the responses of the
blacks to the provocation. Not only have they kicked the black but they have also
told him how to react to the kick. For a long time the black has been listening with
patience to the advice he has been receiving on how best to respond to the kick.
With painful slowness he is now beginning to show that he realizes it is his right
and duty to respond to the kick in the way he sees fit.

The call for Black Consciousness is the most positive call to come from any
group in the black world for a long time. It is more than just a reactionary rejection of whites by blacks. The quintessence of it is the realization by the blacks
that, in order to feature well in this game of power politics, they have to use the
concept of group power and to build a strong foundation for this. Being an
historically, politically, socially and economically disinherited and dispossessed

group, they have the strongest foundation from which to operate. The philosophy of Black Consciousness, therefore, expresses group pride and the determination by the blacks to rise and attain the envisaged self. At the heart of this kind of thinking is the realization by the blacks that the most potent weapon in the hands of the oppressor is the mind of the oppressed. Once the latter has been so effectively manipulated and controlled by the oppressor as to make the oppressed believe that he is a liability to the white man, then there will be nothing the oppressed can do that will really scare his powerful masters. Hence thinking along lines of Black Consciousness makes the black man see himself as a being, entire in himself, and not as an extension of a broom or additional leverage to some machine. At the end of it all, he cannot tolerate attempts by anybody to dwarf the significance of his manhood. Once this happens, we know that the real man in the black person is beginning to shine through.

I have spoken of Black Consciousness as if it is something that can be readily detected. Granted this may be an overstatement at this stage, yet it is true that, gradually, the various black groups are becoming more and more conscious of the self. They are beginning to rid their minds of imprisoning notions which are the legacy of the control of their attitudes by whites. Slowly, they have cast aside the "morality argument" which prevented them from going it alone and are now learning that a lot of good can be derived from the specific exclusion of whites from black institutions. Of course it is not surprising to us that whites are not much aware of these developing forces since such consciousness is essentially an inward-looking process.

We are aware that the white man is sitting at our table. We know he has no right to be there; we want to remove him from our table, strip the table of all the trappings put on it by him, decorate it in true African style, settle down and then ask him to join us on our terms if he wishes.

I seethed with annoyance as I thought of the gross unfairness of much of this theory. The bland generalization lumping together all whites in condemnation was in itself an outrage. Liberals like Patrick Duncan, Peter Brown and many others had suffered imprisonment, banning and house arrest for their commitment to the nonracist cause. Alan Paton had been hounded for years by Security Police. By what twisted logic could they be accused of secretly or subconsciously taking comfort from apartheid government? Many liberals boycotted apartheid amenities and specifically did not enjoy "whites-only beaches, restaurants and cinemas," and by what aberrant thinking could any individual baby be condemned for being "born into white privilege"? The most charitable interpretation I could put on this outburst was that it was the product of youthful immoderacy.

Although, on reflection, it had to be admitted that there *were* some liberals who took advantage of all-white restaurants, cinemas and beaches.

Me, for instance . . .

Nevertheless, as I drove toward my first meeting with Steve Biko I resolved to challenge him about his entire approach to white liberalism, in that this approach appeared to be based on a black requirement of inordinate sainthood among white foes of apartheid as a prerequisite of acceptance in the future South Africa he envisaged. After all, it was not *entirely* his country. It was at least to some partial extent mine as well, and I was certainly not disposed toward apologizing for any pigmentational accidents of birth in this respect. It promised to be a lively encounter . . .

OUR FIRST ENCOUNTER

As I DROVE into King William's Town I reflected on the irony of this small colonial city with its Victorian buildings as a setting for the headquarters of South Africa's radical black resistance movement. The good burghers of "King" were doubtless unaware of the viper they harbored in their midst. I had been told to meet Biko at number 15a Leopold Street, at the offices of the Black Community Programs where he worked as executive director for the Eastern Cape after his banning order in 1973 had restricted him to the King William's Town magisterial district.

I found Leopold Street easily enough, right in the heart of the town. Leopold Street was a pretty, tree-shaded avenue, but where number 15a should have been was a little church whose main door was uncompromisingly closed. Yet close investigation revealed that the church was indeed number 15a, and I knocked on the door to rouse the churchwarden in hopes that he might solve the mystery. The door opened almost immediately and I was beckoned in by several young blacks who appeared to be expecting me. Entering the building I found it was not a church at all, but that the interior was a well-carpentered pattern of administration offices complete with desks, filing cabinets, typewriters, Roneo machines and shelves. I asked for Steve Biko and was ushered through these offices toward the backyard of the "church."

I was conscious of a certain tension. I had never met a "banned" person before and knew only that he could not speak to more than one person at a time, could not be quoted, and was carefully watched by the Security Police. Besides, I wasn't clear as to why Biko should want to meet me – an orthodox white liberal of the type his movement rejected along with the entire white group, regardless of liberal opposition to apartheid.

The backyard of the church was small and overgrown with weeds. A tall tree dominated the yard and towered over a small building in the corner diagonally opposite the church. This building contained three offices and a veranda, and in front of it stood Biko. My first impression was of his size. I am slightly under six feet tall, but he stood at least a couple of inches over me, and had the bulky build of a heavyweight boxer carrying more weight than when in peak condition. His features were pleasant but his expression was one of appraisal rather than welcome. He greeted me with reserve, with a firm, dry, rather fleshy handshake, and motioned me into what I took to be his office, indicating a sofa where I could sit. He sat opposite me on the extreme forward edge of a chair, with his elbows on his knees and fists bunched together between wide-planted legs. It was, I thought, an attitude of challenge, and as I was in a mood of challenge myself I opened up by telling him I had come to find out more about this Black Consciousness business which had in my view too many overtones of black racism. I remember concluding with the phrase: "I don't have to bloody well apologize for being born white or for racial policies I don't support!"

His reaction astonished me. He had listened throughout with a solemn expression, but as I finished speaking his entire face was suddenly animated by a huge, total grin, and his body adopted a posture that was to become familiar in the years ahead – he slid down in the chair until he was almost reclining on his spine. It was an attitude of complete relaxation, and was later to become a telltale sign that Steve wanted to settle down for a long, long chat. He conceded immediately that his "antiliberal" article in *Student Perspectives* had been written in the heat of his early twenties and that it had some "overkill, actually," but defended the basic principle underlying it on tactical grounds, repeating that black liberation had to start with black psychological self-reliance, and that this could only be initiated in isolation from allies whose good intentions were an obstacle to such self-realization. "I don't reject liberalism as such or white liberals as such. I reject only the concept that black liberation can be achieved through the leadership of white liberals," he said.

"But why should it be white liberal leadership?" I asked. "Why can't the leaders be black liberals?"

"It's not as easy as that. The entire political structure of the country is against it. The concept simply isn't practical politics. For example, the laws forbidding multiracial political association."

"But for heaven's sake, your obvious worst enemy is the white racist, the pro-apartheid Nationalist or United party man, not the white liberal or Progressive who rejects apartheid. Why attack these first?"

"Sure, the white racist, the Nats or UP, is the main target, but to equip ourselves to challenge the enemy we first have to distance ourselves from the friend who inhibits us. The liberal is no enemy, he's a friend – but for the moment he holds us back, offering a formula too gentle, too inadequate for our struggle."

"Well, that's all very well, but I'm not happy about the general direction of all this blacks-alone business. Having achieved this Black Consciousness among young blacks today, how do you slam the brakes on it tomorrow? How do you prevent it from becoming black racism or anti-white hatred?"

"Because it isn't a negative, hating thing. It's a positive black self-confidence thing involving no hatred of anyone, not even the Nats – only of what they represent today. Okay, you may have cases where a fringe element retains anti-white bitterness. We'll do what we can to restrain that, but frankly it's not one of our top priorities or one of our major concerns. Our main concern is the liberation of the blacks – the majority of South Africans – and while we want to work to establish a country in which all men are free and welcome citizens – white as well as black – we have to concentrate on what means most to blacks. So at this stage we are preoccupied with black sensitivities, not white sensitivities."

I asked why he had wanted to speak to me, and he replied with another broad grin: "Man, I wanted to see what you look like in real life. Most of the blacks think you're a terrific guy and you've got a big following among blacks because of your editorials – but I wanted to find out if you're a terrific enough guy to start giving some decent coverage to the Black Consciousness movement, which means a lot more to blacks than all the Bantustan stuff your reporters cover." He said SASO and Black Consciousness people generally felt the newspapers did not provide fair coverage of their projects and attitudes and hoped the *Daily Dispatch* would give a lead in this direction. I replied that we'd be glad to give as much coverage as possible in this direction, since our news columns were open to all legitimate news and our letters columns to all shades of opinion. I promised there and then to assign a reporter to the Black Consciousness beat, a black reporter, and asked that this reporter be given the full cooperation of the Black Consciousness officials who could be quoted.

"Okay, so much for news. Now what about views? Your paper runs viewpoint columns by all other groups – Nats, UP, Progressive, Homelanders and Coloured Labour Party spokesmen. What about a column for Black Consciousness?"

"Right," I said. "Find me a columnist who can write such a column within the limits of publishing law and I'll print it regularly."

After a full discussion of these and other matters, I realized we had been speaking for some hours, and prepared to leave. He walked with me to my car, and as we came out of the little yard he saw my brown Mercedes parked outside the church and started extravagantly, making a great show of shielding his eyes with his arms from this capitalistic symbol of automotive opulence.

"My God," he said, elaborately averting his head as if dazzled by such splendor, "how can a champion of the people be driving around in that thing!"

"Look," I said, "you do your black thing and I'll do my white thing. The days of white privilege are numbered, and I'm enjoying it while I can." He was still laughing at this as I turned the corner out of sight and headed for home.

That was my first meeting with Steve Biko, and it was enough to convince me that I had met an unusually gifted man. His quick brain, superb articulation of ideas and sheer mental force were highly impressive. He had the aura and stature of a leader, and on my way home I concluded that in a journalistic career in which I had met and interviewed some of the great figures in British, Canadian, American and German politics, this man Biko might conceivably be the most impressive of them all. In the months and years that followed, in which we became close friends, I soon lost all doubt on that score. Steve Biko, I later came to realize, was the greatest man I ever had the privilege to know.

WE BECOME FRIENDS

My next meeting with Steve was at the place where most of our subsequent meetings took place, the Zanempilo Clinic. The Black Community Programs, based at the Leopold Street "church," ran a number of projects aimed at black self-help schemes such as literacy classes, dressmaking, and health education. The Zanempilo Clinic was one of the main health projects. Built on a hill several miles outside King William's Town, the clinic served thousands of rural blacks who couldn't get to the city hospital. Run by a small staff under Dr. Ramphele, it had an operating theater, a maternity ward and facilities for instruction classes in basic nutrition. During our first meeting Steve had mentioned that he would like to show me around the clinic, and some days later he phoned to invite me to bring Wendy and the children to Sunday dinner there and to spend the day. I pointed out that we had five children, and would therefore constitute quite a multitude. He said that sounded like a "good big African family" and we were all welcome. On the Sunday, Wendy and I and the kids, ranging in age from three to eleven, piled into the car and drove to King William's Town. As arranged, we met Steve at Leopold Street and he, after what seemed to be a now requisite grimace of horror at the sight of my car, drove ahead to guide us to the clinic.

Dr. Ramphele was there to welcome us. She went through her own parody of astonishment at the appearance of the Mercedes and speculating aloud as to where it could be concealed to prevent the damaging impression being conveyed to local blacks that Black Consciousness devotees might be associating with the wrong kind of people.

"It's the smallest, cheapest kind of Mercedes there is," I pointed out.

She replied in her loud brand of raillery: "That's no excuse, man, it's still a Mercedes! What are we coming to here! Our people won't speak to us again if they see this thing here!"

I give the account of the joshing over the Mercedes in some detail, because although the kidding around was good-humored, there was in Steve and his followers a strong antipathy toward what they regarded as luxury items, and I later discovered that Steve had avoided buying something like a television set for the organization because most of "the people" didn't have television and it wasn't a necessity.

We were welcomed into Dr. Ramphele's little house adjoining the clinic, about twenty of us altogether, and over drinks we had a marathon discussion. Although the atmosphere, socially, was friendly, with the smaller children casually taken onto various laps in the totally uninhibited way of Africans where children are concerned, it was quite clear that both Wendy and I were on some sort of trial. It was a most searching session of questions on our complete political stance, private and public. Satisfactory answers drew a responsive ripple of pleasure from our questioners, and unsatisfactory ones a barely perceptible stir of unease.

We held firm to our reservations about the unavoidably racist aspects of Black Consciousness, but generally must have passed muster, because from that day we were increasingly taken into that circle as fully trusted confidants. In the years that followed deep friendship was forged among us all – a friendship that went beyond political considerations, so that, while having initially a political base, it was a personal relationship among people drawn to each other as compatible human beings.

For Wendy and me this was a uniquely enriching experience, because in our country with its countless barriers based on race, deep friendships among blacks and whites were rare. While there were mild friendships involving blacks and whites, societal circumstances generally saw to it that few whites ever met interesting blacks – that is, blacks who interested them as people rather than as blacks.

The striking thing about Steve and his followers was that ironically, for purveyors of Black Consciousness, their blackness was the easiest thing about them to forget. I should explain this statement fully. There was undeniably among the Black Consciousness people a full sense of self-worth – a poise and a confidence which few blacks in South Africa exhibited in their relationships with whites. They walked, talked and slouched in chairs "like us." Conversation wasn't stilted or self-conscious. Long silences didn't bother them if they had nothing to say for the moment. They "walked tall" in all things, without deference or apology. To most people in most countries this would be an extraordinary thing to regard as extraordinary, but our South African society is a highly abnormal one. No observer of it should underestimate the Black Consciousness achievement in producing self-confident attitudes in blacks in an environment which, from cradle to grave, is designed either to denigrate black worth or to channel incipient manifestations of it into stereotyped tribal responses for the political convenience of white racists.

In a certain sense it might seem offensive to record that Wendy and I both felt these people surrounding Steve walked, talked and acted "like us." It might seem condescending, paternalistic and even racist. But in fact the observation is made in the opposite sense. For privileged white South Africans to meet in their own largely unprivileged country blacks liberated into psychologically emancipated attitudes was both a revelation and an education. It was rather, one imagines, like encountering in the middle of Russia a group of dissidents whose entire bearing and behavior is that of persons who have never known repression. It was like discovering an oasis of freedom in a desert of enslavement.

Some years ago I visited Zambia, and was impressed there with the similarly confident bearing of young blacks – particularly young black girls. It had been a decade since I had previously visited Zambia, in that country's year of independence, and now there was a whole new generation of

Zambians who had never known servility or the psychological denigration of second-class citizenship. The girls sat on the arm of one's chair and said: "Now what sort of work do you do?"

Pitifully few white South African males have ever met a black female who could communicate with them on any basis of racial and sexual equality. For them, black women are either unobtrusively performing domestic chores in the kitchen or hurrying by in school uniform, with heads deferentially lowered. Few white males in South Africa have met a Dr. Ramphele who could say quite casually: "Now you're really talking nonsense – here, let me get you another drink."

In the early days of our friendship with Steve there were many adjustments to make, on both sides. He had to adjust to my capitalist assumptions and liberal approach, and I had to adjust to his radical sensitivities. One example will illustrate this. Soon after I first met him, I drove up to King William's Town for a talk. There was an excellent restaurant in the town called "Jack's Place," and on the way up I thought it would be a good idea to crash the apartheid barrier by taking Steve to lunch there.

To avoid any embarrassment to him if we were refused, I went first to the proprietor and told him of my intent. He said he had nothing against the idea personally and that the authorities were starting to allow that sort of thing if one obtained permission. To make sure there were no hitches, I agreed that he should go ahead and seek such permission. He did a certain amount of telephoning of government departments, then informed me with obvious pleasure that I could bring my black guest to lunch.

To think of it all now, I blush at my own naivety, but I recall inviting Steve casually (but inwardly pleased with myself) to lunch at Jack's Place. He declined politely, saying that on principle he would not enjoy going into a place just because he was with me if it was a place he couldn't take his black friends to any time he pleased. Then, with his sensitive insight, he must have perceived what this had meant to me, because he suddenly changed his mind and said: "Okay, let's go. It'll be fun."

Quite a lot was now unsaid on both sides. I hadn't told him I had got "permission" because I felt this would be an insult to him, and he hadn't told me that he and Mamphela had prepared a particularly good meal for me to have with them at the clinic. When Mamphela came into the room he said rather loudly to her, signaling with his intonation that she shouldn't ruin his act: "Mamphela, Donald and I are going to lunch at Jack's Place. What do you think of that?" She hit the roof.

"I think it's a lousy idea! What? Go to that place? Are you mad, Steve? How can you compromise your principles? You'll have lunch here, both of you! Besides, it's ready. Come on!"

And that was that. It was only later that I learned that Steve had already been to Jack's Place himself, once, just to see what it was like, but had found it "too fancy – not a 'people' place." I never repeated the mistake of contemplating such "token integration" again. It was part of the learning process.

SOME PERSONAL MEMORIES

I SAID EARLIER that Steve Biko was the greatest man I ever met. What determines greatness? How does one measure it? Each of us has his own criteria. When I say that Steve Biko was the greatest man I ever had the privilege to know, I mean quite literally that he, more than any other person I have encountered, had the most impressive array of qualities and abilities in that sphere of life which determines the fates of most people – politics. This doesn't mean he was merely a superb politician. He was much more than that. He was a statesman, in that sense of the word in which it is applied to Abraham Lincoln, having that breadth of vision and that wider comprehension of the affairs of men and nations that is conveyed to the listener through more than mere words. He could impart understanding. He could enable one to share his vision and he could do so with an economy of words because he seemed to communicate ideas through extraverbal media – almost psychically.

As a journalist I had interviewed many prominent personalities in various countries, but for me none of them approached the stature of Steve Biko. The one who came the closest to him in "charisma" was Robert Kennedy, with whom I had long discussions both in South Africa and the United States. But the charisma of Kennedy was born of circumstance, background and events. The charisma of Steve Biko was entirely his own. He had from an early age the unmistakable bearing and quality of a unique leader. I say unique because the style of his leadership was his own – it was un-pushy, un-self-promotional, yet immediately acknowledged by his peers. Father Aelred Stubbs, who knew him as a youth, says the greatness of Steve was apparent even in boyhood. Father Stubbs, an erudite Old

Etonian who became principal of the Federal Theological Seminary at Alice, was thus able to acknowledge and defer to the leadership of a youth half his age. I know what Father Stubbs meant. I was thirteen years older than Steve, yet I always had the feeling I was talking to someone older and wiser, and like many others I often sought his advice on all manner of problems.

He had the gift of being able to cut through to the core of a problem and to find the only and best solution, even on topics beyond his personal sphere of experience. For example, he knew little about newspaper administration, yet a staff problem I consulted him about after days of soul-searching was straightened out between his lighting a cigarette and stubbing it out.

Fellow students at Natal University described how he exercised unobtrusive but firm dominance of their deliberations. They say he never sat up front but invariably took a seat at the back of the room, and spoke little. Yet inevitably, it seemed, after they had all had their say they would turn to him and his suggestions always carried the day.

He had excellent qualities beyond charisma, personality and wisdom. He had rocklike integrity and a degree of courage that sent one's regard for the potentialities of the human spirit soaring skyhigh. Incidents related in this book will illustrate this in due course, but it will suffice at this stage to say that his brand of courage was the kind that made the very idea of recantation before a firing squad unthinkable.

Like most truly great men, Steve Biko had no trace of arrogance in him. Arrogance is incompatible with a good sense of humor, and this he had in full measure. And while he had an uncompromising contempt for the Nationalist mentality, he had at no time any ounce of hatred or bitterness toward his persecutors. In fact, he spoke at times almost affectionately about his jailers and interrogators.

Hearing or reading that Nationalist spokesmen described Steve (whom they had never met) as a hater of whites was a particular irony for a number of Steve's close friends who happened to be white – people like Father Stubbs, Francis Wilson, David Russell, Trudi Thomas and others including Wendy and me. Certainly as far as Wendy and I were concerned, it was a matter of the deepest satisfaction that we knew, as any of his close friends knew, that we had his total trust. Had the man been a racist, which he most comprehensively was not, this might have enabled us to think that at least we had helped in some small way to redeem white South Africa in his eyes. But such redemption was never necessary where he was concerned. He simply wasn't a hater of people. Not Vorster, not Kruger, not even the arch-extremist Treurnicht. Steve understood them and their hangups too well to hate them. It was only their racist ideas that he hated. And he hated these to such effect, and opposed them to such effect, and rallied opposition to them to such effect, that because of their merciless rigidity his final collision with the System was inevitable.

I could write endless thousands of words about Steve's qualities as a man, and I can quote his ideas and opinions. I wish it were possible on the printed page to include as well a complete record of his vocal inflections and speech mannerisms exactly as they sounded. They were so distinctive, and so characteristic of him. He tended generally to slur his words, almost to mumble, especially when talking quickly in excitement. His front teeth were spaced, and this did not make for clear diction unless he made a special effort at it – and much of the time he was too bound up with the words and thoughts at issue to bother about niceties of diction. He had a deep, pleasing voice, and employed, like many Black Consciousness people, a number of Americanisms in conversation. He invariably greeted one, whether on the phone or in person, with "Hi!" In such greeting it was drawn out, drawled, almost Southern. Men of all description were "guys." All except the Security Police, who were referred to, even singly, as "the System."

His English was outstanding, and his vocabulary impressive even in his customary quiet understatement. His pronunciation was easy, unstrained and only slightly accented with African intonation, except for words like "burn," "turn," and "colonel," which like many black South Africans he pronounced "ben," "ten," and "kennel." On one occasion Wendy and I couldn't understand what he meant when he told us of how his Security interrogators had "brought in the kennel" and how he had been "surprised to see a kennel in the room." Fortunately we didn't interrupt to ask about this, because a moment later when he started telling us how the "kennel" had put several questions to him we realized . . .

The name "Biko," correctly pronounced, rhymes with "seesaw." "Bee-kaw" is a rough approximation. To be absolutely exact, in terms of perfect Xhosa pronunciation, the *B* is not pronounced "hard." It is a soft *B* – the sort of noise a pipesmoker makes when puffing, drawing in air, to light his pipe. And the emphasis is on the first syllable. But Steve usually pronounced his name simply as *BEE*-kaw, with a hard *B*, to make it easier for non-Xhosas to pronounce. I told him once that he was consistently mispronouncing his own name as a political expedient, whereupon the next few phonecalls from him started with an exaggerated implosion of the *B* and an elaborate drawing out of the first syllable. If the pipe-puffing sound is written as "Bh," what he said on the phone was: "*BHEEEE*-kaw speaking!"

He had a deep sense of humor and could laugh quite immoderately at some subtlety which really touched the innermost chords in his sense of fun. Steve's laugh was especially memorable. I remember how delightedly he laughed one day when my youngest son, Gavin, rushed into the room and burst out with: "Dad-there's-a-boy-at-school-who's-got-a-watch-that's-waterproof-shockproof-and-magnetic-proof!"

"Hey, man!" Steve said to Gavin. "That sounds like one hell of a watch! I think your dad should get you one!" The "Hey, man!" was also characteristic. Some mornings he would phone me in sheer good spirits to say: "Hiiii! Hey, man, that was a damn good editorial this morning! Kwewuku! Ubabetile!" ("Gee! You hit them!") Or he would phone and say: "Hiiii! I'm sending a message by a small-nosed courier who should be with you in about five minutes." That would be Malusi Mpumlwana, a close friend and colleague of Steve's. "Mpumlwana" is the diminutive of "mpumlo," meaning nose.

If you related an amusing story to him he needed no elaborations but seemed to comprehend all the subtle implications. He was most amused once when I told him of my brother's remark on a certain occasion. My brother, like many Transkei traders, often resorted to Xhosa expressions if English seemed inadequate, and on one occasion back home in Elliotdale at a golf club meeting, my brother, who had had a few drinks, noticed that the committee seating was such as to place next to each other two pillars of the community who were widely rumored to be having an affair. Using a Xhosa Anglicism, my brother remarked: "Ngati i 'arrangiwe' le nto!" ("It looks as if this thing is 'arranged'!") In our family this phrase came to be applied to any situation that seemed set up. One day when Steve was having lunch with us I prompted him, while Wendy was out of the room, to ask her on her return whether the two of us would play a tune for him on our two pianos. (I knew such requests irritated her but knew he'd enjoy the piece we had recently learned.) When she came back in, he duly made the request, whereupon she shot a suspicious glance at me, murmuring: "Ngati i arrangiwe, le nto." Steve promptly replied: "Hayi [no] – kodwa [but] i suggestiwe!" This really broke us up, especially the way he drew out the Xhosa pronunciation of "suggest" – "sah-gest."

Incidentally, he did enjoy the playing. We gave him a medley of music on our two pianos consisting only of the work of black composers, kidding him that to play white composers to a "Black Conshahssness" proponent would be inappropriate. So we played him Scott Joplin, Fats Waller, Dollar Brand and Duke Ellington, as well as his beloved Xhosa composer Tyamzashe, who lived right beside the Zanempilo Clinic. Steve often visited the old man, and particularly liked his choral work. Once when I played him a cassette recording of my own composition, "African Overture," as performed by the Cape Provincial State Orchestra, he was deeply moved and at the end of it he had tears in his eyes. "That's pure African music. It's authentic. It's as good as Tyamzashe's work." When I told him it was dedicated to him he was touched beyond words and was quiet for a considerable time. He asked me for a copy of it, and I said he should wait for a later recording scheduled after some re-orchestration, but this had not been done by the time he died.

He also loved a recording I had come by, through a journalist friend, of "Nkosi Sikelele i Afrika" (the African Anthem) sung by President Kaunda, Bishop Muzorewa, Joshua Nkomo, Ndabaningi Sithole and other signatories to the Lusaka agreement whereby the African National Council had united in a common front on the Zimbabwe question. I thought back to this recording at Steve's funeral, when twenty thousand mourners sang "Nkosi Sikelele" – to my mind the most beautiful anthem in all the world.

Steve loved most kinds of music, and had a large range of records in his home, but he had a special liking for African "gumba" music, which relies more on harmony than inventiveness of melody.

He also loved a party, if the occasion was right. I remember one joyous evening, soon after his release from his third (101 days) detention. Wendy and I brought a dozen bottles of champagne to celebrate, and about fifteen of us crowded into the tiny lounge at Zanempilo for a marathon spell of wassailing that lasted to the early hours. Steve had a lot of fun kidding one of the Zanempilo workers for horning in on a televized session with a German television team. "The guy kept drifting in front of the camera asking if anyone wanted tea – just to get his face on the screen," he laughed.

The only sad part of the proceedings was that a close friend of Steve's had been restricted the day before, to the Cape Town area, shortly before he was due to visit Steve in King William's Town. But Steve, who had a lively sense of drama, left the room at midnight and came back in with his arm around the banned man! We were flabbergasted, then delighted, then nonplussed in turn. How could it be possible? We plied him with questions. I remember the look of sheer delight and pride with which he replied: "It's our country, man! We move about as we like, man!"

Steve traveled about the country extensively from time to time, despite his banning, going as far afield as Cape Town and Durban, and more than once to Johannesburg. He once traveled there quite legally. He had to give evidence at the trial of SASO and BPC leaders and had permission to drive himself all the way for this purpose.

On the way through the arid, flat Orange Free State he grew bored and lonely and gave a lift to two young whites. They had seemed reluctant to talk, and as company and conversation had been his aim in giving them a lift (they were hitch-hiking all the way to Johannesburg) he decided to draw them out.

"Are you boys English-speaking or Afrikaans-speaking?" he asked.

After some hesitation one of them said: "We're both English-speaking." But Steve thought he could detect from their accent that they were Afrikaners.

"What a pity," he said, "I was hoping you were Afrikaans-speaking because I want to improve my Afrikaans and I hoped to get some practice."

No response.

"Kom, praat met my (Come speak with me)," he said in Afrikaans.

"No, we don't know Afrikaans much," one of them replied. But the more English he spoke the more they struggled, until eventually he challenged them with a smile: "Come on, you're Afrikaans-speaking, aren't you?" With great reluctance they admitted it.

"Why did you deny it?" he persisted. Well, they said, they know that black people didn't like Afrikaners. Typically, Steve then delivered a long lecture to the effect that people should never, under any circumstances, be ashamed or reticent about their origins or race or culture. "There's nothing to be ashamed of in language or culture. In fact you should be proud of these things!" After that they became relaxed and friendly, and chatted all the way to Johannesburg. In Afrikaans!

Steve enjoyed reminiscing about the trip. "They were nice little guys, actually," he said. Also typically, he had had the sensitivity not to go into politico-racial depths with them. "It would have been too traumatic, really. They couldn't have handled it. As it is they lost a fair amount of their race prejudice on the trip without my having to work too hard at it."

I'll bet they did.

Sensitivity was one of Steve's greatest gifts. Sensitivity and thoughtfulness. This aspect of his character was well illustrated in an article shortly after his death by a mutual friend of ours, Dr. Trudi Thomas. In a cameo piece which captured the essence of his humanity in only a few words, she wrote:

Steve was special. Being with him made a special occasion. Knowing him was an enriching experience.

He was delightful company, full of charm, large and easy and gentle and courteous and humorous. He was always completely in command, completely self-possessed – and completely unassuming. There was, of course, no need for statement or pretense, he was so obviously the real thing. He always seemed to be in buoyant spirits and lifted yours with his.

He was no ascetic – he loved life and its good things and imparted this relish. But he thought that everyone should have a fair share.

I can see him now, resplendent in a new checked winter shirt; looking good; basking in the compliments; a little concerned that it might be a trifle loud. I can see him quaffing a beer provided by a student – one of the endless stream of visitors who beat a path to unlikely King William's Town to talk and listen to this remarkable man – and patting a paunch that was just beginning.

He enjoyed appearances, although he registered impressions rather than details and was often in trouble with his wife when she tested him about what she had been wearing the previous day.

People were important (after all that was his central philosophy) and that included you. When you were with him you had a sense of your own worth – and your responsibilities. He hobnobbed with the great and the influential who sought him out in his banishment, which rather neatly turned his intended Siberia into a Mecca.

But he was always equally available and concerned about the very least. Just released from 101 days in detention (no charge) he helped to organize the annual Christmas party of a creche run by the Black Community Program. I could not attend as I had hoped, and he later gently reproached me for not being at what he regarded as a very important event.

While the Program's clinic doctor was in detention he rushed around arranging locums for weekly out-station work, concerned that sick people would turn up and find nobody to treat them. It is impossible to reconcile this man with the image of a rabid revolutionary. His preferred path was always peaceable and constructive and creative.

I first met him when he was in charge of the Black Community Programs, as we shared an interest in cottage industries and comprehensive medicine and child welfare. He was a most active and effective worker.

He established a community health center with Dr. Mamphela Ramphele, realizing a dream they had had as medical students. I remember his unconcealed pride as he showed us around the beautifully conceived project, typically modest but uncomprisingly adequate. That was just three years ago.

Those were the flag-flying days, full of hope and promise. Now Mamphela is banned and Steve is dead. Is this what we do to black visionaries? Is this the price of black dreams and competence and effectiveness?

Steve was brilliant. With him you had a remarkable sense of being in the presence of a great mind. Strangely, the word "clever" did not suit him. He never indulged in intellectual gymnastics for show. His mind was simply a tool to chisel out sense and truth and order.

With Steve around, ideas flowed and each was scrupulously examined in the light of objectivity. He could not be seduced by popular sentiment or emotionalism or gratuitous association. He remained maddeningly fair-minded even about his greatest opponents or under the most relentless harassment.

He was invaluable in committee. If issues became obscured or irrelevances began to creep in he could provide an instant and masterful analysis and lucidly reveal the essential substance and set the proceedings on the right track toward progress again.

All this adds up to a brilliant, concerned, efficient, human and attractive person. But, there is still more. Much more. His greatness lay in the quality of his spirit, unstintingly and unswervingly served by his personality and his mind.

Despite his towering stature, despite constant harassment and frustration, he remained the most modest and most moderate and tolerant of men. After every meeting with Steve you wanted to go out and say to people: Come and meet this man. Come and talk to him, you will find the right balance again, you will get the true perspective.

Steve was motivated purely by the search for good and truth. There is plenty of scope for this in our South African society, grown dark and murky with hatred and greed and prejudice and overindulged insensitivity.

He searched steadfastly and single-mindedly. His special inspiration was Black Consciousness, the passionate conviction that a black man is as worthy as any other. This insight, however, was not for him merely grounds for recrimination. Certainly it meant that black men should have exactly the same rights as any other, but also that they must fearlessly claim them. Full personhood meant full personality responsibility which it was imperative to shoulder (even unto death) or compromise human status.

Steve had perspective – direction – equilibrium. Steve had a sure center.

In a mad, confused world, he remained normal and sane and good. These were his reference points, his beacons and signposts. These, and not any imported or ready-made ideology, were his policy makers. Everyone who met Steve in good will experienced a sort of magnetism. I attribute it to his triumphant, unassailable normality, a touchstone you were welcome to share.

There are those who suggest that he is being artificially lionized and that his death is being exploited for political gain. They are wrong. The great multitudinous roar of protest springs entirely from the deepest grief and anger and despair. Surely it is obvious that there is no need at all for external prodding. And after the noise has died down there will remain in our hearts an implacable dissent.

It has been said that if Steve had lived he would probably have been charged with preparing inflammatory pamphlets. It is dishonorable to accuse a man who cannot answer for himself. It also does not justify death nor detention without trial. We have an excellent qualified judiciary which can handle these problems completely.

It has been suggested that only one in a hundred black people had ever heard about Steve Biko before he died. That makes about 160,000 people – not a bad tribute to a man who was prevented from meeting and speaking to the people at twenty-six and died at thirty. However, even if the percentage of people who knew him was small, there are few who are unfamiliar with his ideas, which are now significantly and increasingly shaping a nation.

I did think of him as indestructible. As it happens I was wrong about his body. I had obviously attributed to it the same qualities as his transcendent spirit. It lives on, setting alight thousands of hearts and minds. May it purify them and strengthen them and light up the right path and lead them to the just and peaceful land he wanted with a fair share for every citizen.

Trudi's reference to the shirt is so right. He dressed in low-key way and had few clothes, but what he had looked right on him. Most of the time he simply wore a sleeveless open-necked shirt, jeans with a broad belt, and a most familiar pair of yellowish shoes. For his many appearances in court he wore a quiet suit.

He was prosecuted many times, and on minor charges he would defend himself quite brilliantly – always knowing when to give rein to his eloquence and when not to be too clever. On one occasion when he was up in traffic court on a speeding charge, he deferred to the magistrate in just the right degree, giving an impression of humility without any trace of sycophancy ("These magistrates need to feel important, man"), and the way in which he put the most telling points while giving every evidence of respect for the court reminded me of the Nelson Mandela speeches from the dock. Although two previous accused on the same charges had received heavy fines, Steve was cautioned and excused.

Outside the courthouse the young white traffic policeman whom Steve had put through a merciless grilling in the witness box had a cigarette with him. I remember noticing on this youngster's face a look which can only be described as hero-worship.

"Tell me, Mr. Biko . . . ," he said. It was possibly the first time in his life that he had addressed a black man as "Mister."

The magistrate, too, was clearly impressed by him, as were many whites on first meeting this black man out of the ordinary. During one of his trials, I overheard the state prosecutor remark to a court orderly: "This Biko is no ordinary man!"

I seldom saw Steve in a tie except for his court appearances. Once on returning from Zambia I brought him a UNIP tie from President Kaunda's United National Independence Party, and he wore it while giving evidence in the SASO–BPC trial. He told me after the trial that the state attorney, during an adjournment, had asked about the tie and where he got it. "From a friend," replied Steve.

"What friend? What is his name, if you are not ashamed to disclose it?"

"On the contrary, I mention his name with great pride – Donald Woods."

But the greater pride was mine.

Because he could not continue his medical studies on account of his ban, there being no university near King William's Town, Steve studied law by correspondence, and was doing well at the time of his death. He had passed a number of examinations, and after his death I had a moving letter from his professor at the University of South Africa, the country's biggest correspondence college, through which Robert Sobukwe and Nelson Mandela all achieved degrees while in captivity on Robben Island. (The government has since forbidden such study in jails.)

The other element of his nature borne out so well in the tribute by Trudi Thomas was his thoughtfulness toward others. It was this which led him to play a leading role in the founding of the Zimele Trust, a fund to care for the families of political prisoners. His thoughtfulness in this regard extended to small matters as well as big ones. Once when some of our mutual friends were in detention, Steve pestered the prison authorities to allow food to be brought to them. (He liked his food and knew what prison food was like!) On visiting day (they were not detained under the strictest of the so-called Terrorism Act provisions) Wendy decided to drive to King William's Town to visit them and phoned Steve to ask what they would like by way of food. "Meat, Wendy, meat! Mutton, if you can manage it," he said.

She duly brought the meat, precooked, to the jail, then called in on Steve before returning to East London. They had quite a long discussion and on her return home she had a phonecall from him.

"Wendy, did you remember that meat?"

"Yes," she told him, "it had already been delivered." He thanked her, saying he had remembered it only after she had left, and felt guilty at not having reminded her because he knew she wanted to bring something.

Steve was not conventionally religious, although he had genuine religious feeling in broad terms, so I asked him whence came the decision to call one of his sons "Nkosinathi" ("The Lord is with us").

"My mother took the decision unilaterally, actually. She is very religious and Ntsiki and I went along with the decision. But when the next one arrived I took my own unilateral decision to call him Samora, after Samora Machel."

When I asked him whether this meant he was in complete agreement with Machel's politics, he said: "Not necessarily, but Machel led the decolonization of Mozambique, and that was enough for me. Besides, a number of his programs are really good."

One cannot give a full account of the personality of Steve without mentioning his powerful sexuality. Steve did, in fact, have a reputation as a womanizer, and it was no doubt well earned. But he had especially close relationships with two women, his wife Ntsiki and his former fellow student, Mamphela. He had a different but special relationship with each.

I admired them both – Ntsiki quiet, loyal, self-effacing, but tough, and Mamphela boisterous, extrovert and equally tough. Each paid Wendy and me valued compliments – Ntsiki, when I was discussing Steve's funeral arrangements with her and explained that we would stay in the body of the crowd away from the family, since we didn't want to seem like "pushy whites" on this supreme day for black South Africa. She said with such feeling that it brought a lump to the throat: "Oh, Donald, you and Wendy are our brother and sister!" Mamphela's gesture of total acceptance was characteristically in contrast to this. She phoned one evening to speak to me, and Wendy told her I was at the chess club, whereupon she said with irritation: "The silly bugger!" In her amused annoyance she drew out the last word to "bah-gah."

Another remarkable friend of Steve's was Thami Zani, who at one stage held the BPC record for solitary confinement (423 days) and was as tough and as dedicated to the cause as it was possible to be. A big, strong man, he looked like a boxing champ but was, and is, one of the biggest brains in the movement. Then there was big, happy Peter Jones, a "Colored" man from Cape Town, who was Steve's constant companion and was actually with him when they were trapped at a roadblock in the detention which resulted in Steve's death. Peter, or "PC" to his friends, was full of fun. His big feet were invariably shod in sandals, and once I inadvertently stepped on his toe. He asked in a tone of scientific inquiry: "Donald, why is it that you persist in stamping on my feet all the time?"

After meeting many of Steve's friends, I once asked him if I could bring a friend of mine, Colin Eglin, leader of the Progressive Federal party, to visit him. He said, as gently as he could: "I'll see any friend of yours. I'll see Colin Eglin if you think it will help him. It won't help me." I said I thought it would help Colin, and thought (but did not say) it would help Steve as well, in some ways. What Steve meant was that although the Progressives had the two attributes of a nonracist policy and association with the great Helen Suzman, his followers were wary of too much contact with white South African politicians of any party. Although they obviously preferred the Progressives to the Nationalists, they still resented any party that functioned in the all-white Parliament and was therefore part of "the System."

Anyway I brought the two together in mid-1977, and listened throughout to their marathon talk. I felt privileged to do so, because it was a meeting of two unusually sharp minds. After an initial reserve, especially on Steve's side, they got on well, and at the end of their discussion both agreed to stay in contact and to initiate talks between their two groups. It was at the end of this discussion that Steve paid me his highest compliment. Colin had asked if there was anything he could do for Steve, and Steve replied: "Yes, Colin – promise me that you will never try to persuade my friend (nodding at me) to stand for Parliament for your party. He can do more good functioning as he is, with the purity of independence he enjoys outside the all-white structures."

Colin laughingly agreed. (No doubt partly because my candidacy would have cost him white votes!) Without revealing details of their conversation, I can say that the general theme was how each in his own sphere could help bring all the elements of the nation together at a conference table. Both stressed the need to do everything possible to avoid violence. Steve said: "When there is violence there is messiness. Violence brings too many residues of hate into the reconstruction period. Apart from its obvious horrors, it creates too many post-revolutionary problems. If at all possible, we want the revolution to be peaceful and reconciliatory. I hope this may still be possible – although the actions of the government make it appear as if the Nationalists are trying to provoke the opposite." Each told me separately after the meeting that he had been greatly impressed with the intellect of the other.

I was coming in for a considerable amount of legpulling from Steve at this time, and this aspect of our relationship will always remain most vivid for me. I had recently acquired a new company car, another Mercedes of the same silver color, Steve learned, as Premier Vorster's Mercedes. He wouldn't let me hear the end of it.

"How much did it cost?" he said mercilessly.

"Actually, it's not mine, you know, Steve, it belongs to the paper."

"How much?" he said.

"Well, it's the smallest of the range, I'm not sure . . ."

"How much?"

"To tell you the truth, I didn't do the actual buying . . ."

"And at the end of all that," Steve said with huge enjoyment, "how much?"

"Umnqundu wakho!" ("Your ass!") was all I could reply.

LIVING IN
A POLICE STATE

THE ZANEMPILO CLINIC, where my family and I had that first memorable Sunday dinner, became an important meeting place for us and our new-found friends. Being reasonably remote, several miles outside of King William's Town, it was a fairly safe place for discussion with several of the Biko group who were banned. Although Security Police raided there regularly, there were all sorts of "distant early warning" signals which could alert us to their approach, so that they would duly find the banned ones in separate rooms with only one other person present as prescribed by the banning edicts.

Often alone, often with Wendy, I met Steve in a variety of places in the years which followed. Because our phones, both his and ours, were bugged, we evolved a sort of code to arrange where we would meet. The Xhosa language figured prominently in this code talk. Security Police on monitor-ing duty might have understood routine Xhosa, but they never stood a chance of decoding our slurred variety of it. In their frustration they invariably gave both Steve and ourselves a silent, heavy-breathing phone-call immediately after one of our conversations. One night we received three or four, and Steve no less than six. But back to our code. Zanempilo Clinic was in a rural district known as Zinyoka ("place of snakes" in Xhosa). We would therefore, in slurred Xhosa, arrange to meet in Ramba-land. In Xhosa a ramba is a puff adder, the r in "ramba" pronounced as the ch sound in "Loch Lomond." This was an impudent codeword because it was fairly identifiable, but the Security Police listeners never caught on to it, and we relied on it on the basis of the dictum: "Never underestimate the inefficiency of the Security Police." If we wished to meet in the back yard at the church where we first met in Leopold Street, we would refer to it as "eyadini" – at the yard. Thus he became "Biko of the Yard," and a couple of times, blatantly, it was acknowledged on the phone as "Scotland Yard here!"

One night Wendy and I had driven many hundreds of miles from

Kimberley, where our eldest son was at boarding school, and were passing through King William's Town on our way home to East London. We had spoken with Robert Sobukwe, who was restricted in Kimberley, and decided to tell Steve of the encounter. I rang him from a callbox, saying I was "Umhleli wa se Monti" (very slurred, and meaning "the editor from East London," but safe because "Umhleli" also sounds like a person's name). We met ten minutes later at "eyadini."

On another occasion he phoned us in an elaborately casual voice to invite us to Zanempilo – in code. On the way there, Wendy said she had detected the excitement in his voice in spite of his casual manner, and we couldn't work out why, since Mamphela had recently been banished to faraway Tzaneen in the Northern Transvaal. She had been driven there, more than a thousand kilometers, under Security Police escort, and we would have expected him to be downcast about it because we knew he missed her greatly. On arrival at Zanempilo we soon realized why there had been a trace of elation in his voice, because there, large as life, was Mamphela. She had promptly borrowed a car and driven all the way back on discovering a technical misstatement on her banning order. Her name had been spelled wrong and her identity number mixed up, so she decided to defy the System on this technicality.

She immediately resumed her medical duties at the clinic, and actually delivered a baby shortly after her return. There was much merriment about whether she, the mother and the newborn child constituted an "illegal gathering," since her ban prohibited her from being with more than one person at a time. Mamphela made us breakfast, Father Stubbs also having appeared out of nowhere to share the occasion, and in spite of the fact that we all expected the Security Police to arrive at any moment we had a happy and relaxed morning.

I remember admiring Mamphela's steely nerve, and that of Steve. Neither gave any indication of tension, although both must have known that informers would have tipped off the Security Police about her return to the clinic, and that a raid might occur at any time. Typically, the Black Peoples Convention (local branch) planned how to exploit the situation, and several days later gave a press statement after Security Police had visited the clinic to verify that she was there. Playing things by the book in the curious way in which they sometimes operate, the Security Police did not take immediate action against her but took legal advice instead, got the minister to sign another (correctly spelled and numbered) banning order, and used this to remove her once more to Tzaneen. But she had had ten days at the clinic, and the satisfaction of defying the System for those ten days.

Steve and his friends often defied the System, taking calculated risks if they thought these were worthwhile, but most of the time they exercised great care to avoid being caught breaking the bans. One night at the clinic there were a number of people having drinks with Steve, and I wondered what would happen if the Security Police arrived. I whispered this question to him and by way of reply he took me outside. It was a dark night, but after my eyes had become accustomed to the dark, he pointed out certain directions to me, and I saw a number of glowing cigarette ends at varying distances at all four points of the compass. "If the System arrives from any direction, we get distant early warning," he smiled. "Then we disperse in prearranged ways, leaving only the unbanned people in the house."

It was remarkable how Steve functioned as a national leader in spite of being confined to such a small town as "King," as we all called it. People beat a path to his door from all over the country and from all over the world, and he undoubtedly functioned in a full leadership capacity as far as many blacks in South Africa were concerned. Sometimes his visitors were "hot" – either on the run from the Security Police, or outside areas to which they had been restricted.

Once Wendy and I met Steve at "the yard" and he had with him his elder son, six-year-old Nkosinathi. I remember how Steve stood talking to us, with one hand on Nkosinathi's shoulder, explaining that he was "baby-sitting" – keeping Nkosinathi with him all day because there was a "hot" visitor in the house and Nkosinathi might mention his name inadvertently while playing with the child of the next-door neighbor – a black policeman. "Yes," said Steve, smiling as he tugged at Nkosinathi's ears. "This fellow has seen things he shouldn't have seen, so he must stay with me all day!"

Although Steve's basic good humor enabled him to deal easily with all types of people, even Security policemen, some of whom called him "Steve," he drew a firm line between what was fun and what was serious. Even in his dealings with "the System."

For example, one night a number of Security officers arrived at his house to search for some papers which were indeed there. He demanded written authority for their search before letting them in (knowing full well they would need no such warrant). Prepared for such tactics, they produced a multipaged document of authorization, and he said: "I'll read it through the window before letting you in." He locked the front door, went and quickly hid the papers in his mother's room, then put his head through the window. They held the stapled document up to him and he affected to read the first page carefully.

Then, keeping a straight face, he said: "Turn over." The Security

Police officer dutifully turned the page and the reading continued by Steve with just his head out of the window. For the next page turn he simply nodded, and the page was turned, although "the poor chap's arms must have been starting to ache." Finally, when the whole charade was over ("Honestly, it was like a damn altarboy holding up the text for the vicar"), he let them in. They searched all but his mother's room carefully, hers only perfunctorily, and never found the papers. That was a sample of his fun with the Security Police. But he would not let them take liberties. Once he admitted them to his house – several of them, led by the notorious Warrant Officer Gerhardus Hattingh (who features prominently in the later parts of this narrative) – and when they were inside the house, Warrant Officer Hattingh made the mistake of producing a revolver. In a flash Steve gave his forearm a karate-type chop while, with the other hand, wrenching the weapon from Hattingh's hand. "No guns in this house!" he said, handing it back to a shaken Hattingh. Somehow he got away with it – on that occasion.

Once, during one of his spells in detention, he was put in an interrogation room, in a chair in the middle of the room, with seven Security policemen standing along the walls all around him. Hattingh entered the room, walked straight to where Steve was sitting, and slapped him hard across the face.

"What happened then?" I asked.

"I hit him right against the wall," Steve replied. "Bust his false teeth."

"Then what?"

"He went straight out of the room. I had the feeling that he didn't know what to do, or how to react, so he just went out – presumably for further instructions from his superiors."

Yet he harbored no personal hatred for Hattingh, nor for anyone else. He realized that the Hattinghs, the Krugers and the Vorsters were prisoners of their environment, their conditioning, upbringing, background. And somehow Hattingh must have sensed this, because on a later occasion when he had tried to assault Steve in detention, and Steve had held him off at arm's length, saying: "Stop this Hattingh! I don't want to hit an older man," Hattingh apologized – "Sorry, Steve. I lost my temper" – and arranged for Ntsiki to bring him some food and a change of clothes.

These incidents were later grossly distorted by a Security Police officer, Major Hansen of King William's Town, who, while giving evidence at the Biko inquest, represented them as one incident of unprovoked assault on Hattingh by Steve. Furthermore, Hansen claimed in his evidence to have been present at the time, but Steve had told me that none of Hattingh's superiors had been present during these scuffles, which, no doubt, was why Hattingh had gone out of the room "presumably for further instructions . . ."

In all, Steve was detained four times – twice briefly, once for 101 days, and finally until he was killed. When I first knew him he was banned but had not ever been detained, and his associates used to tease him about being the only member of the group who had never been "inside." At the time I asked him how it was that the government had never detained him.

"I think the bastards are trying to discredit me," he laughed.

Part of the reason was undoubtedly his own careful precautions regarding political matters. He never took chances on important issues, staying within the letter of the law so that they couldn't prosecute him successfully. Heaven knows, they tried, repeatedly. In all, he faced five prosecutions on charges ranging from breaking his banning orders (by talking to more than one person at a time) to traffic offenses (not stopping completely at an intersection; exceeding the speed limit) and to "defeating the ends of justice" by allegedly persuading witnesses to change their sworn statements.

He won all these cases, the last being the biggest in terms of seriousness, length of time in court and court fees. The State's objective was clearly to bring every possible charge against him so as to drain the cash resources of the Black People's Convention through heavy legal fees. In the latter case, in which one of the charges was subornation to perjury, he was accused of telling a number of black schoolchildren charged with setting fire to their school to renege on statements they had made to the police. But what had really happened was that these youngsters had come to him for advice, saying they had been beaten by Security Police and forced to sign confessions they had not even been permitted to read. They said they were taken one by one and made to sign at the bottom of a document, most of which was covered with a sheet of paper, and these were now being presented in the Supreme Court as genuine confessions.

Steve advised them all to go into the witness stand and tell the judge exactly what they had told him. This they did, and were acquitted.

Now Steve was charged with "persuading them to perjure themselves by contradicting their free and voluntary confessions to police officers!" Defended by Dr. Wilfrid Cooper and Advocate Denis Kuny, Steve was confident he would win, although the State promptly detained all the schoolboys concerned under the Terrorism Act and said they would only be released if they testified satisfactorily.

Fortunately, there being more than a dozen of them (this was done by the State to prolong the proceedings and push up defense costs) the police-coached story (dictated by none other than Hattingh) could not stand up under cross-examination. The witnesses contradicted each other to such an extent that eventually the true story emerged and Steve was acquitted. He had a hard time raising the fees for the lawyers. I managed to raise some of the money from friends, but most of it came from black associations and contributions, depleting the BPC coffers and thereby giving at least some satisfaction to the government.

It took Steve a considerable time to pay for some of his legal costs, and for this we also evolved a code. I had a number of law books from my studies which I no longer needed, and if I were able to raise a thousand rands (approx. $1200, £600) I would phone Steve and tell him I had a book for him. He would send a courier and would get the book with the money parceled in with it. Once we were jubilant because I was able to send him two books (thanks to some philanthropic white friends I used to put the screws on from time to time).

Once Helen Suzman, the Progressive MP and for many years the only Progressive in the entire South African Parliament, sent me some money for Steve on condition that he was not to know where it came from. Helen, who has been a close friend of mine for many years, stipulated this anonymity because she was reluctant to appear to be a condescendingly benevolent white liberal. For a long time she had run a private fund, out of her own resources, for political prisoners, and this amount came from the fund. When I delivered this money to Steve he was delighted, but intrigued about the donor's identity. Yet, when I told him the donor wished to remain anonymous, he didn't press the point beyond saying: "Well, I only wanted to write and say thanks." I thought what the hell, and said: "Actually the donor is a member of Parliament." This really intrigued him.

"A South African MP! Hell, I'd love to know who it is, but I won't go on about it."

"Well, you see, she wishes to remain anonymous," I said. And Steve, knowing there was only one woman MP in the South African Parliament, grinned appreciatively. "Please tell the anonymous lady I am deeply grateful to her without knowing who she is!"

Because the Security Police monitored all of Steve's phonecalls and ours, they seemed to get particularly incensed when we phoned each other. Often, after such calls, we would both receive abusive calls from them, "anonymously" of course, or "silent" calls with heavy breathing – just to let us know that "they" were listening at all times.

One night Steve and I were chatting on the phone and I mentioned to him that I was going to Durban for a newspaper meeting the next day. The following night, at about midnight, Wendy received an anonymous phonecall in these terms: "We know you are alone in your house tonight. We are coming to get you later." She called friends and discussed the threat, but it was decided among all concerned that as so many such threats proved to be hollow, this one should be disregarded.

At about 4 A.M. she heard five pistol shots ring out – one, then four in rapid succession. The following morning five bullet holes were found in the front of the house and spraygunned on the wall in large letters was "BIKO–COMMY HQ" with a hammer-and-sickle sign. A private investigator later established that the bullets had been fired by Security Police Sergeant B. Jooste, and the painting done by Security Police Lieutenant G. Cilliers, but the uniformed police declined to follow up the evidence.

This attitude was repeated later, after Steve's death, when a T-shirt bearing Steve's picture was sent to my five-year-old daughter Mary. It had been sprayed with an acid-type irritant by Security Police Warrant Officers L. Van Schalkwyk and J. Marais, and again the uniformed police declined to investigate the available evidence.

These incidents arose out of the rage the Security Police seemed to experience over our friendship with Steve. And not only the Security Police. Many white South Africans are enraged at contemplation of a friendship across the color line. At one of Steve's court appearances after Mamphela Ramphele had come out of detention, she saw Wendy at the courthouse and the two embraced and kissed affectionately. A young white policeman glared angrily at Wendy and said audibly to his colleague: "She should be shot!" In his view, no doubt, Wendy was a traitor to the white tribe.

I was never able to visit Steve during his periods of detention, but on one occasion when he was in jail on the subornation to perjury charge, before we got him bail, Wendy managed to see him. This is her account of that visit:

We heard that Steve was "inside" again – it was something one was not too surprised to hear. But this time there was something to be pleased about. He had been arrested and not detained. In South Africa there is a clear distinction. A detention usually means that the detainee is inaccessible to anyone but the Security Police. An ordinary arrest means that a person is charged and becomes an awaiting-trial prisoner under the full authority of the prison, and Security Police have no access to him.

Steve had been charged with "defeating the ends of justice" and had been brought to East London jail – "our" jail. So I decided to go and see him. I had often driven past the jail before, but had never been inside. In fact, a few months before I had driven past many times because I was helping to fight a white municipal election in that area, and I knew every time I drove past that Steve was in solitary confinement in there somewhere – geographically so close but effectively so far. And I would silently say "hello" to him, trying at the same time to sustain my enthusiasm for my white municipal candidate. I drove through the jail gates, past cottages and blocks of offices, past vivid green lawns and obedient garden beds, and eventually found what I assumed to be the actual jail – a dark redbrick building, double-storyed, old and forbidding. There were no welcome signs for visitors – no obvious parking places, no helpful arrows pointing anywhere – not even a sign saying "Jail."

I stopped the engine and stared and listened. There was an enormous wooden double door in the middle of the building and the only other apertures were many small windows at regular intervals covered by thick wire mesh. From these windows came singing, shouting and laughing. I began to feel nervous – as if by now someone would have come up to me, demanded to know what I was doing there, and said that I should move my car and that I should have applied four months ago to the Department of the Interior to be there in the first place. Nothing happened, so I scanned the building again, trying to decide how to get inside. Those doors looked ridiculous. They were reinforced with crossbeams; they had huge studs in them and, best of all, at their center were two round cast-iron doorknockers. I couldn't bring myself to walk across the gravel, raise the knockers and bang them down without dissolving into hysterical giggles.

Then I noticed that one of the windows on the left was slightly larger than the others and had a sign "Blankes" (whites) above it. I went over, peered through the mesh and saw two young men walking around in an office. They both had guns at their hips.

"How do I get inside to see a prisoner?"

"Just bang on the door, lady."

So there it was – I banged the knockers and, to my delight, a small panel slid open and an eye stared at me.

"I want to see a prisoner," I said to the eye.

The panel slid closed and there was a lot of vigorous and hollow clanking. The doors were being unlocked. One side opened. I stepped inside and found myself in a caged vestibule. The turnkey was locking the door again. He was white and middle-aged. He had a gun at his side and attached to his belt was a chain on which hung several huge keys. He was good-natured and friendly and stupid. I looked around and found the office with the two young men.

"I want to see the man in charge."

"You can't, lady. He's in court."

"Well, can I see the person under him, then?"

One of them came into the vestibule and motioned to the turnkey, who loped forward to unlock a gate in the cage which separated the vestibule from the main body of the prison. The young man disappeared and I waited, looking up and down the corridor. It was very noisy in there. Prisoners, black and white, walked past looking surprisingly cheerful. It reminded me of a hospital – the only apparent difference being the lack of wheelchairs and trolleys and the fact that there was more rowdiness. An official-looking white man walked slowly up to me and stared at me curiously. Determined not to state my case with my face pressed to bars I said, as imperiously as I could: "I'd like to see you in your office, please." He nodded and again we had the turnkey letting me out of the cage into the corridor.

In the official's office (which was not his office but the office of three people) I said: "I've come about a prisoner called Steve Biko. I believe he is an awaiting-trial prisoner and I'd like to know what his privileges are."

"Oh yes, lady, he is allowed to have letters," he said. "He is allowed visitors. He is allowed to read newspapers and books. He is allowed to receive food and cigarettes and he is allowed to receive money."

I wrote all this down and thanked him and then asked if I could see the prisoner. He was about to say "yes" when one of his colleagues who had wandered in during our talk said very quickly: "No, lady. Whites are not allowed to vist Bantus (blacks) in this jail." My official and I looked at each other, shocked – he because it had never occurred to him that I could possibly be visiting a black man, and I because I had not realized that he had misunderstood me.

"But don't you ever have whites visiting blacks in this jail?"

"Never, lady." They were emphatic, but embarrassed.

"But don't blacks ever have white doctors or priests visit them?"

"No, lady, they have their own people to do that."

"But I have visited blacks in the King William's Town jail."

"Yes, well, they have the facilities there, lady. That's a new jail."

"But don't you have facilities here?"

"No, lady, there's no facilities here for that."

By now they were both very uncomfortable, avoiding my eyes and moving about awkwardly. I gave up and let them escort me to the turnkey, who locked me out.

Outside on the gravel, my frustration surged forward, took hold of me and propelled me back to the "Blankes" window and the two young men in the office.

"Who's in charge of this whole place?" I demanded.

They told me: "The commandant."

"Where can I find him?"

"Down the road in the main office."

I walked down and came to what was obviously the main office, because it had a flagpole with the South African flag flying at the top of it in the surrounding garden. Two important-looking uniformed policemen stood on the verandah. I introduced myself and asked to see the commandant. They were both charming and one stepped forward, identified himself and asked me into his office. He had a large desk, a picture of Vorster hung on the wall, and the floor was thickly carpeted.

Before I could start talking, his genteel secretary walked in, was introduced to me and said in Afrikaans to him that she had all the invitations to the coming performance in East London of the Orange Free State Police Band, and seeing that "the editor" and his wife were getting one, and seeing that "the editor's wife" was here in person now, could she not hand it to her?

Yes, she could, said the commandant, and expressed the hope that the editor and his wife would come to the performance. Being prepared to endure even this, provided he would let her see the prisoner, the editor's wife accepted graciously.

I looked at the secretary. Her reality was here with this carpet and desk and picture, and not thirty yards away was the world I had just left, the world of the inmates, which she had probably never seen.

The commandant and I got on with our negotiations, and to my amazement he agreed to let me see the prisoner. He called his second-in-command to escort me back to the jail and organize the visit. Back again to the turnkey and the vestibule, but this time with the second-in-command hurrying things up.

The prisoner Biko was called. I heard the imperious shouts, "Biko, Biko," getting fainter down the passage.

He was a long time coming and, as I waited, I noticed a young black prisoner in regulation prison khaki shorts and overshirt standing a little way down the passage. He looked anxious and submissive – the look I have seen on a thousand black faces in this country – the look of someone waiting to accommodate the mood or whim of the white "Baas." He stood there as if he had been told to stand there and wait. A white, fat, sleek warder appeared, and as he strolled past him suddenly made a threatening lunge at him and started shouting at him in Afrikaans. There was no anger in this warder – he was merely teasing, having some fun. The man's arms lifted at once to shield his body from the expected blows. One arm curved around the stomach and the other rose to the head, and the man stammered out answers to the questions and taunts being thrown at him. Then the warder strolled on, walking toward me. He saw me staring at him and, as he looked at me, I realized that not only was there no shame or even defiance in his bearing, but that, in his eyes, my white skin made me an implicit and automatic collaborator in what he had just done.

He strolled past, bored, disappeared for a few moments and then came back toward the black man. As he got near, the black man started cringing, his arms taking their positions again in what was now a conditioned reflex action. The warder was enjoying himself hugely. The audience (me) was making it that much more pleasurable. But this time he only shouted something and then disappeared around the corner. The black man dropped his arms and continued his anxious vigil.

I heard noise from the other direction and pressed my face to the bars to catch sight of Steve. I couldn't see him, but I could see a group of warders and policemen and I knew he must be in there somewhere. And then I saw his face and, with a slight sense of shock, I realized that I had never seen him look like that before. He was looking down, his expression sullen, withdrawn and angry. If he was curious as to why he was being summoned, he didn't show it, and then as he got closer I suppose curiosity did get the better of him because he looked up and peered round one of the heads and caught my eye.

I will never forget the change that took place in his expression. It seemed to take place in slow motion, starting from total withdrawal to reluctant curiosity, to intense curiosity and then a huge, naked smile of recognition. But that did not last long. He had been caught unprepared, and as they let me through the cage he had collected himself and the old reserve had taken over. We shook hands stiffly, like two strangers, and mouthed social platitudes with all those people milling around. We were shown into a visiting room with a long bench along one wall, a small table near it and one steel kitchen chair with a blue seat drawn up to the table. This was obviously the visitor's chair – it looked like a throne in that dingy room. The bench was meant for the visitee. I avoided the kitchen chair and went around the table to sit on the bench. So did Steve. The second-in-command stayed in the room to listen and took up his position near the door, facing slightly away from us and trying to retain some dignity while playing the role of eavesdropper.

So there we were – three awkward people trying to be normal in a bizarre situation. I think I asked Steve about five times how he was and didn't listen to any of the answers. He told me that he didn't expect to be there long (as it turned out he wasn't) and that I should tell his mother that he was all right. We talked about his "privileges" as an awaiting-trial prisoner and arranged for me to bring some reading matter and food. At one point he asked the second-in-command a question about visiting hours, and his tone was so rude and abrupt that it shocked me. The second-in-command answered very politely. It was only afterward that Steve told me the reason for this. He knew that, while I was there, he could speak like that and get away with it. It was his way of scoring some points in the psychological warfare. He knew that when I left the second-in-command and all the others would drop their pretense and treat him the same way they treated all the other "Kaffirs" in the jail.

His sullen expression was another defense. At the inquest much mention was made by the Security Police of the way he drew a veil between himself and his interrogators. This is what I had seen. He shut them out. They didn't exist for him and they could not get at him. They could hurt him – they could even kill him – but they could not get at him, and this is what must have driven them mad.

I said good-by and left after about twenty minutes. The visit had not really been a success in terms of proper communication. I had been ill at ease and Steve had sensed this and kept talking. I hadn't listened to half of what he'd said and felt dissatisfied at the end of it all. I felt as if I hadn't used the time well, but looking back now, I realize that in spite of the clumsiness it succeeded in terms of sheer human contact, and that is all that matters.

Some time afterward I told Steve about my impressions of the jail and he laughed gently and said: "Yes – it's one of the old ones." And that was all. No anger, no bitterness – only an acceptance of things as they were.

I knew that he read fiction only when he was in jail. He was too busy when he was not. So the day after the visit I took him six paperbacks. Four were light reading, and the other two were *Brave New World* and *Nineteen Eighty-four*.

He read them all during the short time he was there and I remember discussing *Nineteen Eighty-four* with him. We talked about a system which consciously and with consummate refinement achieves the debasement of the individual in order to retain power.

What I find so painful now is that the Security Police reduced him to a cabbage lying naked on a concrete cell floor. They stripped him of the very dignity we had spoken about in discussing *Nineteen Eighty-Four,* and they did it not because they were consciously concerned to do so but because, to them, he was "just another Kaffir" – and that is what I will never forgive them for.

Once, when questioning Steve about what it was like to be banned, I asked him, naively, whether the prohibition against being with more than one person at a time was to prevent political conspiracy; whether at any rate, this was the theory.

"Not at all," he replied. "Don't you realize what a ban is? It isn't a preventive measure. It's a way of punishing people the State cannot punish under normal law. Many of the banning restrictions are designed simply to inconvenience or exasperate. At first it doesn't seem too inconvenient to have to report to a police station once a week – but after a year it seems an intolerable inconvenience. Talking to one person at a time is designed to inconvenience you by making you repeat everything you said to the last person to the next person as well. It is to keep you looking over your shoulder, even in your own home. It is to maintain that kind of tension. Besides, all these provisions are designed to make one commit technical crimes – by breaking the ban. They couldn't make you a criminal before, so they set up artificial provisions, and if you are caught contravening these you are technically a criminal."

All very true, as I have subsequently discovered for myself. How he would have laughed if he had known I would come to incur the identical banning orders he had!

He believed I was immune to such punishment, because of my whiteness and what he regarded as my "national prominence as a journalist." He also believed that he himself would not be physically manhandled if he was detained, because "they haven't beaten me up on previous occasions." He thought the Security Police were aware of his political significance among blacks and wouldn't try any rough stuff on him because of that, and he also believed that my articles about him (which, on grounds of genuine modesty, he had more than once tried to discourage me from writing) provided a measure of protection for him. He was wrong on all these counts.

Another reason why he thought he was safe from torture in detention was that he believed the Security Police knew he wasn't an extremist or an advocate of violence, nor indulging in any serious subversion. When I asked whether he thought such niceties of logic counted with the Security Police, he replied that the regime still appeared to show occasional vestigial regard for what was left of law. "They're not completely fascist yet, you know," he said.

In August 1975, I put an idea to Steve. I told him that I had known the new Minister of Police, James Kruger, before he was appointed to the cabinet, and asked if Steve would have any objection if I made a personal plea to Kruger to lift, or at least relax, Steve's banning orders. He said he had no objection, and that it would help him considerably to function constructively if he had freedom of movement and freedom to speak and write publicly. He couldn't suggest any line of petition, since he had never been given a reason for his ban in the first place. Theoretically, a banned person is entitled to ask the minister the reasons for his ban, but what happens is this: every banning order begins with words to the effect that whereas the minister is satisfied that you are engaging in activities which endanger public safety, he hereby bans and restricts you from this, that and the other. When you apply to him for his reasons, his reply is that the reason for the ban is that he is satisfied that you are engaging in activities which endanger public safety . . .

I traveled to Pretoria and made an appointment to see Minister Kruger, whom I had first met in 1969 at a party at the British Embassy in Pretoria. He had then struck me as rather a pleasant fellow at a party. Inevitably we got into a verbal political clash, but he maintained his good humor and by the end of the evening, thanks to generous amounts of whisky all round, I was calling him "Oom Jimmy." Afrikaners often call older people "Oom" (Uncle) as a sign of friendly respect. "Oom Jimmy" must have been in a convivial mood, because at some stage of the evening, in the course of attacking my political views, he mentioned that Prime Minister Vorster had remarked in his hearing that I seemed "a pleasant sort of chap," but that my political views were "too far left of center."

In those days newspaper editors and cabinet ministers had at least a fairly informal relationship, and observed certain niceties even across political barriers, such as the exchanging of Christmas cards or letters of condolence on bereavement. Accordingly, a couple of years later when "Oom Jimmy" was made Minister of Police, I sent him a congratulatory message and received a friendly acknowledgment, and later a Christmas card from him and his wife. When he paid his first visit to the city of East London as minister, I was among the civic guests, and he told a public joke at my expense, quite benevolently, and chatted to me in a friendly enough fashion after the luncheon in his honor. Therefore, when I set off to see him about Steve, I had unrealistically high hopes that I might persuade him to lift or relax Steve's banning orders.

South African cabinet ministers live in the Pretoria suburb of Bryntirion, where all the main official residences are, and Mr. Kruger had invited me to see him at his home, as the only time he could fit in an appointment was a Saturday afternoon. It was a perfect Transvaal winter's day, warm and sunny. It was also the day of the big interprovincial rugby final between the Pretoria-based team, Northern Transvaal, and the Bloemfontein-based team, Orange Free State. I knew that "Oom Jimmy" was as interested in rugby as I was, and that if the final were being played in Pretoria instead of Bloemfontein I might not have managed to get the interview! It was such a fine day that I walked from my hotel to Bryntirion, and arrived at the gate of the Kruger residence about ten minutes ahead of my appointment, so I sat on a garden bench just inside the gate to wait.

I was surprised to see no security guards, and said as much to Mr. Kruger when he opened his front door to let me in. He laughed. "You may not see them, but they're there," he said.

He beckoned me into his study and offered me a drink. We both had a whisky. Normally I don't drink at that time of day, but I felt I should on that occasion as I was on a diplomatic mission, so to speak.

He was informally dressed and wore carpet slippers, slacks and an open-necked shirt. His son had arrived for the day to play tennis, and he came in and was introduced to me. We discussed the impending rugby final, due to be broadcast a short while later. After a certain amount of smalltalk, his son left the room, and Kruger said: "Well, what did you want to see me about?"

"I want to talk to you about a friend of mine, Steve Biko," I said. His reaction was curious. He lifted both hands to his head and lifted both feet off the floor in a gesture of comic consternation. "Ooh!" he said. "My God, Steve Biko! He's all tied up in knots. I know all about Mr. Biko!" He then added either that Biko was "the most dangerous man in the country" or "a most dangerous man for the country" – I don't recall his precise wording.

"Why?" I asked. "What makes you say that?" Kruger just sipped at his whisky, smiling to himself and shaking his head as if reviewing private information of a sad kind. I said: "But what has he ever done? What has he done that is wrong or dangerous?"

Kruger mentioned Steve's founding of SASO and said something about "this black power business." I pointed out that SASO was not banned or an illegal organization, and that Steve had never been convicted of a crime. "He is a close friend of mine," I said. "I have grown to know him very well and I can tell you he's no extremist. In fact, he is one of the most genuinely moderate people I have ever met." I went on at some length, saying that I wished "Oom Jimmy" could meet Steve and that he should do this and judge the man for himself; Steve was the kind of black leader the government should permit to function openly even in their own interests, because the government had no genuine and significant leaders to negotiate with if the younger blacks should turn to violence in the townships. (This was seven months before Soweto.)

"You can't negotiate with leaderless mobs," I pointed out. I made a big thing of having five small children and wanting to seek a nonviolent solution for the country through negotiation. There was no sense in suppressing natural leadership, especially moderate leadership such as Steve could provide, I added, ending my short tirade with: "Hell, Oom Jimmy, you have a thousand laws to prosecute the man under if he advocates violence or subversion. Why not lift the restrictions on him and let your police jump him if he breaks these laws?"

He seemed to think about this, then promised he would look into the Biko file again and review the situation. "But I can't promise anything," he said. "I can give you no undertakings."

I then raised with him the question of his Security Police. I told him that he as minister should "clean out the bad elements," of whom there were quite a number in the Security Service. He replied that his Security Police did "a damn fine job in difficult circumstances," to which I said he was obviously unaware that a number of Security Police officers were vicious, sadistic and had criminal tendencies. I mentioned Warrant Officer Hattingh as an officer in King William's Town who was hated by the blacks, and said that I had been informed by someone who wished to remain anonymous that Hattingh was connected with the burglary of the Black Community Programs' offices in Leopold Street, in which documents were stolen, typewriters smashed and furniture slashed.

"You should get someone to look into these matters," I said, adding that I had discussed all these points about Steve Biko, Hattingh and Security Police excesses with the chief of the Bureau of State Security (BOSS), General H. J. van den Bergh, the previous day. The reaction of both van den Bergh and Kruger to my remarks about Hattingh reflected concern. Both gave me to understand that such behavior, if true, was not wanted in the Security Police.

I left Pretoria in the belief that my raising of both these matters, Steve's restrictions and the Security Police excesses, with the two top officials in the country connected with Security might well prove helpful to all concerned – especially Steve. Also I gained the impression that both van den

Bergh and Kruger had appreciated my raising the matter of Hattingh privately instead of through banner headlines in my newspaper. Actually, in this case, I had no choice, as my informant could not be named, and I was more interested in getting these excesses curbed than in getting "a juicy story."

Twice during my visit to Kruger's house I got up to leave, knowing that he would want to listen to the rugby broadcast and that his son had arrived to be with him, but twice he waved me back to my chair, offered me another drink and chatted on about a variety of matters. Eventually I took my leave, and when he saw that I had not come by taxi, he got his own car out and drove me to my hotel – with some difficulty, because his two small dogs in the back seat kept jumping up and licking at his ears and neck. I was touched by his hospitality and kind gesture in driving me back, and on my return to East London wrote him a thank-you letter, adding that I was hopeful of some relaxation of Steve's banning order.

The first shock I received after this was a stiffly formal letter saying that after reviewing the Biko file, the minister "could not see his way clear to lifting the restrictions." The next shock was that Steve's restrictions were actually increased, with a prohibition on his performing any further work for the Black Community Programs. Steve's reaction was one of amusement: "Look, it was worth a try. You did your best. This new restriction won't stop my work – it's just a petty thing that will do the regime more harm than it does me."

The third shock was that I received a visit from the Security Police and was required to name the person who told me of Hattingh's break-in at the offices of the Black Community Programs. I was later sentenced to six months in jail for refusing to disclose this name. I appealed against the prison sentence, all the way to the highest court of appeal, winning on a purely technical point two years later. The magistrate who had signed my subpoena had not been the magistrate who sentenced me to jail, and this was mistake enough on their part to have the sentence set aside.

I soon established that General van den Bergh had not initiated the action against me, and that it had in fact been initiated by Kruger's Chief of Security, General Geldenhuys, who had consulted Kruger before taking action. He had seen from my thank-you letter that I had written "Dear Oom Jimmy," and did not want to proceed against a personal acquaintance of the minister without consultation, whereupon, obviously becoming politically nervous of the implications of this, Kruger washed his hands of the matter and told Geldenhuys to let "the law take its course."

Through incidents such as these I became more and more involved in what Steve called "the struggle." It was like some inexorable process whereby friendship with an activist like Steve increasingly drew one into activist involvement in turn. My jail sentence did not disturb him. In fact Steve was delighted with this development, saying it would "do wonders" for my "political credibility." He laughed hugely at my rueful response.

My response was in fact the Xhosa phrase "Umnqundu wakho!" (your backside) and for some considerable time after this, whenever Steve phoned me, I would greet him with this phrase. His wife, Ntsiki, told Wendy that Steve used to be so amused by this salutation of mine over the phone that he would collapse on the bed laughing, saying: "Imagine a white guy beginning a phone conversation in such a Xhosa way."

From time to time Steve would lecture me on my role as an activist: "You must never apologize for being unable to keep an appointment. Activists don't have to apologize for such things. If you fail to keep an appointment, I will know it must be for a good reason."

One of Steve's closest friends was Mapetla Mohapi. He walked into my office one day and offered to write a Black Consciousness column. I readily agreed to publish such a column, and he did it excellently. Mapetla was a handsome man with striking eyes. He had great reserve at first, and in fact I detected certain feelings of hostility and suspicion on his part. At that time Steve was experiencing a fair amount of criticism from his followers because of his friendship with whites who were not radical enough for the Movement. I suspect that Mapetla had reservations of this sort. But as time went on he came to trust me and we got on very well. He came to reveal, like Steve, a terrific sense of humor, in spite of constant harassment. For example, he was banned shortly after the column had got into its stride, and although he and his family were confined to Zwelitsha township, the authorities would not provide them with a place to live there. Eventually, after they managed to get a little house there on their own initiative, the authorities had them evicted.

Then Mapetla was detained. It happened like this: three young blacks kept pestering Mapetla to get them scholarships in Botswana, knowing that he went there every few months to visit a friend. Mapetla asked Steve's advice and Steve told him to have nothing to do with the request. He regarded the youths as dreamers and said any involvement with them would spell trouble. But the youths persisted and Mapetla eventually relented. Without telling Steve about it, even while borrowing money from Steve for the trip, Mapetla took them with him on his next visit and dropped them inside the Botswana border.

Within a week, their parents were at the police station, accusing Mapetla of "stealing" their children. To the Security Police this meant only one thing – recruitment of youths for terrorist training abroad – and they detained Mapetla. But he remained in good spirits, smuggling letters out to say that his wife, Nohle, was not to worry about him. Mapetla, like Steve, was a convinced survivalist. Both had experienced detention and solitary confinement and knew they could take it. Mapetla often spoke of the need to survive all the efforts of "the System" – especially "inside" – so as to be able to emerge and continue the struggle.

Then one horrible night Steve phoned Wendy and me to tell us that Mapetla was dead, and that the Security Police alleged that he had hanged himself. Immediately after this call our phone rang several times and all we could hear was maniacal, cackling laughter. Steve had the same treatment. The Security Police were enjoying themselves while on midnight telephone surveillance duty.

We drove to King William's Town the following day, and it was impressive to see Steve and his associates at work and to note the relentless way they planned to expose the truth about Mapetla's death. Steve suspected the Security Police would begin the post-mortem as soon as possible, to prevent the Mohapi family physicians from attending. He telephoned the officer in charge, feigning great certainty in his voice, and said that he had been in touch with Pretoria and had arranged for two black doctors to attend the post-mortem. Steve then added sharply: "The post-mortem is to start promptly at eleven o'clock. That is the decision!" He did not add that it was his decision, not Pretoria's, and the officer did not question "the decision." Amazingly, Drs. Ramphele and Msauli, two black doctors, were permitted to attend throughout the post-mortem by the District Surgeon.

It was both chilling and moving for Wendy and me to see how Steve and Mamphela, deeply grieved about their close friend, were single-mindedly and apparently detachedly analyzing technical medical details of the appearance of Mapetla's eyeballs, tongue and so forth, and particularly some abrasions to the sides of the neck rather than under the chin, which is where they would have appeared if he had died by hanging. Their first priority was not mourning – that could come later – it was to uncover the facts and to see how Mapetla's death could advance the cause.

Throughout Mapetla's inquest, which was brilliantly handled for the Mohapi family by Dr. Wilfrid Cooper, a Cape Town barrister, Steve maintained the closest contact with the medical team. "The verdict doesn't matter," he would say. "The magistrate will whitewash the Security Police. The System won't convict the System. But what matters is the evidence – the facts must be published; Security Police methods must be exposed to the public." They certainly were. The *Daily Dispatch* carried full and detailed reports of the inquest, and for the first time there were comprehensive published accounts of Security Police being skillfully cross-examined in the witness stand.

Steve maintained that there were still vestiges of legality in South Africa which the Nationalist government had not yet got around to removing, and that these had to be exploited. "We must make the fullest use of what law is left," he said. The Mohapi inquest was a prophetic foretaste of Steve's own. Predictably, the Security Police were absolved of blame – yet significantly not even the State's magistrate could bring himself to rule that death was by suicide. This, in the circumstances, was a victory of sorts for Dr. Cooper.

I had a special interest in one of the witnesses at the Mohapi inquest – Thenjiwe Mtintso, one of my own reporters. This remarkable girl was sent to me by Steve in response to my request for a suitable person to cover the Black Consciousness beat. "Tenjy," as she came to be known in the office, responded well to training and became an able journalist. But there was never any doubt about her commitment or her standing in the Black Consciousness movement. I later came to realize that she was one of the leading heroines of the national movement. "Tenjy" was tiny and pretty. Like Mapetla, she took a long time to thaw out and lose a reserve of suspicion of whites, but like Mamphela, once she accepted you there was no more reserve.

One day she came into my office looking worried and preoccupied. "Kuteni, mta' kwetu?" I asked her in Xhosa. ("What's the matter, our child?") She smiled at this, but looked worried again as she told me she feared she would soon be detained, because Security Police had intensified their surveillance of her home and were now openly following her everywhere. Her mother was ill, and Tenjy was worried that she would have no money without her salary. I reassured her that if she was detained, we would send her salary every month to her mother. We then had quite a long discussion about the Security Police surveillance.

She was detained two days later. I made several demands to Security headquarters to be allowed to see her, but it was only months later that I was permitted to do so. In the interview room at the jail, she was careful about what she said because the place was obviously bugged, but she later told me she had been beaten and tortured, and that on the first day of her detention the interrogating officer had pressed a button on a machine, and she had heard my voice saying: "Kuteni, mta' kwetu?" Our entire conversation had been recorded. At the Mohapi inquest she gave evidence about her torture, naming the officers involved. She gave a chilling demonstration to the court of how a towel had been thrown over her face and the ends tightened about her throat to a point just short of unconsciousness.

It was while we were attending the Mohapi inquest that Wendy and I realized that there was a state of war in South Africa between the Nationalists and the real black resistance people like Steve, Mapetla, Mamphela, Tenjy and all their friends – a state of war few whites in the country knew of or could perceive. Later events were to ensure that, whether we liked it or not, we were drawn into this war.

One experience with Tenjy was particularly moving. She idolized Steve, and one day when he had just been released from 101-day detention (looking much slimmer than usual!) he met Wendy and me at King William's Town jail. We were there to visit Tenjy, Mamphela, Malusi Mpumlwana (a special pal and lieutenant of Steve's) and others still "inside." Steve was looking very dashing in a light-colored suit, and was chatting to Wendy at the entrance to the jail while I was visiting Tenjy. As the guard let Tenjy out of the interview cubicle she was for a brief second or two in sight of the entrance. I signaled Wendy, she hurriedly summoned Steve, and for one moving moment Tenjy had her first sight of Steve for many months. I remember how her eyes filled with tears and how this slim, tiny little figure joyously held her fist up defiantly in the BPC salute before the guard led her away.

We saw Malusi there the same day. Malusi was a real character, always bubbling over with high spirits, always smiling – and as tough as nails. His own adventures would fill a book, but as he is still in detention that book is better left to a later date.

That day at the jail, on a glorious sunny morning, Wendy, Steve and I broke his banning order in full view of the world. We were so pleased to see each other after Steve's long detention, and he had so much to tell us about, that we just stood there laughing and talking. It was the day he told us about the "kennel" being brought in . . .

He was in tremendous spirits, but sobered considerably to tell me: "They're after you, you know. They're after you in a big way. You seem to enrage them, and while they can handle that from a black, they can't take it from a white. Man, most of my interrogation was about you. They think you are an agent of Moscow or something terrible. I said to them: 'Can't you recognize an old-fashioned liberal when you see one? Woods is a liberal, man, he is concerned with individual human rights.' But they kept asking what you were up to. The more I said your whole standpoint was published every morning openly in your editorials, the more they were skeptical. They think your writing is a cover-up for more sinister activities. They asked me what blacks thought of you, and I said they love you, they think you're great, and this seemed to upset them."

Steve said that on occasion the Security Police would take him out of the jail and drive him around various parts of the city of East London while interrogating him. On a couple of occasions they drove past my house ("It seemed so near and yet so inaccessible"). They would say to him: "There's the house of your white friend. Wouldn't you like to visit him?" Steve kept saying that the degree of Security Police hatred of me and of my newspaper had been quite remarkable. "During my time in detention they asked me more about you than they asked about me," he said.

He described the tiny cell in which he had been kept in solitary confinement for more than a month. It was six feet by eight, but with a high ceiling, which increased the claustrophobic effect. Steve said he found that by putting the blanket over his head he could pretend the walls were further away and all the dimensions of the room bigger. Father Aelred Stubbs records that Steve told him that while he was in detention he felt no urge for sexual gratification of any kind, because he associated sex with happiness and felt all thoughts of it to be incompatible with captivity.

Steve had told me that while in solitary confinement he found that his memory became quite remarkable, and he could remember details, in sequence, of specific days he had long thought forgotten, and exact events in chronological order. The food had been plentiful but revoltingly served, he said. If the fare was bread and porridge, the dish would be pushed into the cell with the bread slopped right into the porridge.

His interrogators had been astonished by his interest in what they regarded as exclusively "white" matters. For example, a rugby tour by the New Zealanders was in progress at the time, and the Security Police asked if he was following the progress of the tour. He told them he was.

What did he think of the Springbok team?

Steve replied: "I wouldn't have Bosch at flyhalf. I'd pick Gavin Cowley." This, he said, appeared to flabbergast them. Such black knowledge of white sport . . .

He also said there had been utterly no assaults on him throughout his detention, and that although the interrogation sessions had been grueling, there were few instances even of a bullying harshness of tone. He had, however, become angry at the degrading nature of some of the sessions when his interrogators appeared obsessed with putting sexual questions to him. The Security Police regarded Steve, possibly enviously, as a Casanova. I once heard one say at one of the trials: "Oh, Biko – he's a great man for the ladies." It was said with such a leer, and in tones which so much suggested some ghastly propensity, that it was clear this was regarded officially by the Security Police as a damning indictment.

HIS POINTS OF VIEW

MUCH HAS BEEN ALLEGED by Steve Biko's persecutors in their attempt to portray him as a man of violence, and this seems an opportune stage of this account to set out his views on a number of subjects. I had access to these views, not only through our long, personal conversations, but also through tape recordings and notes made by others to whom he spoke candidly "off the record." During the last two years of his life, Steve was so busy leading his followers with advice and guidance that his popularity threatened to hamper his work, and I virtually became his appointments secretary. Diplomats, academics, politicians and journalists from all over the world approached me to arrange interviews with him, and because I knew how busy he was I screened him as much as possible from all callers except those who seemed important as conveyors of his stance to the world media or to foreign governments.

Two such persons were Bruce Haigh of the Australian Embassy in South Africa and Bernard Zylstra of the Canadian Institute for Christian Studies. Both had extensive conversations with Steve, some elements of which are recorded here. I have included these recorded words of Steve Biko at some length because whenever possible and appropriate it seems fitting to use his own actual phrases – as Bernard Zylstra puts it, to let him speak for himself.

The first of Bruce Haigh's conversations with Steve was on January 13, 1977, and Bruce gave me a detailed account of it:

We discussed the current political and economic situation in Australia. He was well informed and questioned me closely on the events which had led to Mr. Whitlam's dismissal. I asked why he had such an interest in Australia and he replied that together with the Scandinavian countries, Britain and America, Australia was a country to which he looked to see how things were being done on a broad range of issues but in particular as to how the process of democracy was evolving and coping with the demands of technocratic society.

On arrival we left the car and sat on the grass under a clump of trees. Biko led the discussion throughout and commenced by giving a brief thumbnail sketch of what he felt would be the likely course of events in Southern Africa. The transition to majority rule in Rhodesia he thought was unfortunately likely to be violent, with the Nkomo-Mugabe faction eventually gaining control. The solution to the problem of government in Namibia was also likely to be violent, but he thought the struggle there would be longer than that in Rhodesia, given the extent of the South African defense commitment. He said the South Africans had built roads, a number of airfields and several large military bases. It was expected that any government that came out of the Turnhalle would request the South African government to maintain its defense forces in Namibia.

Nonetheless whether South Africa was fighting in Namibia or along a future border with that country it would be faced with an unbroken line of hostile neighbors once Rhodesia came under the control of the blacks. South Africa was virtually on a war footing now; after the establishment of Zimbabwe she would be at war. Biko said that with this commitment and faced with organized internal unrest it would only be a matter of time before blacks achieved majority rule in South Africa.

Bruce Haigh's interview with Steve was shortly after the latter's first spell in detention, and he discussed this readily:

Biko gave what he felt were the reasons for his detention. It had become apparent after the first few interviews with the Security Police that they were trying to find out how many students had fled to Botswana and Swaziland after the Soweto riots, and what they were doing there. They knew very little, and he had been unable to help them in their inquiries. He claimed that several thousand students had fled to Botswana and Swaziland and that many had left for other African states, where they were receiving scholastic and military training. He said that a considerable number of students in Botswana were engaged in preparing the way for change in South Africa. Lines of communication had been established between them and the students in South Africa.

Biko said he thought the students in the townships were gradually becoming better organized. It was their intention to avoid unnecessary bloodshed. He believed that in future, demonstrations would be smaller in order to avoid loss of life. Whereas during the unrest in 1976 it was not uncommon, in a demonstration consisting of several thousand students, for over one hundred to be shot with perhaps half that number being killed, in order to avoid this bloodshed in the future he felt the aim would be to create as much disruption as possible with fewer numbers of people involved.

Given the present attitude of the Nationalist government, Biko felt the prospect for peaceful change in South Africa was not good. He believed, however, that protests and boycotts had helped to some extent, and he cited the sport policy adopted by most countries toward South Africa as an example. Despite National party statements he believed they were sensitive to outside pressure, although a lot more was needed before they would consider making the basic changes necessary to remove the system of apartheid.

He listed contact with diplomats and visiting world figures as sources of protection for him against the Security Police. Biko might also have added the strength of his own personality and character. He is a man who would stand out in any company.

Biko believed that foreign embassies in South Africa were far too conservative in their approach to the events unfolding here. He felt that many of them were either negligently or willfully presenting a distorted view of developments to their foreign ministries. Commenting on Andrew Young, Biko said he thought Young understood the plight of the urban black in South Africa. His recent statements were a welcome relief from the views put forward by Kissinger and others on Southern Africa. Biko hoped that Young had now secured a strong place for himself within the Carter administration.

The BPC were adopting a low profile over the period of the anniversary of the first Soweto riots. Biko said they were doing this in order to avoid the unnecessary arrest of BPC officials, who were fulfilling a far more useful role in an organizational capacity than they would as activists if, as a result, they were to be banned or imprisoned.

I made notes of these remarks by Bruce Haigh because Steve told me he had taken a liking to Bruce and had been completely candid with him. I might add that the feeling was mutual, and that Bruce became a firm friend of us both.

Bernard Zylstra's record of an extensive conversation with Steve in July 1977 now follows. Bernard later gave me his notes, and they are worth extensive reproduction as verbatim replies by Steve. Bernard introduces the discussion as follows:

In the fall of 1976 I had spent nearly a month in South Africa, and a similar period this past summer. I spoke with numerous whites (especially Afrikaners, whose language I understand and read) as well as with blacks about the political and economic future of their country. My interview with Steve Biko in July was one of the most lucid exchanges I engaged in. It may well have been his last major recorded interview, in which he speaks for himself.

This is how the interview proceded:

ZYLSTRA: What precisely do you mean by Black Consciousness?
BIKO: By Black Consciousness I mean the cultural and political revival of an oppressed people. This must be related to the emancipation of the entire continent of Africa since the Second World War. Africa has experienced the death of white invincibility. Before that we were conscious mainly of two classes of people, the white conquerors and the black conquered. The blacks in Africa now know that the whites will not be conquerors forever. I must emphasize the

cultural depth of black consciousness. The recognition of the death of white invincibility forces blacks to ask the question: "Who am I? Who are we?" And the fundamental answer we give is this: "People are people!" So "Black" Consciousness says: "Forget about the color!" But the reality we faced ten to fifteen years ago did not allow us to articulate this. After all, the continent was in a period of rapid decolonization, which implied a challenge to black inferiority all over Africa. This challenge was shared by white liberals. So for quite some time the white liberals acted as the spokesmen for the blacks. But then some of us began to ask ourselves: "Can our liberal trustees put themselves in our place?" Our answer was twofold: "No! They cannot." And: "As long as the white liberals are our spokesmen, there will be no black spokesmen." It is not possible to have black spokesmen in a white context.

This was realized readily in many black countries outside of South Africa. But what did we have here? The society as a whole was divided into white and black groups. This forced division had to disappear, and many nonracist groups worked toward that end. But almost every nonracist group was still largely white, notably so in the student world. Thus here we were confronted with the same shortcoming: the context of getting rid of white-black tensions was still a white context. So we began to realize that blacks themselves had to speak out about the black predicament. We could no longer depend upon whites answering the question: "Who are we?" There had to be a *singularity* of purpose in that answer. The white trustees would always be *mixed* in purpose.

ZYLSTRA: How does Christianity fit in with Black Consciousness?

BIKO: I grew up in the Anglican church, so this matter is an important one for me. But it is a troublesome question, for in South Africa, Christianity for most people is purely a formal matter. We as blacks cannot forget the fact that Christianity in Africa is tied up with the entire colonial process. This meant that Christians came here with a form of culture which they called Christian but which in effect was Western, and which expressed itself as an imperial culture as far as Africa was concerned. Here the missionaries did not make the proper distinctions. This important matter can easily be illustrated by relatively small things. Take the question of dress, for example. When an African became Christian, as a rule he or she was expected to drop traditional garb and dress like a Westerner. The same with many customs dear to blacks, which they were expected to drop for supposed "Christian" reasons while in effect they were only in conflict with certain Western mores. Moreover, although the social hierarchy within the church was a white/black hierarchy, the sharing of responsibility for church affairs was *exclusively* white. This meant that the nature especially of the mainline churches was hardly influenced by black fact. It cannot be denied that in this situation many blacks, especially the young blacks, have begun to question Christianity. The question they ask is whether the necessary decolonization of Africa also requires the de-Christianization of Africa. The most positive facet of this questioning is the development of "black" theology in the context of Black Consciousness. For black theology does not challenge Christianity itself but its

Western package, in order to discover what the Christian faith means for our continent.

ZYLSTRA: Tell me about the Black People's Convention.

BIKO: In the 1960s, the African National Congress and the Pan-Africanist Congress had been banned, so the main realities we were confronted with were the power of the police and the leftist noises of the white liberals. Faced with these realities, we had to solve the question of how a new consciousness could take hold of the people. The government controlled the schools. There was a low output from the schools as far as Black Consciousness was concerned. We knew we had to seek for participation among the intelligentsia. But we also knew that the intelligentsia tend to look upon the masses as tools to be manipulated by them, so the change of consciousness among graduates of the black universities that we sought focused on an identification of intellectuals with the needs of the black community. Here lies the origin of SASO – the South African Student Organization. It challenged the injustice of the existing structures, but it did this in a new way. As a matter of fact, since we stressed *Black* Consciousness and the relation of the intellectuals with the real needs of the *black* community, we were at first regarded as supporters of the System. The liberals criticized us and the conservatives supported us. But this did not last very long. It took the government four years to take measures against us. Even today we are still accused of racism. This is a mistake. We know that *all* interracial groups in South Africa are relationships in which whites are superior, blacks inferior. So, as a prelude, whites must be made to realize that they are *only* human, not superior. Same with blacks. They must be made to realize that they are *also* human, not inferior. For all of us this means that South Africa is not European, but African.

Gradually this began to make sense. Black Consciousness gained momentum, but we were still faced with the practical issue that the people who were speaking were mainly students and graduates. There was no broad debate. For this reason we had to move from SASO to the organization of the Black People's Convention so that the masses could get involved in the development of a new consciousness. The BPC was established in 1972. It was then that the government began to go into action. It banned individual leaders of the BPC. But today the BPC is getting wide support. The people are willing to sacrifice for it, with their money and with their time, as you can see from the packed courtrooms at trials of black leaders and inquests into their "mysterious" deaths in backrooms of police stations. In a sense, the Black People's Convention is the most powerful organization among blacks, but this is hard to determine exactly, since the ANC and the PAC are banned as organizations, which means that they have a kind of generation-gap problem: there is a whole generation now that has not been influenced by the ANC and the PAC. In any case, the actual identification of people with the BPC is strong. When I put it this way, I do not want to give the impression that the relation between these organizations is one of competition. There will be *one* movement of revolt against the system of injustice. To be sure, there are the usual divisions due to background, but in terms of the revolution there is unity.

ZYLSTRA: What about the homelands policy?

BIKO: Some blacks support the government policy of separate development in the homelands for the sake of peace, but not as a movement. Here we have to look carefully into the kind of support that Gatsha Buthelezi gets. He has a *tribal* following among the Zulus. He has managed to combine many elements as a *traditional* chief in a *nonurban* setting. He speaks up strongly against apartheid, but today he is the governmentally paid leader of the Zulus. In this way he manages to gain a following. We oppose Gatsha. He dilutes the cause by operating on a government platform. Because of this I see the danger of division among blacks. But we hope to avoid a real split on the basis of the BPC's great appeal to the younger generation. Gatsha is supported by "oldies," for good reason, since Gatsha protects the stability that the older persons need. But we are young. We do not look upon the solution to injustice as an expectation but as a duty. Here lies the dilemma of the old – between duty and bread.

ZYLSTRA: Where is the evidence of support among the younger generation for BPC?

BIKO: In one word: Soweto! The boldness, dedication, sense of purpose, and clarity of analysis of the situation – all of these things are a direct result of Black Consciousness ideas among the young in Soweto and elsewhere. This is not quantitatively analyzable, for the power of a movement lies in the fact that it can indeed change the habits of people. This change is not the result of force but of dedication, of moral persuasion. This is what has got through to the young people. They realize that we are not dealing with mere bread-and-butter issues. In view of this the real momentum is on their side. I realize that the BPC has a problem of strategy in comparison with the homeland leaders. Gatsha can use the machinery of the government when he wants to organize a meeting. But this is not real power.

ZYLSTRA: What is your attitude to communism?

BIKO: This theme confronts us with many, many complexities. Let me mention a number of things, more or less at random. We within the BPC have made up our minds that we must operate within the confines of the law or we will not operate at all. This means that the BPC is not and cannot be a communist organization. To some extent organizations can operate underground, but for our kind of organization it is much more effective to work openly aboveground. Moreover, an aboveground movement must have an element of compromise about it, and we look upon that as an advantage. Further, a Communist in South Africa today will be an instrument of Moscow, not of the black people. Some Marxists are more pliable, more realistic, but then we have to know precisely about whom we are talking.

While the BPC is nonviolent, it should not be forgotten that we are part of a *movement* which will be confronted with new situations that may require different strategies. We begin with the assumption that rapprochement is necessary. The BPC is not a third wing among the blacks, next to the ANC and the PAC.

ZYLSTRA: Do South African blacks display the differences that have divided the blacks in other African nations, like Angola and Rhodesia?

BIKO: Let me at least say this: we are not divided because of *personal* ambitions among the leaders. What are my own ambitions? I have no personal ambitions. I have *hopes*. I know my limits. I am not an administrator. My hope is to engage in doing justice in the South Africa of the future.

ZYLSTRA: What is your attitude towards the USA?

BIKO: Ah, this is a quick change! We begin with the assumption that from the international point of view South Africa is a pawn in the politics of pragmatism, in the game of power between the US and the USSR. We have no illusions about the African policies of either the US or the USSR. Russia has won the show so far in Southern Africa. This is evident in Angola and Mozambique. So now the USA seems to be waking up and asks itself the question: "Why are we so far behind Russia in gaining friends?" The reason, of course, is quite simple. The US has in the past maintained its links with the minority governments in Angola, Mozambique, Rhodesia and South Africa. The situation within the first two has changed drastically in the last few years. It is rapidly changing in Rhodesia. This means that the main focus of Washington with respect to Southern Africa is on Pretoria. This has the effect of making South Africa feel important. Investments must be protected. Trade must be expanded. Cultural exchanges must be maintained.

These developments of the last few years have placed the US in a vulnerable position. It realizes that it hasn't done too well, so it now looks around to ask: "Where do we get support?" And when Washington asks that kind of question, as a rule it puts the question in the context of the rift between communism and capitalism, between East and West, between the "First World" and the "Second World." Can the problems of the "Third World" be properly understood in the context of that rift? In any case, the Third World liberation movements have received support from Moscow, not from Washington. Moreover, many persons within the liberation struggles look upon the Marxist analysis of oppression as the proper diagnosis of their situation. And on top of all this there is the over-whelming evidence of America's involvement in the Third World for the sake of its own economic self-interest. Russia has no investments to protect in Johannesburg. America does.

ZYLSTRA: Does the Carter administration represent a basic change in American foreign policy toward the Third World?

BIKO: The emphasis on human rights appears to spell a shift away from the policies of Nixon and Ford. It seems to us that the USA is now elevating morality to a higher level in its own power struggle, in its present attempt to recover influence in the Third World as a whole. With respect to South Africa, in order to realize its long-term policy America has to find a group with which it can be allied. In order to find such a group, the US is becoming more outspokenly critical of Ian Smith's regime in Rhodesia and also of Vorster's in Pretoria. It appears to us that this is also the reason why Carter chose Andrew Young as ambassador to the UN, and why he sent him to Southern Africa. In this way Carter hopes to develop a new complexion, acceptable to the Third World in general and to South Africa in particular. Carter uses Andrew Young's color as a special passport to the Third World. But Young has no program except the furtherance of the American system. That's why he plays tennis in Soweto. Carter is doing more skillfully what Nixon and Ford did: to make the American system work more efficiently.

But in being so critical of the economic self-interest in the Third World on the part of American capitalism, I at the same time have no illusions about Russia. Russia is as imperialistic as America. This is evident in its internal history as well as in the role it plays in countries like Angola. But the Russians have a less dirty name: in the eyes of the Third World they have a cleaner slate. Because of this, they have had a better start in the power game. Their policy *seems* to be acceptable to revolutionary groups. They are not a "taboo." Here we are probably faced with the greatest problem in the Third World today. We are divided because some of us think that Russian imperialism can be accepted as purely an interim phase while others, like myself, doubt whether Russia is really interested in the liberation of the black peoples.

ZYLSTRA: Would you explain black communalism?

BIKO: The Black Consciousness movement does not want to accept the dilemma of capitalism versus communism. It opts for a socialist solution that is an authentic expression of black communalism. At the present stage of our struggle it is not easy to present details of this alternative, but it is a recognition of the fact that a change in the color of the occupier does not necessarily change the system. In our search for a just system we know that the debate about economic policy cannot be "pure," completely separate from existing systems. In our writings we at times speak of *collective* enterprises because we reject the individualistic and capitalist type of enterprises. But we are not taking over the Russian models. I must emphasize that in our search for new models we are necessarily affected by where we are today. For this reason also it is impossible to present details about the transition stage that will be here after the dissolution of white domination. It is far too early for that.

ZYLSTRA: Has black Christianity influenced black communalism?

BIKO: Only indirectly. Perhaps we should look toward developments in South America, where the Christian-Marxist dialog seems to move toward an alternative, a middle position. You should not forget that in dealing with these highly complex questions we are intensely handicapped because our best thinkers are outside of the country or banned or imprisoned.

ZYLSTRA: What of the future. Any predictions?

BIKO: This again is a difficult issue. I am now getting to the position where I expect an overall escalation of the conflict. Just consider the various angles. To begin with, the Afrikaners have maneuvered themselves into an extremely vulnerable position. They have made up their minds that sharing of political power with the blacks is out of the question. Since a sharing of power is imperative if we are to have a just society, this position of the Afrikaners makes conflict inevitable. If Afrikaner leaders backtrack, they come into conflict with earlier positions and lose credibility among their supporters. Hence the Afrikaner is committed to maintain a *lie*. Because of the position that the Afrikaner has got himself into, conflict seems inevitable. The conflict will not be a result of the black position. For the same reason, a round-table situation seems impossible, since that presupposes the political equality of the blacks. Then there is another complicating factor for the Afrikaner. They have no "homeland" to go to, as the Portuguese did when Angola became independent. And these Afrikaners control political power. They are thus a *vital* part, not only of the problem but also of the solution. After the solution to our problem, the Afrikaners will be here. And therefore goodwill has to be maintained.

ZYLSTRA: Can't the Afrikaners change?

BIKO: In part, yes. But they need fifty years, and that simply is too long. And the Afrikaners are not the only element in the dynamics of change. The second factor in looking at the future is the escalation of conflict at the borders of South Africa. In the past there were border states that acted as a kind of buffer. But that is changing rapidly now. The change has occurred in Angola and Mozambique; it is occurring in Namibia and Zimbabwe today. This means that external military pressures on South Africa will increase. To this we must immediately add the third component: the protracted activities inside South Africa, especially within the numerous Sowetos. The masses of black people within the country will become increasingly defiant. A new generation of blacks is coming to the fore which is not motivated by fear. This internal pressure from the blacks will strengthen a fourth component that will favor change, namely, international public opinion. This is already a most important factor which the Pretoria government has to take into account. Finally, the fifth element that one will have to look at is real change among whites in South Africa. In our struggle, useful coalitions between blacks and whites can be formed, with a view to the elimination of race as the basis of our society. This will be mainly with English-speaking elements of the population, but also with some Afrikaners – not those who occupy positions of leadership in the churches but those in the universities. They are beginning to sense already today that the age of Afrikaner nationalism is over. They know that the future should not be dictated by the *volk* but shaped by the best that can be maintained by meaningful compromise.

ZYLSTRA: In the light of all these factors – which are certainly not exhaustive – what can one expect of the government?

BIKO: As I said, I expect an escalation of conflict, also on the part of the police. And if the Afrikaner regime becomes even more intransigent, we as blacks will have to reassess our strategy. It is true that the government is powerful and that it can last a long time, but precisely because it, too, is aware of the escalation of conflict on all sides, the *sobering* effect of force (at the borders and in the urban townships), the pressure from international public opinion, and a change of attitude among whites – all of these factors combined may well make the Afrikaner regime change its mind. Once people begin to flex their muscles, they won't stop.

ZYLSTRA: What about the pressure for a one man, one vote political system of representation, especially from abroad?

BIKO: Today the one man, one vote solution would spell disaster, economically, for the black masses. For the white man it would be the greatest solution! It would encourage competition among blacks, you see, and it would eliminate the most important ground for critique from abroad of the present regime. But it would not change the position of *economic* oppression of the blacks. That would remain the same.

ZYLSTRA: Why can't the blacks do today what the Afrikaners did in the forties and fifties with respect to their economic position in South Africa?

BIKO: Because they had an organized vanguard. The blacks need this before a transition is possible. Hence restraint among blacks today is necessary. The frustrating difficulty is that the situation does not allow blacks to develop an organized vanguard. This is not only a result of the fact that many of our leaders are imprisoned or banned but also because of the fact that blacks are excluded from many of the essential disciplines needed for the formation of a vanguard: the natural sciences, engineering, and many other areas. Without a competent, organized vanguard the black population cannot properly assume the responsibilities which by right they ought to exercise.

But if the future transition is not to end in chaos, the white population must also be prepared for radical change within their midst. The whites will have to accept a political constellation in this country in which the blacks have full participation. What I mean can perhaps be illustrated by the struggle for civil rights by American blacks in the fifties and sixties. *They* demand the implementation of the existing constitution. *We* demand a new constitution. Such a new constitution cannot be imposed upon blacks by whites. It must be the result of mutual exchange. It must stipulate the role of all South African citizens, including the white man, after transition. White participation is imperative. We favor proportional representation. The future political system of this country must not be racist in any way. This also means that blacks must not revenge themselves on the whites, but equity will require a substantial economic sacrifice on the part of the whites. It is impossible to say today precisely what that sacrifice would mean. It might require that the salaries and wages of whites be frozen for a period of five years. It does not mean that blacks would take over the homes of whites, but it certainly would entail the opening up of residential areas to all groups, as in Gaborone, the capital of Botswana. These are only a few suggestions. An economic upheaval must be avoided.

ZYLSTRA: What can the United States and other nations do to contribute toward the necessary transition?

BIKO: Let us look once again at the relationship between the United States and South Africa. The most important phenomenon in South Africa today is the blacks' legitimate struggle for freedom. What is needed in Washington and in the other capitals of the Western world is an open acknowledgment of this, and in the context of that acknowledgment, the US can and must influence the political direction within South Africa. But it can do so meaningfully only if its concrete steps aid the blacks' struggle for freedom. Here are a few suggestions: In the first place, if that struggle is to be forthright, well directed and consistent, the blacks need proper literature and freedom of mobility. If the Carter administration means business in its human rights policy, it should put pressure on Pretoria to guarantee freedom of the press for blacks and freedom of movement for blacks. Moreover, if the Carter administration is to know what spirit lives among the blacks, it will have to establish contacts with those persons who are the accepted leaders of the blacks, even if they are imprisoned on Robben Island.

In the second place, Washington can exert such economic pressures on South Africa that it will become considerably less profitable to invest in South African industries. The argument is often made that loss of foreign investment would hurt blacks the most. It would undoubtedly hurt blacks in the short run, because many of them would stand to lose their jobs, but it should be understood in Europe and North America that foreign investment supports the present economic system and thus indirectly the present system of political injustice. We blacks are therefore not interested in foreign investment. If Washington wants to contribute to the development of a just society in South Africa, it must discourage investment in South Africa. We blacks are perfectly willing to suffer the consequences. We are quite accustomed to suffering.

Thirdly, in the diplomatic arena it would be a tremendous psychological boost for the blacks in this country if the USA downgraded its diplomatic presence in Pretoria from the ambassadorial level to the consular level. That would have to be done in piecemeal fashion. Moreover, the US should never use its veto power in the UN Security Council in favor of the present regime in Pretoria. South Africa must learn that it is losing friends in the West.

That was the essence of Steve Biko's conversation with Bernard Zylstra.

After Steve's death the pro-Vorster newspapers did their best to smear him by putting a certain slant on a report of a report. They quoted, with their own interpretation, a report in the *New York Times* by that newspaper's highly respected correspondent in South Africa, John Burns, emphasizing in particular one sentence which Steve uttered to Burns. Steve had said that if the Nationalist government remained intransigent, young blacks would almost certainly turn to more extreme forms of violence: "Blacks are going to move out of the townships into white suburbs, destroying and burning there. It's going to happen, it's inevitable . . . a faceless army which destroys overnight will introduce far greater feelings of insecurity (among whites) than an organized military force on the border."

The Nationalist newspapers took this, not as a prediction by Steve, but as his advocacy of this sort of violence. They implied that he wasn't merely saying it would happen, but that it should happen. But knowing that John Burns is a highly conscientious and methodical journalist who would have a full record of the interview, I got in touch with him and he readily supplied the following verbatim report:

The interview took place on August 2, 1976, at the offices of the Black Community Programs in King William's Town. Although under a banning order, Mr. Biko waived the requirement that he speak to only one person at a time, and saw me together with my wife over a period of about three hours. Mr. Biko said that among members of the Black Consciousness movement there were disagreements on the use of violence to promote political ends. "The spectrum goes from peaceful to completely violent," he said. However, he said, the organization was not currently organized for violence. "We don't have any armed struggle wing at the moment," he said. "We are not going to get into armed struggle. We'll leave it to the PAC and ANC. We operate on the assumption that we can bring whites to their senses by confronting them with our overwhelming demands."

He then added: "We haven't debated violence so far. We are confined to operating peacefully precisely because we operate aboveground. That doesn't mean that we preclude it. But there are other ways for us to promote our Liberation, such as crippling the economy."

Mr. Biko said that the question of SASO's attitude and of the Black Consciousness movement's attitude toward violence had been an issue at the SASO trial, and pointed out that the police had not succeeded in providing any documentary support in their contention that SASO was involved in a revolutionary conspiracy. He then gave a rundown of the terrorist trials then in progress around the country, saying that there had been frequent attempts to link the Black Consciousness movement to terrorism, but without success. Again, he emphasized that it was the ANC primarily, and to some degree the PAC, that was involved in the promotion of violence. Speaking of the SASO-BPC trial in Pretoria, he said: "Our position at the trial is that we will have to negotiate," meaning negotiate a political settlement between blacks and whites. "We are for a bargaining process," he said. He added: "But there is no doubt that all other facets of change are being considered, and will progressively find more favor, depending on the intransigence of the system toward change."

Violence, he said, seemed inevitable. "There will be sporadic outbursts, like Soweto, and in time they will change from being sporadic to being organized. Eventually the crucial point will arrive where whites will decide whether our liberation is to be negotiated or forced. I think there will be a sufficiently conservative influence for them to opt for force, for a last-ditch struggle. What happens from our side will depend on the option they choose.". . .

Mr. Biko added: "Even if the whites negotiate, they will want to negotiate on their terms," which would mean essentially coopting the black middle class, and manipulating leaders like Gatsha Buthelezi. There would also be an attempt to divide blacks among themselves, to isolate the Black Consciousness movement and other black radicals. He said that these divisions would undoubtedly occur, and that this would stretch out the process of black liberation "over a long period." He went on: "No matter how you look at it, armed struggle is difficult to discount as a possibility." He said that, as he had indicated, whites were likely to opt for a negotiated solution that would favor their interests, meaning that they would negotiate with black "moderates" only. But, he said, if whites were "sufficiently intelligent" to negotiate with more influential blacks, meaning the Black Consciousness movement and those who took a similar stand, "there would be a breakdown (of negotiations) anyway. So the end is the same."

When asked again about the question of violence, and how imminent it was, Mr. Biko replied: "Sporadic outbursts are going to increase in significance and the white community, which so far has been very well protected, is going to realize how thin its security really is. Blacks are going to move out of the townships into white suburbs, destroying and burning there. It's going to happen. It's inevitable. When that happens, there will be white panic." At this point, Mr. Biko pointed out that there was already considerable insecurity in the white community, reflected in desperate attempts to get money out of the country. He continued: "A faceless army which destroys overnight will introduce far greater feelings of insecurity than an organized military force on the border, which you can confront and defeat."

Mr. Biko predicted that the government would forge closer ties between the police and army, preparing both for the coming struggle, and that white newspapers would be more and more inclined to press the government to make adequate preparations for the threat. In the meantime, money would continue to flow out of the country. "I think a real crisis point may be reached in three or four years' time. I am not saying that change will occur then, but the point will come when real panic is no longer an abstract thing."

Elements of this interview appeared in summarized form in the *New York Times*, and when I showed a clipping to Steve, he commented that it read much "tougher" than he had meant it to read. He said he had "laid it on thick" to John Burns, to try to jolt public opinion in the United States to some sense of urgency on the South African question, but had expected the summarized report to be toned down somewhat, as foreign journalists usually did because of his banning. He chuckled ruefully: "John Burns didn't tone anything down. He was disturbingly accurate, really . . ." However, Steve expressed himself satisfied that the points he had made in the interview were fairly reflected and hoped that they would have the desired impact in view of the high international repute of the *New York Times*.

ARGUMENTS AND DISCUSSIONS

Steve Biko and I had many animated discussions about politics and other matters. It is hard to imagine, for people who do not live under a repressive regime, that a simple chat about opinions could land both participants in trouble. However, this was certainly the case for both of us, and because of this we always tried to make certain we were safe from hidden microphones before we talked candid politics.

One place Steve liked taking Wendy and me to was a small forest glade north of King William's Town, where we could speak in normal tones without fear of bugging. He also liked going out there on his own sometimes to get away from everyone and simply think, but one day the Security Police followed him there and discovered the place, and he never went back again.

It was in this glade one day that I had a long dispute with him about his critical attitude toward the United States. He, for his part, thought I was too blindly pro-American and that I had an unrealistically idealistic view toward Western democracy. Not that he was pro-East or in any way pro-communist, but he felt the East was more ready to censure the Nationalist government in the United Nations and to institute sanctions than the West was, and this accorded with the view of most blacks.

On this occasion, and on another occasion at "the yard," we thrashed the whole thing out. There was much about American ideals that he liked, but he was cynical about Western capitalism and the West's protective attitude toward its investments in South Africa. He explained that young blacks in South Africa were becoming increasingly anti-West because the Western countries merely "slapped the wrist" of the Vorster government when they felt an anti-apartheid gesture was called for, but maintained their diplomatic and economic links which helped to bolster up the regime.

I based my argument on the democratic values of the American Constitution, with its guarantees of individual liberty and its checks and balances which had produced the glorious chapter of Watergate, in terms of which even the highest officer in the State could be toppled from power for misdemeanors. In reply Steve surprised me by saying that individual liberty was both admirable and desirable, but that it wasn't his highest priority. "When people are starving, unemployed and exploited, food, work and social security are higher priorities for them than individual liberty," he said.

I replied: "That's a real Third World argument. Surely all other benefits flow from individual liberty. Look, Steve – one day you and I will travel the world. We'll go to the East, where your image as a black leader will be my protection, then we'll go to the West, where nobody needs protection!" He laughed appreciatively, and said he looked forward to such a journey of discovery. Thereafter we often spoke about this trip and what it would be like, and whom we would visit. We planned, after visiting both East and West, to journey throughout the length and breadth of Africa. He had never been outside the country and always enjoyed my accounts of travel to faraway lands – especially the United States.

He used to emphasize the importance of the Black Peoples Convention commitment to the principle that the South Africa – "Azania" – of the future should be dominated by neither East nor West. "We have a lot to learn from both, but we must be slaves to neither," he said. When I railed at Eastern cynicism in backing the liberation movements of Africa he agreed only partially. "Cynicism, yes, but accompanied by effective material assistance, which is more valuable than speeches and wristslappings," he said.

I pointed out the number of African states that had accepted aid from the Easterners only to boot them out afterward. "But that is precisely my point," he said. "You are missing my point, which is that the Russians don't stick fast afterward. Their record in Africa is one of material aid, then disengaging or being ousted. On the other hand Western aid against colonialism has several times led to Western economic imperialism. Look, I'm not starry-eyed about the Russians, and I reject their basic ideology – it's just that their brand of intervention has been more beneficial in Africa. Of course it is to suit their own cynical ends – but it is of more practical assistance than the oratory of an Andy Young. The Andy Youngs are nice enough guys, but their approach is doing us no damn good. If we are to have a peaceful solution here the Andy Youngs must stop talking and start really getting tough with Vorster – sanctions, blockades if necessary, the lot. We blacks reject the theory that sanctions will harm us more. It's always whites who say that. If people want to be our friends they must act as friends, with deeds."

Steve talked candidly of many other things, but to repeat all of these while a Nationalist government controls South Africa would be to imperil a fair number of people. There was, however, one cabinet minister whom he thought was convertible in time to possibly playing a future role in the nation's government. He said of the Minister of Sport and Recreation, Dr. Piet Koornhof, that he appeared to have "human qualities not totally stifled by his Nationalist environment." He added: "It seems there is quite a nice guy there trying to get out!"

It was hard for me to reconcile such statements as these from Steve with some of the opinions he expressed about his political stance. In the interview with John Burns he also said at one stage that one-party rule was appropriate for Africa. We had argued for hours on this point one day, I waxing loudly vehement that this theory was "totalitarianistic tripe" and he needling me that my viewpoint was "good old Gladstone liberalism." My main points were, first, that if there was such unanimity among citizens of African states, then there was no need for legislation limiting the system to one-party only, and, second, that a no-party state would make more sense than a one-party state anyway, since the one party recognized duplicated the state's government machine needlessly.

Unlike most human beings, Steve was big enough to concede an argument, and on this point, after more than two hours of debate, he did so. He did more. He said I had raised aspects of the subject that had never occurred to him, that they had a validity which altered his stance on the issue considerably, and then proceeded to develop my argument more lucidly and convincingly than I ever could! I always regarded with pride Steve's at least partial conversion thereafter to the basic principles of the Westminster ideal – the permitting of free men to organize any number of associations or platforms to promote legitimate policies. In fact, I like to think to this day that Steve, who taught me so much, was genuinely influenced by me on at least two issues – the one mentioned above, and the adoption after much advocacy by me of a less cynical attitude toward the United States in particular and the Western democracies in general.

At about the time of the Burns interview, or rather shortly after it, Wendy and I were at Zanempilo and we told Steve of how John Burns, who had lived for some years in China, had described the labor camps there, the summary way in which people were consigned to them for minor and often imaginary "ideological errors," and other repressive aspects of life under the Peking regime. Steve responded provocatively: "I suppose it's hard for an American, coming from a country with such a high standard of living, to imagine how the Chinese would be prepared to sacrifice civil liberties in exchange for social security and enough to eat." And that, as he knew it would, led to another long argument . . .

Looking back on it now, it seems that "argument" is not the right word for many of those discussions. Steve wasn't a cheap puller of debating tricks to score petty points. Although some of his remarks were provocative by design, this was invariably to open up a process of thinking aloud and listening intently – a process of verbal and mental dissection of an issue. His repartee was always telling but never, never, offensive. In all the time I knew him he never once hurt my feelings.

I regret to say the same could not be said by him of me, because I did hurt his feelings on one occasion. Steve had come to lunch and was patting a little pup we had acquired for the children. The pup was pitch-black and his name was "Charley." Steve said: "what do you call him?" "Well," I said. "He's very black so we considered a Black Consciousness name like Saso."

He tried to hide his annoyance and I remembered in a flash that the African attitude to dogs and their names has none of the jocular tradition known to whites. In fact, the Xhosa word for dog, "inja," is a deeply insulting term of opprobrium – much more so than in English. But he let the incident pass with the response: "You should rather call him Vorster."

I thought of this incident later, at Steve's funeral, as the crowd chanted:
"Vorster! – Inja!"
"Kruger! – Inja!"
"Hattingh! – Inja!"
And when they burst into song: "Ama–Bhulu a–zi–zinja!" ("The Boers are dogs!")

When we used to drive out to the glade north of King William's Town, Steve, Wendy and I, we would be in two cars, because of the ban on Steve being with more than one person at a time. One of us would go in Steve's car on the way there, and the other would come back with him. Sometimes the three of us would talk in the yard of Leopold Street, Steve and I in chairs under the big tree, Wendy in the car parked within easy hearing distance but arguably separate from us – in case the Security Police drove in. It was during one such session in the yard that Steve shocked me by saying that there could in certain circumstances be a case made out for detention without trial. "What?" I said. "Do you mean that if you took over government of this country you might detain people like Kruger and Vorster?"

He said: "It could well be necessary as a stabilizing measure during a delicate period of unstable transition. Yes, in such a case I would."

I said: "Then I'd be the first to scrap you on their behalf and to demand that they be charged or released!"

He smiled at the thought and said: "I know you would."

At about this time, I had written a speculative piece in my weekly column, aimed for educational purposes at white readers. It was called "Prepare to meet ALF," and read as follows:

This is a letter of introduction for my fellow South Africans, and it is intended to prepare them for a meeting with ALF. As an actual letter of introduction it is somewhat premature, because ALF isn't born yet, but it will prepare the ground for ALF's appearance on the South African scene.

ALF, I believe, will be the letters of the name of the political movement which will soon be formed to articulate the aspirations of a large number of blacks. I believe it will seek to unite all the black political groups, including those rivals of the past the PAC and ANC, and that the main drive for such black unity will come from the young leaders of the present BPC.

They will want a new name, to get away from the divisions of the past, and they will want to incorporate in it a reference to the new kind of South Africa they want to bring into being. They will see it as a common black front, so the word "front" will come into it. They will see it as a movement for liberation, so the word "liberation" will come into it. They will want it to mark the new name they have in mind for the country – Azania.

Hence, Azania Liberation Front. Or ALF for short.

I believe the black unity born out of a desire to avoid the fragmentation that has retarded black politics in Rhodesia will find its expression in such a movement, and that its influence will be formidable.

No doubt the Azania Liberation Front will be banned soon after its formal inauguration – but the likelihood is that its formal inauguration will come so long after its actual launching that its effectiveness will not be seriously curtailed.

On the contrary, since a large measure of effectiveness of any black opposition to white control depends these days on recognition by the frontline states, by the OAU and by the UN, such a ban will help establish the credibility of the ALF.

This movement is in any event unlikely to be revolutionary in the sense of being committed to violence. Its basic function is more likely to be to create an unchallengeable mandate for men like Mandela, Sobukwe and Biko, by that time in probable alliance with the Inkatha movement of Gatsha Buthelezi, to speak for the black nonhomeland masses in negotiation with the white leaders.

This, of course, presupposes there will be such negotiation.

But so does a logical look at the probable sequence of events in Southern Africa – majority rule in Rhodesia (Zimbabwe) and South West Africa (Namibia); increasing pressure from both West and East, including veto-withdrawal, trade embargo and possibly massive military intervention.

Any decision by white Nationalism to take on the whole world will fail in the long term – no matter how many bullet factories P. W. Botha officially opens – and it is inevitable that the day will come when white leaders will have to negotiate with black leaders.

The major difference between such talks and the ones the government now hold is that the black leaders concerned will not only have the mandate of the massive black majority but will be recognized as so mandated by the rest of Africa and the rest of the world.

And that, I suggest, will be the major role of the Azania Liberation Front – and the extent to which its leaders will be generous in their approach to white fears will depend on how soon the white leaders will be prepared to talk real business with them.

As matters now stand, there is no guarantee that ALF will be magnanimous, benevolent and beneficial for everyone concerned – although all the existing evidence indicates this as a reasonable probability.

But what is certain is that any increase in hardness of black attitude will be in direct proportion to white delay in negotiating with properly mandated black leaders.

This is what has happened elsewhere in Africa, and there is no reason why it shouldn't happen here.

We should therefore hope that when ALF finally surfaces officially, the white government will have the common sense to acknowledge the significance of the fact realistically and to negotiate realistically, rather than to react with bans, threats, war drums and other evasions doomed to have no permanent validity.

Steve chided me for writing this article: "Hey, man, the damn Security Police will take it all seriously and think we are engaged in a deep plot. You know what they're like." I replied that as a journalist I had to write what I honestly believed, and to predict openly what I thought was a probable future course of events.

"Yes, but you know their mentality – they read all sorts of sinister implications into anything like that, no matter how speculative it is. Those guys love conspiracy theories." Little did we realize as we chuckled over this that that same article would be introduced into his own inquest by the Security Police.

My last visit to Steve, and our last long conversation, took place only two days before he was detained for the last time. I spent the morning with him at Zanempilo. I had recently had talks with the nonracist South African Council on Sport, which was affiliated to the Supreme Council for Sport in Africa but had no actual power to confer the prospect of international acceptability to any South African sports code, no matter how non-apartheid. Nor would the Council achieve this power without BPC backing.

I put it to Steve that the BPC should provide this backing so that opponents of racist sport would have a double-edged sword – being able on one hand to punish a racist sports association with ostracism and on the other to reward it with international acceptability if it shed all traces of racism. At first he opposed the idea, saying that the BPC position was one of opposition to all recognition of South African sports bodies while political apartheid persisted. But after going into all aspects of the issue he came to agree that there were more advantages than disadvantages in the suggestion. The idea was to hold off the proposed formation of a blacks-only sports council, throw major black support behind SACOS, and give the sports integrationists a last chance for several months (we decided on six months) before the final breach.

He said he would sell the idea to his colleagues, and added: "Give me some time, though. I will have to make a long trip."

Whether he was on this trip when he reached the fatal roadblock, or whether he was combining it with another to sort out BPC problems in Cape Town, or whether he was simply going along on one of his tours of contact, no one can say. But what can be said, by anyone who knew Steve, was that he was not going on that trip for the purpose suggested by the Security Police in connection with pamphlets calling for political murder and general bloodshed. That simply wasn't his line. It wasn't his style. The crude language in the pamphlet cited simply wasn't in the Biko manner. He wasn't a pamphleteer, and scorned sloganeering.

But against this smear, and many others, he was not to have the opportunity to defend himself. The manner in which he would have handled himself in the dock when confronted by such accusations can be gauged by the following off-the-record exchange with a Nationalist sympathizer during an adjournment while he was giving evidence in the 1976 SASO/BPC trial. The exchange went like this:

QUESTIONER: Why do you seek confrontation?
BIKO: There is nothing wrong with confrontation as such.
QUESTIONER: Confrontation leads to violence. Do you approve of violence?
BIKO: No, confrontation does not necessarily lead to violence. You and I are now in confrontation, and there is no violence implied.
QUESTIONER: Why do you emphasize Black Consciousness? You people are not even really black – more a dark brown.
BIKO: Why do you call yourself white? I would describe you as rather pink.
ADVOCATE ASIDE TO COLLEAGUE: This isn't a confrontation – it's a massacre!

Steve was always so quick to take the route of humor, and his basic inclination was so clearly to respond to what was human, even in speaking of his persecutors, that later claims by the Security Police that he was associated with a pamphlet campaign calling for bodies and blood seemed to me to be particularly obscene. Besides, he knew Security Police tactics so well that he would never have been fooled by the corny ploy of "confessions" by associates.

He used often to talk of this sort of thing. "You know," he would say, "they come in and say that your pal so-and-so has told them everything. They even show you statements 'voluntarily' supplied by other detainees, but it's so bloody stupid because even if the chap has written it out himself and even if there's a grain of truth in some of the stuff, what do they hope to achieve? Even if they beat you up into admitting anything they want you to admit, you just wait until you're in court and tell the judge the whole damn thing is nonsense. You were forced to say it, and it's meaningless because it becomes inadmissible evidence."

The Port Elizabeth Security Police must have been particularly keen to get Steve to make some such confession while he was in detention for the last time. After his death they tried to smear his name with allegations they never confronted him with in public during his lifetime. And the method they employed, the very method he had described to me, formed part of their own evidence during the inquest which followed his death at their hands.

3: THE TRIAL

In 1976 Steve Biko played a leading role in one of the most remarkable trials in South African history. A group of nine young blacks were prosecuted in the Supreme Court for alleged subversion by intent. That is to say, in a sense their thoughts were placed on trial. The State sought to establish that their philosophy, the Black Consciousness philosophy as enunciated by SASO and the BPC, was a danger to public safety in that it was likely to lead to a mobilization of black opinion against the established white order in a manner calculated to cause "racial confrontation."

As a mobilization of black opinion against the established white order was precisely what Black Consciousness was all about, the accused had the complex problem of defending themselves without renouncing their basic philosophy. The prosecutor took the line that the SASO/BPC style of mobilization of black opinion involved the inculcation of violent anti-white feeling which encouraged interracial hostility with the ultimate aim of revolution. The defense took the line that blacks needed no inculcation of resentment against white racism; that such resentment was already widespread among blacks; that even within the country's statutory curbs on anti-apartheid expression blacks had the right to mobilize opinion to seek peaceful redress of their grievances and that Black Consciousness was a constructive rather than a destructive philosophy.

Since the accused were all disciples of the philosophy and since Steve Biko was the foremost proponent of it, he was summoned by the defense team to give evidence on their behalf. This was ironical, in that it is virtually certain that he would have been among the accused had he not already been banned. But as a witness for the defense he came to dominate the trial, and in the style of Nelson Mandela of a previous generation he turned the courtroom into a platform for the articulation of black grievance.

The following excerpts from the abridged court record are given to illustrate, in Steve Biko's own words, on one of the few occasions permitting him to give public utterance, how he saw the role of articulate black leadership in the struggle for liberation. His replies under questioning by defense lawyer David Soggott, state prosecutor K. Attwell, and the notedly pro-government Judge Boshoff, are given in chronological sequence as the trial progressed.

SOGGOTT: Mr. Biko, I think we should first go through the essential elements of your personal history. You were born in 1946 in King William's Town, is that correct?

BIKO: Yes.

SOGGOTT: And you matriculated at Marianhill, which is near to Pinetown, in 1965?

BIKO: That is correct.

SOGGOTT: From 1966 you went to medical school?

BIKO: I entered the University of Natal as a preliminary-year student in 1966 and stayed on to June 1972, when I was expelled from the university. I was then doing third-year medicine.

SOGGOTT: Can you tell us why you were expelled?

BIKO: The reason given by the administration was inadequate academic performance.

SOGGOTT: And what do you say about that reason?

BIKO: It was challengeable, that is all I am prepared to say.

SOGGOTT: Were you interested in medicine?

BIKO: By the time I was expelled I had already made up my mind to leave.

SOGGOTT: And you left in 1972, is that correct?

BIKO: That is correct.

SOGGOTT: And what then did you do?

BIKO: I worked for the Black Community Program.

SOGGOTT: BCP?

BIKO: The BCP, yes, from the beginning of August 1972.

SOGGOTT: Where did you work?

BIKO: In Durban, until I was banned in March 1973.

SOGGOTT: And then where did you go?

BIKO: I then went to King William's Town. I was asked by the Black Community Programs to start a branch of the same organization in that town.

SOGGOTT: And you then started working for them?

BIKO: That is correct.

SOGGOTT: Is that from February 1973?

BIKO: Effectively from April 1973 to December 9, 1975.

SOGGOTT: Why did you cease working for them in December 1975?

BIKO: I was so directed by a variation to my restriction order.

SOGGOTT: Now apart from your Community Program work, have you become interested in the study of law?

BIKO: Yes I have. I registered in 1973 with the University of South Africa.

SOGGOTT: Could you describe the circumstances surrounding the formation and rise of SASO? When you got to the University of Natal was NUSAS, the National Union of South African Students, the dominant student body there?

BIKO: That is correct.

SOGGOTT: Would you tell His Lordship how the black students fitted into the NUSAS framework?

BIKO: Where do I start? Do I start from the differences with NUSAS?

SOGGOTT: I think that might be appropriate.

BIKO: Right, well when I got onto the campus I was interested initially in NUSAS and I accepted fully their nonracist approach. I then began to debate in favor of this with people who were of other views, who were critical of the kind of allegiance that whites in general have to nonracialism.

SOGGOTT: Can you just elaborate on that a little bit, who were these other people who had that view?

BIKO: Well, there were several students on the campus, some of them my friends, like Dr. Mokoape, and others who were not friends of mine but were politically motivated people on the campus.

SOGGOTT: When you say Dr. Mokoape do you mean accused number 4 sitting there?

BIKO: I do not know his number. Yes, he is that man.

SOGGOTT: What was their attitude?

BIKO: Their attitude was one of deep distrust of the attachment of whites to the concept of nonracism. They felt this would always be propounded as an idea only, but that in effect whites were satisfied with the status quo and were not going to move away from this. I did not agree. I believed there were committed whites who wanted the situation changed, who wanted to share with us everything the country could produce.

SOGGOTT: This view which criticized NUSAS, did it fix on any specific examples as demonstrating their view of the white students' role?

BIKO: Well, I cannot remember now specific examples quoted then, but it was common cause among students that in the history of the students' organizations, certain of the NUSAS leaders had done things that black students looked on with contempt.

SOGGOTT: Such as?

BIKO: Sometimes they would mention a statement by a particular NUSAS president in a situation where he did not suspect that he was being overheard, sometimes they would talk about segregation, for instance during NUSAS conferences, there would be private student parties in the residences where blacks were not allowed to come in, and there you would find officials of NUSAS. These were the things that made blacks begin to feel that the attachment of liberal students to nonracialism was shaky.

THE JUDGE: Was that the policy of the university or was there social equality at the university, the official policy?

BIKO: The official policy of the university was that blacks should not come into the residences, but then the NUSAS officials were free to decide where to throw their parties, and in many instances they were known to hold these parties in the white students' residences where they knew blacks could not come.

SOGGOTT: And now I want to ask you this – was there ever an occasion where there was a NUSAS conference and any dissatisfaction was expressed as to the accommodation of black students?

BIKO: Yes, it was the 1967 conference at Rhodes University, Grahamstown. We had been given to understand that residences would be completely integrated for the first time at a NUSAS conference, and on our way to the conference in the train we had a discussion as a delegation from the Natal University (Black Section) to the effect that if this condition was not met we would register our protest, withdraw from the conference and go home. When we got to Rhodes University the conference organizer could not quite say where we were going to stay, we were all put out at the hall in different places and we eventually noticed that all the white students first went, then some of the Indian students, then eventually he came back to us to say he had found a church where we could stay. At that moment I felt we had ample reason to stick by our decision in the train.

SOGGOTT: Mr. Biko, who took that decision in the train, can you mention any names?

BIKO: Well, there was the then president, Rogers Rabavan, there was Ben Nqubane, Johnny Masonwane, Paul David and myself. There were also, I think, other students from other campuses in Natal, like Shan Maraj.

SOGGOTT: Very well, you were about to say that night something happened?

BIKO: Yes, that night we were outwitted by the executive of the organization, in that just as we started the session the executive brought in a resolution condemning the Rhodes University Council for not allowing them to have blacks in the residences. This tended to split the attitudes of some of the black students to the whole question, because they felt that the blame devolved not on the NUSAS executive but more on the University Council. My view was that NUSAS had known for a long time that this was a difficult aim to achieve, and should therefore have made more preparations, and that anyway the time had come when if they could not get an integrated venue they should simply postpone the conference. We debated this in my delegation and because there was no agreement I moved a private motion proposing that the conference adjourn until we could get a non-racist venue. I think the motion was introduced at 12 o'clock at night and the vote was finally taken at 5.30 in the morning, and during the intervening debate a lot of attitudes became clear and new ideas came to my mind.

SOGGOTT: What do you mean by that now, new attitudes and new ideas?

BIKO: I realized that for a long time I had been holding onto this whole dogma of nonracism almost like a religion, feeling that it was sacrilegious to question it, and therefore not accommodating the attacks I was getting from other students.

But in the course of that debate I began to feel there was a lot lacking in the proponents of the nonracist idea, that much as they were adhering to this impressive idea they were in fact subject to their own experiences back home, they had this problem, you know, of superiority, and they tended to take us for granted and wanted us to accept things that were second-class. They could not see why we could not consider staying in that church, and I began to feel that our understanding of our own situation in this country was not coincidental with that of these liberal whites.

SOGGOTT: Yes, and subsequent to this NUSAS gathering can you tell us what further developments there were?

BIKO: Well, firstly one must mention that I began to share the Rhodes experience with a number of black students, first on my campus and then elsewhere, and at that time there began to emerge some kind of creative thought to say, well we cannot blame the white students for what they do, they have got their experiences in their homes, we have to look positively at what we do as black students, and we began to feel there was a need for some kind of consultation among black students which focused on their problems as black students on the campuses, and which allowed NUSAS to continue as it did, but operated specifically for black students.

SOGGOTT: And this group of people who were opposed to NUSAS, did it become greater or fewer as time went on?

BIKO: It became greater. More and more black students began to hive off from support for NUSAS to accommodate, you know, the new thoughts that were beginning to crystallize.

SOGGOTT: There was a University Christian Movement conference in 1968?

BIKO: That is correct.

SOGGOTT: Was any expression given to new thinking then?

BIKO: Yes, we had decided, when I say we I am referring to the students who were beginning to think more in terms of black dialog among the relevant black universities, were beginning to think that we should sound out this idea a bit more, and a number of us went to several conferences. We went to the NUSAS conference in 1968 in Johannesburg, but found that few black students were participating at that conference. We then went to UCM, which was at Stutterheim in July, following the NUSAS conference, and at that conference there were a number of black students from all over the country, from universities and colleges, and in fact they were in the majority at that conference. We felt that the platform had somewhat widened, and that we could talk more authentically to a group which was reasonably representative in the sense of random sampling of students from several universities. So we shared this idea with the students, we allowed for situations where black students met alone to discuss this particular idea, and a decision was taken at that conference to press for a conference to look specifically at this question.

SOGGOTT: This decision was taken by whom?

BIKO: As I said, we created a situation for black students to meet alone.

SOGGOTT: How did you do that, or how did that come about?

Biko: Well, we were faced with a legal problem at Stutterheim. It is an urban area, and there exists what they call the 72-hour clause in the Group Areas Act, a provision which allows a black man to be in an urban area for only 72 hours without permit. So this problem confronted the conference and it was thrown at the students by the leadership of UCM. There was a very intense debate on this point, with some students saying that we should as a means of protest not observe this rule, and others saying we should observe it by just walking symbolically across the border of the town and coming back for a fresh period of 72 hours. Now I was among those students who felt this would be a bit hypocritical. I thought we should take the stance that this law was objectionable and that we black students should allow ourselves to be arrested, and that the white students who were there should either be arrested with us or protest against our arrest. There was a debate about this strategy and eventually we froze the situation where blacks had to decide upon it on their own because they were the ones who were affected. The conference eventually accepted this and the blacks met on their own to look at this. And when we met on our own we began to talk about problems affecting us uniquely as black students, which we felt were not given full consideration in organizations of a wider nature. Eventually a formal decision was taken to work towards a conference in December to deal with this specific issue of a black student organization as such.

Soggott: Would you say that that was the first organizational germ of SASO?

Biko: Yes.

Soggott: And when was the first conference of that organization as such?

Biko: It was called in early July 1970 – sorry, 1969, at the University of the North, commonly called Turfloop.

Soggott: Now the question of Black Consciousness, did that figure at all at your 1968 conference?

Biko: Not in the final form as defined, but I think traces of it were beginning to creep into the thinking of the student leaders.

Soggott: Would you now deal with the conference at Turfloop in July 1969?

Biko: Yes. This was mainly a structural conference. We looked at the final draft which had come from the previous meeting, the December meeting, and adopted it as the constitution of SASO. We then considered basic policy questions, the pressing one being what our relationship to existing student organizations would be. There was much debate about this. Some people were for a complete break while others were for retention of some links. As a result we decided that we would not affiliate with NUSAS but that we would recognize NUSAS as the national student organization. I must explain that the dichotomy here arose out of the differences in attitudes of the various students because of their university situations. Some of the black campuses were actually debarred from participation in NUSAS by their various authorities. This tended to make NUSAS some kind of romantic attraction to them, and they felt that it would be a complete letdown to join the bandwagon with their administrations in criticizing NUSAS, so they preferred to leave it loose like that.

SOGGOTT: Now, were elections held?

BIKO: Yes, elections were held, and a new executive was put up.

SOGGOTT: Were you elected to any position?

BIKO: Yes, I was elected as first president of the organization.

SOGGOTT: Who else was on the executive at that stage?

BIKO: Well, I had Pat Matshaka as vice-president, I had Wuila Mashalaba as secretary and a man called Denamile as treasurer. Those I remember, I cannot remember the others.

SOGGOTT: Were any of the accused involved at that stage?

BIKO: No, none of them were involved then.

SOGGOTT: Of the nine accused before court, which of them did you know before their arrest?

BIKO: Before their arrest I knew Mr. Cooper, Mr. Myeza, Mr. Lekota, Dr. Mokoape and Mr. Moodley.

SOGGOTT: Did you as president go around addressing the campuses?

BIKO: Yes, I did.

SOGGOTT: And what sort of response did you find from black students to the idea of SASO as conceived at that stage?

BIKO: There was encouragement wherever I went.

SOGGOTT: Now I wonder whether at this stage it might not be appropriate for you to tell His Lordship, was there among the black students themselves still opposition against the formation of SASO?

BIKO: Yes, I would say perhaps the best experience had come from my own campus, where I had a day-to-day interest in the students. There was ambiguity in the attitude of some students who were essentially pro-NUSAS, who felt that what was happening now was against the whole spirit of nonracism that NUSAS advocated. On the other hand there were other students who felt that SASO was not going far enough, and that the involvement of Africans with Indians and Coloreds was going to lead essentially to the same amorphousness that the nonracist organizations found themselves in.

SOGGOTT: They wanted a purely African organization?

BIKO: Yes, some students wanted a purely African organization.

SOGGOTT: When did you break off with NUSAS?

BIKO: I think the formal decision was taken in 1970, but even in between the two conferences there was a drastic shift of attitude. On the one hand NUSAS felt threatened by the emergence of SASO, and thought they should try to block its growth on the various campuses, and we on our part became more critical of NUSAS. It became quite clear that we were competing for attention on campuses, and therefore in order to survive we had to say what was latently at the back of our minds about NUSAS, to make the students see exactly why they should fall in with us.

SOGGOTT: And was this accepted?

BIKO: This was accepted and then in 1970 a decision was taken to withdraw our recognition of NUSAS.

SOGGOTT: Was the question of the term "nonwhite" raised at all, do you know?
BIKO: Students took a decision that they would no longer use the term "non-white," nor allow it to be used as a description of them, because they saw it as a negation of their being. They were being stated as non-something, which implied that the standard was something and they were not that particular standard. They felt that a positive view of life commensurate with the build-up of one's dignity and confidence should be contained in positive description, and they replaced the term "nonwhite" with the term "black."
SOGGOTT: Now, Mr. Biko, in 1970 in Port Elizabeth you people had an executive meeting of SASO?
BIKO: Correct.
SOGGOTT: Would you tell His Lordship what significant decisions if any were taken there?
BIKO: There were a number of decisions taken. I remember two specifically. We looked at our program for the forthcoming year, 1971, and recognized in the program certain days that we thought we should incorporate as days to be remembered by the various campuses for their significance. In the first instance there was what we called the "suffer" day, I think it was on May 10, and secondly there had already been on various campuses a commemoration of Sharpeville. At that meeting we decided to incorporate this as a formal day within the SASO calendar.
SOGGOTT: Any other decisions?
BIKO: We decided also to organize what we called compassion day.
SOGGOTT: Was anybody sent to what is known as an international common-wealth students' conference in Ghana?
BIKO: Yes, we had received an invitation from the Commonwealth Students Association, which was having its meeting in Ghana. The invitation we received was a joint one with NUSAS, so we sent a telegram saying we were not prepared to go on a joint delegation with NUSAS but if they wished to they could invite us on our own. We eventually got an invitation saying we could come, and we appointed Lindelwe Mabandla to represent us.
SOGGOTT: Was any other decision taken in relation to black organizations?
BIKO: Yes, we felt at that stage that we were exponents of a particular philosophy that was important not only for students but for the entire black community, and we felt that we needed to share this with existing black organizations within the country.
SOGGOTT: What philosophy was this?
BIKO: We had already begun to realize that our attitude, which constitutes Black Consciousness, was a unique approach in the country, and that we wanted to share it with other organizations. The focal point was that of coordination of efforts. We felt there were a number of organizations which were doing important work among blacks in the country, and that they could achieve better results if they shared their efforts and delineated fields of endeavor so that they did not overlap in their activities.

SOGGOTT: And what decision was taken in relation to this?

BIKO: We decided that we would set up a series of meetings with these organizations individually. We would send a delegation in the course of the ensuing year to share our view of, you know, coordinated efforts to uplift the position of the black man in the country.

SOGGOTT: Now, Mr. Biko, historically viewed can one say that this set the ball rolling in the direction of BPC, the Black Peoples Convention?

BIKO: Yes.

SOGGOTT: May I bring you back to the question of the holding of the Sharpeville day? What was the thinking behind that?

BIKO: There were two main reasons. Firstly, we had people who had been killed in pursuit of the struggle of the black man within this country, and it seemed only proper for us as black students to remember these occasions in honor of these people who died for our cause. The second reason was that we were in a particularly weak position as black people in the country, faced with an all-powerful institutionalized governmental machinery, and that if we showed our abhorrence of this through constant remembrance services whites might feel persuaded to restrain their police force, who were most to blame for such deaths. Those are the two reasons, the first one factual and the second psychological.

SOGGOTT: Before the establishment of SASO had you gone to Sharpeville commemoration services?

BIKO: I had.

SOGGOTT: Would that have been simply as a student or in any official capacity?

BIKO: No, no, it was as a student.

SOGGOTT: As a result of what was said there did you find that any racial hostility against the white race was encouraged or inflamed?

BIKO: I would say no, I would say on the contrary that these services tended to give a certain amount of serenity, you know, they gave a certain amount of content and identification with those people.

SOGGOTT: And looking into the future, did you attend subsequently SASO commemorations of heroes' day?

BIKO: Yes I did.

SOGGOTT: And at those services or commemoration services, was racial hostility encouraged or inflamed?

BIKO: Definitely not. The prevailing theme was a sense of serenity in being united over a particular aspect of our history, and there were religious overtones. We had sermons by various distinguished ministers and I have no doubt that the majority of people there were moved by the way the whole thing was handled. In a way they tended to relate it to a biblical sacrifice, you know, in the sense that these people died for us, and that we should therefore rededicate ourselves to our struggle, so to speak.

SOGGOTT: Yes. Now, Mr. Biko, compassion day, would you briefly tell us what that was about?

BIKO: Compassion day was meant for the remembrance of specific situations of affliction that the black man was subjected to from time to time, things like starvation in places like Dimbaza, things like the floods in Port Elizabeth.

SOGGOTT: Now you said starvation in places like Dimbaza, is that what you said?

BIKO: Yes.

SOGGOTT: Where is Dimbaza?

BIKO: Dimbaza is a resettlement area outside King William's Town where I stay.

SOGGOTT: And when you say starvation there can you tell us what you mean by that?

BIKO: Well, one had there the plight of families moved from the Northern Cape, North Western Cape and Western Cape, and in most instances the man was not in a state to work, the woman of the family did not have work when she arrived there, they were given government rations which in most instances lasted for sometimes two or three weeks although they were supposedly monthly rations. The church had to move in. I went there once with the minister of the Anglican church, and visited three or four houses. I could not take it any more. In all the houses there was no furniture except perhaps a chair or some old bedstead, a stove and some pots, and there was clear evidence of suffering on the part of kids there. That is what I mean by starvation.

SOGGOTT: Now, you have mentioned Dimbaza, what else?

BIKO: The flood situation in and around Port Elizabeth.

SOGGOTT: What was the purpose of holding compassion day, apart from the mere fact of recalling these disasters?

BIKO: The main idea of compassion day was to get students to develop a social conscience, to see themselves as part of the community, and to direct their energies to solving problems of the nature we were thinking about on compassion day.

SOGGOTT: Merely to get some details relating to you, in 1971 did you and Barney Pityana attend a conference known as the Institute of Interracial Studies under Professor Van der Merwe in Cape Town?

BIKO: That is correct, yes.

SOGGOTT: And did you address that conference?

BIKO: I did.

SOGGOTT: What did you address the conference on?

BIKO: I spoke on white racism and Black Consciousness, and Barney Pityana spoke on Black Consciousness broadly.

SOGGOTT: Subsequently a book was published called *Student Perspectives on South Africa*, is that right?

BIKO: That is correct, yes.

SOGGOTT: Did your address there figure in that book?

BIKO: It did, yes.

SOGGOTT: Now, I want to refer to the SASO resolution: "SASO is a black student organization working for the liberation of blacks first from psychological oppression by themselves through inferiority complex and secondly from the physical oppression accruing out of living in a white racist society." Now, the

concept of Black Consciousness, does that link up in any way with this resolution?
BIKO: Yes it does.
SOGGOTT: Would you explain that link-up?
BIKO: Basically Black Consciousness directs itself to the black man and to his situation, and the black man is subjected to two forces in this country. He is first of all oppressed by an external world through institutionalized machinery and through laws that restrict him from doing certain things, through heavy work conditions, through poor pay, through difficult living conditions, through poor education, these are all external to him. Secondly, and this we regard as the most important, the black man in himself has developed a certain state of alienation, he rejects himself precisely because he attaches the meaning white to all that is good, in other words he equates good with white. This arises out of his living and it arises out of his development from childhood. When you go to school, for instance, your school is not the same as the white school, and the conclusion you reach is that the education you get there cannot be the same as what the white kids get at school. The black kids normally have shabby uniforms, if any, or no uniform at school, while the white kids always have uniforms. You find for instance even the organization of sport, these are things you notice as a kid, at white schools to be absolutely so thorough and indicative of good training, good upbringing, you could get in a school fifteen rugby teams, we could get from our school three rugby teams. Each of those fifteen white teams has got togs for each kid who plays, while we have to share the togs among our three teams. Now this is part of the roots of self-negation which our kids get even as they grow up. The homes are different, the streets are different, the lighting is different, so you tend to begin to feel that there is something *incomplete in your humanity*, and that completeness goes with whiteness. This is carried through to adulthood when the black man has got to live and work.
SOGGOTT: How do you see it carried through to adulthood, can you give us examples there?
BIKO: I remember specifically one example that touched me, talking to an Indian worker in Durban who was driving a van for a dry cleaner firm. He was describing to me his average day, how he lived, and the way he put it to me was: "I no more work in order to live, I *live in order to work*." And when he went on to elaborate I could see the truth of the statement. He described how he had to wake up at 4 o'clock, in order to walk a long distance to be in time for a bus to town. He worked there for the whole day, so many calls were thrown his way by his boss, and at the end of the day he had to travel the same route, arrive at home at 8.30 or 9 o'clock, too tired to do anything but to sleep in order to be in time for work again early the next day.
SOGGOTT: To what extent would you say that this example is typical or atypical of a black worker living in an urban area?
BIKO: With I think some variance in terms of the times and so on and the work situation, this is a pretty typical example, precisely because townships are placed a long distance away from the working areas where black people work, and

the transport conditions are appalling. Trains are overcrowded, taxis are over-crowded, the whole traveling situation is dangerous, and by the time a guy gets to work he has really been through the mill. He gets to work, there is no peace either at work, his boss sits on him to eke out of him the last effort in order to boost production. This is the common experience of the black man. When he gets back from work through the same process of traveling conditions, he can only take out his anger on his family, which is the last defense that he has.

SOGGOTT: Why is there this sense of inferiority, as perceived by you people?

BIKO: I have spoken a bit on *education*, but I think I must elaborate on that. As a black student you are exposed to competition with white students in fields in which you are completely inadequate. We come from a background which is essentially peasant and worker. We do not have any form of daily contact with a highly technological society. We are foreigners in that field. When you have to write an essay as a black child the topics prescribed tally well with the white experience, but you as a black student writing the same essay have to grapple with something which is foreign to you – not only foreign but superior in a sense, because of the ability of the white culture to solve so many problems in the sphere of medicine and other spheres. You then tend to look at it as a superior culture to yours. You tend to despise the *worker culture*, and this inculcates in the black man a sense of *self-hatred* which is an important determining factor in his dealings with himself and his like.

And of course to accommodate the existing problems, the black man develops a *two-faced* attitude. I can quote a typical example. I had a man working on one of our projects in the Eastern Cape on electricity. He was installing electricity, a white man with a black assistant. He had to be above the ceiling and the black man was under the ceiling and they were working together pushing up wires and pushing through the rods in which the wires are and so on, and all the time there was insult, insult, insult from the white man. "Push this, you fool." That sort of talk. And of course this touched me. I knew the white man very well, he spoke well to me, so at tea time we invited them to tea and I asked him: "Why do you speak like this to this man?" And he said to me in front of the guy: "This is the only language he understands, he is a lazy bugger." And the black man smiled. I asked him if it was true and he said: "I am used to him." This sickened me. I thought for a moment that I did not understand black society. After some two hours I came back to this black guy and said to him: "Did you really mean it?" The man changed. He became very bitter. He was telling me how he wanted to leave his job but what could he do? He did not have any skills, he had no assurances of another job, his job was to him some form of security, he had no reserves. If he did not work today he could not live tomorrow, he had to work, he had to take it. And as he had to take it he dared not show any form of what is called insolence to his boss. Now this I think epitomizes the *two-faced* attitude of many black men to this whole question of existence in this country.

SOGGOTT: The use of the word "black" in literature and as part of Western culture, has that figured at all?

BIKO: Sorry?

SOGGOTT: The use of the word "black," what does black signify and how is it used in language?

THE JUDGE: Is it a comprehensive term?

BIKO: If I understand you correctly, the reference I think of common literature to the term black is normally in association with negative aspects. You speak of the black market, you speak of the black sheep of the family, you speak of – you know, anything which is supposed to be bad is also considered to be black.

THE JUDGE: Now the word black there, surely it has nothing to do with the black man. Isn't it just idiom over the years because darkness usually, the night was a mystery for the primitive man, I mean I include the whites when I talk about primitive man, and when he talks about dark forces, he refers to magic, black magic, isn't that the reason for this?

BIKO: This is certainly the reason, but I think there has been created through history and through common reference the attitude whereby exactly that kind of association is perpetuated even for the black man. The black man sees this as being said of black magic, of the black market, precisely because, like him, it is an inferior thing; it is an unwanted thing; it is a thing rejected by society. And of course, typically, and again in the fact of this logic, whiteness goes with angels, goes with, you know, God, beauty, you know. I think this tends to help in creating this kind of feeling of self-censure within the black man.

SOGGOTT: When you have phrases such as "black is beautiful," now would that sort of phrase fit in with the Black Consciousness approach?

BIKO: Yes.

SOGGOTT: What is the idea of such a slogan?

BIKO: That slogan serves a very important aspect of our attempt to get at humanity. It challenges the very roots of the black man's belief about himself. When you say "black is beautiful," what in fact you are saying to him is: "Man, you are okay as you are. Begin to look upon yourself as a human being." Now, in African life especially, it also relates to the way women prepare themselves for viewing by society. The way they dress, the way they make up and so on, tends to be a negation of their true state and, in a sense, a running away from their color. They use skin-lightening creams; they use straightening devices for their hair, and so on. They sort of believe, I think, that their natural state, which is a black state, is not synonymous with beauty, and beauty can only be approximated by them if the skin is made as light as possible and the lips are made as red as possible, and the nails are made as pink as possible. So in a sense the term "black is beautiful" challenges exactly that belief which makes someone negate himself.

THE JUDGE: Mr. Biko, why do you people then pick on the word "black"? I mean "black" is really an innocent reference which has been arrived at over the years, the same as "white." Snow is regarded as white, and snow is regarded as the purest form of water and so it symbolizes purity. So "white" there has got nothing to do with the white man?

BIKO: Right.

THE JUDGE: But now, why do you refer to you people as blacks? Why not brown people? I mean you people are more brown than black.

BIKO: In the same way as I think white people are more pink than white. (Laughter.)

THE JUDGE: Quite. But why do you not use the word "brown" then?

BIKO: Because, historically, we have been defined as "black" people, and when we reject the term "nonwhite" and take upon ourselves the right to call ourselves what we think we are, we have got available, in front of us, a whole number of alternatives, starting from Natives to Africans to Kaffirs to Bantu to Nonwhites, and so on, and we choose this one precisely because we feel it is the most accommodating.

THE JUDGE: Yes, but then you put your foot into it. You use "black," which really connotates dark forces over the centuries.

BIKO: This is correct. Precisely because it has been used in that context, our aim is to choose it for reference to us and to elevate it to a position where we can look upon ourselves positively; because even if we choose to be called "brown," there will still be reference to "blacks" in an inferior sense in literature and in speeches by white racists in our society.

THE JUDGE: But would you still refer to black magic if you refer to witchcraft?

BIKO: Oh yes, we do refer to black magic.

THE JUDGE: Now, do you use it in a good sense or a bad sense?

BIKO: We do not reject it. We regard it as part of the mystery of our cultural heritage. We feel it has not been sufficiently looked into scientifically.

THE JUDGE: But I am not asking you about witchcraft. I am referring to the term. Would you refer to it as black magic?

BIKO: Yes. We do refer to it as black magic.

THE JUDGE: But now, why do you use "black" there? In what sense do you use "black"?

BIKO: Well, when we talk of black magic in this country – unlike in London, for instance, where people talk of black magic meaning a kind of witchcraft, there being no connotation that it comes from black society – when you talk of witchcraft or superstition in this country, automatically it is associated with "black" in the minds of most people. Whites are not superstitious; whites do not have witches and witchdoctors. We are the people who have this.

SOGGOTT: I am not sure he is right there.

(Laughter.)

THE JUDGE: Yes, we have a lot of witchcraft.

BIKO: Well, it is certainly not our type of witchcraft, I must say.

THE JUDGE: Well, how many whites go to witchdoctors?

BIKO: You mean to our witchdoctors? Oh well, this is fine. They go, but the witchdoctors are ours and the witchcraft is ours.

THE JUDGE: But you take it amiss. I mean the fact that the white man blames the witchcraft on the black man. Or don't you take it amiss?

BIKO: Well, in certain instances, yes. I think there tends to be a certain derogatory connotation in reference to blacks as superstitious beings.

THE JUDGE: But does that not cause you people a lot of grief – witchcraft? I mean, when I go on circuit and I do murder cases near Sekukuneland, or even near Tzaneen, we always have witchcraft cases and they do the most terrible things. When a child dies they think that somebody must have bewitched the child and they just kill a few people. Well, you cannot justify that?

BIKO: No, we do not. We do not accept superstition. We do not accept witchcraft. But all we are saying is that there are certain things within this whole sphere of black magic which can be usefully investigated. I mean, I would reject it as much as you do, because I do not believe in it myself, but I do not have disdain for the people who believe in it like most of society seems to have. I understand it from the cultural roots. This is through my education; my exposure to so much more literature and other, I would say, cultures in the world. I have decided that there is no place for this in my belief, but the person who believes in it, I can still talk to him with understanding. I do not reject him as a barbarian.

THE JUDGE: But I suppose witchcraft is deprecated by reason of the fact that people do irresponsible things and harm people?

BIKO: This is correct – yes.

SOGGOTT: Is your concern so much the restructure of the word "black" in the world of linguistics so as to alter the response of black people to their own blackness?

BIKO: It is certainly directed at man – at the black man.

SOGGOTT: And I think you were talking about your understanding of the black man's own sense of inferiority and self-hatred and all that?

BIKO: Yes.

SOGGOTT: In the world of language, how does the black man figure? How does he feel?

BIKO: Yes, I think this is another area where experiences of, well let me say, difficulties, are experienced. We have a society here in South Africa which recognizes in the main, two languages, English and Afrikaans, as *official languages*. These are languages that you have to use at school, at university, or in pursuit of any discipline when you are studying as a black man. Unfortunately the books you read are in English. English is a second language to you. You have probably been taught in a vernacular, especially during these days of Bantu Education up to Standard Six. You grapple with the language to matriculation, and before you conquer it, you must apply it now to learn disciplines at university. As a result, you never quite catch everything that is in a book. I mean I am talking about the average man now. I am not talking about exceptional cases. You understand the paragraph but you are not quite adept at reproducing an argument that was in a particular book, precisely because of your failure to understand certain words in the book. This makes you *less articulate* as a black man generally, and this makes you more inward-looking. You feel things rather than say them, and this applies to Afrikaans as well. Much more to English than to Afrikaans.

Afrikaans is essentially a language that has developed here, and I think, in many instances, it is idiom. It relates much better to African languages, but English is completely foreign, and therefore people find it difficult to move beyond a certain point in their comprehension of the language.

SOGGOTT: And how does this relate to the black man or in particular to the black students as inferiority?

BIKO: An example of this, for instance, was again during the old days of NUSAS where white students would be discussing something that you, as a black man, had experienced in your day-to-day life, but your *powers of articulation* were not as good as theirs. Also you have among the white students a number of students doing M.A., doing Honors, highly articulate, very intelligent. You may be intelligent but not as articulate. You are forced into a subservient role of having to say "yes" to what they are saying, even when talking about what you have experienced, and which they have not experienced, because you cannot express it so well. This in a sense inculcates also in many black students a sense of inadequacy. You tend to think that it is not just a matter of language. You tend to tie it up also with intelligence, in a sense. You tend to feel that that guy is better equipped than you mentally.

THE JUDGE: But why do you say that? Isn't English the official language of SASO?

BIKO: Yes it is.

THE JUDGE: Well now, but your complaint is against the language, but it is just the very language that you are using?

BIKO: No, no, I am not complaining against the language. I am merely explaining how language can help in the development of an inferiority complex. I am not complaining against the language itself. The point at issue is that we have something like ten languages. We cannot speak all ten languages at one meeting. We have got to choose a common language. But unfortunately in the learning process this is really what happens – you do not grasp enough and therefore you cannot be articulate enough, and when you are side by side with people who are more articulate than you, you tend to think that it is because they are more intelligent than you; that they can say these things better than you.

THE JUDGE: But your language is very idiomatic. Is it not easier for you people to speak Afrikaans than English because Afrikaans is like your language, very idiomatic?

BIKO: This is true, actually, but unfortunately Afrikaans has got certain connotations historically that provoke a rejection from the black man, and these are political connotations.

SOGGOTT: But your point, as I understand it, is that the black man feels a bit of a foreigner in the linguistic field?

BIKO: Right.

SOGGOTT: Mr. Biko, still talking about the question of inferiority. This article "I Write What I Like" by Frank Talk, Annexure Eight to the Indictment – "Fear – an important determinant in South African politics." Who wrote that?

BIKO: I wrote that.

THE JUDGE: You say you wrote it?

BIKO: I wrote it.

THE JUDGE: Is it Annexure Eight? Is this by Frank Talk?

BIKO: That is right.

THE JUDGE: Isn't accused number 9 Frank Talk?

BIKO: No, no. He was never Frank Talk. I was Frank Talk.

(Laughter.)

SOGGOTT: M'lord, the indictment alleged that he compiled it, but in fact it was never ever suggested that number 9 wrote it.

BIKO: No, I wrote that.

SOGGOTT: In it you say: "Township life alone makes it a miracle for anyone to live up to adulthood." What do you mean by that?

BIKO: This refers to the degree of violence in the townships, which tends to introduce a measure of uncertainty about what tomorrow will bring. If I am in a different type of life and I spend a night at your place, somehow I feel unexposed to what I would call the bad elements of society. But when you are in a township, it is dangerous to cross often from one street to the next, and yet, as you grow up, it is essential that kids must be sent on errands in and around the township. They meet up with these problems; rape and murder are common aspects of our life in the townships.

SOGGOTT: And at night time what is the position?

BIKO: It is especially bad at night time. I mean in the few days I have spent up here in Mabopane I have seen two cases of grievous assault with no relationship between the persons assaulted and the person assaulting. You see an old man being assaulted by a number of young men for apparently no reason whatsoever except that it is the end of the month and possibly he might have some money on him. This does not surprise me. It is a common experience. But I have never learned to accept it all the same, because it is a bitter reminder of the kind of violence there is in our society. Now when I use that term there, that it is a miracle to live to an adult age, the precise meaning of it is exactly that – that one escapes all these possible areas of pitfalls where one might die without any explanation. It is not because you are well kept. It is not because you are well protected. It is just a miracle. It happens.

THE JUDGE: It would be interesting to know what your attitude here is. Isn't that a justification for influx control? Isn't the difficulty that you have a lot of people seeping into such an area and you find your bad elements among those people because it is an uncontrolled element that comes in? To give you an illustration, years ago I was counsel for the black people here when they wanted to move Newclare black township, and at that time I think that 37,000 people were there who were not entitled to be there, that just came into the township, and they were there illegally. Now isn't that type of thing the cause of this type of crime that you get in a township?

BIKO: Yes, M'lord, if one looks at it superficially, but there is a much more fundamental reason. It is absence of abundant life for the people who live there. With abundant life you get discipline, people get the things that they want. And because, of course, you do not get a society here which offers this to the people, the State introduces measures like influx control.

THE JUDGE: Another point. You can continue but I just want to make this observation now. Influx control ensures that the people who are there in the township have employment?

BIKO: Right.

THE JUDGE: But now these people who are there illegally, they are people without employment, and they probably have to steal to live. I mean otherwise they do not know how to exist?

BIKO: I do not want to canvass the point of influx control too much.

THE JUDGE: No, no, I am just asking you as a matter of interest because influx control is given as one of the reasons why the black man is oppressed.

BIKO: Yes, because the real point about influx control is that if it is necessary it must be applied equally to everybody. It is conceivable that urban influx control may be necessary in society, but where it is applied it should be applied without reference to color. It should be applied to everybody. It must not be that a white guy is free to move to Cape Town tomorrow, to Durban tomorrow, and some other place without being indexed, while I have got to go through a whole rigmarole of red tape in order to move from one area to another just because I am black.

THE JUDGE: But with the white people you do not have that situation in the sense that usually white people have full employment; is that not so? You cannot say that, unfortunately, for the black man, so the position is that when black people come into an area where there are already conditions of overcrowding, then you find that crime comes with it?

BIKO: Equally, M'lord, there are large numbers of black people who do have full employment where they are going. When I had to be employed in Durban, I had to go through the whole system of influx control. Now in the first instance I had a job; I had no competitor; I was wanted; I was going to be assisted in getting a house, but somehow or other it was made difficult for me to move, and in the second instance – and this is part of the complaint about influx control – it is a very degrading system.

THE JUDGE: Well, usually it is the manner of application that causes difficulty.

BIKO: Quite right. You are made, in some instances, to stand naked in front of of some doctors supposed to be running pus off you, because you may be bringing syphilis to the town. It is inhuman, the way it is done. Three people are lined up in front of him, all naked, and he has just got to look at all of you. Now I must feel that I am being treated as an animal, and as you enter the room where this is done in Durban there is a big notice saying: "Beware – Natives in a state of undress." They are trying to put you in your place. I mean, if it is applied equally, then fine.

SOGGOTT: Whatever the causes, what you are saying is that there is an insecurity in one's physical life in the townships. Does this have an effect on the black man in relation to his sense of confidence or inferiority or whatever it is?

BIKO: Yes. It contributes to a feeling of insecurity which is part of a feeling of incompleteness. You are not a complete human being. You cannot walk out when you like, you know, that sort of feeling. It is an imprisoning concept in itself.

SOGGOTT: Now, Mr. Biko, were you ever involved in actually monitoring ordinary people's conversations?

BIKO: You mean for purposes of research? Yes.

SOGGOTT: Would you tell His Lordship briefly what that was?

BIKO: M'lord, this was a research carried out in 1972. The purpose was literacy. Now this particular method we were using placed a lot of emphasis on syllabic teaching of people. You did not just teach people the alphabet in isolation, you had to teach them syllables, and you had to start with words that had a particular meaning to them, what we called generative terms. Now the preamble to it was some kind of research in a specific area in which you were going to work, which carried you to several segments of the community, to particular places where the community congregated and talked freely. Your role there was particularly passive. You were there just to listen to the things that they were talking about, and also to the words that were being used. We also used pictures to depict the themes that they were talking about. Now I was involved in this with Jerry Modisane and Barney Pityana.

SOGGOTT: Who were you doing this research for?

BIKO: We were doing it for ourselves. I had been asked to participate in a literacy program that was drawn up by SASO.

SOGGOTT: In what circumstances?

BIKO: Well, we chose available circumstances. In this particular instance we listened to women in queues waiting to see a doctor or nurse at a clinic. Some of them had babies in their arms or on their backs. We listened to people in shebeens. I went around buying beer in a lot of shebeens, and we listened to people in buses as well, and trains.

SOGGOTT: What was it that people were saying, if anything at all, about their condition of life? And the white man, did the white man or the white government come up at all?

BIKO: The most noticeable thing in such situations was the constant recurrence of what I would call "protest talk" about the oppression that the black man is exposed to. Sometimes it was general, sometimes it was specific, but always it contained what I would call a round condemnation of white society. Often in very, very tough language, some of which is not suitable for repetition in this court. I remember, for instance, a bus in which I was traveling and in most instances the topic was dictated by the position of the bus, on the way to town. As you are coming out of Umlazi, you pass a hostel for adult male blacks. Now there are certain restrictions in hostels, like they may not bring in women and so on, but each time we passed there in the morning, of course there was a stream of women coming out of the hostel and people started talking about this, saying that those bachelors had lots of women, and from there onwards the theme built up almost automatically as to why they were disallowed. "Where does the white man think these guys are going to get their sex from?" That sort of thing, and from there it blows up. And then again, the bus goes through the industrial area called Jacobs; you pass through the southern part of Jacobs, and there you have a constant stream of people getting in and out of factories, and the talk centers around problems of labor and so on. I cannot remember specifically what was said, but they started from there again and always, central to this theme, was the condemnation of white society. You know when people speak in the townships, they do not talk about the government; they do not talk about the provincial council, or city councils; they talk about whites, and of course the connotation there is with reference to obvious structures – but to them, it is just whites. And, as I say, the language is often hard, you know; sometimes to the point of swear-words which would not be repeatable in this court.

SOGGOTT: And you, yourself, have lived in Ginsberg Location in King William's Town. Is that right?

BIKO: Yes, I have.

SOGGOTT: And is that a rather poor rural location?

BIKO: Yes, it is a small township of about a thousand houses, very poor.

SOGGOTT: So you are familiar with life there?

BIKO: That is correct.

SOGGOTT: Now the echoing of this sort of sentiment, did that take place while you lived there?

BIKO: Oh yes. It was very common.

SOGGOTT: And is there reference to oppression at all in any shape or form by these people in their ordinary thinking?

BIKO: Yes, often.

SOGGOTT: Now, Mr. Biko, when you set out to conscientize people, is that then to bring to them the ideas of Black Consciousness?

BIKO: That is correct.

SOGGOTT: Can you tell us, when you do this, do you relate what you say to their condition and the various aspects which you have told His Lordship about, the question of starvation and labor and so on?

BIKO: This is correct. We do make reference to the conditions of the black man and the conditions in which the black man lives. We try to get blacks to grapple realistically with their problems, to attempt to find solutions to their problems, to develop what one might call an awareness of their situation, to be able to analyze it and to provide answers for themselves. The purpose is really to provide some kind of hope. I think the central theme about black society is that it has got elements of a defeated society. People often seem to have given up the struggle, like the man who was telling me that he now lives to work. He has given himself to the idea. Now this sense of defeat is basically what we are fighting against. People must not just give in to the hardship of life. People must develop a hope.

People must develop some form of security to be together to look at their problems, and people must, in this way, build up their humanity. This is the point about Black Consciousness.

SOGGOTT: The question I want to put to you is this. Haven't these people got used to their existential conditions, their grievances, insecurity, the absence of food and so on?

BIKO: That is understating the position. I think it is possible to adapt to a given hard situation precisely because you have got to live with it, and you have got to live with it every day. But adapting does not mean that you forget. You go to the mill every day. It is always unacceptable to you. It has always been unacceptable to you, and it remains so for life. But you adapt in the sense that you cannot continue to live in a state of conflict with yourself. You sort of accept, like the man who was working with the electrician was saying to me, you know: "Oh, he talks in this way." This is his explanation of it. This is his sort of glib adaptation to it, but deep inside him, he feels it. He cannot keep on answering back every day: "Don't call me 'boy.' Don't shout at me. Don't swear at me," because there is the job he has to keep. He has adapted but he does not forget it, and he does not accept it, which I think is important.

SOGGOTT: When in a document of BPC or SASO you refer to the whites or the white government as "oppressors," does this not alter black people's feelings or their attitudes in relation to the white government or the whites?

BIKO: No, it only serves to establish a common basis for discussion because what is contained in that expression is usually what the black man himself normally says about the whole problem in even stronger terms. But when we talk about the problems that the black man faces, what you are merely doing is to establish a point of departure for what you are talking about, and the goal for BPC or SASO usually is that of a build-up of membership especially for BPC.

SOGGOTT: Now would you tell His Lordship the SASO desire in relation to foreign investment?

BIKO: The desire is a rejection of foreign investment which is nothing but an exploitation of the blacks in this country by companies which belong to governments critical of apartheid in this country. In other words, on the one hand Harold Wilson stands up to criticize the system here, and several of his firms come to invest in this country among other reasons precisely because there exists in the country cheap labor from the blacks.

SOGGOTT: And what would SASO's desire have been as far as that investment goes?

BIKO: Our desire was that an ideal form of operation in this country by foreign investors would have been one negating the concepts within white society about the black man, which reduced them to the position of completely nonskilled worker seen as an extension of the machine.

SOGGOTT: Yes, and if they did not do that?

BIKO: Well, we just felt that they were selling out on us, and they might as well get out.

SOGGOTT: Then they might as well get out?

BIKO: That is right.

SOGGOTT: Were there any other themes or thoughts behind the rejection of foreign investment, the one being that they participated in exploitation in hypocritical circumstances, that you have described?

BIKO: Right.

SOGGOTT: Any other features?

BIKO: Yes, there was another one, in a sense the relationship between a foreign government and its companies which invest in this country. We believe South Africa is particularly sensitive to criticism by the world of its policies. We believe that part of our political campaign is to make sure that as many people as possible criticize South Africa for its policies. Putting pressure on foreign companies about their participation in this immoral setup was also calculated to make sure that the foreign governments began to feel unhappy about participation of their firms in this country, and to assist generally in building up pressure to make South Africa shift its attitudes gradually to a more acceptable stance. It was a political stance which was calculated to bring pressure to bear on South Africa to shift policies to make them more acceptable to the world and to us as blacks.

SOGGOTT: You have already mentioned to His Lordship some of the reasons why you people reject foreign investment. Are there any other themes which are connected with it?

BIKO: The wealth of the country must be enjoyed by the people of the country. Foreign investors come and exploit the wealth of the country with more advanced technological means than those we have in South Africa to siphon off profits which rightfully belong here, and these go to profit societies other than out own societies.

THE JUDGE: Were there any pushers of the anti-foreign investment line whose aim was to achieve a weakening of the South African economy?

BIKO: No, this was not considered by SASO as an end of what you are talking about there.

THE JUDGE: Or the creation of widescale unemployment?

BIKO: Certainly not.

SOGGOTT: What do you people believe could be accomplished as far as the actual withdrawal of foreign investments were concerned?

BIKO: We never, for a moment, thought that foreign firms would, as a result of this kind of stance, withdraw.

SOGGOTT: What was your belief as to their ability to withdraw, even if they wanted to?

BIKO: Well, our understanding at the time, and I think it still appertains at this moment, is that certainly after Sharpeville, the whole question of investment or participation in the economy of the country by foreign firms was tightened to make it impossible for anybody intimately involved with the South African economy to withdraw at will.

SOGGOTT: Yes?

BIKO: And, of course, if you are investing in machinery in factories and so on, you won't take this to England with you. You will leave them here, so if any particular investor feels uncomfortable, all he can do is to sell it to the next investor, or to a South African concern. And in this sense, you know, it was impossible to foresee even if one wanted to anyway, disruption of the economic system. Jerry Modisane suggested that this was a colorless stance. It served nothing. It did not commit us to anything. His view was that we should adopt a program of discouraging foreign investment capital. The argument against it was that we were not interested in mounting a program of de-investment, in mounting a campaign of de-investment, because, in the first instance, we didn't believe that those who invested here did so without being aware of the situation.

SOGGOTT: So it was defeated.

BIKO: It was defeated, yes.

SOGGOTT: Can you explain to us why foreign investment concerns you people?

BIKO: We believe that if we are to move toward a peaceful solution, our efforts must be coupled with support from other people, from other governments, and we see this whole foreign investment question as a vehicle for generating pressure to sympathize with our point of view so that South Africa can listen, not only to us but also to other people talking about the same thing. I refer now to the argument often put up by some foreign investors to the effect that foreign investment offers job opportunities and therefore helps the black man. This is like the attitude taken by Polaroid to say they are going to be involved in the future problems of the black man by donating part of their profits to welfare programs. We felt this was paternalistic. We felt that the point of application of foreign investors must be the humanity of the men they employ rather than pandering to considerations of materialism, like giving him a token increment here, or giving him token assistance at social welfare level.

There is no way in which established industry which has been set up with foreign capital in this country is going to be killed, just because one proprietor pulls out, because there is always going to be another one who takes over. So from the point of view of jobs and job situations, those blacks who are employed in firms directed by foreign investment are going to continue in employment. What we attack is precisely the fact that when these people have got a point of leverage, because they are not South Africans, because they are subject back at home, probably, to more liberal attitudes, they don't make use of this. This is what we attack. They don't alleviate the lot of black people, and certainly even if they withdraw themselves, we are not going to suffer, because there is no difference whether it is a South African proprietor or a foreign proprietor.

SOGGOTT: What about the resolution which "condemns the black puppets who go overseas under the cloak of leadership and persuade foreign investors to stay in South Africa with the belief that it is for the betterment of the black man"?

BIKO: This is an attack essentially on Bantustan leaders. I think of Gatsha Buthelezi especially. He did this. Sebe of the Ciskei also did this. They go out into the world to invite foreign investment without any understanding of what we, the representatives of the black people, think. We believe they are puppets, puppets to those who work against our interests for the interests of white society, and when I say white society, I mean society's government power structures. So we are attacking them for speaking as if they are speaking for black people, when they merely say what they are expected to say by those they serve.

SOGGOTT: Mr. Biko, would you refer to Resolution 42: "SASO believes that South Africa is a country in which both black and white live and shall continue to live together." Now what does that mean?

BIKO: Well, this means that we accept the fact that South African society is a plural society with contributions having been made to its development by all segments of the community.

SOGGOTT: As you understand the position, on the accession to an open society, how will people be able to vote? What rights will the white man have to vote?

BIKO: We emphasize to our membership that it is not our intention to generate a feeling of anti-whitism. We are merely forced by historic considerations to recognize the fact that we cannot plan side by side with people who participate in their exclusive pool of privileges.

THE JUDGE: Now you say you people stand for one man, one vote?

BIKO: Yes.

THE JUDGE: Now is it a practical concept in the African setup? Do you find it anywhere in Africa?

BIKO: Yes, we find it, even within this country, for whites.

THE JUDGE: Now apart from this country, I mean, now let us take any other country in Africa. Do you have one man, one vote in any other country?

BIKO: Yes.

THE JUDGE: Which country?

BIKO: In Botswana, not to go too far.

THE JUDGE: Yes, Botswana is under the influence of the South African background and traditions. Now take it away from the South African traditions?

BIKO: Where to, My Lord, for instance?

THE JUDGE: Well, now anywhere outside South Africa?

BIKO: You have it in Ghana.

THE JUDGE: Didn't that disappear in Nkhrumah's day already?

BIKO: It didn't disappear. What has happened is that in Ghana now there is a military regime, but the concept of elections, be it for city council, for provincial council, or any of the governmental structures that they have, is on a basis of one man, one vote.

THE JUDGE: Well, that may be the subordinate bodies, but now when it comes to the important vote, affecting the country, is there any country in Africa where you have one man, one vote?

BIKO: Well, Kenya, for instance.

THE JUDGE: Just recently I read that there are forty-six countries in Africa and of the forty-six, I think only five countries have a democratic form of government and they are just around South Africa?

BIKO: I saw the same thing. I think what they said was that there were twenty-nine with nonmilitary government, but of that twenty-nine, a lot of them were one-party states. Now a one-party state is not necessarily undemocratic, if it is selected by the people.

THE JUDGE: Yes, but now just to test that, Russia also operates on that basis.

BIKO: Yes.

THE JUDGE: And of the two hundred, I think, and forty-five million, only fourteen are communists, and they are the people who really govern and decide who the people should vote for?

BIKO: I have not gone into the Russian society. I won't be able to dispute that.

THE JUDGE: Yes, but you see, there again it is a one-party state and they also argue like you. Everybody has the vote, but now what is it worth?

BIKO: Yes, My Lord, but let us take the Kenya situation for instance, where there has been a recent development of the opposition.

THE JUDGE: But I thought that disappeared when Odinga Oginga [sic] was assassinated?

BIKO: No, Oginga Odinga has not been assassinated. He is still alive.

THE JUDGE: Tom Mboya?

BIKO: Tom Mboya was with the governing party and that party is still governing.

THE JUDGE: Yes, but then they found out that he had a certain adherence among the people and . . .

BIKO: I think, My Lord, you are confusing Tom Mboya with Kariuke. It was Kariuke who was murdered, and it was Kariuke who had generated among the people a certain thought, but Kariuke was also operating from inside the governing party. You see in Kenya there is a very good demonstration of what a one-party state can achieve by way of differing thought within the party. Kariuke was the advocate on the one hand of the common man, the worker, the servant in Kenya, against this whole development in Kenya of a bourgeoisie within the ruling party. You had Kenyatta on the other hand who felt constantly attacked by Kariuke. Okay, Kariuke was allowed to air his views in Parliament; he was allowed to hold meetings throughout the length and breadth of the country, but still operating from within KANU, which is the ruling party. This is the essence of a one-party state, that there is no need to divide your men and let them lead other parties to . . .

THE JUDGE: Yes, but Kariuke didn't survive all this?

BIKO: Oh well, My Lord, several politicians don't survive. Verwoerd didn't. (Laughter.)

THE JUDGE: Yes, but now you have mentioned Kenya, are you prepared to say that there is one man, one vote in other African countries?

BIKO: Yes, I am.

THE JUDGE: Democracy, doesn't it presuppose a developed community? Democracy where you have one man, one vote?

BIKO: Yes, it does, it does, and I think it is part of the process of developing the community.

THE JUDGE: Yes, but democracy is really only a success if the people who have the right to vote can intelligently and honestly apply a vote?

BIKO: Yes, My Lord, this is why in Swaziland, for instance, where they have some people who cannot read the names of the candidates, they use signs.

THE JUDGE: Yes, but do they know enough of the affairs of government to be able to influence it by a vote? I mean surely you must know what you are voting for; what you are voting about? Assuming now they vote on a particular policy, such as foreign investment, now what does a peasant know about foreign investment?

BIKO: I think, My Lord, where democracy is allowed to work, one of the principles normally entrenched is a feedback system, a discussion between those who formulate policy and those who must perceive or reject policy. In other words there must be a system of education, political education, and this does not necessarily go with literacy. I mean Africa has always governed its peoples through various chiefs, Chaka and so on, who couldn't write.

THE JUDGE: Yes, but government is much more sophisticated and specialized now than in those days.

BIKO: And there are ways of explaining it to the people. People can hear. They may not be able to read and write, but they can hear and they can understand the issues when they are put to them.

THE JUDGE: Well, take the gold standard. If we have to debate whether this government should go on the gold standard or go off the gold standard, would you feel that you know enough about it to be able to cast an intelligent vote about that?

BIKO: Me, personally?

THE JUDGE: Yes.

BIKO: I think probably much better than the average Afrikaner in the street, My Lord.

THE JUDGE: Yes, well, that may be so. Now do you think you know enough about it to be able to cast such an intelligent vote that the government should be based on that vote?

BIKO: Yes, I think I have a right to be consulted by my government on any issue. If I don't understand it, I may give over to someone else that I have faith in to explain it to me.

THE JUDGE: Well, how can you? I mean that it is your vote, and what about the ten other people who have votes?

BIKO: The same applies to everybody else, and this is why there are political processes whereby things are explained. I mean, the average man in Britain does not understand spontaneously the advantages or disadvantages of Britain becoming involved in the European Economic Community, but when it becomes an issue for public decision, political organizers go out to explain and canvass their points of view, and the man in the street listens to several people and decides to use what he has, the vote.

THE JUDGE: But isn't that one of the reasons why Britain is probably one of the most bankrupt countries in the world?

BIKO: I think I prefer to look at it more positively and say it is one of the most democratic countries in the world.

THE JUDGE: Yes, but now it is bankrupt?

BIKO: I think it is a phase, My Lord. Britain has been rich before. It may still get up on the ladder again. I think it is a phase in history.

THE JUDGE: Yes, but something went wrong somewhere along the line, and it is because of its democracy probably.

BIKO: I don't think so. I think it has been partly the whole decolonization process which has robbed Britain of a fixed life, of what they used to get before. Now they are forced back on their own resources and they don't have much. It is geographically a small country with 56 million people, no land to cultivate.

THE JUDGE: But she must have had good government at one stage.

BIKO: I think she could have had good resources at one stage and she could have tightened the belt so that the distribution of wealth did not touch the lower man at some stage, like during the time of Adam Smith; even the time of the laissez-faire policy when you know the few people who controlled industry in Britain went rampart throughout the country, manufacturing, making themselves rich, and of course the government got rich, but the people didn't get rich. The people got poorer.

THE JUDGE: They had a vote.

BIKO: They obtained the vote, and they have been gradually returning a more socialist government which is against the exploitation of people. People are restoring the whole process; the wealth must come back to the people.

SOGGOTT: Mr. Biko, if I may just perhaps explore some of the questions further which His Lordship has put to you. As far as this country is concerned, do you visualize any particular impediment to the adoption and functioning of the one man, one vote system?

BIKO: I would say basically that the South African black man is in many ways different from the stage at which several African countries took up independence. I think he is a highly Westernized man in the first instance, and his accommodation of the whole Western system becomes that much greater. I can say only the degree of literacy, functional literacy and beyond that, education, is that much higher, and thirdly I think he is faced with a different problem, unlike any other country in Africa, which has been inhabited by colonialists. We have a situation here where whites are part of this country, and are not simply colonial settlers. So I think, My Lord, the whole process of political development in this country is going to accommodate the various factors that make up our society. Our stance is we want a one man, one vote system. Whites are suspicious about that. Now in the process of bargaining, surely some middle situation must be achieved. You can't bargain without a stance, you know, but our stance is not exclusive of the white man. We must reach somewhere in the middle.

SOGGOTT: Now, would you indicate to His Lordship the concept of black economic values? Can you tell us what economic society you people want to bring about?

BIKO: All right. From the economic point of view the starting point is that we, as Africans, have had a form of economy, even in our rudimentary culture (I use the term "rudimentary" now because the whole scope of knowledge has so widened you know, in latter years), we had an economy which was mainly an agrarian economy centering around crops and centering around cattle, sheep and so on; small stock and big stock. Now the whole operation of that society had certain basic tenets, the first one being that we did not believe in apportioning land for private ownership by individuals. The land belonged to the tribe and land was held for the tribe in trust by the chief. The chief could say that over there we are going to have our grazing area, and you are going to sit over here, and have your farmstead here, and you are going to live here. Now when he does that, he is not giving you what is commonly held very dear by Western society, a title deed over something that you have bought or have been given. He is merely giving you a right to stay there. If the tribe, for one reason or other, may require to use that portion, he gives you another place, and there is no question about it. But, of course, he does not do this completely arbitrarily. You know, he consults with the people and everybody is free to consult in the various meetings that are called by the chief, but the central point of what I am saying is that the economic system has certain basic tenets.

Now we are advocating black communalism, which is, in many ways, similar to African socialism. We are expropriating an essentially tribal background to accommodate what is an expounded economic concept now. We have got to accommodate industry. We have got to accommodate the whole relationship between industry and politics. But there is a certain plasticity in this interpretation precisely because no one has yet made an ultimate definition of it. You get Kenya, for instance, saying they believe in African socialism, but Kenya is almost a carbon copy of the old British society, highly capitalistic in approach.

SOGGOTT: In what direction does your economic policy lead?

BIKO: What we have accepted is the introduction of the concept of sharing in the present society, right? Now I have given a rudimentary explanation for what we believe. We know that we are dealing with a society which is basically capitalism-oriented, although it does embrace a lot of socialistic attitudes. I mean in South Africa, for instance, there is nationalization of several things like the radio and the railways. Now again, we are talking of bargaining. We are talking of dialog from two different standpoints between two sides both interested in the future of the country. We would be developing our standpoint from this side, which is the platform from which we are going to talk to a people who hold dear a free enterprise system, and out of these two clearly the synthesis would come.

THE JUDGE: Is there any part of your program which suggests that all private property must be expropriated?

BIKO: No.

SOGGOTT: Now, Mr. Biko, can we now get on to the question of the achievement of your freedom?

BIKO: First of all, in our analysis, the cardinal point is the existence in our society of white racism which has been institutionalized, and also cushioned with the backing of the majority of whites. In other words, a white child does not have to choose whether or not he wants to live with the system. He is born into it. He is brought up within white schools and institutions, and the whole process of racism is somehow with him at all levels, privileges that they hold, and they monopolize these away from black society.

Now then comes the analysis. Can we, in fact, crack this cocoon to get whites away from the concept of racism, away from the concept of monopolizing the privileges and the wealth of the country to themselves? Can we preach to them as individuals? Our belief is that white society will not listen to preaching. They will not listen to their liberals. Liberalism has not grown within white society, and we blacks cannot stand idly by watching the situation. We can only generate a response from white society when we, as blacks, speak with a black voice and say what we want. The age of the liberal was such that the black voice was not very much heard except in echoing what was said by liberals. Now has come the time when we, as blacks, must articulate what we want, and put it across to the white man, and from a position of strength.

We certainly don't envisage failure. We certainly don't have an alternative. We have analyzed history. We believe that history moves in a particular logical direction, and in this instance, the logical direction is that eventually any white society in this country is going to have to accommodate black thinking. We are mere agents in that history. There are alternatives. On the one hand we have groups that are known in this country, who have opted for another way of operation, who have opted for violence. We know that the ANC and PAC have done this, but we don't believe it is the only alternative. We believe there is a way of getting to where we want to go through peaceful means. And the very fact that we decided to form an aboveboard movement implies that we accepted certain legal limitations to our operations. We accepted that we were going to take this particular course. We know that the road to that particular truth is fraught with danger. Some of us get banned, like I am. Others get arrested, like these men here. But inevitably the process drives towards what we believe history also drives to, an attainment of a situation where whites have to listen.

I don't believe that whites will be deaf all the time. This government is not necessarily set on a Hitlerized course. I think it is buying time. From their interpretation of the situation at the moment. Mr. Vorster can postpone some problems, but I believe that as the voice which says "no" grows, he is going to listen. He is going to have to accommodate the feelings of black people.

After his exposition in evidence as led by Mr. Soggott and questioned by Judge Boshoff, Steve Biko was now placed under cross-examination by the state prosecutor, Mr. K. Attwell, who tried to gain damaging evidence against the SASO/BPC accused by wringing from Biko some adverse admissions about the nature of these organizations and in particular about the extravagant wording of some of their literature.

ATTWELL: Mr. Biko, would it be correct to say that you are one of the founding lights of both SASO and BPC and one of the foremost protagonists of the Black Consciousness idea?

BIKO: Correct.

ATTWELL: And that in no small measure you were responsible for the constitutional framework of these organizations and many of their basic policies as we have come to know them through their documents?

BIKO: To a great extent, yes.

ATTWELL: Now, certain tendencies had exhibited themselves to you and certain of the other founding members at a stage which pressed you into the idea of forming a body like SASO, is that correct?

BIKO: Correct.

ATTWELL: And this was at that time something of a unique organization to found, was it not?

BIKO: Correct.

ATTWELL: In fact it had no parallel in our history before? In fact I think one can say in history there has been no parallel to the SASO organization?

BIKO: Outside the country I do not know, but inside the country certainly not.

ATTWELL: And that it was a venture which must have been fraught with numerous dangers and one which you approached, I should imagine, with great caution?

BIKO: Correct.

ATTWELL: In the past, organizations which had worked primarily for the black people had had a somewhat difficult path and history in this country?

BIKO: This is correct.

ATTWELL: And there are references in the documents to the past organizations described in terms such as "which stood high in the defense of black dignity and righteousness and which were banned during the sixties." I gather that is a reference to the banned African National Congress and the Pan-Africanist Congress?

BIKO: You must understand one thing about the black community, that the ANC and PAC are important movements in the history of the black community in the sense that they affected people's lives and they created allegiances. When you are a new movement and you want to be in favor with everybody, any untoward reference to past organizations to which people may have some rudimentary allegiance may harm you, so that BPC and SASO never adopted any critical attitude toward any past movements. We spoke positively about ourselves and as little as possible about anybody else except existing groups, you know, like white society and its power structures.

ATTWELL: Would you agree with me that SASO and BPC concentrate to a large extent on psychological oppression in their approach?

BIKO: Yes, but I think as I said in my evidence-in-chief the whole community development program is in fact directed also at alleviating suffering, which is a form of physical oppression, and by physical liberation we also imply liberation from those actual living conditions which are oppressive.

ATTWELL: In your own view at the moment, do you consider that the blacks are in a position to overthrow the State by violence?

BIKO: I do not think so.

ATTWELL: One of the military expert witnesses expressed the view that South Africa was militarily too strong, and would repulse any such attack by the inhabitants. Do you go along with that?

BIKO: Well, I have not studied the strength of the white army lately.

ATTWELL: But you do not think it feasible?

BIKO: I do not think it feasible.

ATTWELL: The military expert also suggested that the most productive sphere in which the blacks in this country could work toward change was the black worker sphere, do you agree with that statement?

BIKO: If you are talking about fundamental change perhaps it is a possibility, but I think there are other spheres which lend themselves to easier use. Take the field of sport for instance, which I think is in the vital interests of society also in that it foreshadows attitudes in other areas. I think the country now is at a stage where considerable pressure can be applied fruitfully in the sphere of sport.

ATTWELL: But in what sphere in your opinion can the blacks exert the most pressure and be most effective?

BIKO: I am telling you now, sport.

ATTWELL: How do blacks exercise great pressure in sport?

BIKO: The importance of groups like the South African Rugby Union, the South African Cricket Board of Control, and various sporting groups within the black spheres that control sport have grown tremendously influential over the years to a point where they command an extensive audience in the external world, and I notice that even people who are regular politicians, like Gatsha Buthelezi, are now joining, and I think it is simply because this is one sphere where the end is imminent. Springboks will not remain all-white for long unless they are going to play inside the country only among themselves.

ATTWELL: And do you foresee that sport can bring about a fundamental change?

BIKO: I think it is a foreshadowing of attitudes. I think unless white people in this country are illogical, if you are going to mix on the sports fields and mix fully, as is eventually going to happen, then you have to think about other areas of your activity, you have to think about cinemas, you have to think about shows and dancing and so on, you have to think about political rights. It is a snowball effect, and the outside world is merely tackling this to bring to the minds of white South Africa that we have got to think about change, and change is an irreversible process, because I believe in history moving in a direction which is logical to a logical end.

ATTWELL: So you would not agree that the black worker sphere is in fact the main sphere in which blacks can be most effective?

BIKO: Not now certainly.

ATTWELL: I think at this stage, Mr. Biko, I would just like to get clear certain terminology which is used by the black organizations if we may, and what you understand by such terms. Firstly you have this word conscientize?

BIKO: Yes.

ATTWELL: Now, I have here a definition of conscientization which I would like to read. "Conscientization is a process whereby individuals or groups living within a given social and political setting are made aware of their situation. The operative attitude here is not so much awareness of the physical sense of their situation, but much more their ability to assess and improve their own influence over themselves and their environment. Thus in the South African setting for instance, it is not enough to be aware that one is living in a situation of oppression or residing in a segregated and probably inferior educational institution. One must be committed to the idea of getting oneself out of the morass, one must be aware of the factors involved and dangers imminent in such an undertaking, but must always operate from the basic belief that one is in a struggle that must be seen through in spite of the dangers and difficulties. Thus then conscientization implies a desire to engage people in an emancipatory process, in an attempt to free them from a situation of bondage. The framework within which we are working is that of Black Consciousness." Now, what is your comment on that exposition of conscientization?

BIKO: I think it is fairly correct.

ATTWELL: Is that how you understand it and is that how SASO and BPC understood conscientization?

BIKO: Yes.

ATTWELL: And if one comes across the term that it is used for conscientization purposes, is that the sense in which it was used?

BIKO: Yes, certainly.

ATTWELL: Then there is talk of the System?

BIKO: Yes.

ATTWELL: What do you mean by the term System?

BIKO: Our fundamental meaning of the term System is those operative forces in society, those institutionalized and uninstitutionalized operative forces in society that control your being, guide your behavior, and generally are in authority over you. Now this is implying government certainly, this is implying the agents of the government, the police especially. There is a tendency in our ranks to regard the police as the System, but the System is also the entire process of oppression.

ATTWELL: Now, I get the impression from SASO and BPC documents that whether one refers to the System or the government or the whites, these three terms seem to be used to mean the same thing?

BIKO: Yes, there is a fair argument for the interchangeability of the terms.

ATTWELL: And if one finds an attack by any particular author in a document and he refers to "the whites have done this" or "the government has done this" or "the System has done this," it all means basically the same thing?

BIKO: Sometimes the term "whites" is used interchangeably with another term which is "white racism," but again the term "white racism" has got to be understood also to be closely tied up with the System. In other words you get institutionalized racism, which expresses itself through agencies of the government, and you get noninstitutionalized racism, which expresses itself in the open street. For instance, outside in the square, the whole relationship between black and white shows a certain form of racism. There is no toilet outside here, and this morning I went into the toilet which is marked "white" and everybody around was looking at me almost wanting to stop me, and I was asked where the black toilet was. Fortunately they did not stop me. But what they were showing me is racism.

ATTWELL: To SASO and BPC the System is white, and the government is a white government?

BIKO: Not true absolutely, there are extensions of the System in the black ranks which are organized as part of the System.

ATTWELL: Like Gatsha Buthelezi?

BIKO: Gatsha Buthelezi is certainly as black as I am in color, and possibly in aspirations, but operates within a system which is created for him by the white government and in that sense he is an extension of the System.

ATTWELL: Would you describe yourself as a freedom fighter?

BIKO: I did use the expression once to Security Police who wanted to know what my profession was, and I said I was a freedom fighter.

ATTWELL: I think that was with tongue in cheek, not so?

BIKO: Well, it was making conversation, and if you have got to live with the Security Police on your neck all the time you have got to devise a way of talking to them, you know, and this is one of the ways. Generally, they understand only one language.

(Laughter.)

ATTWELL: Have you noticed that South Africa's regime has been criticized for its involvement in South West Africa as the illegal regime in South West Africa?

BIKO: Well it has been criticized and I have been party to this myself.

ATTWELL: In what sense is South West Africa considered a foreign country to South Africa?

BIKO: Actually, SASO does not include any technical college or institution of higher learning in Namibia precisely because we regard Namibia as another country, which has been colonized.

ATTWELL: All right, we will talk about it as Namibia then. Do you consider Namibia to be a foreign country?

BIKO: Yes, foreign in the sense of being another country.

ATTWELL: Is that how SASO understands it?

BIKO: That is correct.

ATTWELL: And BPC?

BIKO: Certainly.

ATTWELL: I see. Now, SWAPO for instance. Would that be a foreign organization?

BIKO: It is a foreign organization.

ATTWELL: Now, Mr. Biko, when did your association with SASO end?

BIKO: Officially when I was banned.

ATTWELL: Now, when you concluded your executive association with SASO, how many executive portfolios of SASO had you yourself held?

BIKO: Only two, actually.

ATTWELL: And they were?

BIKO: First was presidency for one year.

ATTWELL: Why did you stand down in the July of 1971 and not continue on the executive of SASO?

BIKO: There are two reasons for it, in fact you can also ask me why did I not stand again for the presidency in 1970. Our belief was essentially that we must attempt to get people to identify with the central core of what is being said rather than with individuals. We must not create a leadership cult. We must centralize the people's attention onto the real message. This is the reason why you notice that all the first presidents of SASO served one year and changed. It was also the reason why that particular column which I was assigned to write, "I write what I like by Frank Talk," was written under a pseudonym, because if you deal with issues all the time people tend to relate to the person in terms of their personal affiliation or disaffiliation to him as a person. We wanted them to focus on the message. I was asked in July 1972 to come back onto the executive by a particular caucus group and I refused, because I thought I had served my purpose, I had made my contribution and it was time for new leadership to emerge. I felt I had already stayed too long by being on the executive for two years.

ATTWELL: Looking at the other accused here, those that you know, I think you have intimated that you know accused number 1, Saths Cooper, number 2, Muntu Myeza, number 3, Patrick Lekota, number 4, Dr. Mokoape, and I think you said number 9, Strini Moodley. Do you know the other accused at all?

BIKO: Yes I know them now, I have met them.

ATTWELL: Apart from here, did you know them before their arrest?

BIKO: No. I only knew three, that is Strini, Saths and Aubrey, before I was banned. Since I was banned and before their arrest I then met Lekota and Muntu. But that is not quite true, Lekota was at the same school as me. Actually, I knew him then as a soccer star on our team.   (Laughter.)

ATTWELL: Yes, he has the nickname "Terror," is that right?

BIKO: Something like that, I think it was "Terror."

THE JUDGE: Did he earn his name "Terror?"

BIKO: As a striker, yes!

ATTWELL: Was there any secrecy about the formation of SASO?

BIKO: No, certainly not.

ATTWELL: Did it enjoy publicity in the press?

BIKO: Well, it did not in 1969. In fact we had a very quiet conference. We were bothered about this. In 1970 we had a lot of press coverage but we had to go out of our way to attract the press to come to the conference.

ATTWELL: Why was so little coverage given or sought by the steering committee for the formation of SASO?

BIKO: The steering committee could not possibly attract publicity precisely because they would have had to give policy considerations which had not yet been formulated by the organization.

ATWELL: So for one and a half years these things were kept hidden?

BIKO: By whom?

ATTWELL: Kept hidden until you felt you were strong enough?

BIKO: Kept hidden from whom by whom?

THE JUDGE: Mr. Attwell, how are you using this in your case?

ATTWELL: M'lord, ultimately I will be submitting to Your Lordship that these people realized that this was a revolutionary concept, and they kept it hidden for quite a long time until they felt themselves strong enough to make it public, and that the reason they kept it hidden was because they were building up their strength, they did not want this thing to get to the press or to any other persons, because they were scared of the reception this type of thing would have and they could have been crushed in the early stages.

BIKO: But this constitution which you say was hidden was in fact given to various student representative councils who in terms of their internal university rules had to approach rectors before affiliating. They had to show the constitution. I spoke to a number of rectors about SASO. They had the constitution, and I remember specifically Mr. Boshoff of Turfloop, I spoke to him in detail about SASO, and he accepted the constitution, and eventually accepted SASO. Now, was that hiding it?

ATTWELL: We will be submitting to His Lordship at the end of the case that there was a progressively militant, more militant use of language by SASO in its documents.

BIKO: I would put it that there was a progressively more positive approach by SASO in its language.

ATTWELL: Now, you are familiar with the language used in the early documents?

BIKO: Yes, since some of the documents were drawn up by me.

ATTWELL: The one "noting with grave concern and disgust the display of naked terrorism?"

BIKO: Right. Well I just find this a usual expression of indignation which you would get from SASO.

ATTWELL: You say that the blacks are being subjected by the white government to "direct terrorism?"

BIKO: Yes.

ATTWELL: Do you think that is a valid statement?

BIKO: I think it is far more valid than the charge against these men here. I think that what we have to experience is more physically depressing than the charge you are placing against these men for the few things they have said.

ATTWELL: Which men are you talking about?

BIKO: The nine accused.

ATTWELL: Well, perhaps you could expand on that, Mr. Biko?

BIKO: I am talking about the violence in which people are baton-charged by police, beaten up, like the people who were striking in March at Henneman. I am talking about police firing on unarmed people in places like Sharpeville, and I am talking about the indirect violence that you get through starvation in the townships. I am talking about the squalor that you find at Winterveld right now. I am talking about the kind of situation you get at Dimbaza, where there is no food, hardly any furniture for people. I think that, all put together, constitutes more terrorism than what these guys have been saying. Now they stand charged, but white society is not charged, this is what I mean.

ATTWELL: What do you understand the charges are against the accused?

BIKO: Well, I have been made to understand that they are supposed to have fanned the feelings of blacks to result in a state of racial hostility, something like that. And I have been interested in this case all along. When I first heard about it I thought there could be something my men had done. After a long time the state closed its case, and what had they done? You produced a mass of documents, and this so-called conspiracy exists only in the minds of the Security Police and probably you, Mr. Attwell.

ATTWELL: You refer to them as your men?

BIKO: They work with me.

ATTWELL: With you?

BIKO: Yes.

ATTWELL: In close contact with you?

BIKO: Actually I do not know some of them, but we share a belief about our society, that is what I mean by saying they work with me.

ATTWELL: Some of them you do not know?

BIKO: Yes.

ATTWELL: But you are ready to defend them, although you do not know what they have done?

BIKO: I defend them because I believe in our organizations. If they are being charged for being in SASO and for being in BPC, I have faith in the validity of SASO and BPC.

ATTWELL: You, of course, together with the rest of SASO and BPC members, have been engaged in a liberatory struggle against the white system?

BIKO: Yes.

ATTWELL: And your sympathies, I gather, lie with the accused in this case?

BIKO: Well, I have been called here by subpoena to come to court and my understanding of that significance is that I must speak the truth under oath. Sure I have sympathies with my men, but I will not stand between my men and the truth.

ATTWELL: While we are talking about evidence in this trial, when were you approached to give evidence in this case, Mr. Biko?

BIKO: I got what one might call a questionnaire from Mr. Chetty, the lawyer, toward the end of last year. This questionnaire contained various questions about the formation of SASO, and about various conferences that I attended up to 1970. I answered all the questions as truthfully as I could, and I indicated voluntarily to Mr. Chetty that should I be required to come and defend any of the assertions I made there, I was available, precisely because I realized on looking around that there were in fact very few people who had been there at the beginning of SASO, certainly not among these guys here, and very few among people who are generally available to give evidence. I subsequently got a subpoena in November, it must have been about the middle of November, to come up, so I came up believing I was going to appear. I did not appear. I went back home, and got another subpoena about two weeks back and that is why I am here.

ATTWELL: So in effect you volunteered to give evidence?

BIKO: I did volunteer to give evidence, yes.

ATTWELL: Because as you say there is a misconception about SASO and BPC and this would be an opportunity to clear the air, as it were?

BIKO: Because I recognize myself as one of the few guys who were there at the formation of these bodies, and who are available at this moment to assist the court on historical questions.

ATTWELL: In the period after your banning did you have any contact at all with any of the accused?

BIKO: As I said, after my banning I met Mr. Lekota and Mr. Myeza.

ATTWELL: Did they come down to King William's Town?

BIKO: Well, they were on business, you see, and my home is in King William's Town, and I am interested in SASO, so they came to chat to me about developments in the organization.

ATTWELL: What did you do to allay the fears of any people that SASO and BPC dissociated themselves with the methods of ANC or PAC?

BIKO: The point is that no such fears were ever expressed within the context of SASO and BPC. I think it was quite apparent to everybody what SASO and BPC were all about, and certainly we spoke of the whole development of the human being, in other words the black man discarding his own psychological oppression. Every day in our meetings they saw this as being the thing that BPC and SASO were promoting.

ATTWELL: Do I understand you correctly, nothing specific was done to allay any fears if they did exist?

BIKO: To understand me correctly you have to say that there were no fears expressed.

ATTWELL: But apparently the whites were scared?

BIKO: Well we did not have white membership, so if you are talking about within the context of BPC certainly there were no whites within BPC.

ATTWELL: There were no whites in BPC but surely you were addressing yourself to the whites indirectly anyway?

BIKO: I have spoken to white audiences about Black Consciousness in the past and I found no such fear. When I addressed a group of white students in Cape Town I spoke about our viewpoint, and incidentally this was found most acceptable by the Afrikaner students present, who said to me that this had been the way Afrikaner nationalism had developed, right we wish you guys well. I became friendly with the president of the Afrikaner Studentebond, Mr. Johan Fick. I met him recently in Johannesburg, and he invited me to his room at Rand Afrikaans University. He wasn't frightened.

ATTWELL: Do you consider that the white man in South Africa is scared?

BIKO: I think the general white population may very well be under the influence of propaganda to a point where they do not realize just how inevitable change is, but I think the white leadership, especially the leadership of the three main white parties in this country, is aware of the inevitability of change, and I think there is a certain fear which is gnawing at them about which direction this change should take. Okay, they certainly do not want to find themselves overtaken by events, they want to be moving with the events. So there is an element of fear certainly in leadership, but I do want to say that the average white man often is not aware. The way he treats black people in shops and post offices indicates that he just is not aware of the inevitability of change.

ATTWELL: What image is BPC giving out about the ANC and PAC?

BIKO: We refer to them as organizations which exist in the history of the black people.

ATTWELL: With approval or disapproval?

BIKO: I think, Mr. Attwell, one thing you must realize is that the struggle concept which is struggle from liberation of yourself, from anything threatening you, is continuous through history. At different times it is picked up by different people in different methods. Okay, but the struggle is what we attach ourselves to. We must recognize that the ANC and the PAC were involved in the struggle, and were not involved in the struggle for selfish purposes, but on behalf of blacks and for the liberation of blacks. We may or may not necessarily approve of their methods, but the fact is they exist in history and for pushing the struggle forward.

ATTWELL: Do you agree with me that this constitutes approval?

BIKO: It is not a passing of judgment. It is a recognition of what has happened in history. An approval implies subjecting whatever has happened to systematic analysis so that you can arrive at a judgment either approving or disapproving. In this case it is just reference to a particular phase in our history as black people.

ATTWELL: And when BPC talks or SASO talks in its documents of "our true leaders who have been banned and imprisoned on Robben Island?"

BIKO: That is correct.

ATTWELL: Who are they referring to specifically?

BIKO: We refer to people like Mandela, we refer to people like Sobukwe, we refer to people like Govan Mbeki.

ATTWELL: And what is the common factor in those people?

BIKO: The common factor is that they are people who have been selflessly pushing forward the struggle for the black man.

ATTWELL: They include the leaders of the ANC?

BIKO: They do.

ATTWELL: Do you know any of these persons who have been on Robben Island?

BIKO: Oh yes.

ATTWELL: Could you name them?

BIKO: I have met Mr. Sobukwe.

ATTWELL: In what connection?

BIKO: Because I wanted to meet him.

ATTWELL: When was this, Mr. Biko?

BIKO: It was in 1972.

ATTWELL Was there anything specific that you wanted to know from him?

BIKO: Well, no, I was on a tour of the country for black community purposes which took me to collect some information from Mr. Stanley Ntwasa in connection with some cases that he had had that year, and because we were in Kimberley we took the opportunity of seeing Mr. Sobukwe.

ATTWELL: When in 1972 would this have been?

BIKO: September.

ATTWELL: Sobukwe is a particularly relevant person in the history of the black struggle in this country, is he not?

BIKO: He is an important figure.

ATTWELL: Can you point to any document of SASO or BPC which specifically and unambiguously rejects violence?

BIKO: You would have to give me a whole lot of documents to look through.

ATTWELL: It is not in the BPC constitution, is it, a rejection of violence?

BIKO: No, it is not there. Nor is it anywhere in the constitution of the Nationalist Party.

ATTWELL: Yes, but you people had a peculiar background, you had prejudice you had to meet?

BIKO: Yes.

ATTWELL: A suspicious bunch of authorities that were keeping an eye on you?

BIKO: Mmmm.

ATTWELL: A difficult time was forecast for both organizations from the start?

BIKO: That is correct.

ATTWELL: And a lot of rejection was expected?

BIKO: That is correct.

ATTWELL: And a lot of resistance was expected?

BIKO: That is correct. So?

ATTWELL: And there is no specific rejection of violence in either constitution?

BIKO: Precisely, because we never thought of it.

ATTWELL: Do you find some of the white students a strange phenomenon?

BIKO: Afrikaner students.

ATTWELL: Yes, your Mr. Nengwekulu in one speech talks about these strange people with their strange logic?

BIKO: Oh yes, he does that, he does that, yes.

ATTWELL: Generally students are going to be the future leaders of society, are they not?

BIKO: Yes of course, but when you talk about students being leaders you do not really talk about every individual student. There are duds at university as well.

ATTWELL: Would you consider SASO to have been the nursery of BPC?

BIKO: I think only in terms of giving a skeleton a bit of flesh to a philosophy that was later to be adopted by BPC, in that sense, yes.

ATTWELL: SASO and BPC were there to articulate the feelings of blacks, do you agree with me?

BIKO: Yes, to articulate their feelings on issues.

ATTWELL: Now, which sentiments would SASO and BPC be articulating, the sentiments of those that are very militant and use very harsh language, or those that use lesser language?

BIKO: Mr. Attwell, I think if you conducted a survey you would find no more than a fraction of 1 percent of black people who are pleased with the situation that exists. Now BPC sees itself as a political pressure group, right? They seek to represent the interests of the majority of black people, and the majority of black people are displeased with what is going on, so BPC therefore seeks to articulate that displeasure with the system. And it takes various forms. There are many complaints. It would take us three weeks to put them one by one.

ATTWELL: Yes, I merely want to know which group of blacks?

BIKO: The majority who are displeased about what is going on right now.

ATTWELL: And if it articulates these feelings would it be the feelings of those people who are viciously anti-white and militant, or the others?

BIKO: They represent all blacks. I think they synthesize all the complaints. Some people complain about squatter conditions because they experience squatter conditions, others complain that they have got small yards, you have got to synthesize all this and come up with the general black viewpoint.

ATTWELL: You say the vast majority of blacks would have these feelings?

BIKO: Yes, sure.

ATTWELL: Now, you know the accused are charged with causing or encouraging or furthering these feelings of hostility?

BIKO: I understand that is the charge.

ATTWELL: And do you consider there is a difference between causing something, encouraging something or furthering something?

BIKO: Oh well, I am sure there is a difference because the actual words have different meanings. I think again that you have a wrong interpretation of black solidarity. We are not envisaging getting a committed membership which constitutes almost what you might call a standing army. No, we are looking forward to getting a majority of black people behind us, behind what we say, in the same way that the Nationalist party has a majority of white people behind them at this moment. They do not constitute a homogeneous mass that can be called to action any day. There are wide differences even among them, but at least there is a central feeling, they constitute what you call *die volk*, and the Nationalist party, the Broederbond, these are their spokesmen. You cannot call them tomorrow to action because they are scattered throughout the country, but they have got an identity and they have got a vanguard in the form of the Nationalist party, the Broederbond and all the other Afrikaner cultural organizations which speak for them. Now the same thing applies to black people, we are trying to create a situation where BPC speaks for the people, gives them a home, gives them dignity, so that they can feel they are human once more, which is not what they are feeling now.

ATTWELL: You want to involve all the blacks, do you not?

BIKO: Not necessarily all. I am sure not all the Afrikaners are in the Nationalist party.

ATTWELL: All right, how many blacks are in South Africa?

BIKO: More than 20 million.

ATTWELL: You see there are references in the documents to thirty million, about a third higher than you estimate?

BIKO: Okay.

ATTWELL: Do you see any significance in this inflated figure?

BIKO: No, I think the only significant thing about it is BPC's knowledge from experience that a lot of black people are in fact not registered. For instance in Soweto, the current official figure is about 800 000. But there are about one and a half million in Soweto, because for every, say, six people who are registered, there are two who are not registered or something like that. Those figures come from that kind of thinking. There is no other significance beyond that.

THE JUDGE: It is because the population figures are taken from a census?

BIKO: That is correct.

ATTWELL: So they do not necessarily go by the number of people who are registered, people who are really counted in households?

BIKO: Well of course, M'lord, when the census official comes around to my home as a black man, he never really says to me: "We are counting the people who are here in the country." It is a typical white approach again. He comes in and he says: "How many people live here?" Now the first thing you think about is registration. If I have got people squatting in my house I am going to be arrested, so if there are ten people but six registered you say: "Six, baas," so he writes six and he goes next door. (Laughter.) So you see this is how it is relevant. If it was explained to people nicely that the officials were only counting, and would not prosecute, people would give the correct figures, but they never know, they are never told.

THE JUDGE: You have said that because of the conduct of the white man there was an explosive position which led to the strikes in 1972 and 1973.

BIKO: Yes.

THE JUDGE: Now isn't there a danger that if this extravagant language is used it can have an agitatory effect on the black man and worsen that explosive situation?

BIKO: M'lord, as I have submitted before, this language with reference to the black man receiving it is indeed quite mild and quite within his experience of white society and the way he himself ordinarily expresses it. If it was the intention of SASO or BPC to arouse people into violent reactions, there were many individual situations they could paint in far more colorful language to achieve their result. They could talk of starvation in highly emotive language which could achieve that result, they could talk of the many murders that one gets in townships, and tie it up somehow with the socio-political order in order to achieve their results, but they never did this. All they do is to look broadly at issues, and certainly it is not the preoccupation of SASO and BPC, as I know them, to go around saying: whites are this, whites are that, whites are enemies, whites are racists. We see these terms in the course of language to articulate existing thoughts among blacks, because it is a starting point in the building up of our membership, in our building up of our humanity within our ranks. And I do not think black people, truly speaking, are incited to violence specifically by this. They look at the central thing, that is we have got a common grievance, we have got common experiences. Let us start from there building our society. I think if you look at it again historically, if you look at the Afrikaner documents describing the whole Afrikaner/English problem you will find equally extravagant language was used to express the common problems of the Afrikaner in terms of their clash with the English. This is what you do when you want to define a starting point, to say what your problem is.

ATTWELL: Can it not have the effect of making the people more hostile than they are?

BIKO: M'lord, I can refer you to typical examples of how blacks react to this sort of thing. There is a document here for instance which you have referred to in which Harry Nengwekulu was talking about violent white society. Now I was at that meeting. My estimate of that crowd was certainly above a thousand, it could have been much more. But for God's sake, when he was talking about this violent white society and in a sense ridiculing white society, the people just laughed. Not one of them stood up to say: "Down with white society." You know, they just felt an inner peace to feel somehow that they had a psychological ascendancy over white society, in that they were able to articulate their problem together, and to talk about it and to laugh over it. I think this is the conduct at many a SASO meeting or BPC meeting. I have never seen a single meeting where people were aroused in the manner suggested.

ATTWELL: Nowhere in these documents do you say that the white government is doing anything good.

BIKO: It does so little good that it is not worth commenting on. (Laughter.)

ATTWELL: Now perhaps you would have a look at this tribute to the late Nthuli Shezi, vice-president of the Black Peoples Convention, issued by the Black Peoples Convention. Will you have a look at the third paragraph of that document for instance: "The violent assassination was inflicted by an agent of protection of white racism, superiority and oppression on our black brother. It should not be regarded as being directed towards him alone, but should be regarded as an assault on the entire black community." And then it carries on: "Who can deny that the ravages of poverty, disease and violation are neither situational nor are they accidental. Who can deny that the thousands of black children and black mothers and fathers who die of starvation represent a deliberate attempt to extinguish from the surface of the earth the entire black nation?"

Now that type of sentiment, do you seriously in BPC and SASO believe that that is the intention of the government and the System to systematically and premeditatively extinguish from the surface of the earth the entire black nation?

BIKO: Well, I think you should know that in African politics, as in poetry, there is license for what one might call justifiable exaggeration. I spoke earlier about various situations in which the black man finds himself at the receiving end of aspects of the System. I spoke about squatter areas, I spoke about blacks being shot by police, and I said this was terrorism. It is political license. Now I want to say also that you may find that kind of talk in BPC/SASO documents, but it is not the kind of thing that BPC and SASO go around saying most of the time. The central message of SASO and BPC is internal within the black community. Extreme things are done to us, and we tend to respond in extreme language. You haven't got the black experience, unfortunately, Mr. Attwell, so I cannot explain this to you. You have got to be black to understand what I am talking about.

ATTWELL: Well, I got that impression the very first time I read this document . . .

BIKO: That is because you are white.

ATTWELL: But this document could have got into the hands of thousands of whites?

BIKO: It was not directed to whites.

ATTWELL: But it could have got into their hands?

BIKO: Well, if you took it and distributed it, yes. That is just theoretical.

ATTWELL: Did you attend Shezi's funeral?

BIKO: I was there, yes.

ATTWELL: Was it an emotional funeral?

BIKO: All funerals are emotional.

ATTWELL: What sort of speeches were delivered?

BIKO: There were speeches to encourage people to continue. It is the typical African situation, when anybody of note dies the normal theme of the speeches there is that what he was doing other people must continue with. That was the theme of the white minister who conducted the funeral.

ATTWELL: You say it was a white minister who conducted the funeral?

BIKO: Yes, it was.

ATTWELL: I submit to you that the speakers brought out all the good in Mr. Shezi, whatever good there may have been, and neglected any weak points that he may have had.

BIKO: This is done.

ATTWELL: And brought out all the evil things they could about the whites, and ignored all the good that there may or may not be. Would you agree with me?

BIKO: I think they have not finished all the evil.

ATWELL: They have not finished all the evil yet?

BIKO: No, no.

ATTWELL: Would you have gone further than this?

BIKO: One could go further if one wanted to.

ATTWELL: Would you have gone further?

BIKO: Not necessarily me, but anybody could have gone further if he had wanted to. If the intention was to try to portray white society as bad, and use that to make everybody who was there angry, a whole further litany of evil could have been produced.

ATTWELL: Did a man called Bokwe Maphuna ever assault a white policeman?

BIKO: I attended a court hearing where he was charged with assaulting a traffic cop, which according to him was the actual reverse of what had happened. He had been hit by a white traffic cop and he went to lay a charge, and apparently the traffic cop on receiving notice of this decided to lay a countercharge, and his case came first, so Maphuna was now in a situation where he had to answer why he beat up the cop, and in actual fact the cop had beaten him up.

ATTWELL: Was he convicted?

BIKO: Yes.

ATTWELL: Now did you write the following?: "*To look for instances of cruelty directed at those who fall into disfavor with the Security Police is perhaps to look too far. One need not try to establish the truth of the claim that black people in South Africa have to struggle for survival. It presents itself in so many facets of our lives. In our crime-ridden townships poverty is so prevalent that even black will kill black to be able to survive. That is the basis of vandalism, murders, rapes, and other crimes that go on while the real source of the evil, the white racists, are suntanning on exclusive beaches or relaxing in their bourgeois homes.*"

BIKO: Yes.

ATTWELL: Are those your real sentiments?

BIKO: Yes.

ATTWELL: Then you say: "*This is a dangerous type of fear, for it only goes skin deep. It hides underneath it an immeasurable rage that often threatens to erupt. Beneath it lies naked hatred for a group that deserves no respect. Unlike in the rest of the French or Spanish former colonies where chances of assimilation make it possible for blacks to aspire toward being white, in South Africa whiteness has become associated with police brutality and intimidation, early morning pass raids, general harassment in and out of the townships, and hence no black really aspires to be white. The claim by whites of monopoly and comfort and security have always been so exclusive that blacks see whites as the major obstacles in their progress toward peace, prosperity and a sane society. Through its associations with all these negative aspects whiteness has thus become soiled beyond recognition. At best therefore blacks see whiteness as a concept that warrants being deposed, hated, destroyed and replaced by an aspiration with more human content in it. At worst blacks envy white society for the comfort it has usurped and at the center of this envy is the wish, nay, the secret determination in the innermost minds of most blacks who think like this, to kick whites off those comfortable garden chairs that one sees as blacks ride in a bus out of town, to claim them for themselves.*" Now what did you have in mind?

BIKO: The article speaks for itself, if you read all of it. It is a commentary on the decadence of our society. I point out the rising animosity between black and white which has been brought about by history, and by three hundred years of oppression, and my warning here is that if this situation is not corrected, it leads to a hardening of attitudes, especially on the black side. Blacks may very well get to a position where they feel permanently that they cannot live side by side with whites. And this is a warning to society to perceive this trend.

ATTWELL: Where is the warning expressed in warning terms?

BIKO: Throughout. You have got to read the whole thing in context, you see, and if you look at the title, right, I am trying to eradicate the thinking that is prevalent in white society which makes them operate from fear as a basis. In other words they do not necessarily look at things that are done by blacks logically. They look at them in terms of to what extent they are threatened in their position as whites, and this is the basis for police brutality.

ATTWELL: So you agree with me that the whites basically are afraid of Black Consciousness?

BIKO: Not all whites.

ATTWELL: Well, if we can talk about whites collectively as you people generally do, would you say that they were afraid of the Black Consciousness movement?

BIKO: I think you are talking collectively now about the majority of whites.

ATTWELL: Yes, what about them?

BIKO: I would say that the majority of whites are not even aware of Black Consciousness.

The accused in the trial, Saths Cooper, Edmund Myeza, Patrick Lekota, Dr. Aubrey Mokoape, Nkwenkwe Nkomo, Pandelani Fefolovidwe, Gilbert Sidibe, Absolom Cindi and Strini Moodley, were convicted and sentenced to imprisonment on Robben Island for minimum spells of five years.

In terms of even statute law, unduly rebellious thoughts in South Africa identified with Black Consciousness had now become a major crime, and the verbal expression of black anger against white rule had now earned the judicial definition of terrorism.

And Steve Biko, having completed his marathon spell of testimony, returned to his area of restriction.

A portrait by *Daily Dispatch* artist, Don Kenyon. It was published in full color on the front page of the issue announcing Steve Biko's death.

Steve Biko ... a typical expression ... a good listener ... a marvellous sense of humor ... a dedicated political leader.

Senator Dick Clark of the United States Senate Committee on Africa made a special visit to see Steve. When they met, Steve had recently been released from one hundred days in detention, and was thirty two pounds under normal weight.

The Editor of the *Daily Dispatch* in his office.

Gatsha Buthelezi, leader of the Kwa Zulu Bantustan.

Robert Sobukwe.

Nelson Mandela: "I have cherished the ideal of a democratic and free society ... It is an ideal which I hope to live for and to achieve. But if needs be, it is an ideal for which I am prepared to die."

Alan Paton and Nadine Gordimer, two South African writers. For Donald Woods "they tore into final shreds any of apartheid's claims to validity."

Helen Suzman, for many years the only Progressive Party member of the South African Parliament. She sent an anonymous donation to Steve Biko from her private fund for political prisoners.

Alon Reininger Percy Qoboza, editor of *The World*, who was detained on the same day that Donalds Woods was banned.

General Geldenhuys, Kruger's Chief of Security. He initiated a prosecution against the author which resulted in a six months prison sentence, which was eventually lifted on appeal.

Daily Dis

After a terrifying night of anonymous, threatening telephone calls and pistol shots fired at her home, Wendy Woods found this slogan sprayed on a wall of the house.

Daily Dispatch

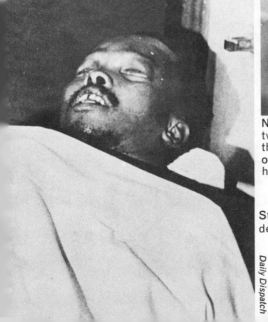

Keystone

Ntsiki Biko and her children, Samora aged two and Nkosinathi aged six, defiantly give the Black Power salute soon after hearing of Biko's death. "Steve may be dead but his struggle continues."

Steve Biko's body immediately after his death.

Thousands of mourners salute the coffin on its way to the memorial service.

Some of the twenty thousand people who stood in remembrance of a great black leader.

Frank Sp
P.

International Defense and Aid Fund for South Africa

Frank Spooner Pictures

Samora Biko at his father's funeral.

Hillelson The coffin containing Steve Biko's body was carried to the funeral in an ox cart.

Bishop Tutu stands before the banner of the Black Peoples Convention during the service.

Sidney Kentridge, barrister for the Biko family: "Any verdict which can be seen as an exoneration of the Port Elizabeth Security Police will unfortunately be widely interpreted as a license to abuse helpless people with impunity."

Mr. Prins, Chief Magistrate of Pretoria.

Lieutenant Wilken: "Biko made no complaints to me."

Major Harold Snyman: "I felt bad about Biko's death. He was worth more to us alive than dead."

Dr. Ivor Lang: " I could find nothing organically wrong with the man."

Captain Siebert: "Biko was beside himself with fury ."

Colonel Goosen, commanding officer of the Security Police in Port Elizabeth: "We have full authority... We don't work under statutes."

Dr. Hersch and Dr. Tucker (right). Both examined Steve Biko before he died; neither expressed any serious indication of brain damage at that time.

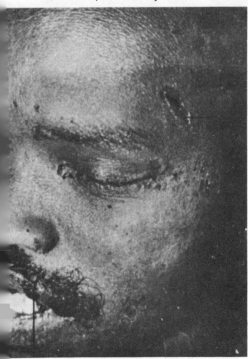

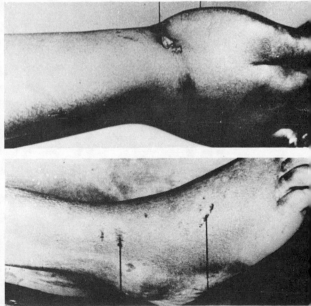

Photographs produced in evidence to show the injuries to Steve Biko's head, wrists and ankles.

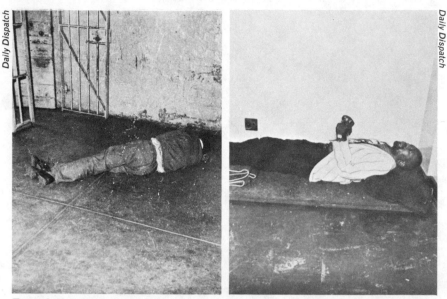

Two of the photographs which were used to indicate the positions in which Steve Biko was found at various times during his detention.

Major Snyman standing in the office in Security Police Headquarters, Port Elizabeth, where Steve Biko was kept naked and in chains for forty-eight hours.

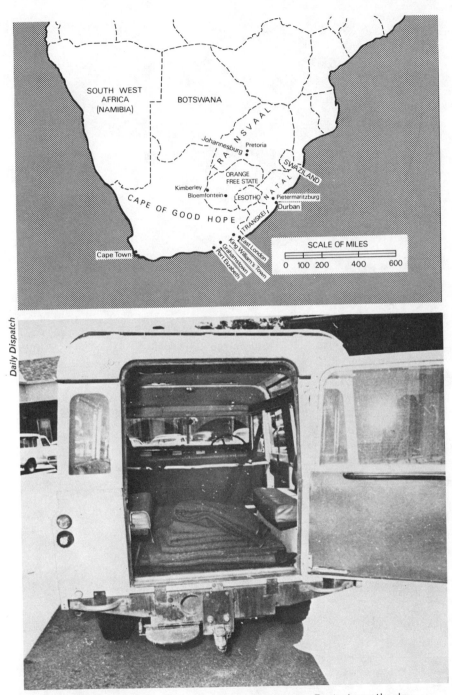

The vehicle in which Steve Biko was taken 750 miles to Pretoria on the day before he died.

Prime Minister Vorster: "The world can do its damndest."

James Kruger, the Minister of Justice: "Biko's death leaves me cold."

4: THE KILLING
STEVE BIKO DIES

ON AUGUST 18, 1977, Steve Biko and his friend Peter Jones were stopped at a Security Police roadblock near Grahamstown, in the Eastern Cape Province.

I heard of their arrest in a phone call from Malusi Mpumlwana the following day. We discussed the matter at some length. Obviously, Steve had been caught breaking his banning order by being outside the King William's Town magisterial district, and we speculated on when he would be charged for this. We also discussed the matter of whether he would be allowed bail, and how we could raise the bail money and fees for his defense. Later Malusi phoned again to say he had heard that Steve was not simply under arrest but had been detained and taken to Port Elizabeth for "interrogation." Yet at no stage were Wendy and I or Malusi or Ntsiki or other members of Steve's family or circle of friends unduly alarmed. Steve had been detained before, and no harm had come to him.

We had slight misgivings about the fact that he and Peter had been taken to Port Elizabeth, because the Port Elizabeth Security Police had a particularly savage reputation under a certain Colonel Pieter Goosen. But although we were uneasy about the interrogation venue, none of us really feared for Steve's life, nor even that he would be assaulted. He was, we assumed, too important a figure in South African politics, and far too well known among key figures internationally, to come to any harm. In addition he seemed to have a way of defusing the violent inclinations of interrogators, turning aside anger with humor, calm reason and sheer personality.

We were totally unprepared for the tragedy when it came.

Steve had been in detention almost a month when we learned of his death. I entered my office at the *Daily Dispatch* about 10 o'clock on the morning of Tuesday, September 13, and found my secretary, Linda Murray, in tears. Malusi had phoned to say there were reports that Steve was dead. I wasn't even upset, I was so sure it could not be true. I told her not to worry, there was some mistake. In fact I laughed at the very thought, saying: "Steve dead? Nonsense! I know the Nationalists are mad – but even they are not so mad as to let him die of *anything* in detention."

Then came the slight but chilling doubt. *Could* they be that mad?

I phoned Malusi. He was out.

I phoned the family.

Dear God, it was true.

Within those first shocked seconds, South Africa became a different place for me. Everything about it was now different. The Nationalists were no longer simply disastrously misguided racists – they were now the mortal enemy, who stopped at nothing, who had committed the ultimate outrage. I perceived them suddenly for what they really were – of the same genre as Duvalier's Tonton Macoutes in Haiti and all political police terrorists of repressive regimes that know no limit in their desperation, and for whom nothing is sacred. So powerful for the Nationalists was their god of white racial purity that no morality any longer attended any aspect of their war in its defense.

I phoned Wendy to tell her. She, too, could not believe it. When she finally came to believe it, she could barely speak. Neither of us really slept that night. Wendy said of the regime: "I feel nothing any more. I'm beyond feeling scared of them. There is nothing worse they can do."

In the early hours of the morning I stared into space, talking with a silent intensity to a mental image of Steve lying dead.

"Who did it? How did it happen? What is the bastard's name? What does he look like? Come on, Stevo! How did it happen? Who is the bastard? What does he look like? How can it all be brought out? Answer, Stevo! Answer Stevo! Answer Stevo! Heh – Stivana! Heh – mta' ka Biko! Pendula, ke-Stivovo! Teta, Sitivi! Kawusi Xelele! Kawusi xelele ngoku! Yini kaloku! Hey – Bhee-ko! Uthini? Steve-you-better-answer-I'm-just-going-to-keep-up-these-questions-until-you-answer! Who did it? What is his name? What does he look like?"

So great is the power of imagination in times of bereavement, so vivid is the faculty of autosuggestion, that after an hour or so of these intense questions I suddenly received clear answers from an acutely real, clear image of Steve. He was sitting in the armchair near the foot of the bed, with his legs crossed, in slacks and open-necked shirt, leaning forward slightly with an animated expression on his face as if on the point of speech.

"What are you doing here?" I asked.

He was now grinning so much that he could hardly control his lips sufficiently to form words with them.

"What I always do – my work." (He pronounced it "*WEK*," with great emphasis, and his eyes widened with elation.) He added, excitedly, waving a hand: "I'm fine, man. Quite all right, really."

"Where are you?" I asked, not quite sure of what I meant by the question.

"At home, man. Everything's quite normal actually."

"What happened? Who did it? What does he look like?"

"There were three of them, as a matter of fact. But the main one was a young guy, very strong. But it doesn't matter, really!"

I had the impression from this that he meant it didn't matter in the sense that the blows (certainly more than one blow) directed at him had done more lasting harm to the System than to him.

Obviously, these words were not spoken aloud, on either side, because they were all emanating from my own imagination, as a result of fatigue, emotional strees and subconscious make-believe. I spoke to Wendy, found she was awake, and told her of my imaginings. "What did he say?" she said. I told her, and she understood, both of us knowing it was sheer imagination. We talked on through the night, aware that neither of us could ever fill this particular void, no matter how vivid the power of imagination might be.

We had both gone through the day more easily than through the night, because up until the early evening we had been preparing articles for publication and I had been working with the layout men at the *Daily Dispatch* for a special front-page design with a large color portrait of Steve and the phrase on either side of it:

"We salute a hero of the nation."

("Sikahlela indoda yamadoda.")

RESPONSE
TO THE TRAGEDY

THE FOLLOWING MORNING, newspaper readers throughout South Africa learned of Steve's death, and many things about him that the Nationalistcontroled radio and television service had omitted to carry the evening before.

Within hours of hearing of Steve's death, various newspapers in South Africa had asked Wendy and me to write our immediate reactions for publication. Still in shock, still barely able to accept that Steve was actually dead, we wrote what follows. South African newspaper readers were able to read these articles the following morning. They were among the last such articles publishable in the South African press in such blunt terms.

My article read:

I have just received the news that my most valued friend, Steve Biko, has died in detention. He needs no tributes from me. He never did. He was a special and extraordinary man who at the age of thirty had already acquired a towering status in the hearts and minds of countless thousands of young blacks throughout the length and breadth of South Africa.

In the three years that I grew to know him my conviction never wavered that this was the most important political leader in the entire country, and quite simply the greatest man I have ever had the privilege to know.

Wisdom, humor, compassion, understanding, brilliancy of intellect, unselfishness, modesty, courage – he had all these attributes. You could take the most complex problems to him and he would in one or two sentences strike unerringly to the core of the matter and provide the obvious solution.

How I wish I could publish for all South Africans his thoughts on all their fears, prejudices and political timidities, and what he saw as the clear and peaceful answers to these – but the government through its banning orders silenced all public statements of his, and even in death he may not be quoted.

His thoughts could be repeated somehow, it is true, and will, but part of their force was that they came directly from him in his uniquely influential position as a black spokesman of major standing.

I once went to Minister J. T. Kruger and begged him to lift the restrictions on Steve and to speak to him. The result of that visit was an increase in Steve's restrictions and a State prosecution against me, culminating in a six-month jail sentence.

Steve's reaction was to burst out laughing – nothing ever daunted his spirit.

He was detained more than once. He experienced solitary confinement more than once. He always came out of such ordeals as tough as ever and as resiliently humorous about the interrogation sessions.

He had a far closer understanding of his interrogators' fears and motivations than they will ever know, and with almost total recall he recounted to me the full range of their questions. Many were simply incredible. I'll say no more than that – at this stage.

Although he was under banning orders for four years, restricting him to King William's Town, he went pretty much where he liked – to Durban, to Cape

Town, to Johannesburg, to Pretoria, to Bloemfontein and other places. He visited my home in East London on a number of occasions. He regarded all of South Africa as his home and he had helpful friends everywhere.

Any contest of wits between him and his many watchers in the Security Police was an absurdly one-sided mismatch.

The only thing that could bring him down was death – and now it has done so.

Whether all the circumstances surrounding his death will ever come to light cannot be known at this stage, but there are enough basic facts known to apportion blame.

The basic facts are that barely three weeks ago, when he was detained, he was completely fit and healthy (I know because I was with him a day or two before his detention) and that this healthy and strong young man was imprisoned without trial by political police, and that he died three weeks later still in such captivity.

Therefore, whatever the cause of his death – I repeat, whatever the cause – I hold responsible all those who were associated with his detention, because his death occurred while under their control, and control exercised through morally wrong powers such as detention without trial is control that is morally unjustifiable, making those who exercise it morally accountable for all that occurs in terms of it.

And because Minister J. T. Kruger heads the department which exercises such powers, I hold him particularly accountable in this tragedy.

As to those more directly concerned with the interrogations to which he was subjected, all things humanly possible will be done to bring their role to light. This can confidently be promised, because without any doubt a great many South Africans have sworn this oath today, and I am only one of these many.

The government quite clearly never understood the extent to which Steve was a man of peace. He was militant in standing up for his principles, yes, but his abiding goal was a peaceful reconciliation of all South Africans, and in this I happen to know he was a moderating influence.

Therefore, to the racists who have gloated over my grief today in anonymous phonecalls and telegrams, even twisting scriptural texts to coat their venom, I reply in the same vein:

"Weep not for me, but for yourselves and for your children."

Wendy's article read:

Steve Biko was once unknown to my husband, Donald, and myself. We had heard of him but did not know him. And then because of persistent urging on the part of various people, we met him and the foundations of a deep and committed friendship were laid.

We were drawn to him at once. Physically, he was an imposing figure, very tall, extremely well-built and with a noble face. He was not an extrovert – one had a sense of great capacity for self-containment. He spoke quietly, generally unemotionally, and all the time one was aware of his acute sensibilities – his ability to listen, to sift and make judgments on what people were saying to know what they were really like.

He had every excuse, perhaps, to fail to notice people and not to remember their names or faces, because as a national leader he was a very busy man. But he never forgot to acknowledge anybody – and this he did because it was in his nature to be like that.

His intellect was razor-sharp. It was thrilling to hear him talk on abstract concepts, ideologies, moralities, people and ordinary everyday happenings.

Someone once said: "With Steve there are no disappointments." There is no exaggeration in that statement. On the first meeting with him we were aware that we were talking to someone out of the ordinary, and with every subsequent meeting yet another aspect of his extraordinary mind and personality would be revealed.

He was a man of inviolate integrity and with an intuitive capacity for wisdom far beyond his years. His profound respect for human dignity precluded any leaning toward the undisciplined and superficial emotionalism of the revolutionary anarchist.

His awareness of his and his people's ideological position made him tough and very disciplined in his dealings with people, but this was offset by his personal gentleness and the warmth which came through in spite of his reserve.

He understood all people and the politics of power. He understood his enemy. He was no mere politician. He was a statesman the likes of which this country will not see for a long time.

Steve and I met many times, once when I visited him here in an East London jail, and in this country where crisis situations are continuously provoked, our friendship deepened.

Our association with him has changed our lives. We are honored to have been among the friends of a man born with unusual leadership qualities and an unrelenting dedication to the liberation of his people.

We loved him dearly and the pain of knowing that he is dead will not leave us for a long time.

A few days later, my syndicated column for that week, a column which appeared every Friday in six South African newspapers with a total readership of well over a million, read:

I have often written about Steve Biko in this column, in an attempt to acquaint as many South Africans as possible with the special qualities of this remarkable man whose close friendship I was privileged to experience for three years.

In a normal society in which he could have spoken and written freely, his unique greatness would have been acknowledged openly by the vast majority of our people. But the ministerial edict banning him meant that he could not speak publicly or be quoted, and consequently that a fairly large proportion of the population, the whites, knew little or nothing of him.

This was foolish of our political rulers in that they are ultimately the main losers thereby, because suppression of a moderate leader intensifies resistance to themselves in the deepest ways.

The Russians experienced this with Solzhenitsyn. They suppressed his words, but his ideas increasingly circulated among the people.

The Nationalists here have a similar misconception of the nature of what they are up against. Like the Kremlin, they think the enemy is words, and that if they prevent certain words being uttered by certain people they have won.

But their enemy is ideas. Thoughts, more than words. Words, after all, are merely the reflection of thoughts. The thoughts are the main thing, and you cannot legislate against thoughts. You cannot detain them or ban them or restrict them.

That is why the creed of our present rulers cannot survive in South Africa. The thoughts of too many are against them, and ultimately they themselves are far too few.

Steve has died in detention, and bitter though the grief is in this tragedy, its fruits will be the most bitter for those who might have believed his death would be to their benefit.

Mr. Vorster thunders out in ringing oratory at his party congresses that South Africa will soon be tested as never before. Wrong, Mr. Vorster. Not South Africa, but the tiny minority – the 10 percent or so who support the National party. Theirs will be the ultimate test, and they will fail it dismally.

One particular myth has led Vorster supporters in South Africa and Smith supporters in Rhodesia to a falsely optimistic evaluation of their chances. Each speaks as if he is a Churchill rallying the nation to its finest hour, promising not comfort but "blood, sweat, toil and tears." They seem to see the looming challenge as analogous to the image of Britain in 1939, girding to repel the invader.

But there is one massive difference. Churchill was rallying a united people behind him – all 50 million Britons, not a small proportion of them in the midst of a large anti-Churchill majority.

The insoluble problem of Mr. Vorster and Mr. Smith is that each represents ideas rejected by a large majority of his own countrymen.

And on top of this there are no international allies.

On the contrary, there is mounting international anger and hostility.

Mr. Vorster's situation is looking increasingly like a Paul Kruger situation, except that this time it is not a question of a small nation against the British Empire, but a small nation against the whole world – and most of its own citizens.

Again it is all because of thoughts. Thoughts that led to apartheid laws, to racist attitudes, to bulldozers flattening squatter shacks, to laws which permit detention without trial and thence to circumstances in which forty-five citizens die in such detention – twenty of them in the past eighteen months.

And these thoughts in turn are opposed by thoughts of indictment, resentment, bitterness and hate.

And a champion of reconciliation, moderation and peace lies dead in detention.

While his death seriously diminishes hopes for the peace he sought for the rest of us, we can only hope and believe his followers will pursue his goal with even stronger zeal.

Will nothing turn our rulers voluntarily away from their disastrous course? Are we really headed for the horrors of war?

These questions are no longer the problems of Steve Biko. He has died having done all he could to help his fellow men.

That is the best epitaph anyone could aspire to.

The first response from Police Minister Kruger was to imply that Steve had died of a hunger strike, but I remembered that Steve had once discussed with me his attitude toward detention. While he believed no harm would befall him in detention, he said that if he were to die in such circumstances I was to know that if it were claimed that he had died by any of four means, this would be a lie. The four were self-inflicted hanging, suffocation, bleeding (through, for example, slashed wrists) or starvation.

He had told me he would never take or endanger his own life while in detention. He was a survivalist, and knew from previous experience that he could take solitary confinement, long captivity or prolonged interrogation without cracking.

I set off the following day on a round of public speeches at large protest meetings in the major cities throughout the country, challenging Kruger's hunger strike theory and accusing him and his Security Police of being responsible for Steve's death. Wendy also hit the public protest speech trail, speaking at Rhodes University while I addressed a similar meeting at Cape Town University.

Steve's death coincided with the Transvaal congress of the Nationalist party, and Kruger, caught up in the spirit of party camaraderie, joined in the generally frivolous reception to the news at the congress. He said, basking in the tough-guy image which callousness confers on Nationalist spokesmen when party delegates are applauding them: "Biko's death leaves me cold." One party delegate from Springs, a certain Christoffel Venter, stood up among sniggers of appreciation to commend Minister Kruger's "democratic principles." Mr. Kruger, said Venter, was so democratic that he allowed detainees "the democratic right to starve themselves to death" if they so desired.

Mr. Kruger, preening himself before the giggling delegates, responded: "Mr. Venter is right. That is very democratic."

Kruger later tried to claim that he had been misquoted in the translation from Afrikaans to English. He claimed that the Afrikaans expression he had used – "*Dit laat my koud*" – did not mean: "It leaves me cold" but rather: "I am sorry, I am neutral about it."

This was but the first of a number of lies Kruger would tell about the death of Steve Biko. The Afrikaans expression *"Dit laat my koud"* means absolutely and utterly nothing other than literally: "It leaves me cold." In fact, Mr. Kruger had gone further. He had extended the bounds of his jocularity at the time. "One feels sorry about any death. I suppose I would feel sorry about my own death," he said. Typically, in seeking to repair the damage of his first statement, he made the damage worse.

As the heat of protest rose, Kruger started to back away from his hunger strike theory. "I didn't say that Biko died of a hunger strike," he said. But everyone knew that he had implied it in announcing that Biko had died "following a hunger strike." Indeed, Kruger had gone into detail in claiming that a number of doctors had examined Biko and found nothing wrong and that Biko had refused all food and drink made available to him.

Kruger made a series of swift appearances on national television at this stage. The first was to claim that Biko had been fed intravenously by drip. In announcing this, Kruger gestured vaguely at his arm, giving a coy impression of a bewildered layman dazzled by medical procedure. "I'm not a doctor," he said spuriously. As protests mounted, he reappeared on television to condition the faithful to an acceptance of the Biko killing, talking at length on the dangers of Black Consciousness to whites and claiming that Biko had been involved in plotting violence and in the drafting of pamphlets advocating violence. The Nationalist press dutifully echoed these smears, the Cape Town organ of the party, *Die Burger*, going so far as to print a prominent front-page headline: *"Lyke en bloed gevra in Biko-pamflet"* ("Bodies and blood called for in Biko pamphlet"). This headline so incensed me that I reported *Die Burger* to the South African Press Council, which after a full hearing in Johannesburg directed *Die Burger* to print a retraction, pointing out that the headline had not reflected fact but only Minister Kruger's claim.

The Nationalist press attacked me personally for addressing protest meetings, and accused me of "stirring up racial animosity against whites" over Steve's death. Then further facts came to my notice via sources close to persons who had attended the Biko post-mortem, and I pressed new charges against Minister Kruger. Would he confirm or deny that pathologists at the post-mortem had found evidence of brain damage? Mr. Kruger, for once, failed to respond.

I had reason at this stage to believe that he was personally displeased with me, to say the least. In fact, he had been for some time. After I had won my court appeal against the prison sentence arising from my ill-fated mission to get Steve's restrictions lifted, Kruger had fulminated against me in the presence of a man who later told me about the incident. Kruger complained that I had "abused his hospitality" at his home, had outstayed the amount of time I had asked for, and had thereby prevented him and his son from playing tennis as they had arranged. And to think, he added, that he had gone out of his way to drive me to my hotel.

After Kruger's early persistence with the hunger strike theory of Steve's death, I had publicly challenged him in these terms: if pathologists found that Steve had died of malnutrition or other result of a hunger strike, I would resign my job and undertake never to write another word for publication, provided that Kruger gave the undertaking that if pathologists found evidence that death was due to factors showing that his Security Police had deceived him, he (Kruger) would resign as minister and go out of public life for good in South Africa.

Kruger declined to respond to the challenge.

Wendy and I approached the funeral day with trepidation. It was being arranged by Malusi and other lieutenants of Steve's. Both of us knew that nothing would stop us from attending that funeral, but we thought it more than likely that we would be caught up in a sudden flare of anti-white feeling on the part of blacks from elsewhere in the country, whose anger and grief on that emotional occasion might know no bounds.

When the pathologists released Steve's body to the family to prepare for burial, I went with Ntsiki to the mortuary. The undertaker led us into a little lobby to what looked like a large double filing cabinet. He opened the top door of the refrigerated cabinet and slid out a long "drawer" on which lay Steve's body, covered with a sheet. I reached forward and uncovered the face.

What I saw was a gross caricature of his features. There was a large bump on the forehead, the features were distorted and the entire area above the nose and eyes was abnormally raised. Ntsiki sobbed quietly, whispering: "Oh, Steve! Oh, Steve!"

We both bent close to inspect the face carefully. It was not possible to know to what extent the altered features were due to the post-mortem operations when the scalp was opened to remove the brain.

Steve's eyes were open, and had a silvery, opaque sightlessness. The corpse was in no way revolting. That massive Biko dignity was still there – but what was striking was the total contrast between those animated features in life, and the flat emptiness of expression in death. Even the full lips had collapsed flat. There was certainly no sign of malnutrition – both Ntsiki and I noted how full and normal the body looked – but this was no surprise, because by this time even Kruger realized that the hunger strike theory was dismissed as nonsensical.

In spite of the fears Wendy and I had about the funeral, the five-hour-long interment ceremony went off without incident, and I was able to report in my syndicated column as follows:

Take a crowd of 20,000 blacks at the funeral of a well-loved leader who has died in detention, add to their sorrow a large measure of anger over the circumstances of his death, anger over certain callous remarks passed by a white politician about that death, anger over the stopping of many thousands of mourners from attending the funeral, anger over the general racial situation, and anger expressed in speeches of a highly emotional nature.

Add to all this several hundred whites personally unknown to any in this multitude – teenagers, students and others – and have them all intermingled in this vast black concourse. Predictably, in this land of racial tension, it requires but one stumble, one jostle, one tactless remark to touch off a tragic racial incident.

Yet no incident of the sort took place at the funeral of Steve Biko last weekend. Through five hours of ceremony and speechmaking by spokesmen of all those allegedly anti-white organizations such as SASO and BPC, not one single white there present was made to feel unwelcome or under direct threat by that emotional multitude.

Harsh and fiery words were said about the Nationalist government and individual ministers of it, especially Minister J. T. Kruger, and about apartheid, and about white racism, and about security laws and about 300 years of bigotry – but no single white, whether in the midst of the crowd or on the VIP podium, was touched other than in friendship. It was a kind of miracle. My wife and I were in the middle of the standing crowd and afterward compared notes about certain moments of apprehension. One came for me when I noticed what appeared to be a hard-bitten township tough-guy standing fairly close and looking at me with stony face through slitted eyes. He had a large knife scar on one cheek and appeared in my imagination to be sizing me up for a cutting job.

One is very conscious of one's whiteness on such occasions . . . However, when he became aware that I was looking back at him that rocklike face broke into a friendly smile and a nod of greeting. I have never been so relieved in my life!

Progressive personalities Helen Suzman, Alex Boraine and Zac de Beer arrived early, and a sea of blacks on one of the packed stands hurriedly made way to find a seat for Helen – but few of the other whites present were as well known. Most were young people, and probably most of them were conscious of the risk they ran.

I think what motivated many of the whites who attended, apart from natural motives of condolence, was a sort of act of faith in the kind of country South Africa could become, with people judged as human beings rather than as members of a race group. That certainly was a point made in many of the speeches. Admittedly it was a minor theme to the major theme of black activism, yet consistent throughout was the message that the end result envisaged is a nonracial, nonethnic society. I have long believed that South African blacks are simply not racist by inclination, and that to the extent that one can ever validly generalize, blacks do not seem as readily disposed toward racial bigotry as so many whites appear to be.

Which, in the circumstances, is also a kind of miracle.

Several whites who had been personal friends of Steve Biko were discernible in the crowd, notably Rev. David Russell and Dr. Francis Wilson, and all the major embassies were well represented, as well as all the major Christian churches. It was a fittingly sad and solemn occasion, but for my wife and me the greatest sadness after all the tributes and speeches were over was the journey home with the renewed realization that the Steve Biko we will miss most painfully is not the revered leader most of the masses will miss, not the young philosopher the academic visitors will miss, not the brilliant conversationalist the overseas journalists will miss, but the lovable friend who always made for the same chair in our house and whose inflexions of voice and gestures in lighting a cigarette and quaffing a beer and greeting a child and slouching for a chat are so vividly remembered.

I think he would say that the reason why there was no racial incident at his funeral is that the people were all known to be there in friendship; that they were intermingled – not standing in separate racial groups – and that just as hostility grows from separateness and isolation, so love grows from closeness and contact.

The total opposite of apartheid.

I AM BANNED

THE FOLLOWING WEEK I made my last prepared public speech in South Africa before being banned. The text of the speech suggests that I had expected to be banned, but in fact the fears of being silenced to which I had referred were in connection not with any formal State action against me but rather in connection with a large number of physical threats I and my family had been receiving from Security Police or right-wing cranks. In one day alone there had been five telephoned bomb threats. Here are some extracts from that speech, delivered at a large gathering on the campus of the University of Natal in Pietermaritzburg:

South Africa today is ruled by fear – the fear of the ruled and the fear of the rulers.

The rulers are fearful because they are a minority, and their fear is increasing because they perceive that the hatred of them by the majority is increasing.

As always, fear breeds hatred and hatred in turn breeds more fear. Increasingly, voices of warning are seen as voices of incitement. Voices of dissent are seen as voices of treachery and treason. Increasingly, moderation is being seen as extremism and the peacemakers are being portrayed as the advocates of violence.

South Africa today is heading for civil war, and we who warn of this endanger ourselves by doing so, because what we intend as a warning motivated by love of all our fellow citizens is seen as a kind of advocacy of the very thing we are trying to prevent.

The danger lies in actually speaking out aloud the things the people don't want to think about. The people hate such thoughts because they fear all the implications behind them. They would rather push the whole subject under into the depths of the subconscious and pretend that today's pleasant sunshine reflects the wishful reality.

Steve Biko foresaw violence and bloodshed in South Africa. Don't we all? He could see it looming ahead. Don't we all? But to suggest that he advocated it or desired it is a despicable lie. The main issue is that a key political figure in this country was detained in good health and within three weeks became the forty-fifth South African to die mysteriously in Security Police custody, and that it is the duty of all free men to question this mysterious death until those responsible have given adequate reply.

I am aware of the physical danger involved in calling for justice in the matter of Steve Biko's death. I am also aware that beyond certain sensible precautions nothing further can be done to minimize such danger, but I want to take this opportunity of saying this: if anything happens to people like myself to silence our voice in this matter, I ask the hundreds of thousands of South Africans who feel as we do to ensure that such a silencing would not succeed in diminishing the chorus of demands for justice but would rather add to it in volume and intensity.

It is highly unpleasant to live under threat, but circumstances have made this necessary at this time and there cannot be the remotest possibility of turning back. But, for the climate of hysteria and hatred that has created these dangers I blame this government and in particular Prime Minister Vorster and Justice and Police Minister Kruger as well as their lackey newspapers.

They are the ones who have not only created the conditions causing violent unrest but have on several occasions by their words lent encouragement to excesses by white extremists, who mysteriously have access to teargas canisters and unlisted telephone numbers. More than this, they have presided over a system of detention under whose dispensation helpless people can be seized, tortured and assaulted without ever having had access to lawyers or friends or family – access not even denied to a criminal. Yet the government can see no reason for a judicial inquiry into deaths in detention.

There are several reasons: the numerous complaints of torture in detention.

Whether or not Mr. Vorster regards these allegations as untrue, I can tell him that literally millions of South Africans believe that Security Police interrogation is often accompanied by torture, including torture by shocks with electrical apparatus and including beating up and tightening of material about necks until a point of near-suffocation is reached. It is also believed that that point has on occasion been exceeded – hence the number of alleged hangings in detention. Surely this matter is more important than several other matters that became the subject of inquiries.

If Mr. Vorster and Mr. Kruger want the Biko tragedy to stop harming this country's image, then several things must be done, and done quickly:

Prosecutions indicated as necessary by inquest evidence must be initiated as soon as possible thereafter.

A judicial commission of inquiry into all detainee deaths and all allegations of torture in detention must be set up as soon as possible.

Detention without trial must be stopped.

Minister Kruger must either resign or be sacked for his grossly inept and callous handling of the entire matter.

And let Nationalists stop trying to find scapegoats for black unrest. The unrest is not due to agitators, it is due to apartheid. They can lock up every single alleged agitator, but lasting peace will come to South Africa only when apartheid is scrapped.

Let me say this to all Nationalists: believe it or not, we, your open critics, do not wish to hate you. We wish to share this country with you as loved fellow citizens with a full appreciation of your culture and your identity. These need not be sacrificed.

But in God's name turn back from the madness of apartheid before it is too late, and honestly learn to see yourselves now as others see you. After thirty years in power you have succeeded in turning everyone against your policies – the blacks, the Indians, the Coloreds and many whites. You have succeeded in turning the whole continent of Africa against you, and indeed the whole world. Is everyone out of step but you? Are all Christian churches out of step but yours?

You pronounce yourselves ready to fight the whole world – yet not even the majority of your own citizens will be your allies in such a fight. It is not your known courage and your sterling qualities that are in dispute – it is your racism. It is your insistence that only you can decide what is good for most of us in this country. But this country isn't your house – it is a house you share with all of us, and the rights you are entitled to exercise in it are by no standard the dominant ones. Yet nobody wants to put you out. There is nobody who disputes your right to be here – there are only multimillions who dispute your right to be here *only on your terms.*

These are dangerous days, and I am saying here all the things I want to say while I can say them, and I am saying them in conscious fear of a number of terrible possibilities that may eventuate in this climate of excessive recrimination by the agents of hatred.

But these things must be said, because there is no fear that can outweigh the need for them to be said.

Shortly after this speech was delivered, the country was plunged into a general election campaign.

By this time Kruger had completely abandoned his hunger strike theory. In fact, he had said in an interview that if it came to light that the Security Police had acted improperly, "heads would roll." He seemed to be pre-preparing to ditch some lower ranks as scapegoats to clear his own sorry role in the tragedy.

Meanwhile a number of us in South Africa, friends of Steve's, journalists and concerned students as well as Progressive Federal party spokesmen, were worried that the government appeared to be stalling off the Biko inquest until after the election.

In the weeks preceding the inquest, government propagandists were hard at work to condition the public through the medium of the State-controlled radio and television service.

One example of this will suffice. In what is left of South African legal procedure, an inquest can only be held once a certain formality is complied with. That formality is a certificate by the attorney-general to the effect that no prosecution of any person for the death is envisaged. In other words, the attorney-general is saying: "I have no certain information which points to any specific person or persons as being responsible for this death, so hold an inquest and determine for me whom I should prosecute, if anyone."

The State propagandists seized on this avidly and sent out repeated "news" bulletins on radio and television in these terms: "The attorney-general has confirmed that no one is to be prosecuted for the death of Black Consciousness leader Steve Biko."

Not a word about the fact that this was a procedural formality. Not a word explaining that the next step was an inquest to determine who *should* be prosecuted.

The "news bulletin" was intended to convey the impression, and succeeded among many members of the South African public in creating the impression, that extensive investigation had cleared the Security Police of all blame even before the inquest, and that Steve's death was either an accident or suicide. There was even talk that there might not be an inquest.

We renewed our calls for an inquest to be held, and held soon. These calls, together with overseas reaction as reflected in the anti-Nationalist newspapers, might well have influenced the government to order the inquest before the end of the election campaign.

In the event, the election showed no evidence that the horrifying details which emerged from the inquest had cost the government any electoral support. On the contrary, the government gained a considerably increased majority and Kruger's own constituency gave him a massive endorsement.

But before the inquest began, a number of people who had been pressing for it to be held were banned or detained. Percy Qoboza was taken away by Security Police and his paper, *The World*, banned without explanation. Beyers Naude, Theo Kotze, David Russell, Cedric Mayson, Brian Brown and I were banned, and Malusi Mpumlwana, Thenjiwe Mtintso, Kenny Rachidi and other BPC officials were detained.

On that day, October 19, Percy and I had been due to fly to America for a conference at Williamsburg, Virginia, of the African-American Institute. The Security Police took Percy earlier that day, and came for me at the airport. I had been on the point of passing through passport control at the airport when three men approached me.

"Mr. Woods?" said one in English. "We are from Security Police head-quarters in Pretoria. You won't be leaving on that plane – please come with us."

In a small office near passport control they handed me three batches of documents signed by the Minister of Police, J. T. Kruger, banning me under terms of the Internal Security Act. The banning orders confined me to the magisterial district of East London, prohibited me from writing or publishing anything and from entering any newspaper or publishing house or school or other educational premises, forbade me to be with more than one person at a time other than my wife and children, and ordered me to report to the local police station in East London once a week. The ban was for five years.

"Kruger has really gone mad, hasn't he?" I said. They were non-committal.

They explained that they were under orders to drive me back to East London immediately, and two of them drove me as far as Winburg, in the Orange Free State, where they handed me over to three other Security Police officers who drove me from Winburg to Aliwal North. From here two more drove me to Queenstown, and from there two more drove me to East London. The trip took twelve hours. During the trip I asked many questions about deaths in detention but received no satisfactory replies.

On reaching East London we went straight to the Security Police offices there, where Colonel J. van der Merwe told me of the implications of the ban. "My men are keen to catch you breaking the ban," he added. "There is nothing they would like more. We know what goes on, believe me, and will come in at any time to your house."

I was then taken to my house and left on the doorstep with my suitcase.

Settling down to a new way of life under the ban, I had to accept that because of it I would not be able to attend the inquest proceedings, which were due to begin on November 14. We made plans for Wendy to attend the inquest throughout, and to phone me regularly to give a description of each day's proceedings.

In one sense it was all academic. We no longer had access to the person we would most have wanted to discuss the inquest with. But it was necessary to take the utmost notice of the inquest. Horrible though the evidence would be, this was our final association with the physical Steve Biko, and we had to involve ourselves as fully as possible in noting down every discernible detail of his last days of life.

5: THE INQUEST
THE SCENE

ON MONDAY, NOVEMBER 14, 1977, the inquest into the death of Steve Biko began in Pretoria. It was conducted in the Old Synagogue building, formerly Pretoria's chief synagogue but long used as a courtroom. The world's press was represented, as was every major South African newspaper.

The chief irony for me was that because of my ban I was prevented from attending the very inquest I had so vigorously demanded, and that the ban had obviously been imposed because of the actions I had taken to publicize the need for a public inquest. So I had to stay at home waiting to receive the reports of others – a frustrating experience which was, however, alleviated by Wendy's detailed and perceptive descriptions of what was going on far away in that Pretoria courtroom. She was present throughout the proceedings, and the following is her description of that inquest and her reaction to the atmosphere that prevailed.

WHEN WE WATCH synthetic drama we suspend disbelief so that when we see something shocking we are willing to go with it and to submit to whatever manipulation the creator of the drama has in store for us. Synthetic drama is always larger than life, however well done, understated or tasteful it is.

Real drama, on the other hand, is a different experience. Real drama is marked by a sense of the mundane. There is no sign of suspension of disbelief. We see and hear things and our senses send all the right messages to the brain, but it turns them away because they are too bizarre for admittance.

For me this was the experience of the inquest. It took three weeks for the story of a killing to unfold. And during that time a strange sense of ordinariness overlaid the painful and shocking facts which came out. On the very first day we heard about leg irons and then we actually saw them. They were brought into court and we heard the chains clanking and saw the heavy rings of iron which rubbed Steve's ankles until they bled. We saw Major Snyman, in the witness stand at the time, look at them quite comfortably as if they were standard office equipment. And we didn't really believe it. Leg irons belong in Madame Tussaud's, Hollywood film sets, horror comicbooks – not in this confusion in which I am sitting, with people shuffling and coughing, with the jeans that I am wearing and which I have worn many times in Steve's company. At this stage I am not at times entirely convinced that Steve is dead and that we are all sitting here because of his death. I feel someone is going to pop his head around the doorway, smile and announce cheerfully that it has all been a good joke but it has gone far enough, and wave us all out of the courtroom.

And then on that same day we heard that Steve had been kept naked in his cell for several days. We heard that when visited by a magistrate who asked him if he had any complaints, he asked for water and soap, a washcloth and a comb and said: "Is it compulsory to be kept naked? I am naked since I have been here."

Again the blocking out process played havoc with this information. Steve drank beer, smoked cigarettes, got in and out of cars and told people what to do. He could never have been in a position which would have caused him to utter those words.

We all knew that the Security Police had killed Steve and that they would concoct a story to match the brain injuries, so the varying accounts of the alleged scuffle did not surprise us. What we were not prepared for were the admissions by Security Police that Steve had been kept at different times naked and in chains – admissions delivered from the witness stand with bureaucratic smugness and with a veneer of the defensiveness of a civil servant who admits that he has filched a dozen ballpoint pens from the office.

In retrospect I suppose this was the shock: that throughout the inquest we were subjected to fact after fact and we had to piece together for ourselves a cohesive story and hang on to it, knowing that the truth was there in the minds of these people, knowing that we would never hear it from them, and, knowing that, hearing them deliver their evidence with all the self-containment of men who know that the System will never let them down.

The Old Synagogue is a gracious building right in the center of Pretoria. Inside there are "pews" for the "congregation" – about two hundred people. Up front are two rows reserved for the press. The holy place has been transformed into elevated thrones for whatever judicial presences preside, with the usual accommodation for legal counsel, court stenographer and the witness. The only remaining trace of religious mysticism was a green and pink light which reflected on different people's faces during the day, as the sun moved over a stained-glass window in the center of the ceiling.

There was a sense of expectation on that first day. Outside television cameras were being jostled into position on shoulders, young short-back-and-sides policemen in their blue uniforms walked about, looking worldly wise and with obvious signs of fed-into and repeated-at-length instructions of "what-to-do-in-case-of." They might have been objects of derision but for the guns they wore.

The Biko family arrived – all dressed in black – wife, mother, sister, brother, silhouetted continuously in the white light of many cameras. They sat submissively and with dignity until the cameras had had their fill, and then relaxed and became people again. The newspaper people stood or walked to and from areas of the courtroom with deceptive familiarity. But really nobody knew who was who, and it was a considerable time before we all settled into one group with at least one common purpose – to hear or participate in another day's evidence.

As the inquest wore on we all got to know each other. Personalities revealed themselves. Empathies and animosities formed. A palpable sense of "we" and "they" developed. "We" were the Biko family and friends, blacks, sympathetic whites, counsel for the family, the South African English-language press, the world press, members of pressure groups. "They" were the Security Police, the doctors, counsel for the police, counsel for the doctors, counsel for the prisons, the magistrate, the policemen inside and outside the courtroom, the interpreters and the informers. The magistrate's two assessors were in a limbo yet to be assigned to either group.

An atmosphere of muted warfare prevailed in the courtroom. It was obvious that the Security Police had been told to reply only in Afrikaans to make it as difficult as possible for the international press to get the day's evidence. After every question put to them they would carefully turn their faces away from the public and obsequiously reply to the magistrate, mechanically prefacing each answer in Afrikaans with "Your honor." The fact that it was the correct thing to do anyway (the court stenographer had to get it down, and after all the magistrate did have to hear) made their unctuous satisfaction more obvious.

The courtroom acoustics were abominable. Not only was most of the evidence in Afrikaans, but it was inaudible Afrikaans. There was no public address system. The proceedings sounded like a private conversation at the end of the room. The State showed no sign of any awareness of responsibility to the public, any sense that this was a public inquest and that the public's right to hear was in fact a right and not a privilege to be scrabbled for. A petition signed by the press to pay for the installation of its own public address system was turned down by the magistrate on the grounds that it would interfere with the microphones for the court record.

The court policemen, ostensibly there to keep order, were actually there to embarrass the odd black who was dozing, by pointing at him or her and making a big show of beckoning and paternal scolding, but not, if noticed, to do the same for the white court interpreter who huddled into himself under the witness stand and dropped off from time to time, or for one white dignitary who was lullabied into a comatose state by a sustained onslaught of specialist jargon during the medical evidence. The court policemen also enjoyed telling the press and public to keep back behind certain courtroom gates strategically placed to keep people just out of earshot.

Every day for about an hour before the court adjourned, blacks would start congregating on the pavements outside the Old Synagogue. The numbers would slowly increase, and by the time people started emerging from the building, they would be jammed shoulder to shoulder, and would start singing songs of freedom and defiance. This would last for about twenty minutes while white policemen stood tensely by, staring at them with unconcealed dislike, and German shepherd dogs barked with vicious anticipation from inside their minute cages in police vans.

The inquest provided a new experience for South Africans. We got a chance to get a good long look at Security Policemen. Millions of people could read what they had to say at the receiving end of interrogation and could see pictures of them in the papers. We at the inquest could see their faces, could watch their demeanor under cross-examination and could hear their words – their version of the story. For the first time, these men, products and inheritors of the Afrikaner Nationalist tradition, were flushed out of their police stations and their little interrogating rooms. For once they were in the position of having to account for themselves.

These men displayed symptoms of extreme insularity. They are people whose upbringing has impressed upon them the divine right to retain power, and in that sense they are innocent men – incapable of thinking or acting differently. On top of that they have gravitated to an occupation which has given them all the scope they need to express their rigid personalities. They have been protected for years by the laws of the country.

They have been able to carry out all their imaginative torture practices quite undisturbed in cells and rooms all over the country, with tacit official sanction, and they have been given tremendous status by the government as the men who "protect the State from subversion." To all this, add the sort of personalities which enjoy inflicting pain on their fellow humans, and we see that they are men with diminished responsibility, victims of a collective mutated psyche, and – with the power they wield – very dangerous people.

The doctors who dealt with Steve are, to a lesser extent, products of white South African society. Although not consciously cruel, they are men whose consciences have been so drastically warped by their society that they are capable, through their negligence, of committing acts of extreme inhumanity. They were obviously not aware that they were acting in that way. Dr. Lang knew about the leg irons, but he did not appear at all shocked by their existence. I suppose he had seen them many times on other people. It also became apparent from all three doctors' testimony that casual and minimal treatment of black prisoners was normal to them, and that they were used to deferring at any time to Colonel Goosen's demands, in spite of the fact that these were in direct conflict with their patients' welfare.

As the days went by we realized that there were not going to be any major breakthroughs. The Security Police had their story, and in spite of all the holes Mr. Sidney Kentridge (appearing for the Biko family) picked in it, exposing both Security Police and doctors as liars, there was not much expectation of any blame being officially attached to anyone.

But in retrospect I now realize that, in spite of logical acceptance, there remained illogical hope. Experience had shown that we should not expect much from legal decisions in political trials in South Africa. But there must have been hope, because the betrayal of that hope showed on people's faces after Mr. Prins, the magistrate, took one minute to announce that Steve had died of head injuries, probably sustained during a scuffle.

What follows is a record of the inquest proceedings based on the notes taken by Wendy; by Roger Omond of the *Daily Dispatch*; by Helen Zille of the *Rand Daily Mail*; and on the detailed reports which appeared in both these newspapers.

THE THIRTEEN DAYS

THE MAJOR PARTICIPANTS in the inquest into the death of Steve Biko were as follows:

MR. MARTHINUS PRINS – Presiding Magistrate
PROFESSOR JOHANNES OLIVIER – Assessor on the Bench
DR. ISIDOR GORDON – Assessor on the Bench
MR. SIDNEY KENTRIDGE – Barrister for the Biko family
MR. GEORGE BIZOS – Barrister for the Biko family
MR. ERNEST WENTZEL – Barrister for the Biko family
MR. SHUN CHETTY – Briefing Attorney for the Biko family
MR. K. VON LIERES – Deputy Attorney General of the Transvaal
MR. RETIEF VAN ROOYEN – Barrister for the Police
MR. J. M. C. SMIT – Barrister for the Police
MR. W. H. HEATH – Barrister for the Prison Department
MR. B. DE V. PICKARD – Barrister for the doctors appearing
DR. MARQUARD DE VILLIERS – Barrister for the doctors appearing

The major witnesses called to give evidence were, in order of appearance:

LIEUTENANT G. KUHN – Police (Port Elizabeth)
SERGEANT P. J. VAN VUUREN – Security Police (Grahamstown)
MAJOR H. SNYMAN – Security Police (Port Elizabeth)
WARRANT OFFICER R. MARX – Security Police (Port Elizabeth)
CAPTAIN D. SIEBERT – Security Police (Port Elizabeth)
MAJOR R. HANSEN – Security Police (King William's Town)
COLONEL P. J. GOOSEN – Security Police (Port Elizabeth)
MR. J. FITCHET – Warder at Port Elizabeth Prison
LIEUTENANT W. E. WILKEN – Security Police (Port Elizabeth)
DR. I. LANG – a District Surgeon in Port Elizabeth
DR. B. TUCKER – Chief District Surgeon in Port Elizabeth
DR. C. HERSCH – Specialist Physician in Port Elizabeth
PROFESSOR J. LOUBSER – Chief State Pathologist in Pretoria
PROFESSOR N. PROCTOR – Professor of Anatomical Pathology,
     Witwatersrand University
DR. A. VAN ZYL – District Surgeon in Pretoria
DR. J. GLUCKMAN – Pathologist for the Biko family

PROFESSOR I. SIMSON – Head of Department of Anatomical Pathology,
     Pretoria University
WARRANT OFFICER J. BENEKE – Security Police (Grahamstown)

Day One: Monday, November 14, 1977
The proceedings began with the tabling of the autopsy report by Chief State
Pathologist Dr. J. D. Loubser. Dr. Loubser's report stated categorically that
Steve Biko had died of "extensive brain injury" resulting in centralization of the
blood circulation to such an extent that there had been intravasal blood coagula-
tion, acute kidney failure and uremia. The report also mentioned abrasion to the
left forehead, injuries to the chest wall and other "numerous but superficial"
injuries.

Leading evidence for the State was the Deputy Attorney General of the Transvaal, Mr. Klaus von Lieres. He read out a statement by Lieutenant Alfred
Oosthuizen of the Security Police at Grahamstown. The lieutenant said in his
statement that on August 18 he received information that inflammatory pamphlets were being distributed – pamphlets inciting blacks to cause riots. He learned
also that Mr. Biko was on his way from King William's Town to Cape Town
and he had reason to suspect Mr. Biko was actively concerned.
     At 8 P.M. he put up a roadblock, and at 10.20 P.M. a white station wagon
stopped. He asked the driver to unlock the trunk, but he was unable to do so,
saying first that he could not because the car belonged to his firm, then that he
could not because it belonged to a friend. Because of these differing explanations, the lieutenant asked the driver to identify himself. The driver and his
passenger were both "cheeky," and the driver asked the lieutenant in a belittling
manner if that was normal procedure. He identified himself as Peter Jones, and
the passenger as Bantu Biko. They would not give further details, and Lieutenant
Oosthuizen decided to take them to the charge office. There he asked Mr. Biko
if he had permission to be outside King William's Town district, to which he
was confined. Mr. Biko said he had no written permission and he could do as he
liked. Mr. Biko laughed at him, and in doing so fell on a bench, which broke.
     Lieutenant Oosthuizen tried to search Mr. Biko and Mr. Jones, the statement
said, but they refused to allow him to, and Mr. Biko grabbed his hands. Finally
he searched them. Mr. Biko wanted to take his private possessions with him to
the cell, but this was not permitted. According to the statement, Lieutenant
Oosthuizen then got in touch with his commanding officer, who told him to take
the two men to Port Elizabeth. This was done the next day.
     Mr. von Lieres also read a statement by Major Andries Michiel Kuhn, of
Grahamstown. He said he had been in charge at the roadblock when the station
wagon was stopped, and later was in the charge office when Mr. Biko and Mr.
Jones were searched.

Lieutenant Gert Kuhn was then called to the stand and read out three statements he had made. In the first, dated October 20, 1977, the lieutenant gave a list of the times when he had visited Mr. Biko in his cell. The first visit was at 8.10 A.M. on August 22, 1977, and he named others on September 8, 9, and 10. In the first statement he said he saw no injuries on Mr. Biko, and had no knowledge of any incident when Mr. Biko could have been injured. The second statement, dated October 18, 1977, concerned a visit to Mr. Biko's cell with a police photographer, when positions pointed out to him were photographed. In the third statement, made on November 9, 1977, the lieutenant changed his first statement. He repeated the list of visits to Mr. Biko's cell, but left out the dates September 8, 9 and 10. He said he had not been told by other policemen that Mr. Biko would not eat, or that he had complained. Lieutenant Kuhn also said that he had never received complaints from Mr. Biko. He did see him lying under a blanket without clothes, but he could not say in what manner Mr. Biko was walking in that period.

Questioned by Mr. Kentridge, Lieutenant Kuhn said he spoke to Mr. Biko in English. He said he knew, when he made his first affidavit, giving the times of visits to Mr. Biko, that it would be required for inquest proceedings. Lieutenant Kuhn said he saw no injuries on Mr. Biko, and in particular had not seen the bruise on the left side of Mr. Biko's forehead which appeared on a photograph handed to him. The lieutenant told the court his statement concerning the times of his visits to Mr. Biko was not false, "just faulty." It was rectified in a later statement. He said the reason for the "mistake" was that when he prepared to make his affidavit he found that the station commander had already made an extract from the record book of the times of his visits to the cells. He inserted these times into the affidavit without checking them. He knew his evidence would be used to show that on those dates there was nothing wrong with Mr. Biko. Lieutenant Kuhn said that he had not seen Mr. Biko after September 6. He realized that the dates in his affidavit were incorrect only when his attention was drawn to this by Mr. von Lieres in consultation. He said he made his statements when General Kleinhaus visited Port Elizabeth to investigate the affair. The general questioned everyone who had had anything to do with Mr. Biko. The statements were made on duplicate forms, but he did not know who duplicated them. They were not brought by the general when he came.

Sergeant Paul Janse van Vuuren then gave evidence. He had visited Mr. Biko daily from August 18 to September 6, and again on September 11, but Mr. Biko never complained. His impression was that Mr. Biko did not want to speak. He gave Mr. Biko meals of soup, magewu, bread, margarine, jam and coffee. Mr. Biko refused the soup and magewu, and the bread heaped up, he said. The prisoner did not ask for any other food. On September 11 he saw in his registers that Mr. Biko, who had been removed from Walmer police station, Port Elizabeth, on September 6, had been returned.

That evening he visited cell number 5, where Mr. Biko was kept, and he seemed to be asleep on his mats. Later he found Mr. Biko on the cement floor with his head toward the cell bars and his feet near the mats. Sergeant van Vuuren said that to get into the cell one had to go through four locked doors. He could not say if Mr. Biko had fallen or crawled to that position. Mr. Biko was lying on his right side looking at the door. There was froth on his mouth and his eyes were glazed. Sergeant van Vuuren said he tried to give him water, but he stayed in the same position. He dragged Mr. Biko to the mats, covered him with blankets, and called the Security Police.

Major Fischer, Colonel Goosen and Dr. Tucker arrived and removed Mr. Biko from the cell.

In a second statement, Sergeant van Vuuren said he pointed out to a police photographer the position in which he found Mr. Biko on the last occasion. On October 20 he made a third statement to General Kleinhaus on a duplicated form, on which particulars were added in ink. He gave a list of visits to Mr. Biko's cell at all hours of the day and night and up to six visits on one duty stretch. He said he saw no injuries on Mr. Biko, in particular not a bruise on Mr. Biko's forehead appearing in the photograph shown to him. Mr. Biko's skin color was much darker than shown on the photograph, he told the court.

In a fourth typed statement read to the court, Sergeant van Vuuren said that Mr. Biko had never spoken to him – he never answered his questions and never showed any reaction when his food was put down in his cell. Mr. Biko ignored him. He left the soup and magewu in the cell, and when it was still there at the next visit he gave it to other prisoners. The coffee mug was usually empty, the sergeant said. He could never tell if Mr. Biko had eaten some of the bread. There was a small possibility that he had. When he found Mr. Biko lying on the cement floor on September 11 he took hold of him under his arms from the back and dragged him to his sleeping mats. Mr. Prins, the magistrate, commented: "Like a lifesaver."

Questioned by Mr. Kentridge, Sergeant van Vuuren said he received orders that Mr. Biko should be kept naked in the cell. Mr. Kentridge then read to the court a report by a magistrate who saw Mr. Biko at the Walmer police cells on September 2 and who said that Mr. Biko had asked for water and soap to wash himself and a washcloth and a comb. According to the magistrate's statement, Mr. Biko said: "I want to be allowed to buy food. I live on bread only here. Is it compulsory that I have to be naked? I have been naked since I came here." Mr. Kentridge asked if Mr. Biko was kept naked in order to humiliate him.

"I cannot say," replied Sergeant van Vuuren. He then confirmed that from August 18 to September 6, Mr. Biko was not allowed out of his cell.

"Isn't a prisoner entitled to exercise in the open air?" asked Mr. Kentridge.

Sergeant van Vuuren said he was acting on instructions from the head of the Security Police in Port Elizabeth, Colonel P. Goosen. He confirmed that when he saw Mr. Biko on September 11 – the day before he died – he had frothed about the mouth, his eyes appeared glassy, and his breathing was hurried. At 6.20 P.M. Sergeant van Vuuren booked Mr. Biko out of the Walmer police station. He did not know where he was taken.

The next witness, Major Harold Snyman of the Security Police in Port Elizabeth, said he was the leader of an investigation team of five appointed to interrogate "the Black Power detainees." Mr. Biko had been detained on August 19, but for strategic purposes others were interrogated first. On September 6 it was decided that Mr. Biko could be confronted with certain evidence. He was taken to office 619 in the Sanlam Building in Port Elizabeth. The interrogation began at 10.30 A.M. and lasted till 6 P.M.

Major Snyman said Mr. Biko had adopted an extremely aggressive attitude toward members of the interrogation team. To make him feel at ease, his handcuffs were removed and he was offered a chair to sit on. During the day Mr. Biko was offered meat pies and milk, which he refused. It was strange, said Major Snyman, that he did not use the toilet. Major Snyman said Mr. Biko evaded questions concerning his visit to Cape Town. He would not answer questions directly, but as the interrogation went on he was more cooperative. Among other things, he said that he had gone to Cape Town to escape his marital problems. Later he said his sole purpose in going was to heal a breach which had arisen in the Black People's Convention.

Asked about the distribution of pamphlets in Port Elizabeth on August 17, Mr. Biko admitted that he and Mr. Patrick Titi, another detainee, were responsible for compiling the pamphlet.

Mr. Kentridge questioned the major about the methods used during the seven-and-a-half hours of interrogation to change Mr. Biko's attitude from one of "extreme aggressiveness" to an admission of involvement in the compiling of pamphlets and other matters. Mr. Kentridge: "What method of persuasion did you use to make an unwilling witness talk to you? That morning Mr. Biko denied all knowledge of a certain pamphlet, and by 6 P.M. he had admitted to drawing it up. What methods of persuasion did you use?" Major Snyman answered that Mr. Biko was confronted with certain evidence the Security Police had, then he admitted it.

Mr. Kentridge: "He first denied it and then admitted it. Why should he answer you at all. Why shouldn't he just whistle at you? . . . Did you make threats?" Major Snyman denied making threats or putting physical pressure on Mr. Biko.

Mr. Kentridge: "How did you break him down?" Major Snyman said he had unlimited time to get the information, and it would not have paid the police to assault Mr. Biko for information. He told Mr. Biko that he would remain in detention until he answered the questions satisfactorily.

Mr. Kentridge said Mr. Biko was detained in 1976 for 101 days. "What sort of a threat do you think it would be to threaten to keep him in detention unless he answered questions? What can you do to a man who insists on keeping silent?" Mr. Kentridge repeated this question several times as Major Snyman outlined the subjects about which Mr. Biko was interrogated. Mr. Kentridge then said to the major: "You are evading my questions. At the beginning he (Biko) gave a denial. Later on he gave proper information. How do you get him from the first stage to the second stage?"

Here Mr. Kentridge was interrupted by Mr. R. van Rooyen, appearing for the South African Police, who said Major Snyman had replied that Mr. Biko admitted his involvement after being confronted with evidence from other sources.

Major Snyman, in his statement concerning events the next day when interrogation resumed, told of a violent struggle between his investigation team and Mr. Biko. Major Snyman said that shortly after Mr. Biko had his leg irons and handcuffs removed, and was offered a chair to sit on, he got a wild expression in his eyes suddenly and jumped off the chair. Mr. Biko threw the chair at Major Snyman, but he jumped out of the way. After this, Mr. Biko charged at Warrant Officer J. Beneke, lashed out wildly at him and pinned him against a steel cabinet. Major Snyman said he and Captain Siebert went to Warrant Officer Beneke's help. They tried to grab Mr. Biko, who was "clearly beside himself with fury." In the process they knocked against the tables in the office.

Two other members of the team came to assist. They overpowered Mr. Biko, and put handcuffs and leg irons on him. The struggle lasted several minutes, though Major Snyman could not say how long exactly. Mr. Biko was fastened to the grille in the office but continued to struggle against his handcuffs and leg irons. "Warrant Officer Beneke told me he got a terrible bump on the right elbow," said Major Snyman.

At 7.30 that morning Major Snyman reported the incident to Colonel Goosen. They both visited Mr. Biko in office 619. Colonel Goosen spoke to Mr. Biko, who, Major Snyman said, still had a wild expression in his eyes, and a visible swelling on his upper lip. He was talking incoherently and in a slurred manner. Mr. Biko refused to react to questions and the wild expression remained in his eyes. At 9.30 the district surgeon, Dr. Lang, gave him a medical check-up. Major Snyman was not present. After the investigation, Major Snyman said, he and the team tried to communicate with Mr. Biko but he would not react to questions. He then gave orders that Mr. Biko was to be allowed to rest on his mat and to be covered with a blanket. He was still handcuffed and the leg irons were tied to the grille. He was offered water repeatedly but mumbled refusal. Mr. Biko was passed into the custody of a night team under Lieutenant Wilken.

The next morning, September 8, Major Snyman and his team returned to find Mr. Biko still lying on the floor. He was awake, but would not react to questions, and there was no point in the investigation continuing. Major Snyman was aware that on the day before Dr. Lang had found nothing physically wrong with Mr. Biko. A medical certificate to this effect had been handed to Colonel Goosen. When he saw that Mr. Biko was still refusing to answer questions, he reported the incident of the struggle in an "occurrence book."

Major Snyman said he was aware that Colonel Goosen called Dr. Lang again on September 8. He learnt that Mr. Biko was taken to the prison hospital on September 8, and that on September 11 he was moved to the Walmer police cells. He was present on September 11 at 6.20 P.M. when Mr. Biko left for Pretoria with Captain Siebert and other members of the police force. He learnt that Mr. Biko had died in Pretoria.

Major Snyman said the amount of violence used on Mr. Biko on September 7 to get him under control was "reasonable, and only as much as was necessary to pin him down on the floor and handcuff him." Questioning the major on this aspect, Mr. Kentridge asked if he had heard the hunger strike statement by Mr. J. T. Kruger (Minister of Justice, Police and Prisons).

MAJOR SNYMAN: I remember it.

MR. KENTRIDGE: How did you feel when you heard that Mr. Biko had died?

MAJOR SNYMAN: I felt bad about it. He was worth more to us alive than dead.

MR. KENTRIDGE: Is that why you were sorry?

MAJOR SNYMAN: I also had sympathy with the death.

MR. KENTRIDGE: Were you surprised he had died?

MAJOR SNYMAN: I was surprised. We did not think there was so much wrong with him as . . .

MR. KENTRIDGE: As what?

Major Snyman replied that they had a doctor's certificate that there was nothing physically wrong with Mr. Biko.

Mr. Kentridge then asked Major Snyman about the minister of police's statement to the National Party congress in Pretoria that Mr. Biko had asked for 15 minutes to consider whether he would answer police questions, and then told them he would go on a hunger strike. He asked whether Major Snyman had given any information concerning this to the minister. Major Snyman replied: "I reported to my commander. He took it further."

Mr. Kentridge then handed in an affidavit by a Mrs. Ilona Kleinschmidt, containing statements by the minister of police on the death in detention of Mr. Biko. Commenting on the relevance of the evidence, Mr. Kentridge said: "The minister has said a number of things which are in serious conflict with the evidence that appeared from the affidavits of the police officers that have been filed. Consequently, this material may turn out to be of considerable importance in testing the credibility of certain police officers. The point is that, if these affidavits are correct, then certain statements made by the minister cannot be correct. We cannot say which are correct. It will certainly be necessary for certain police officers to explain the discrepancies."

In another statement, Major Snyman said he was told that the post-mortem examination had revealed that Mr. Biko died as a result of an injury which caused brain damage. Major-General Kleinhaus conducted the investigation to find out how Mr. Biko received the injuries. Major Snyman made a statement that at no stage had he noticed a mark on Mr. Biko's forehead, and could not say how it occurred. Mr. Biko was not assaulted by anyone while he was present, Major Snyman said in his statement on October 20.

Mr. Kentridge asked why Mr. Biko was kept naked in the Walmer police cells. Major Snyman said he had acted on instructions given to prevent the recurrence of suicide in police cells. Mr. Kentridge then commented that the prisoner was left naked but with a blanket and said: "People have commited suicide with their blankets."

Major Snyman said they had no experience of this in the Walmer cells.

Mr. Kentridge then asked why it had been necessary to put Mr. Biko in leg irons on the 6th when he showed no sign of violence before the morning of the 7th. Major Snyman said the office was not locked.

MR. KENTRIDGE: Could you not have locked it? I think you will have to give a better answer. Why did you put him in leg irons? Was it to break the man down, or only to prevent escape?

MAJOR SNYMAN: It was the custom.

(Adjournment)

Day Two: Tuesday, November 14, 1977

Major Snyman told the court that Mr. Biko had fallen, hitting his head against a wall, during the scuffle with the five security interrogators about which he had testified the previous day. Major Snyman had said when he reported for duty on the following morning, September 8, he had noticed that Mr. Biko's speech was still slurred. He was also aware that a doctor had been summoned.

MR. KENTRIDGE: When you found that he had not recovered you decided to cover yourself by writing down what happened in the occurrence book. Yet you did not regard it as necessary to make an entry in the occurrence book on the 7th. Did you think he was shamming?

MAJOR SNYMAN: I had no reason to think he was suffering from anything serious.

MR. KENTRIDGE: What made you change your mind between the 7th and the 8th?

MAJOR SNYMAN: Because he stubbornly refused to answer.

MR. KENTRIDGE: But that was exactly the same on the 7th.

MAJOR SNYMAN: I made a verbal report to my commanding officer, Colonel Goosen, before I made the entry in the occurrence book.

MR. KENTRIDGE: In your entry you said, among other things, that he went berserk, that he threw a chair at you and that after a struggle he fell with his head against the wall. Which wall did he knock his head against?

MAJOR SNYMAN: Against the northern wall.

MR. KENTRIDGE: Was it between the cabinet and the chair on which he had been sitting?

MAJOR SYNMAN: That is correct.

MR. KENTRIDGE: What part of his head hit the wall?

MAJOR SNYMAN: The back of his head, he fell several times.

MR. KENTRIDGE: Did you report to Colonel Goosen that he fell with his head against the wall?

MAJOR SNYMAN: Yes, I did.

MR. KENTRIDGE: Were all five of you in the room when he fell with his head against the wall?

MAJOR SNYMAN: Correct.

MR. KENTRIDGE: Yet Colonel Goosen did not tell the doctor that he fell with his head against the wall. He only said he feared Mr. Biko might have had a stroke.

MAJOR SNYMAN: I do not know what Colonel Goosen reported to the doctor.

MR. KENTRIDGE: There were 28 affidavits made in connection with the incident and in no one of them is mention made of Mr. Biko falling with his head against a wall.

Mr. Kentridge asked Major Snyman whether Major-General Kleinhaus, when he went to Port Elizabeth for his investigation, had told him (Major Snyman) that Mr. Biko died as a result of a brain injury and had drawn his attention to an injury on Mr. Biko's left forehead.

MAJOR SNYMAN: That is correct.

MR. KENTRIDGE: You were then invited to add anything you thought necessary in your affidavit, but in that affidavit you did not mention that he fell with his head against the wall?

MAJOR SNYMAN: I did not regard it as necessary.

MR. KENTRIDGE: You say in your affidavit that nobody assaulted Mr. Biko in your presence.

MAJOR SNYMAN: That is correct.

MR. KENTRIDGE: Did General Kleinhaus question you about the bump on his head?

MAJOR SNYMAN: General Kleinhaus asked us and we demonstrated to him how it happened.

MR. KENTRIDGE: Did you demonstrate to General Kleinhaus how Mr. Biko fell with his head against the wall?

MAJOR SNYMAN: I explained to the general how the struggle had taken place, where we all fell and how such a thing could possibly have happened.

MR KENTRIDGE: Did you specifically tell the general and point out to him that Mr. Biko bumped his head?

MAJOR SNYMAN: Yes.

MR. KENTRIDGE: I suggest that answer is false. General Kleinhaus took a number of affidavits from your men and not in one of them is it mentioned that Mr. Biko fell with his head against a wall. When police photographs were taken of your office were you asked to point out the place on the wall?

MAJOR SNYMAN: No.

MR. KENTRIDGE: I submit you did not think Mr. Biko would die and that you made the entry in the occurrence book in case there was to be a court case.

(Major Snyman's reply was inaudible.)

MR. KENTRIDGE: When Colonel Goosen saw Mr. Biko he already showed symptoms indicative of brain damage. I suggest the probability is that by 7.30 A.M. on September 7 he had already suffered brain damage.

MAJOR SNYMAN: Mr. Biko did not complain of a headache or ask to see a doctor.

MR. KENTRIDGE: I suggest the brain injury was probably suffered between the evening of the 6th and the morning of the 7th.

MAJOR SNYMAN: I deny it.

MR. KENTRIDGE: Then I suggest he sustained it in your presence.

MAJOR SNYMAN: The only injury I saw on Mr. Biko was a mark on his lip.

MR. KENTRIDGE: Before the post-mortem results were out we had statements by the minister of police about hunger strikes and so on, but nothing about his head bumped against a wall. Did you not think it your specific duty to tell your superiors that he bumped his head against the wall?

The magistrate, Mr. Prins, at this stage interrupted and asked Major Snyman whether he had actually seen Mr. Biko bumping his head against the wall or whether it was a deduction he made from what had happened.

MAJOR SNYMAN: Yes, I could not observe it myself because I was involved in the struggle.

MR. PRINS: The possibility therefore exists that he did not bump his head against the wall?

MAJOR SNYMAN: That is so.

MR. KENTRIDGE: Yet in the occurrence book you said he fell with his head against the wall. I submit that no value can be placed on your statement.

MAJOR SNYMAN: I think he must have sustained the injury after the last time I saw him on September 8.

Earlier, Major Snyman denied they had kept Mr. Biko in their offices to prevent word leaking out about how Mr. Biko had been treated. He said Mr. Biko was a violent revolutionary who had gone berserk when he realized he had been betrayed by his friends. Major Snyman said Mr. Biko had been told immediately before he went berserk at the Special Branch offices in Port Elizabeth that the police knew of his plans and activities. The plans included the formation of a united revolutionary front of the Black People's Convention and the banned African National Congress and Pan-Africanist Congress. This body would have had terrorist branches both within South Africa and overseas, Major Snyman said. Trained men would have been brought into the country for the armed overthrow of the government.

Police had affidavits showing Mr. Biko's involvement in the drafting and distribution of a subversive and revolutionary pamphlet in black Port Elizabeth townships on August 17, Major Snyman said he had confronted Mr. Biko with statements by his friends, whose handwriting he knew, testifying to Mr. Biko's involvement in subversive activities. Mr. Biko had been told that the police knew he had not gone to Cape Town as he claimed, to get away from marital problems, or because of a breach in the Black People's Convention. "I put it to him . . . that the primary purpose was actually to contact Neville Alexander and others of the Unity Movement. There were discussions on the establishment of a revolutionary front with ANC and the PAC, which are terrorist organizations, the Unity Movement of South Africa and the BPC. I further put it that we had information that plans had already been made for him (Mr. Biko) to go overseas so that these four organizations could come together in a united front. I put it to him that he had had discussions with Robert Sobukwe, the president of the PAC, who is restricted."

Major Snyman said he had told Mr. Biko that, should Mr. Biko himself not be able to go abroad, his place would be taken by someone who would represent him and go under cover of studying theology in England. This confrontation had followed Mr. Biko's admission the previous evening that he had been involved in the drafting of a subversive pamphlet.

Mr. Biko had also been questioned about Mr. Donald Woods, the editor of the *Daily Dispatch*, Major Snyman said. Mr. Woods had written an article about the establishment of a new organization, the Azania Liberation Front, and Mr. Biko had been asked if he had had discussions with Mr. Woods.

Major Snyman said that, when he was told what the police knew, "a look" had come into Mr. Biko's eyes. "He immediately jumped up like a man possessed, grabbed the chair and threw it at me. I attribute this to the facts with which we confronted him that morning." Major Snyman said he could not give a detailed description of the violent struggle in which first three policemen, then five, had tried to bring Mr. Biko under control. He had not before seen the bruise on Mr. Biko's forehead shown in a photograph of the body. All he had noticed after the struggle was a bruise on Mr. Biko's upper lip and a scratch on his chest.

Asked what reaction he would have expected from a man confronted with evidence against him as Mr. Biko had been, Major Snyman said a number of things had counted against Mr. Biko that morning. There were possible charges he could face in connection with breaking the conditions of his banning order. He had been connected with a revolutionary pamphlet, and connected with the establishment of a new revolutionary front. His own people had left him in the lurch and his public image would have been seriously damaged had he been sentenced.

Questioned by Mr. van Rooyen about Mr. Biko's public image, Major Snyman first said Mr. Biko definitely did not have the image of a peaceful person, but presented himself as a revolutionary. The Port Elizabeth pamphlet called on the people to stay away from work the following day and to wear black or a black item in sympathy with those who had died or were exiled or jailed.

Mr. Kentridge said there was no evidence that Mr. Biko had compiled the pamphlet. He would not contest its admissibility at this stage, but might argue later on its relevance. The pamphlet was then read out in full by Major Snyman.

Mr. Kentridge then stated: "Having looked at this pamphlet, it would appear that it has no relevance to this case at all. It is in dispute whether Mr. Biko made a confession about this. The only man who could tell us about this is no longer with us. It is not the case that if a man writes a subversive pamphlet one is free to kill him. I can understand there has been an effort to find Mr. Biko guilty post-mortem, but I am sure Your Worship will not be a party to this."

Questioned by Mr. van Rooyen, Major Snyman said the evidence in the hands of the Security Police would destroy Mr. Biko's image as a peace-loving man and betray him as a violent person. Asked if he had anything that would prove to the world that Mr. Biko's image was false, Major Snyman replied that he had a newspaper cutting from the East London *Daily Dispatch* of an article written by Mr. Donald Woods about the merging of a new front under the name "Azania Liberation Front." He also had statements "from his (Biko's) own friends, the people who worked with him."

MR. VAN ROOYEN: It would then have been clear to him that his friends had left him in the lurch?

MAJOR SNYMAN: We had to confront the man with facts. He had to know that his friends had spoken and we wanted to hear the words from his own mouth.

MR. VAN ROOYEN: You were there, why did he go berserk?

MAJOR SNYMAN: I confronted him with these facts. He jumped up immediately like a man possessed. I ascribe that to the revelations that I made to him.

Mr. van Rooyen then asked permission to hand in the pamphlet and the statements by other detainees as evidence. Mr. Kentridge said he had just read the documents and would withdraw his objections. He said he understood the sworn statements put to Mr. Biko were part of the reason for his outburst.

Mr. Kentridge then asked whether these sworn statements were put to Mr. Biko on September 6 or on the morning of September 7. Major Snyman replied that it was the morning of the 7th. Mr. Kentridge then checked with the magistrate that the dates on the affidavits ranged from September 15 to September 30, and said that the statements would not have been put to Mr. Biko during his lifetime. "What we have got here is a smear prepared after Biko's death."

Mr. van Rooyen said it was the contents of the documents that had been put to Mr. Biko. Mr. Kentridge replied that it had been made clear and confirmed that the actual sworn affidavits were put to Mr. Biko. He called on the witness to put it beyond doubt.

The magistrate then ruled that the statements would not be permitted in evidence and Mr. van Rooyen agreed.

When asked by Mr. van Rooyen about the struggle between Mr. Biko and the five policemen, Major Snyman repeated his previous day's account and added that at one stage Mr. Biko had shouted: "You people are harassing me, you are intimidating me." Mr. van Rooyen asked if Mr. Biko had hit the back of his head against the wall. "Yes, the back of his head," Major Snyman replied.

Warrant Officer Ruben Marx, another member of the interrogation team, was the next witness. In his first statement he said that at about 7.20 A.M. on September 7, as a result of a hard bang, he and Detective-Sergeant Nieuwoudt, who had been working in the room next door, charged into the interrogation room. There he saw Major Snyman, Captain Siebert and Warrant Officer Beneke struggling with Mr. Biko, who was "raving with fury." Questioned by Mr. von Lieres, Warrant Officer Marx gave a graphic description of the struggle with Mr. Biko: Detective-Sergeant Nieuwoudt charged Mr. Biko and his shoulder hit Mr. Biko in the middle of his back. Mr. Biko then fell to the floor but jumped up and continued struggling. Then he fell over a chair and landed in a sitting position in the chair. Then Mr. Biko jumped up and screamed: "You are harassing me and you are intimidating me." He was furious and raving. Mr. Biko was then pinned down and handcuffed.

Examining him, Mr. Kentridge referred to the words: "You are harassing me, you are intimidating me."

Mr. Kentridge: This morning Major Snyman used those same words. Do you know that?

Warrant Officer Marx: I don't know anything about this.

Mr. Kentridge: Eleven statements have been made about what happened in that room on the morning of the 7th. In not one of these statements is there anything about Mr. Biko shouting out, and now this morning for the first time we have the exact same words from you and Major Snyman. I put it to you that this is an invention.

Warrant Officer Marx: It is not a fabrication.

Mr. Kentridge then drew Warrant Officer Marx's attention to an entry in the occurrence book on September 8 in which Major Snyman had reported the struggle on the 7th during which Mr. Biko fell with his head against a wall and his body on the ground and in the process suffered an injury to his lip and body.

Mr. Kentridge: Is that true?

Warrant Officer Marx: I know of an injury to his upper lip.

Mr. Kentridge: I am asking you whether the statement by Major Snyman is true or not.

Warrant Officer Marx: I didn't see him hit his head against the wall.

In a second statement of October 10 – an unsworn statement – Warrant Officer Marx said he had not noticed any mark or wound above Mr. Biko's left eye as was shown on photographs. Mr. Kentridge asked whether he was interested in what caused the death.

Warrant Officer Marx: I guessed. I am not a doctor . . . possibly as a result of the skirmish we had. That was a possibility, there was a heavy struggle.

Mr. Kentridge: As a result of a skirmish you had? What gave you that idea?

Warrant Officer Marx: In that skirmish any reasonable person can believe that he may have got an injury.

Mr. Kentridge: Really? Did you tell that to General Kleinhaus?

Warrant Officer Marx: Questions were put to me and I answered them.

Mr. Kentridge: Did you put this theory of yours to General Kleinhaus?

Warrant Officer Marx: I answered his questions and he didn't ask me to elaborate.

Mr. Kentridge: Didn't you think the scuffle was one of the reasons why he was not behaving in a normal manner when the doctors came to see him in Port Elizabeth?

Warrant Officer Marx: I didn't have much to do with him.

Mr. Kentridge: He fell twice. Did you see him fall on his head?

Warrant Officer Marx: No.

The next witness to take the stand was Major R. Hansen from King William's Town. Mr. Kentridge asked that the court keep to the schedule for witnesses and call Captain D. Siebert, who was also involved in the scuffle with Mr. Biko. The magistrate upheld the ruling and Captain Siebert was called.

Captain Siebert handed two statements to the court, one dated September 17 and the other October 10. In his first statements, Captain Siebert repeated the details contained in the other statements. In his second statement he said he had not seen the mark on Mr. Biko's left forehead, but it was "not impossible that this injury could have been sustained when they were forced to overpower him on September 7." On September 8 Mr. Biko was able to walk normally without help, Captain Siebert said.

Addressing the court after Captain Siebert's evidence, Mr. Kentridge said: "I note with great surprise that my learned friend Mr. von Lieres (who led the evidence) has not chosen to take this witness through a full description of what happened in that office as he did the last witness. May I ask Your Worship to note the fact." Questioning Captain Siebert on the interrogation of Mr. Biko before the scuffle, Mr. Kentridge mentioned words allegedly used by Mr. Biko that he was being intimidated and harassed. Captain Siebert said Mr. Biko made that claim before the struggle broke out.

Captain Siebert confirmed the evidence of a previous witness that no documents had been shown to Mr. Biko during that interrogation.

He said Mr. Biko had fallen twice – the first time in the area of the chair in which he had been sitting and the second time face-down near the bed. When Mr. Kentridge questioned him on Major Snyman's entry in the occurrence book, Captain Siebert said he did not know the entry had been made. Mr. Kentridge read the entry to him, and asked him if it was true. Captain Siebert replied that it was not impossible that he had bumped his head against the wall.

MR. KENTRIDGE: Did you see him fall with his head against the wall?
CAPTAIN SIEBERT: No.

(Adjornment)

Day Three: Wednesday, November 16, 1977

Continuing the cross-examination of Captain Siebert, Mr. Kentridge asked him whether he had heard anyone tell his commanding officer (Colonel Goosen) that Mr. Biko had bumped his head against a wall during interrogation in Port Elizabeth on the morning of September 7.

CAPTAIN SIEBERT: I cannot remember.
MR. KENTRIDGE: You did not tell Colonel Goosen yourself that he had bumped his head?
CAPTAIN SIEBERT: It is a possibility.
MR. KENTRIDGE: You could have, but did you?
CAPTAIN SIEBERT: No, I cannot say that I did.

Captain Siebert said he did not mention to the investigating officer, Major-General Kleinhaus, that Biko had fallen twice during the interrogation because he stood by the statement he had made earlier to Colonel Goosen. In the statement to General Kleinhaus he had only replied to questions put to him.

On the morning of September 11, he and certain other officers had been told to take Mr. Biko to the Pretoria prison in a Land Rover for medical treatment.

CAPTAIN SIEBERT: I was told that as the doctors could not find anything wrong with him and the local hospitals did not have the necessary facilities, he had to be taken to Pretoria for observation and investigation.

MR. KENTRIDGE: Why was he not taken in an ambulance?

CAPTAIN SIEBERT: They tried to make arrangements for an aircraft to fly him to Pretoria, but no aircraft was available. Therefore the Land Rover was used.

MR. KENTRIDGE: Was the purpose that nobody outside your service could have access to this person?

CAPTAIN SIEBERT: No. He was seen by various doctors and in my opinion they would not have given permission for him to be transported if his condition did not allow it.

(Mr. Biko was put in the back of the Land Rover and lay on some cell mats.)

MR. KENTRIDGE: What was he wearing?

CAPTAIN SIEBERT: He was naked.

In reply to further questions, Captain Siebert said he understood Mr. Biko was in a half berserk state. In the limited space of the Land Rover, it would have been even more difficult to control him than it had been in the interrogation room.

MR. KENTRIDGE: Did considerations of common humanity not count with you?

CAPTAIN SIEBERT: Yes, I think so.

MR. KENTRIDGE: According to Colonel Bothma (of the Prisons Department in Pretoria) you told him Mr. Biko had studied medicine for four years, that he practiced yoga and that it was easy for him to mislead other people. Did you say that?

CAPTAIN SIEBERT: I could have said it.

MR. KENTRIDGE: Why did you take it upon yourself to tell Colonel Botha this?

CAPTAIN SIEBERT: I don't believe I said it was easy for him to mislead other people.

Captain Siebert said that he personally had believed Mr. Biko was shamming, but that he no longer thought so.

MR. KENTRIDGE: Another prison officer, Colonel Dorfling, made a statement that you told him Mr. Biko had been on hunger strike.

CkPTAIN SIEBERT: I said I saw him refuse to eat.

MR. KENTRIDGE: Colonel Botha also said you told him Mr. Biko had not eaten since his arrest.

CAPTAIN SIEBERT: I deny that. I only saw Mr. Biko for the first time on the 6th of September.

MR. KENTRIDGE: Colonel Dorfling also said you told him Mr. Biko was a medical student and that he practiced yoga. He understood that to mean Mr. Biko could pretend that he was sick.

CAPTAIN SIEBERT: He was examined by two doctors who could find nothing wrong.

MR. KENTRIDGE: I want to know why you went out of your way to tell the two colonels that Biko was shamming?

Captain Siebert's reply was inaudible.

Asked whether he had told Colonel Dorfling that Mr. Biko was an aggressive type of person and that before he went on a hunger strike he had struck a major with a chair, Captain Siebert replied: "I said he threw a chair at him. As far as the hunger strike is concerned, I think the colonel is making a mistake." Captain Siebert said when he handed Mr. Biko over to the prison authorities in Pretoria his condition had not changed from the previous night.

MR. KENTRIDGE: According to the medical orderly who took Mr. Biko over from you, Sergeant Pretorius, he looked seriously ill and he feared for his life. The medical orderly was correct, wasn't he?

CAPTAIN SIEBERT: If one looks at it now, yes.

MR. KENTRIDGE: The medical orderly also said one of the security men told him Mr. Biko studied medicine and yoga. What was the purpose of that – to put the medical men off the scent?

CAPTAIN SIEBERT: There was no purpose behind it.

In reply to further questions, Captain Siebert said in his view Mr. Biko had feigned illness to prevent further interrogation.

A King William's Town Security Police officer then described how Mr. Biko had slapped another Security Police officer who was questioning him. The officer, Major Richard Hansen, said he had known Mr. Biko since early 1975. Mr. Biko had often complained that the Security Police harassed him and other members of the "Black Power" organizations.

On August 31, 1976, Mr. Biko was arrested at the home of Mrs. E. Mtintso, and detained for questioning. Major Hansen described an incident which took place during this: "On our arrival at the security offices in King William's Town, I instructed Warrant Officer Hattingh to get the personal particulars while I reported the arrest. After a while Warrant Officer Hattingh came to me and told me that Mr. Biko was adopting a cheeky attitude and refused to provide the information required. I accompanied Warrant Officer Hattingh to the office where Mr. Biko was. I told Mr. Biko not to be childish and to give the particulars. When Warrant Officer Hattingh put a question to him he sprang past me and gave Warrant Officer Hattingh a heavy smack with his open right hand against the left cheek and also hit at Warrant Officer Hattingh with his clenched fist. Warrant Officer Hattingh warded off the blow and I grabbed Mr. Biko from behind. In the process I asked him what he was doing. He suddenly calmed down and said: 'Sorry, captain, I lost my temper.' "

Asked by Mr. Kentridge whether Warrant Officer Hattingh had done anything to provoke Mr. Biko, Major Hansen said not as far as he knew. Asked whether Warrant Officer Hattingh had laid a charge of assault against Mr. Biko, Major Hansen said he had advised Warrant Officer Hattingh not to lay a charge of assault at that stage because certain allegations concerning the editor of the *Daily Dispatch*, Mr. Donald Woods, and Mr. Biko were being investigated. Mr. Kentridge asked if it was not because he (Hattingh) would have been cross-examined? Major Hansen said it was not.

Major Hansen then said he had made a statement and an affidavit after Mr. Biko's death about the incidents in King William's Town because he was asked to.

MR. KENTRIDGE: Did they ask you to describe the assault by Mr. Biko on Mr. Hattingh? Did they say they wanted it?

MAJOR HANSEN: Yes, but they didn't say why they wanted it. I was asked to describe his personality in the affidavit.

MR. KENTRIDGE: Mr. Biko was held in detention for 101 days and afterward no charge was laid. Do you know about that?

MAJOR HANSEN: I know that he was held, possibly for that time. No charges were laid.

Colonel P. J. Goosen, the head of the Eastern Cape Security Police, was the next witness. He said the Security Police, on the strength of the information they had, regarded Mr. Biko as nothing else than a terrorist leader in South Africa. Elaborating on an affidavit which he made on September 17, Colonel Goosen said· "At about 7.30 A.M. on September 9 Major Snyman reported to me that Mr. Biko had become very aggressive and had thrown a chair at him and had attacked Warrant Officer Beneke with his fists. A measure of force had to be used to subdue him so that he could be handcuffed again. I immediately visited Mr. Biko. He was sitting on the sleeping mat with his hands handcuffed and the leg irons fixed to an iron grille. I noticed a swelling on his upper lip. There was a wild expression in his eyes. I talked to him but he ignored me."

Colonel Goosen then immediately tried to get hold of the district surgeon, Dr. Lang, by telephone. After several other phonecalls he left a message for Dr. Lang who phoned him back later that morning. At about 9.30 A.M. Dr. Lang arrived at his office. Colonel Goosen continued: "I gave him a short sketch of Mr. Biko's personal background and asked him to examine the detainee. After Dr. Lang's examination he issued me with a certificate which read as follows: 'This is to testify that I have examined Steve Biko as a result of a request from Colonel Goosen of the Security Police who complains that the above-mentioned would not speak. I have found no evidence of any abnormality or pathology on the detainee. Signed: Dr. Lang. Time: 10.10 A.M., September 7, 1977.'"

As a result of a report from Major Fischer, who headed a second interrogation team, at 9.15 P.M. on September 7 he again visited Mr. Biko, Colonel Goosen said. "I spoke to Mr. Biko. As before, he mumbled incoherently. At this stage I was honestly of the opinion that Mr. Biko was playing the fool with us as neither the district surgeon nor I could detect any scars or signs of illness. While I was in the office, I again asked whether Mr. Biko had partaken of any food or drink. It was reported to me that he flatly refused to eat or drink. On the morning of September 8, on arriving at my office, I immediately visited Mr. Biko. He was lying on the cell mats. I spoke to him. He mumbled. I immediately telephoned Dr. Lang and asked him to come and examine Mr. Biko again as he did not react to our questions. At about 12.55 P.M., the chief district surgeon, Dr. Tucker, and Dr. Lang reported to my office. I made a brief report to them on Mr. Biko's condition and again expressed concern because he did not eat or drink. Both doctors then examined Mr. Biko in my absence. After the examination I was informed by Dr. Tucker that neither of them could find anything physically wrong with Mr. Biko. Dr. Tucker suggested Mr. Biko be taken to a place where there were better facilities for a proper examination and that a specialist's opinion be obtained." (Arrangements were then made to take Mr. Biko to a prison hospital where he could be examined by a specialist, Dr. Hersch. Later that evening Mr. Biko was examined by Dr. Hersch and Dr. Lang.)

"After the examination Dr. Hersch informed me that he, like Dr. Lang and Dr. Tucker before him, could find nothing physically wrong with Mr. Biko. It was then agreed that Mr. Biko should be kept in the prison hospital for observation and that further tests, including a lumbar puncture, should be performed on him by Dr. Hersch on the morning of September 9. On September 9 Dr. Lang informed me by telephone that the lumbar puncture had been performed and that he would like to keep Mr. Biko in the hospital block for further observation. On September 11 Dr. Lang informed me by telephone that neither he, nor Dr. Tucker nor Dr. Hersch could find anything physically wrong with Mr. Biko and that I could remove him for further detention in the police cells of Walmer. The necessary arrangements were made with Major Fischer. At about 2 P.M. on September 11 Major Fischer asked me by telephone to come to the Walmer police station, where a report was made to me. I visited Mr. Biko in his cell. He was lying on his cell mats and his breathing was reasonably irregular. A little foam could be seen around his lips. I immediately telephoned Dr. Tucker and asked him to come and examine Mr. Biko. Dr. Tucker examined Mr. Biko at 3.20 P.M. Both of us expressed concern, because the nature of any possible illness could not be diagnosed. It was mutually agreed to transfer Mr. Biko to an institution with all possible facilities for a proper medical examination. I informed Brigadier Zietsman of Security Police headquarters in Pretoria telephonically of the state of affairs. Instruction was received to transfer Mr. Biko to the central prison in Pretoria. However, I first had to ascertain whether any military aircraft were available. If not, I had to use road transport if the chief district surgeon had no objection.

"No military or other flights were available. I consulted Dr. Tucker, who had no objection to Mr. Biko being transferred to Pretoria by road provided we let him lie on a mattress or something soft. Brigadier Zietsman was again informed telephonically and the necessary arrangements were made for Captain Siebert, Lieutenant Wilken, Warrant Officer Fouche and Sergeant Nieuwoudt to transport Mr. Biko in this office's comfortable Land Rover to Pretoria as speedily as possible. At about 6.30 P.M. on September 11, Captain Siebert informed me telephonically that they were departing for Pretoria with Mr. Biko. Everything possible was done by me to ensure the comfort and health of Mr. Biko while in detention."

Mr. Biko had been held in chains and kept naked in police cells to prevent him from committing suicide or escaping, said Colonel Goosen. "What right have you to keep a man in chains for 48 hours or more?" Mr. Kentridge asked. Colonel Goosen said that as divisional commander he had authority to do so to a man detained under Section 6 of the Terrorism Act to prevent him committing suicide or injuring himself.

MR. KENTRIDGE: Where do you get your authority from? Show me a piece of paper that gives you the right to keep a man in chains – or are you people above the law?

COLONEL GOOSEN: We have full authority. It is left to my sound discretion.

MR. KENTRIDGE: Under what statutory authority?

COLONEL GOOSEN: We don't work under statutory authority.

MR. KENTRIDGE: You don't work under statutory authority? Thanks very much, Colonel, that's what we have always suspected.

Mr. Kentridge asked why Mr. Biko had been kept chained in the Security Police offices on the night of September 6 instead of being sent back to the Walmer police station cells. Colonel Goosen said there were adequate sleeping and toilet facilities at the offices, Mr. Biko might try to escape, and if he were transported there might be attempts to free him. Colonel Goosen added that Mr. Biko had been kept in chains because not all the offices had burglar-proofing.

MR. KENTRIDGE: Would you keep a dog chained up in this way for 48 hours? I want to know what sort of man you are.

COLONEL GOOSEN: If I regarded him as absolutely dangerous, I would have done so.

MR. KENTRIDGE: We have been told Mr. Biko was kept naked at the police cells at Walmer. Can you confirm that? It has also been said this was by your order.

COLONEL GOOSEN: That is so.

Asked about fears that detainees would use clothing to commit suicide by hanging, Colonel Goosen said there had been two examples recently of detainees hanging themselves by tearing up shirts and other articles of clothing.

MR. KENTRIDGE: Is there any reason why, for decency's sake, a man should have no underpants?

COLONEL GOOSEN: For a specific reason. It is to eliminate suicide.

MR. KENTRIDGE: Have you ever had a man commit suicide with strips torn from his blankets?

COLONEL GOOSEN: In twenty-three years I do not think I have had one occasion where that has happened. Blankets have been used for escapes.

Colonel Goosen said he was unaware of Special Branch allegations that men had hanged themselves with their blankets, and could not comment on whether he believed this was possible. The magistrate, Mr. Prins, then said: "The question is whether you ever thought it was possible for a man to commit suicide with a blanket." Colonel Goosen replied: "I have never thought about it." Asked whether he had given orders that Mr. Biko be kept naked in the prison hospital, Colonel Goosen said he could not remember giving such an order. Asked if he would accept that Mr. Biko had clothing at the prison hospital, Colonel Goosen said he was aware Mr. Biko had pajamas, among other items.

Colonel Goosen said that police investigations had connected Mr. Biko with the drafting, typing, duplicating and distribution of a subversive pamphlet distributed in Port Elizabeth black townships on the night of August 17. "Had he lived, serious criminal charges would most definitely have been laid against the deceased."

Colonel Goosen put forward the theory that Mr. Biko had sustained his fatal head injury while in Port Elizabeth prison hospital on September 8 or 9. He was aware that Mr. Biko had been found in the bath twice and on the floor in front of his bed there. He said: "If one takes into account that these incidents took place during the night of September 8 or 9, I wish to express the serious supicion that the deceased possibly sustained the wound on his forehead and brain damage at the time of these incidents. The deceased was apparently determined on self-destruction, even with his method of breathing during his detention."

Colonel Goosen also said that Mr. Biko had deliberately breathed in an un-natural way, later observed and diagnosed by Dr. Lang as hyperventilation. This method, used by deep-sea divers to get as much oxygen as possible, could be dangerous, leading to light-headedness and even death, he had read in medical books. "This fact and the fact that the deceased was found in his clothes in a full bath of water in the prison in an apparent attempt at suicide could have resulted in his hitting his head hard, for example, against the bath, causing the brain damage," Colonel Goosen said.

(Adjournment)

Day Four: Thursday, November 17, 1977

The cross-examination of Colonel Goosen continued. Mr. Kentridge said he had understood that during the time Mr. Biko had been in the Walmer police cells he had not been allowed any exercise on the instructions of Colonel Goosen. Colonel Goosen replied that he was being wrongly interpreted. Mr. Biko had been alone in a cell and as such had had enough fresh air and could get enough exercise, he said. He admitted that Mr. Biko had not been allowed out of the cell.

Mr. Kentridge said that according to the warrant under which Mr. Biko had been detained certain special provisions had been made that nobody should be allowed to visit him, that he should receive no food from outside and that he should receive no reading matter. The warrant also specified that Mr. Biko should be treated as an awaiting-trial prisoner, he said.

According to prison regulations prisoners who did no work outdoors should be allowed one hour's exercise in the open air whenever the weather permitted, Mr. Kentridge said. Colonel Goosen said the reason for his instruction was to prevent Mr. Biko communicating with anybody outside. Mr. Kentridge asked him: "What right did you have to override a standing instruction?" Mr. van Rooyen, for the police, objected saying that the questions had nothing to do with the cause of death but were part of a "vendetta" against the Security Police. The inquest should not be used as a platform for propaganda against the Security

Police. Its only purpose was to investigate if anybody could be blamed for Mr. Biko's death. "While the whole world knows what is going on in this room, this goes a bit far," he said.

Mr. M. J. Prins, the presiding magistrate, said that the state of mind of Mr. Biko during his detention was a relevant matter. It was also relevant that a certain state of mind could have been brought about and could have triggered Mr. Biko's emotions.

Mr. van Rooyen said a question of whether Mr. Biko was allowed to exercise in the open air was relevant, but, when Colonel Goosen was asked if his instructions had been against standing orders, or whether anything had been written in an occurrence book, this had nothing to do with Mr. Biko's state of mind and should not be allowed.

Mr. Kentridge said: "I don't think Your Worship has heard any criticism of the Security Police except for those in Port Elizabeth or those who were concerned with Mr. Biko. I would have expected the police to have disassociated themselves from these members." His questioning was all part of showing that there was a process of breaking Mr. Biko down by keeping him naked and by keeping him in his cell. His questions about the use of chains, the failure to allow Mr. Biko to exercise and the failure to enter occurrences in the occurrence book were meant to show that the Security Police showed, in their treatment of Mr. Biko, no concern for legality and did not consider themselves bound by regulations. He was not concerned with what Colonel Goosen did with other prisoners, only with showing that in this instance he had paid no attention to ordinary legality. A number of police witnesses had testified that there had been nothing untoward in their treatment of Mr. Biko. The magistrate would have to decide what sort of men he was dealing with.

Mr. Kentridge then referred to Colonel Goosen's affidavit in which he said that Dr. Tucker (the chief district surgeon of Port Elizabeth) came to his office to examine Mr. Biko on September 8. The colonel had said that he had told the doctors of his supicions. Mr. Kentridge wanted to know what these had been.

COLONEL GOOSEN: I told them of my suspicions because Mr. Biko had not taken food or liquid. We had here a man who would not react or talk and who used no toilet facilities. This had been unnatural behavior. I was not satisfied that his behavior was that of a normal person. I still thought he was shamming. I had had experience before with this tendency.

MR. KENTRIDGE: Do you think it shamming if a man does not go to the toilet for three days?

COLONEL GOOSEN: He did not take any liquid. I thought perhaps the need was not so great. I am just a layman. This man was in my care. He was my responsibility.

Colonel Goosen said he had never told the doctors that he thought Mr. Biko was shamming. He had called Dr. Lang and Dr. Lang arrived with Dr. Tucker because he had thought it necessary to get a second opinion. He might have told Dr. Tucker that he was afraid Mr. Biko might have suffered a stroke, Colonel

Goosen said. After the doctor's examination, the colonel said, he was still convinced that Mr. Biko was shamming illness. Later on he was not satisfied. He was in two minds about it and wanted to make one hundred percent sure. On the 8th he knew there had been a violent struggle but did not know for certain what injuries could have been incurred.

MR. KENTRIDGE: Were you worried that Mr. Biko had had a head injury?

COLONEL GOOSEN: At that stage I paid no attention to it. I did not know for certain. I always had to consider the probability.

MR. KENTRIDGE: Why did you not mention this to the doctors? Did you have any certainty that he had suffered a stroke? You told the doctors you were worried about a stroke but never that you were worried about head injury.

(Colonel Goosen said that the possibility that Mr. Biko's speech was impaired had made him think that Mr. Biko had suffered a stroke.)

MR. KENTRIDGE: My submission will be that you knew Mr. Biko might have suffered a head injury but wanted to draw the doctors' attention away from it.

COLONEL GOOSEN: That is not so.

Colonel Goosen said that when the doctors arrived Mr. Biko was still shackled hand and foot. After they had left he was again shackled.)

MR. KENTRIDGE: Do you accept that at that time he had had a brain injury?

COLONEL GOOSEN: I now know it to be possible.

MR. KENTRIDGE: I will submit that a man with a brain injury was left lying in chains for 48 hours.

COLONEL GOOSEN: If I had known at the time that he had a brain injury I would not.

MR. KENTRIDGE: On your own admission you did not know what was wrong with Mr. Biko, yet he was left lying on the mat.

COLONEL GOOSEN: The medical doctors could find nothing wrong.

MR. KENTRIDGE: That is not quite true. Dr. Tucker was sufficiently worried to recommend that Mr. Biko should be sent to the prison hospital to be examined by a specialist. In spite of that you left him lying on the mat.

COLONEL GOOSEN: I was responsible for the man's safety. I had reason to believe he was shamming. Therefore, I had to keep him like that.

MR. KENTRIDGE: There is a good precedent for your behavior. I understand that in the eighteenth century this was exactly how they treated mental patients.

Mr. van Rooyen then rose and said that this was the sort of comment which hit the headlines and which should not be allowed.

Mr. Kentridge replied: "We make no secret of the fact that we will submit that Mr. Biko was treated with the utmost callousness. If Mr. Biko had been properly treated he might not have died at all." Mr. Prins intervened. Mr. Biko might not have had a head injury at the time, he said. Mr. Kentridge then said he would leave out this sort of comment until he addressed the court.

He put it to Colonel Goosen that from the morning of September 7 until Mr. Biko left the care of the Security Police he had received not so much as a dab of ointment for his swollen lip. Colonel Goosen answered that when he handed

Mr. Biko to the prison department he was no longer under his control and the prison regulations then applied to him, except that a special request was made that Mr. Biko should be kept in isolation while in hospital. While Mr. Biko was his responsibility two doctors saw him, and it had been their prerogative to prescribe medicine.

Mr. Kentridge than pointed out that in fact Dr. Lang had noticed on the 7th that Mr. Biko's ankles were swollen. Colonel Goosen answered that he himself had seen marks on Mr. Biko's wrists and ankles. This was not unnatural. Mr. Biko had strained against his chains like a madman only a few hours before, he said. Colonel Goosen said that he still believed that he did everything possible for the comfort of Mr. Biko while he was in detention.

"Mr. Biko went to the Port Elizabeth prison on the evening of the 8th only after dark. You gave certain specific instructions to Colonel Bothma, the prison commander," Mr. Kentridge said. Colonel Goosen replied that he had briefly sketched the background to Colonel Bothma. He had asked Colonel Bothma to keep Mr. Biko for observation and to see to it that he did not communicate with other prisoners. Mr. Kentridge then quoted Colonel Bothma as having said that Colonel Goosen gave him instructions for Mr. Biko to be guarded only by white members of the police force. He asked Colonel Goosen if he did not trust the black members of the force. The colonel answered that this was one of his standing instructions in all these cases of detention. Black policemen were not always available. The prison hospital was manned by whites and this order had been given to prevent any messages being passed.

MR. KENTRIDGE: Doesn't this and the fact that Mr. Biko was taken to the prison only after dark seem as if you didn't want anybody to know that Mr. Biko suffered from an ailment?

COLONEL GOOSEN: Quarters used for awaiting-trial prisoners had to be cleared for Mr. Biko. I had to consult with Colonel Bothma and I was told that the doctor could see Mr. Biko only late that night.

Mr. Kentridge quoted prison regulations as saying that in cases of death, serious illness and injury, the prisons department had to notify the next of kin of a prisoner. Mr. Biko's illness had been serious enough to warrant examination by a specialist and to send him seven hundred miles to a hospital in Pretoria.

MR. KENTRIDGE: Why didn't you notify his next of kin?

COLONEL GOOSEN: After the doctors had examined him it was their opinion that there was nothing physically wrong. I had no reason to inform his family. I had reason to believe he was shamming.

(Mr. Biko had been sent to Pretoria for a diagnosis, he said.)

MR. KENTRIDGE: You thought there was nothing wrong, yet on the Sunday night you tried to get a military plane to take this malingerer to Pretoria?

COLONEL GOOSEN: This shows the attention we gave him. Even when a prisoner has only a headache we get a doctor. I tried to get Mr. Biko to Pretoria as soon as possible.

MR. KENTRIDGE: Do you know that Dr. Hersch took a lumbar puncture and that the finding was positive? Red blood cells were found in the spinal fluid.

COLONEL GOOSEN: To my knowledge the three doctors said they could find nothing wrong.

MR. KENTRIDGE: If all these doctors told you there was nothing wrong, why try to get a military plane?

Colonel Goosen said that this showed the care they took to avoid criticism.

MR. KENTRIDGE: I put it to you that the dictates of common humanity and decency would have impelled you to inform the family unless you had something to hide.

COLONEL GOOSEN: The circumstances were special. We were trying to prove that Mr. Biko was somebody quite 'different from what he had seemed to be. Had we known he was ill the family would have been told.

Mr. Kentridge said that in his affidavit Colonel Goosen had said that Dr. Lang had come to the conclusion that Mr. Biko was shamming a slight paralysis.

COLONEL GOOSEN: Dr. Hersch and Dr. Lang told me they could find nothing physically wrong and strengthened my suspicion that he was shamming illness.

MR. KENTRIDGE: In your affidavit you said that you were present on the evening when Dr. Hersch examined Mr. Biko. Dr. Lang was also there. You say that when Drs Lang and Tucker examined him he pretended that his one arm was slightly weak but at the prison he indicated the other arm was slightly weaker, but that you couldn't remember which arm was shown.

Mr. Kentridge said he could find no mention of this in Dr. Lang's evidence, although this had certainly made an impression on Colonel Goosen.

COLONEL GOOSEN: I can't remember which arm it was but for me it was very noticeable that he showed another arm. It was just observation. I made no note of it.

MR. KENTRIDGE: Surely that can't be true? If it made such an impression on you, you must have a picture of it in your mind? I find it strange that you cannot say which arm it was.

Mr. Kentridge said Dr. Tucker had also made an affidavit in which he said that Mr. Biko, when asked to move his limbs, could not move his left limbs properly.

COLONEL GOOSEN: I wasn't present at Dr. Tucker's examination.

MR. KENTRIDGE: I will suggest that this evidence of yours is a complete invention. I'll show you why. In your affidavit you said: "It was noticeable that during Dr. Lang's and Dr. Tucker's examination on the 7th and the 8th Mr. Biko pretended that one arm was slightly weak." Yesterday you told us you had not been present. So this statement must be a falsehood.

COLONEL GOOSEN: Drs. Lang and Tucker came to my office and there was a discussion. I wanted to know what the diagnosis was. During the discussion I was told that he pretended that one arm was weak. Dr. Lang again drew my attention to it at the prison.

MR. KENTRIDGE: Why didn't Dr. Lang mention this?

COLONEL GOOSEN: He will probably give evidence.

MR. KENTRIDGE: Dr. Lang said in his affidavit that Mr. Biko had refused water and food and had displayed a weakness of all four limbs. Why should he tell you something different from his report?

Colonel Goosen said that this discussion took place immediately after the examination. He was present at the examination of Drs. Hersch and Lang.

Mr. Kentridge said that according to the report, when the reflexes were tested, different arms were shown as weak, but the doctors did not regard this as sinister. One could not pretend reflexes, he said. He put it to Colonel Goosen that this alleged discrepancy was an invention on his part.

MR. KENTRIDGE: You said in your affidavit that at the time when you decided to send Mr. Biko to Pretoria he had been examined by three doctors and you had been assured by them that there was nothing wrong and that it was the general view that he was shamming illness. Are you trying to tell us that Dr. Hersch also could find nothing wrong?

COLONEL GOOSEN: I had a discussion with Dr. Hersch. I was very eager to know his diagnosis. He said that he could find nothing physically wrong and he suggested that a lumbar puncture should be taken the next day.

MR. KENTRIDGE: On what basis do you say that Dr. Hersch was also of the opinion that there was nothing wrong with Mr. Biko?

COLONEL GOOSEN: I did not say that this was a general view of the doctors. I was giving my own opinion. Dr. Lang agreed with me to a large extent.

Mr. Kentridge reread the paragraph in the affidavit. Was that not intended to include Dr. Hersch? he asked. Colonel Goosen replied that he meant that Dr. Lang was of the opinion and other people may have been of the opinion. Dr. Lang had told him that neither he, Dr. Tucker, nor Dr. Hersch could find anything wrong and that he could return Mr. Biko to the Walmer police station.

MR. KENTRIDGE: Did Dr. Lang ever tell you that Dr. Hersch thought that Mr. Biko was shamming illness?

COLONEL GOOSEN: Not in those words.

MR. KENTRIDGE: It did not happen, did it? I will suggest that you put the paragraph in your affidavit in order to deliberately mislead. Did not Dr. Lang tell you that Dr. Hersch had found red blood cells in the spinal fluid? What did he tell you?

Colonel Goosen said that he was told that a lumbar puncture had been done and that Dr. Lang and Dr. Hersch wanted to keep Mr. Biko in the prison hospital for observation. He said he ordered Mr. Biko to be sent to Pretoria because they had the facilities for a proper examination there.

MR. KENTRIDGE: What was wrong with Port Elizabeth? There are very good hospitals in Port Elizabeth.

COLONEL GOOSEN: With Mr. Biko's background there were good reasons why he could not be kept there.

MR. KENTRIDGE: Often in hospitals, prisoners are kept under a 24-hour guard? I know you made a lot of the fact that he studied yoga. Did you think he was a magician?

COLONEL GOOSEN: I still thought he was feigning. I thought it was possible that he could be assisted to escape and leave the country. I have often had prisoners under guard in hospitals who succeeded in escaping.

MR. KENTRIDGE: Wasn't the real reason that you did not want anybody to see Mr. Biko in that condition? You did not think he would die and until he recovered you wanted to keep him out of sight.

COLONEL GOOSEN: I had no reason to hide him. Neither I nor any of my colleagues, nor the doctors saw any external injuries.

MR. KENTRIDGE: Do you know that General Gericke, the officer commanding the Pretoria prison, said in an affidavit that if he had not had the proper facilities in prison Biko would have been sent to a public hospital for treatment?

COLONEL GOOSEN: Had I known what his condition was I would have agreed to that but I thought then he was feigning illness.

Colonel Goosen said that when he could not get a military plane he asked Dr. Tucker if he could convey Mr. Biko by road. Dr. Tucker said that provided they allowed Mr. Biko to lie on a soft mattress there was no reason why not.

MR. KENTRIDGE: What facilities was Biko to have?

COLONEL GOOSEN: A relatively luxurious Land Rover was used. Seats were removed to put the mattress on the floor.

MR. KENTRIDGE: We understand that the only facility available was a container of water.

COLONEL GOOSEN: We still thought he was shamming. The doctors did not prescribe anything.

MR. KENTRIDGE: Do you know that Mr. Biko went to Pretoria without even a medical history accompanying him?

COLONEL GOOSEN: I phoned Brigadier Dorfling of the Central Prison and asked who would treat Mr. Biko. He told me it would be Dr. Brandt. He told me to tell Dr. Brandt to contact Drs. Lang and Tucker in Port Elizabeth. Colonel Dorfling was phoned twice. I think everything possible was done to inform Pretoria.

The colonel could not say if the medical history was properly conveyed, he said. He later heard that Dr. Brandt had not phoned Drs. Lang and Tucker but he had done everything possible from his side. He was "reasonably upset" when he heard Mr. Biko had died because he had been a detainee of the Security Police and he realized what a terrible tragedy it was that Mr. Biko could not be placed before a court and shown for what he was. The sad situation now was that Mr. Biko was regarded by the foreign press and foreign countries as a martyr. Instead of being able to expose Mr. Biko a veil had been drawn over his activities.

Mr. Kentridge said: "You have certainly tried to expose him in this courtroom." Colonel Goosen said that when Mr. Biko died he realized that he had not been shamming at all. Mr. Kentridge replied: "Unluckily this realization came too late for Mr. Biko." Colonel Goosen said this was a tragic occurrence for the police of South Africa because of the propaganda that could follow it. He had discussed Mr. Biko's death with his colleagues but nobody put up any theories. He had no idea of what the cause of death could have been.

Mr. Kentridge read from Colonel Goosen's affidavit in which he described an incident when Mr. Biko was found in a bath. Colonel Goosen had said in his affidavit that he would like to express a serious suspicion that Mr. Biko had suffered brain injury during this incident. Colonel Goosen had also said that Mr. Biko had been bent on self-destruction even in his method of breathing during detention. The injury on Mr. Biko's forehead had never been noticed by the doctors and he did not know how it could have been caused. He had since learned that the photograph handed into the court showing the injury had been overexposed and that the injury could have consisted of just a few scratches which showed up more clearly in the photograph.

Mr. Kentridge then said: "Are you seriously suggesting that the incident in the bath was an attempt at suicide? Are you saying that a normal person would sit in a bath of water with his clothes on? Don't you think he might already have had a brain injury?" He went on to say that when Warder Coetzee found Mr. Biko in a bath full of water he had asked him to get out and he eventually did so. When the warder asked him what he was doing there at that time of the morning he did not say anything but just gave a groan.

Colonel Goosen replied: "Many of Mr. Biko's methods had seemed strange to me." He agreed that it was not normal for a man to get into a bath with his clothes on and to turn on a tap and when asked to close it to calmly close it with his foot.

Mr. Kentridge said: "Does that not sound as if he had a brain injury? Why do you only mention it as your serious suspicion that Mr. Biko had been bent on suicide? Isn't the real explanation that when you made the affidavit you probably realized that the wound had been suffered before he reached the hospital?" He asked if Colonel Goosen, when he made his affidavit, had not connected Mr. Biko's brain injury with his mumbling and the fact that he wet his blanket.

COLONEL GOOSEN: I gave a lot of thought to where the brain injury could have been incurred.

MR. KENTRIDGE: When you made the affidavit you still had in mind that Mr. Biko might have been pretending the effects of brain injury on the 7th and 8th and actually had it on the 9th.

COLONEL GOOSEN: I thought the man might be shamming so as to be allowed into a hospital where he might have had the opportunity to commit suicide.

MR. KENTRIDGE: What about your view that Mr. Biko had been deliberately hyperventilating as part of his suicide attempt?

COLONEL GOOSEN: I was concerned at this stage that the injury had been incurred elsewhere than in our care. I was satisfied that the breathing could have been part of his attempt at self-destruction.

Colonel Goosen said that he had thought of the possibility that Mr. Biko might have been injured while in the care of the Security Police.

MR. KENTRIDGE: Do you have any theory?

COLONEL GOOSEN: I would say now that there is a great possibility that he incurred the injury in room 619.

Mr. Kentridge then turned to the question of a hunger strike and the allegations contained in some police affidavits that Mr. Biko was on such a strike. He asked Colonel Goosen what the meaning of the words "hunger strike" was, and the colonel replied that it had many meanings. Mr. Kentridge said that it was important to get certainty. If a man did not eat because he felt unwell, would the colonel say that the man was on a hunger strike?

COLONEL GOOSEN: No.

MR. KENTRIDGE: If someone does not eat because he says he is not hungry would you say he is on a hunger strike?

COLONEL GOOSEN: Yes – not in that English . . .

MR. KENTRIDGE: The man was just not eating?

COLONEL GOOSEN: Yes.

Mr. Kentridge said that he wanted to put it to the colonel that he had not been entitled to say that Mr. Biko had gone on a hunger strike at all. Mr. Kentridge read extracts from the colonel's and the doctor's affidavits and a number of other affidavits where mention was made of Mr. Biko taking food and water and where he thanked some of the people concerned. Mr. Kentridge pointed out that Mr. Biko had partaken of the bread, coffee and magewu. He suggested to Colonel Goosen that his observation that Mr. Biko had started a hunger strike was based on the fact that the colonel had seen pieces of bread in his cell. The reply was inaudible.

Mr. Kentridge said there was nothing to show that Mr. Biko had not partaken of some coffee and bread on September 6, except that some of Colonel Goosen's officers said that while they were interrogating him he took no food or water. The colonel said that was so. Mr. Kentridge then said that on the 8th, when doctors examined Mr. Biko, he had asked for water and that he had drunk it. Colonel Goosen said he was not aware of it.

Mr. Kentridge then pointed out that the affidavits referring to the 8th and 9th and the affidavits from the warders mentioned that Mr. Biko had drunk water. After reading from the affidavits referring to Mr. Biko partaking of food and drink, he said: "That does not sound like a man on hunger strike in any sense." Colonel Goosen said the strike that he had mentioned had been brought to his attention. Mr. Biko had just not eaten.

Mr. Kentridge drew the attention of the court to an incident on September 9 after Mr. Biko had been found in a bath full of water. Warder Du Preez had taken food to Mr. Biko and told him to eat. Reading from Warder Du Preez's statement, Mr. Kentridge said: "He (Biko) would not hold the spoon to eat although he moved his fingers strongly. I then fed him. After he had had half his porridge he said he didn't want any more because he had had enough. I then gave him his mug of coffee and he drank it up."

Mr. Kentridge then drew Colonel Goosen's attention to the first official statement made by Mr. Kruger, the minister of justice, after Mr. Biko's death. In this statement the minister said that Mr. Biko had been on a hunger strike since September 5. Mr. Kentridge then read sections of the statement to the court.

MR. KENTRIDGE: You see, in the first place it says that since September 5 Mr. Biko refused his meals and threatened a hunger strike. It is quite clear from the evidence that he never made any threats in connection with a hunger strike and secondly it is not correct to say that by Sunday (September 11) Mr. Biko had still not eaten . . . Colonel, there are a number of substantial errors in that statement. You realize that, don't you?

COLONEL GOOSEN: There are contradictions, Your Worship, if those are the minister's words. I cannot say it is accurate.

Mr. Kentridge said that the minister had used this statement as a basis of a complaint to the Press Council against the *Rand Daily Mail* and had attached his signature to a letter accompanying the statement.

MR. KENTRIDGE: There are at least two errors.

COLONEL GOOSEN: Provided it is the minister's statement I cannot comment on that.

Mr. Kentridge then referred to the statement made by the minister at the National Party congress on September 14 in which he said that on September 5 when the Security Police had finished with the other man (Peter Jones) they then came to Mr. Biko and started questioning him. He then said he would go on hunger strike. He first said he would answer questions, but first asked for a quarter of an hour to think. After that he said no, but threatened a hunger strike.

Mr. Kentridge asked the colonel if "you know of no evidence to support that statement?" He said that earlier Major Snyman had said that the passing of such information to the minister was the duty of his commanding officer. Colonel Goosen denied he had contact with the minister but said he had made contact through the normal channels via Security headquarters. Mr. Kentridge said: "But information of what happened in Port Elizabeth obviously had to come from you as head of the Security Police in Port Elizabeth? You see if the statement I have read to you were in fact made by the minister then it must follow that someone misled the minister."

At this stage Mr. van Rooyen, for the police, objected to the handing in of an affidavit containing statements by the minister. He said they were hearsay and inadmissible. The magistrate allowed Mr. Kentridge to ask further questions before hearing arguments on the relevance of the minister's statement.

Mr. Kentridge asked Colonel Goosen who reported to the minister and he replied: "I have no idea. I take the matter to the Security headquarters, then I presume it goes to the commissioner and then to the minister."

Mr. Kentridge then addressed the court on the objection raised by Mr. van Rooyen: "We have put before the court the dossier containing a number of statements made by the minister of police regarding the treatment of Mr. Biko. The minister was not in Port Elizabeth. The minister had no personal knowledge of what took place. He must rely on reports given to him by his officers, as Colonel Goosen had said, through Security headquarters. The starting point of the information is Colonel Goosen. The point about these statements, which we can prove are accurate and which I am sure the minister will in no way dispute, is that they purport to describe in detail how Biko on September 5 threatened a hunger strike. Another statement by the minister said Biko had asked for a quarter of an hour before saying he would go on hunger strike. This is a very detailed account of what happened, and even later, as appears from the dossier, it was reiterated by the minister that although he never said Biko died of hunger strike, he went on a hunger strike. This is completely unfounded. It is contrary to the evidence given by Colonel Goosen and Major Snyman. It is very clear from the extract I read from statements by the prison warders that it is wrong to say that from September 5 Biko refused food.

"Your Worship, it is absolutely clear therefore that when he made the statement the minister was misled, and two questions arise – who misled him and why? Not only is there no mention of the hunger strike, but nowhere is there any mention of the scuffle (on September 7). Nowhere is there any mention of the fact that the colonel suspected he had a stroke. Nowhere is there any mention of a lumbar puncture and the somewhat disquieting result. My submission is that the story of the hunger strike, false as it was, was obviously an excuse, it was a cover-up.

"There are only two questions that arise out of that which are as important as any other questions in this inquest. Where did the cover-up start and how high did the cover-up go? If we have answers to those questions it will tell us a great deal about what really happened to Steve Biko while in the custody of Colonel Goosen. There is only one way of ascertaining that. He (Colonel Goosen) has denied he gave this information. Very well, we must speak to the man to whom he gave the information and if necessary the next in the chain until we have discovered how and why this false story was propagated to the minister so that he could propagate it to the country and the world.

"You will not fail to observe that whoever gave the minister this incorrect information was obviously quite unconcerned with the embarrassment it would cause the minister and the country, and this is what we must investigate."

With regard to Mr. van Rooyen's objections that the statements of the minister contained in newspaper reports were hearsay, Mr. Kentridge said it would be no problem at all for the investigating officer to take the dossier to Mr. Kruger and ask if they were correct or not. In any event, Mr. Kentridge said he was unaware that the inquest court was bound by the hearsay rule. The court had discretion in this regard.

"If Colonel Goosen denied he gave the wrong information and we call the next man in the chain and the next man, either someone will place the responsibility on the previous link in the chain, or if that is not so, I fear we must go as high as the minister himself and ask him to come here and tell Your Worship who gave him the false information. I have wanted to avoid anything like that. I did not want the minister's statement to be in dispute. It is not my intention to trouble the minister unnecessarily. Nor did I think it would be necessary to go higher than Colonel Goosen. But there is nothing left for the court other than to test his evidence."

Mr. Kentridge then asked to hand in the dossier provisionally while the investigating officer went to the minister to find out if any of the passages of his statement were wrong. "If the minister is satisfied I don't see why my learned friend should not be."

Mr. van Rooyen replied: "I have the sneaking feeling that I have been listening to a consummate piece of artistry. My learned friend (Mr. Kentridge) has succeeded in speaking up on those things on which he could not lead evidence because it would be inadmissible. I can only object in the most strenuous fashion against this methodology."

Mr. van Rooyen said the purpose of the inquest court was to establish the cause of death and to find out if any living person was responsible . . . (partly inaudible). Mr. van Rooyen said he had read reports that Mr. Biko had been murdered and that his head had been bashed in. Newspaper reports were hearsay evidence and not admissible, he said. There was not the slightest evidence that Colonel Goosen had made any inconsistent statements in the court. "It is a fishing expedition. In terms of the law Your Worship will determine the cause or likely cause of death." In a trial by newspaper hundreds of alleged statements could be brought.

Mr. K. von Lieres, leading evidence for the State, said that anything that fell outside the scope of the inquest was basically irrelevant. The minister could not contribute any evidence relevant to the inquiry because he was not an eyewitness. "This affidavit is an attempt to introduce derogatory evidence which is not admissible in terms of the normal rules." Mr. von Lieres suggested that there had been an attempt to turn the court into a political platform for the general election of November 30. "This court is not instituted in terms of the Electoral Act but in terms of the Inquest Act." Even if the dossier were relevant it would endanger the objectivity of the inquiry, Mr. von Lieres said.

Replying, Mr. Kentridge said he was not surprised at the attitude taken by Mr. van Rooyen because it was his job to protect the police. But, he was most surprised at the attitude of the Deputy Attorney General, Mr. von Lieres, in view of the undertaking that there would be the fullest possible inquiry without any suggestion of a cover-up.

In reply to questioning by the magistrate Mr. Kentridge said: "We are not dealing here with a misunderstanding. We are dealing with the minister of police who made a statement on what happened and which is absolutely incorrect and which contains things which never happened." Mr. Prins said that some reports had only alleged that the minister had made the statements. Mr. Kentridge replied: "The investigating officer can fix that up by bringing the minister here." When asked by the magistrate how this could assist the court, as "the minister can say that he said it and that nobody told him about it," Mr. Kentridge replied that it was not a wild goose chase. Suppose the minister did make a statement and he said in court the brigadier had given him the information. Then the brigadier would be called to give evidence to corroborate that.

Mr. Prins said that if it was found that Colonel Goosen was lying, did it help him to determine the cause of Mr. Biko's death? Mr. Kentridge said: "Yes, if they are found to lie then it tells something very important. It shows that they have something to hide, that something happened."

Mr. Prins wanted to know how relevant the minister's statement was. "We have tried to show," Mr. Kentridge continued, "that there were certain very strange aspects in the affidavits of Colonel Goosen and his staff. I said to Colonel Goosen that this was very strange and referred to the fall in the bath and the hyperventilation. We say they have something to hide. What have they to hide which will avoid them getting the blame? We have significant evidence that the official information to the minister contains palpable untruths. If we find that someone in the Security Police went to the trouble of planting it on the minister, it is the clearest possible proof of guilt.

"We have official channels of communications here. We know the information the minister had was not casual. We know he must have had an official report which started off from Colonel Goosen. If Colonel Goosen was not responsible (for the wrong information) why did he not react and correct it? It was never corrected.

"The minister was allowed to continue repeating the statement. A man must have very strong motives if he allowed a statement of this nature to continue to be repeated."

Mr. Kentridge said if the story that Mr. Biko had died of a kidney disease had come from official sources it would have been highly relevant. "What makes this relevant is that the primary source must have been the Security Police in Port Elizabeth. The interest of the parties that I represent could never be satisfied if this line of investigation is now stifled."

Mr. B. de V. Pickard, representing the medical doctors, said his clients had no interest in the credibility issue involving Colonel Goosen. He was opposed to Mr. Kentridge's line because his clients were concerned about sitting at the court day after day.

Mr. von Lieres said that they all wanted a full inquiry but they did not want irrelevant evidence to be presented to the court, and it was his duty to object to it. Mr. Prins adjourned the court, saying he would give his findings next day on the admissibility of the reports handed in by Mr. Kentridge.

(Adjournment)

Day Five: Friday, November 18, 1977
Magistrate Prins rejected Mr. Kentridge's application and refused to allow transcripts of Minister Kruger's public statements to be admitted as evidence. He gave four reasons for his decision:

1 According to the rules of evidence the dossier of reports, if relevant only to Colonel Goosen's credibility, should not go in;
2 It should not go in because it was irrelevant to the circumstances of Mr. Biko's death;

3 It should not go in because it was hearsay evidence;

4 It should not go in because it was hearsay evidence "so far removed that it was dangerous."

Mr. van Rooyen rose and told the court that to refute the possibility of any allegation that these proceedings were being stifled, he had been in contact with the commissioner of police, and to test if there had been inconsistent statements he had been advised to make the two brigadiers available for consultation to the counsel for the family. If counsel were then not satisfied they could reapply for the admission of further evidence.

Mr. Kentridge said that this was a "very strange and surprising offer," and asked: "Why not have a public consultation so that they can be asked questions in the witness box?" He did not know what the value of a private consultation was. He appreciated the offer, however, "as far as it goes," and would consider it, he said, adding that counsel for the family could not present any eyewitnesses and could only suggest on the basis of circumstantial evidence.

Mr. Kentridge then resumed his questioning of Colonel Goosen. He asked Goosen why he did nothing to correct the minister's statement when he saw it reported. The colonel replied that it was certainly not his duty and lay outside his function to do so. To the suggestion that he must have made a written report to his superiors, he answered: "I made several affidavits which were in the possession of my head office. They included everything which could have been said in a written report." He could see no reason why anybody would have given wrong information to the minister. He could name legions of times when the minister had been wrongly quoted by the press.

MR. KENTRIDGE: Can you tell us of any way in which such a remarkable error could have crept into the report?

COLONEL GOOSEN: I never said Biko threatened a hunger strike. I cannot comment on how the error reached the minister.

Colonel Goosen said he discussed the "hyperventilation" theory with Colonel Bothma at the Port Elizabeth prison about a week later. "They spoke about the strange breathing exercise," and Colonel Bothma took out a medical book. Mr. Kentridge asked if Dr. Lang agreed with his theory of hyperventilation as part of a suicide attempt. The colonel replied that he did not think Dr. Lang went into the question. Dr. Lang was present when he spoke of the possibility, and he stressed that hyperventilation could be dangerous if practiced for long enough. This was what Colonel Goosen had meant when he spoke in his affidavit of "research in medical books," he said. This discussion took place long before General Kleinhaus came to Port Elizabeth, about five days after Mr. Biko's death.

Mr. van Rooyen, for the police, then rose to re-examine Colonel Goosen. Mr. van Rooyen said the contention had been put to the colonel that his men would not hesitate to assault detainees. Colonel Goosen said that in all cases of Section 6 the aim of the Security Police was to interrogate them thoroughly to establish their activities, the source of their funds, and a legion of other circumstances. All measures were taken to ensure the safekeeping of such a detainee and to ensure that he did not escape, injure himself, or suffer injury. It would be of no avail if the detainee made an admission and the next moment said that he had made it because he had been assaulted.

"We have a lot of time," Colonel Goosen said. A detainee was detained until he had answered all the questions. It sometimes took days and weeks to build up communication, and communication sometimes started in a laughable manner. "Our technique is almost that of Mr. Kentridge – sometimes we talk nicely, sometimes we use sarcasm. We have no reason to assault a detainee."

Colonel Goosen then said that no assault charges had ever been laid "against my assaulting team." Laughter followed, and he changed the phrase to "the interrogation team."

The members of an interrogation team were all selected men. They were selected on the grounds of their personality, and ability to communicate with others and to contain their team members. A member of the force with a personality defect had very little chance of becoming a Security policeman.

Colonel Goosen said sections of the press and liberalists had created a climate of revolt against security legislation among the general public: "It has developed so far that South Africans are getting guilt feelings that we might have acted incorrectly." Therefore the Security Police were very careful not to give any reasons for criticism. "We are very disappointed by this criticism because we are aware of the politeness and concern with which we treat detainees. We buy them cigarettes, cold drinks, and nice things to eat." Assault charges would harm the image of the Security Police.

Because there was a tendency to suicide in police cells, "like the Baader-Meinhof cases in Germany," they did their utmost to prevent this. If a detainee complained of so much as a headache, a doctor was called. If a prisoner suffered, for instance, from high blood pressure, it was arranged that he should be regularly visited by a doctor.

Continuing, Colonel Goosen said that Mr. Biko's health had been of the greatest importance to him. Because of information in his possession he had realized that it was of primary importance to bring this "peaceable" man before a court. He knew that the Black People's Convention had been concerned with training terrorists and that Mr. Biko had financed the conveyance of trainees to Botswana. He had been creating "a climate for bloodbath and revolution in South Africa."

Also, it was important to him to find Mr. Biko's associates. "His death would have placed an absolute damper on the investigations," he said. He would have been "disappointed" if Mr. Biko had been released and had afterwards alleged that he had been assaulted because he knew how carefully and politely Mr. Biko had been treated.

Mr. van Rooyen asked why Mr. Biko was kept naked and in chains, and the colonel replied that this was on orders from head office and in order to prevent the continuation of "a pattern of suicides." On the morning of September 7, Mr. Biko had been "like a madman" and the colonel had been concerned to prevent a repetition of this.

Mr. Prins then asked: "If this was so, would the things they had attached to him not have led to injury and harmed the image which you guarded so jealously?" Colonel Goosen: "These things are standard equipment. They only curbed his movements." There were bars in front of the window of the office on the sixth floor where Mr. Biko was kept but not on the window of other offices nearby, he said. There had recently been an accident where a man had jumped through one of those windows. All the offices had ordinary doors. It would not have been sufficient for Mr. Biko's safekeeping merely to lock a door. While Mr. Biko was being interrogated he wore clothes because he was then better guarded than he was in his cell. There had been two instances immediately prior to the Biko incident where prisoners in cells had hanged themselves by their shoelaces and trouser legs.

Colonel Goosen said that his instructions required detainees not to be moved from one place to another unless they were either handcuffed or held by the arms by officers, and to be kept on the ground floor wherever possible. He had wide discretion about their treatment. It had not been part of his instruction to keep a detainee shackled and handcuffed when on a higher floor. That had been left to his discretion. His instruction had been only that a detainee should be treated with the utmost care.

Mr. Biko had been dressed and not shackled during interrogation but he had given orders that Mr. Biko should be handcuffed and leg-shackled during the night and that there should be a night guard consisting of Lieutenant Wilken and two warrant officers. In the morning the shackles and handcuffs were removed, and had nothing happened on the morning of the 7th Mr. Biko would have been left free. But something happened that made him realize that Mr. Biko was wild and dangerous, and he ordered that he should be shackled.

Had Dr. Lang said that Mr. Biko were ill he would have had him removed to an institution with the necessary medical facilities. He would not have kept him handcuffed and chained to a grille. Dr. Lang had said that there was nothing wrong and Colonel Goosen had thought that Mr. Biko was shamming. He had kept Mr. Biko shackled because he had caused a violent struggle. Colonel Goosen said he went into Mr. Biko's room periodically during the day. Mr. Biko's attitude had not changed except that he was no longer very aggressive.

Colonel Goosen said he did not release Mr. Biko for fear he might injure himself. Mr. Biko would have spent the night in chains in any case. His orders had not been changed because Mr. Biko had been chained during the day. He had been convinced that Mr. Biko was feigning illness to win concessions which would enable him to escape. In a public hospital he could escape or be freed by a group of persons, because the colonel would have no control over him. He had thought that the prison had all the necessary facilities.

It had been of the utmost necessity for Colonel Goosen to find what was wrong with Mr. Biko. To get a diagnosis he had had no objection to his being seen by a specialist in internal diseases. He could see no external injuries. He had welcomed the suggestion that Mr. Biko be kept longer for observation because he had wanted to make one hundred percent sure. He had still subconsciously thought that Mr. Biko might have had a stroke, he said. He had been eager to have Mr. Biko examined by a private specialist and had been satisfied he should be kept in the hospital unit of the prison.

Colonel Goosen said the police had standing orders which prescribed that registers should be kept. This had nothing to do with statutes. An occurrence book was just a register for good administration. The Security Police were not above the ordinary police. There were other branches of the force which also did not keep occurrence books.

Mr. Prins then asked: "If that was so, what was the use of making an entry in an occurrence book at all?" Mr. Goosen replied: "It is advisable in many cases for the purposes of good administration to keep an occurrence book. A prisoner might be injured while playing football, there might be an inquiry, a civil action might follow." Ordinary prisoners were allowed to take exercise in an open space and could then communicate with adjoining cells. In Mr. Biko's case, however, communication had to be prevented at all costs, and he had therefore thought that Mr. Biko could get sufficient fresh air and exercise in his cell. After receiving a report from Major Snyman on the morning of the 7th he had visited Mr. Biko and had seen that he was extremely aggressive but could see no injury. He had called a doctor but the doctor, too, could find no injuries.

He had tried to communicate with Mr. Biko, Colonel Goosen said. Mr. Biko had spoken incoherently. From previous experience, and because he was a layman, he thought that Mr. Biko could possibly have suffered a stroke.

Colonel Goosen said he had been present when Dr. Lang had examined Mr. Biko. Mr. van Rooyen then quoted Dr. Lang's statement as saying: "Colonel Goosen strongly emphasized the fact that he did not want any harm to befall Mr. Biko . . . Mr. Biko was able to give me a good account of himself and was unable to give other symptoms than weakness of the limbs and the lack of a desire to eat."

Argument about the admissibility of the handwritten document then resumed. Mr. Kentridge said that he was objecting to the document being handed in which had allegedly been shown to Mr. Biko during the interrogation. Major Snyman had said that he had shown some unsworn handwritten statements to Mr. Biko. These had not been put to Major Snyman but were now being put to Colonel Goosen, who was apparently being asked to say that they had been shown to Mr. Biko during the interview. It was interesting that counsel for the police wanted to hand in documents not properly proved in the light of the strong opposition to his application to hand in statements by the minister, which at least he could have properly proved.

Mr. van Rooyen argued that to prove the documents he did not necessarily have to bring to court the persons who made them. He was interested in a state of mind. Mr. Kentridge had said that the police had brought Mr. Biko from denial to admission by assault, but the police said they confronted him with the documents. The state of mind of both interrogator and detainee was relevant. If the evidence about the confrontation was true it could have caused a violent reaction. If he did not hand in the notes it could be said that there were no notes. If it were possible for it to be argued that no documents existed and that there had been no confrontation he would suffer irreparable harm if he were prevented from handing in these statements. Objectively seen, the contents may even have been false, but the only question here was the state of mind.

Mr. von Lieres intervened. The only question here was if the documents existed before the scuffle. It did not matter if the facts were true or false if Mr. Biko believed them to be true.

The magistrate then ruled that the case had been made out for handing in the documents to prove their mere existence but not to prove the veracity or the truth contained in them. They could be placed in court on the basis that they existed.

Mr. van Rooyen then continued with his examination. Questioned about the statements, Colonel Goosen said that he had had the documents before September 6 and that he had discussed their content with his staff. He believed that the information they gave about the BPC was the truth and that he recognized the handwriting in which these documents were written as being that of Patrick Titi and Peter Jones. These and other documents were in the hands of Major Snyman's interrogating team. He felt that there was enough material in them to confront Mr. Biko with.

Dr. I. Gordon, one of the two assessors, asked Colonel Goosen a number of questions involving his suicide theory.

DR. GORDON: Say the man got a head injury on the 6th or 7th. Could he not have sat on the bath as a confused man?

COLONEL GOOSEN: Till that stage I did not know there were problems with his head. I now concede that he may have hurt himself in room 619, but I called the doctor immediately. It is unnatural that a man goes to have a bath at 3 A.M.

DR. GORDON: How could he commit suicide if there were other people around?

Colonel Goosen replied he did not think that Mr. Biko had been under personal supervision but he was talking under correction.

DR. GORDON: If he was not under guard, then it was against your instructions.

COLONEL GOOSEN: (Reply inaudible.)

DR. GORDON: You have no medical knowledge and (inaudible) then you are the first to say hyperventilation can lead to suicide?

COLONEL GOOSEN: No, it is my own theory.

DR. GORDON: I also want to learn something, if you can tell me that a man can commit suicide by that method.

COLONEL GOOSEN: No, I can't say that.

DR. GORDON: Am I right in coming to the conclusion that you have no firm grounds for stating a man can commit suicide in this way?
COLONEL GOOSEN: It is not on firm ground at all. It was wrong. It was my own layman's approach.

After lunch Captain Daniel Siebert was recalled. He was shown the handwritten documents containing alleged statements by Mr. Jones and Mr. Titi. Questioned by Mr. van Rooyen, Captain Siebert said that during the interrogation the team asked Mr. Biko if he recognized the handwriting as that of Mr. Jones and Mr. Titi. Magistrate Prins then asked the captain when Mr. Biko was confronted with the documents. Captain Siebert said it was during the afternoon of September 6. On the evening of September 7 no further documentation was shown to Mr. Biko.

The next witness was Mr. J. Fitchet, a warder at Port Elizabeth prison, who made three statements before the court. In a statement dated September 15, Mr. Fitchet made the following points: on September 9, while he was watching over Mr. Biko, he gave him a mug of puzamandla which he drank; Mr. Biko then asked for water and drank two full mugs; he then said he wanted to kiss Mr. Fitchet because Mr. Fitchet had given him magewu and water.

Mr. Fitchet also said that Mr. Biko stated he wanted exercise, got out of the bed and walked around his cell. He walked without any aid and without holding on to anything. He did not appear unsteady on his feet. He kept his head down with his eyes fastened to the ground. After about twenty minutes he said he was tired and sat on his bed.

In answer to a question by Mr. Fitchet, Mr. Biko said his people lived at Fort Beaufort. In answer to Mr. Fitchet's question as to why he was arrested, Mr. Biko said he had been traveling in his car. Asked what sort of car, he said it was a Passat, which was now in Queenstown. Mr. Biko would say nothing more.

Questioning Mr. Fitchet on these statements, Mr. Wentzel, for the Biko family, said: "I am told that in the light of his medical condition it is inconceivable that on September 9 he could have walked around in the manner you describe. What would you say to that?" Mr. Fitchet held on to the microphone in the dock and remained silent.
MR. WENTZEL: You won't get inspiration from the microphone.
MR. FITCHET: I cannot answer that question.

Mr. Wentzel also drew Mr. Fitchet's attention to the fact that other witnesses had said Mr. Biko's speech was slurred on occasions before September 9, and that at a medical examination on September 7, Dr. Lang, the district surgeon, had found Mr. Biko was staggering. Mr. Wentzel also pointed out that none of Mr. Biko's family came from Fort Beaufort and that he was arrested while traveling in a Peugeot, not a Passat, in King William's Town, not Queenstown.

Mr. Wentzel also questioned Mr. Fitchet on a duplicated statement that he had been asked to fill in by General Kleinhaus. The affidavit contained statements in connection with Mr. Biko's detention and the person filling it in had to cross out incorrect statements, let correct ones stand, and add further comments if he felt it necessary. Mr. Wentzel said that a large number of affidavits in this form had been sworn as evidencé in this inquest. Mr. Fitchet crossed out the following words: "Besides what I already said in my statement(s) I noticed no injuries of any kind on Stephen Biko." He also crossed out the statement: "I noticed the following injury(s) on Steve Biko during my visit to him." The following statement remained standing in the Roneoed form: "I noticed no injury of any description on Stephen Biko." Mr. Fitchet had added the words ". . . except handcuff marks on both wrists."

The other statement left standing in the form was: "I was shown a mark on a photograph taken during the post-mortem on Mr. Biko. I have not noticed such a mark or injury on Stephen Biko."

MR. WENTZEL: Did General Kleinhaus give you instructions to cross out what didn't apply while you were alone or with other warders?

MR. FITCHET: He gave us no instructions.

MR. WENTZEL: Did he give you the explanation about what he wanted you to do with Roneoed forms when you were alone or when your colleagues were with you?

MR. FITCHET: I am not sure.

MR. WENTZEL: It is less than a month ago. Do you have a particularly bad memory?

MR. FITCHET: Yes.

At this stage Lieutenant Winston Eric Wilken was called to the stand by Mr. von Lieres. On September 6 at 6 P.M. he was on night duty with Warrant Officers Coetzee and Fouché. He found Mr. Biko lying in the interrogation room on two cell mats underneath two blankets, with one under his head as a cushion. One of Mr. Biko's feet was lightly cuffed to the lower end of the grille in front of the door and his hands were also cuffed. He could, however, move easily.

Lieutenant Wilken noticed that a carton of milk and a meat pie had been placed on the cabinet. Major Snyman told him that Mr. Biko would not eat. Asked whether he had any complaints, Mr. Biko was aggressive and answered negatively. He also did not want to take any food or water. Mr. Biko slept most of the time and never wanted to use the toilet facilities in spite of being asked by Lieutenant Wilken. During the night he visited him regularly and the night passed by quietly.

The next day Major Snyman mentioned to him that Mr. Biko had acted violently earlier in the day and had attacked him and other officers and that it had taken a short time before they could calm him. He was informed that Mr. Biko had been examined by a doctor who could find nothing wrong with him. Major Snyman had also mentioned that Mr. Biko would not eat or drink anything.

Mr. Biko was asleep when the lieutenant took over duty that night and was still lying on the same cell mats underneath two blankets, with one blanket as a cushion. His foot was cuffed to the grille. His hands were also cuffed. "I noticed a swelling on his upper lip and accepted that it was a result of the trouble earlier in the day," Lieutenant Wilken said.

Mr. Biko woke up at about 7.30 A.M. and Lieutenant Wilken talked to him: "I offered him food but he refused it. I said to him that he might as well come out with the truth because he was wasting everybody's time. He answered me by saying that I must give him fifteen minutes and then he would make a statement. I sincerely believed that he would do it and left him there. When I arrived back a little while later I saw that he was asleep and I left him.

"At about 9 P.M. Mr. Biko woke up and he talked with a slurred tongue. I did not know what was happening and phoned Major Fischer, my section head, and informed him that Mr. Biko was to have made a statement earlier in the evening but now was speaking with a slurred tongue."

Lieutenant Wilken then described the Land Rover used to take Mr. Biko to Pretoria. The back seats had been removed and five cell mats were placed in it. Mr. Biko was wrapped in four blankets and he used another as a cushion.

Lieutenant Wilken's lengthy statement was dated September 17.

In his second statement, dated October 20, Lieutenant Wilken said that he had that day been informed by General Kleinhaus that he was investigating the circumstances which led to the death of Mr. Biko, which a post-mortem had established as resulting from an injury that had caused brain damage. A photograph was shown to him where an external mark above the left eye was pointed out. "It was put to me that it is possible Mr. Biko received this injury while he was under my control. I was warned by General Kleinhaus that I was not obliged to make any further statement."

The lieutenant continued: "Now that the photo of Biko's face was shown to me with the mark above his left eye, I remember that when I arrived on duty on the evening of September 6 just after 6 P.M., and while Mr. Biko was lying on his back with his face to the ceiling, I saw a darkening of the skin, similar to a birthmark, dark brown, above his left eye and more or less in the same position as that on the photo. I placed no value on it. It did not look like an injury to me. Biko made no complaints to me."

Lieutenant Wilken said the guard team was not with Mr. Biko in the office where he was being detained but in an adjoining office from where they visited him every now and then. He said he had not cross-examined Mr. Biko at any stage. Mr. von Lieres then asked whether Mr. Biko was "assaulted" by the lieutenant or any of the others on duty. He answered: "No."

Mr. Kentridge then cross-examined Lieutenant Wilken.

MR. KENTRIDGE: When you took over from Major Snyman did he keep you informed of the progress of the interrogation?

LIEUTENANT WILKEN: I was aware they had made a certain breakthrough.

MR. KENTRIDGE: Did he say how they were getting on with Biko?

LIEUTENANT WILKEN: I can't think that he mentioned any progress but he looked satisfied.

MR. KENTRIDGE: When you took over on September 6 were you there to continue the interrogation?

LIEUTENANT WILKEN: No.

MR. KENTRIDGE: Does it not seem strange that a lieutenant and two warrant officers should be detailed to stand watch over a man chained hand and foot?

LIEUTENANT WILKEN: Yes probably under normal circumstances. That was the colonel's instructions.

MR. KENTRIDGE: During the earlier part of the evening you said to Biko that he must come out with the truth.

LIEUTENANT WILKEN: If you refer to Wednesday the 7th, then it is correct.

MR. KENTRIDGE: The truth about what?

LIEUTENANT WILKEN: It is general that if you come to a detainee, then you tell him to tell the truth. You sometimes don't even know what the case is about.

MR. KENTRIDGE: Why did you say he was wasting everybody's time?

Lieutenant Wilken said if Mr. Biko had told the truth they would have taken him back to his cell.

MR. KENTRIDGE: Major Snyman agreed with me that you were on the night interrogation team with your two assistants.

LIEUTENANT WILKEN: That is not so.

MR. KENTRIDGE: What did he mean when he said give me fifteen minutes?

LIEUTENANT WILKEN: Biko said give me fifteen minutes.

MR. KENTRIDGE: You must have been pretty pleased that he was prepared to give you a statement.

LIEUTENANT WILKEN: I was surprised and pleased.

MR. KENTRIDGE: That was very good for a non-interrogator.

LIEUTENANT WILKEN: Yes.

MR. KENTRIDGE: Did you then get a sheet of paper and a pen?

LIEUTENANT WILKEN: It was too early for pen and paper and we would first have to get a verbal story.

MR. KENTRIDGE: Did you go back after fifteen minutes?

LIEUTENANT WILKEN: Yes, he was asleep.

MR. KENTRIDGE: Why did you not wake him up?

LIEUTENANT WILKEN: It was . . . (inaudible) not my instructions to wake him up.

MR. KENTRIDGE: You made a big breakthrough. You said you were pleased.

LIEUTENANT WILKEN: My instructions were to leave him and let him rest and when it seemed he was asleep, I left him.

MR. KENTRIDGE: Did you not think it strange that he said fifteen minutes and then you find him asleep?

LIEUTENANT WILKEN: He may have taken me for a ride.

MR. KENTRIDGE: Then about an hour later he woke up?

LIEUTENANT WILKEN: Right.

Mr. Kentridge then questioned Lieutenant Wilken on the mark on Mr. Biko's forehead. Lieutenant Wilken said he had first seen the mark when he had sat next to Mr. Biko on a chair in the dark.

MR. KENTRIDGE: Were you not sitting there on the chair, like a night sister, to ask him a few questions?

LIEUTENANT WILKEN: I don't like the remark, Your Honor, about the night sister, but I did not ask him any questions.

Lieutenant Wilken said he just sat on the chair to pass by a few minutes of time. Mr. Kentridge pointed out there were many ways of passing the time. Besides he had two companions, and what about newspapers? Lieutenant Wilken confirmed that there were some newspapers. He explained that the light in the office next door was on and it was not all that dark. Mr. Kentridge asked what he was really doing that evening, to which he replied: "I don't know what you are insinuating, but nothing happened."

Mr. Kentridge told him that he was the only one of a number of officers who had admitted seeing any sort of mark on the left side of Mr. Biko's forehead. Lieutenant Wilken replied that he had discussed the matter often with his colleagues but that he had not told his colleagues about the mark because he had never attributed any importance to it.

The magistrate then adjourned the proceedings until Monday and announced that he had decided, in consultation with the counsels involved in the inquest, that the three documents handed in before lunch would not be made available for publication because they had been accepted on the clear understanding that they were just to serve as proof that the documents existed and not as proof of the content matter of the documents.

(Adjournment)

Day Six: Monday, November 21, 1977

Mr. Kentridge reported on his private consultations with the two brigadiers to whom Colonel Goosen said he had reported. The consultations followed the refusal by Magistrate Prins to admit press reports of statements by the minister of police, Mr. J. T. Kruger, as evidence. It was then arranged that Mr. Kentridge could have private consultations with the two brigadiers – Brigadier C. F. Zietsman, head of the Security Police, and his deputy, Brigadier P. J. Coetzee. The brigadiers were thought to be links in the chain of information on Mr. Biko's death which passed from Colonel Goosen to Mr. Kruger.

Dealing with his meeting with Brigadier Zietsman and Brigadier Coetzee, Mr. Kentridge said: "The two brigadiers consulted with us separately. Both consultations were held in the presence of the investigating officer, Major-General Kleinhaus. The information and explanations given by the brigadiers have cleared up many of the problems which existed when we first made our application for the calling of these and other officers whom we referred to as the links in the chain of communication reaching from Colonel Goosen to the minister.

"We did not then know how many links there were in the chain, or who they were. We are now able to eliminate Brigadier Coetzee from the inquiry entirely. He was away from Pretoria on September 13, and Colonel Goosen did not speak to him on that day. We accept that he can have no responsibility in the matter, and there is no need to call him as a witness.

"The officer to whom Colonel Goosen spoke on September 13, in the morning, was in fact Brigadier Zietsman. We are satisfied that Brigadier Zietsman did no more than to note down the information which Colonel Goosen gave him. Brigadier Zietsman asked the questions, and Colonel Goosen gave the answers, which the brigadier wrote down. The brigadier then conveyed the information to the commissioner of police, General Prinsloo, who presumably reported to the minister, as it would be his duty to do.

"We do not think that there can be any question of General Prinsloo's having distorted the information given to him; nor do we believe that the minister did so.

"What is most important, it is clear to us, having spoken to him, is that Brigadier Zietsman did not do so either. Nor, as he has related it to us, can there have been any room for misunderstanding, at least not for any misunderstanding which could possibly have led to the seriously incorrect version of events published by the minister on September 13 and 14. It seems, therefore, that it is necessary only to call Brigadier Zietsman. He can briefly clarify the whole issue. Moreover, he has told us that subsequent to his conversation with Colonel Goosen, the Port Elizabeth office did in fact send telexes to Security Police headquarters in Pretoria in connection with the detention of Biko. We have asked for these telexes but Brigadier Zietsman cannot produce them to us without the consent of the commissioner. Of course, this court has the power to call for the production of these telex messages, subject to any claim of privilege which may be made in respect of portions of them which do not refer to the facts of the Biko case.

"We therefore ask the court in due course to call Brigadier Zietsman, and to request him to bring with him the relevant telex messages from Port Elizabeth."

He wanted to hand in affidavits verifying the minister's reported statements on September 13 and 14. These were by a *Rand Daily Mail* journalist, Mr. Patrick Laurence, and a lawyer who acted for the *Rand Daily Mail* in a recent Press Council hearing on the statements, Mr. William Lane.

Mr. van Rooyen, for the police, objected to the procedure, particularly to the affidavits by Mr. Laurence. He said it appeared that Mr. Kentridge wanted "a second bite of the cherry." Mr. Prins had already ruled that documents relating to statements by the minister were hearsay and inadmissible, and the affidavit from a journalist was irrelevant and inadmissible.

Mr. Prins said that any affidavit verifying what was said by the minister could not change the matter. What was published as having been said by the minister was accepted as correct. Until the court had some indication of which aspects of Colonel Goosen's evidence were incorrect it would not consider ordering an affidavit from Brigadier Zietsman and would only then decide on whether to call him to give evidence or to make any telexes available on his reports to the minister.

Lieutenant Wilken then continued his examination under Mr. Kentridge and said he had made a point of visiting Mr. Biko from time to time during the night of September 6. He said he believed he was alone when he spoke to Mr. Biko in room 619 and he believed that Mr. Biko was asleep most of the night.

Mr. Kentridge asked whether Lieutenant Wilken seriously believed a man could sleep through the night with leg irons and handcuffs on him. Lieutenant Wilken said a person generally woke up in the night in any event even if they did not have on leg irons and handcuffs. Lieutenant Wilken then said that he had testified that Mr. Biko had only one foot in the leg iron, which gave him a lot of mobility. When he said Mr. Biko was asleep he meant that his eyes were not open. Mr. Biko was loosely manacled, and he denied that the pressure of the leg iron would always be felt as a weight on the leg. The pressure would be the same as that on a person who was wearing sunglasses – he would be aware of them.

Lieutenant Wilken agreed that Mr. Biko's foot and ankle were swollen.

Mr. Kentridge stated that according to medical evidence to be introduced it appeared probable that Mr. Biko suffered head injuries either during the night of September 6 or in the early morning of September 7, before 7.30 A.M. If that was the case the responsibility would appear to lie with Lieutenant Wilken's night squad or Major Snyman's day squad.

Lieutenant Wilken said he could not throw any light on how Mr. Biko might have suffered an injury while under his care or how an injury to his head could have occurred on September 6.

He had accompanied Mr. Biko on the Land Rover trip from Port Elizabeth to Pretoria and had sat at the front of the vehicle. Mr. Biko's condition was normal, except that as they approached towns, Mr. Biko's breathing became much heavier. Mr. Biko apparently slept most of the way. When they stopped for gasoline he did not give Mr. Biko a chance to get out to stretch his legs. He was given an opportunity to relieve himself, but he did not want to do so. He could not remember when the offer was made to Mr. Biko.

When they arrived in Pretoria Mr. Biko's condition was the same, which, in Lieutenant Wilken's opinion, was normal.

MR. KENTRIDGE: He was normal, and now we are speaking of some twelve hours before his death.

LIEUTENANT WILKEN: That is correct.

Mr. Kentridge said a medical orderly in Pretoria Prison, Sergeant Pretorius, had said: "Biko seemed to be seriously ill and I was afraid for his life." Did Lieutenant Wilken remember hearing this remark? The lieutenant said he did not remember hearing it.

Mr. Kentridge asked him whether, while at Pretoria Prison, he remembered one of his party saying to the others that Mr. Biko had studied medicine for four years, that he practiced yoga and that he could deceive people easily. Lieutenant Wilken said it was quite possible that he had said it himself, because at that stage he believed Mr. Biko was shamming. While they were in the Land Rover Mr.

Biko would breathe normally, but when there were lights and people around he would breathe more deeply.

Mr. Kentridge said he would ask the magistrate to reject this answer as a basis for Mr. Biko shamming.

MR. KENTRIDGE: What right did you have to say this man could deceive people and was probably shamming?

LIEUTENANT WILKEN: It was an opinion.

MR. KENTRIDGE: Why is it that you Security people insist on telling people all the time that he was shamming?

LIEUTENANT WILKEN: The case was that the doctors had said there was nothing wrong. We had to assume they were right.

MR. KENTRIDGE: Is not the obvious reason that there was something you wanted to hide in connection with this man?

LIEUTENANT WILKEN: No, we had nothing to fear or hide.

Mr. Kentridge said it became clear from affidavits that warders in Port Elizabeth were concerned about Mr. Biko's condition and had treated him in a humane and considerate manner. One or two had even fed him when he could not feed himself. Lieutenant Wilken said he had also treated Mr. Biko humanely.

MR. KENTRIDGE: We have the situation that you are sent on an urgent journey to Pretoria on a Sunday night to take a man to hospital. He had, according to you, refused food and water and had not taken any opportunity in the course of a twelve- to fourteen-hour journey to relieve himself. He said, as far as we know, not a word during the journey and then when you get to Pretoria you take it upon yourself to tell people there that this is a person who can easily deceive others and you think he is shamming. Is that a reasonable summary of what happened?

LIEUTENANT WILKEN: It is one-sided if you don't take in the background, but basically, yes, it's correct.

MR. KENTRIDGE: I suggest that it was not Biko that was shamming but members of the Security Police. I am going to suggest that this constant refrain was to draw attention away from what the Security Police had actually done.

LIEUTENANT WILKEN: (Reply inaudible.)

Lieutenant Wilken said Mr. Biko had not always worked with the Security Police, since he saw them as enemies, and that he had a different attitude to the prison warders. Mr. Kentridge said there was another reason for this different attitude since, perhaps, the prison warders did not assault Mr. Biko.

Lieutenant Wilken said Mr. Kentridge had not been there and could not say this. Mr. Kentridge said Lieutenant Wilken was right but Mr. Biko had been assaulted during a particular period and he left it to the lieutenant to explain how Mr. Biko came by this injury. Mr. Kentridge added that this pointed to the limitations imposed by holding a man incommunicado.

Mr. van Rooyen, for the police, said he wished to complain bitterly about Mr. Kentridge's reference to an alleged assault. So far there was no basis for these remarks.

Mr. Kentridge said it would be the Biko lawyers' submission that Mr. Biko had probably suffered a head injury between 6 P.M. on the evening of September 6 and 7.30 A.M. on the morning of September 7. It was natural to suggest that some violence had been applied to him and the court had not heard any explanation of this injury. The court was entitled to draw its inferences.

Mr. van Rooyen said there had been the clearest evidence of an incident of violence initiated by Mr. Biko and not by the police on the morning of September 7 when Mr. Biko's "head could have connected with the wall."

Mr. Kentridge replied: "I would be vastly interested to hear from my learned colleague on whether the head came to the wall or the wall came to the head."

Mr. van Rooyen asked whether Lieutenant Wilken had seen any injury on Mr. Biko which could have given the slightest suspicion that he had been assaulted. Lieutenant Wilken said when he saw the mark above Mr. Biko's left eye it appeared only to be darker than the rest of his skin, but did not seem to be the mark of an assault.

Mr. Pickard, for the doctors, then made an application for the postponement of the inquest after all the "laymen's" evidence had been given. He suggested possible postponement dates as January 9 or 15. He said Drs. Lang and Tucker had only arrived in Pretoria last Thursday and he found it extremely difficult to prepare evidence adequately for the proceedings since there was a wide range of information to be canvassed from various medical experts.

There was a distinct possibility that the Biko family would level criticism at the doctors who had treated Mr. Biko during the last days of his life. He added that the entire professional careers of the doctors he represented were at stake.

After a discussion and a short adjournment Mr. Prins refused the application.

Dr. Ivor Lang, a Port Elizabeth district surgeon, was then called to the stand by Mr. von Lieres. His evidence included the following points.

He visited Mr. Biko, at the request of Colonel Goosen, on September 7. In a background report he gave the time of this visit as about 12 P.M. but changed this in a later affidavit to 9.30 A.M. Colonel Goosen, he said, had expressed concern that Mr. Biko might have suffered a stroke. He carried out a lengthy and complete examination and before departing he informed Colonel Goosen that he "could find no organic cause for Mr. Biko's apparent weakness and that (he) was satisfied that he had not suffered a stroke, nor was there any paralysis of any kind."

In cross-examination, Mr. Kentridge drew attention to the fact that Dr. Lang had been asked by Colonel Goosen to make out a certificate following this first visit to Mr. Biko. This certificate stated that Dr. Lang could find no evidence for any abnormality or pathology on Mr. Biko. Mr. Kentridge then referred to a clinical report which Dr. Lang had handed to the pathologist conducting the post-mortem on Mr. Biko. This report included the facts that there was a small laceration on Mr. Biko's inner upper lip and a superficial bruise over the breast-bone "at approximately the second vertebra." (In a subsequent correcting affidavit Dr. Lang said that the word "vertebra" should read "ribs.") A pigmented mark was present around each wrist and his hands, feet and ankles were swollen.

Mr. Kentridge pointed out that in the report for Colonel Goosen none of these injuries had been mentioned. Dr. Lang would not explain this, and said that he presumed the first report was "merely for record purposes."

MR. KENTRIDGE: Being wanted for record purposes, wasn't it important to have a complete and correct record?

DR. LANG: In retrospect, yes.

MR. KENTRIDGE: Why not at the time?

DR. LANG: I didn't think of it.

Dr. Lang admitted that the first part of his certificate made at the request of Colonel Goosen was incorrect. Mr. Kentridge then turned to the sentence that read: "I have found no evidence of any abnormality or pathology on the detainee." Dr. Lang admitted that he had found the injuries mentioned in the later report.

MR. KENTRIDGE: None of this is mentioned in your certificate. Wouldn't a person who later read your certificate have taken it to mean there was no sign of injury on Biko, so that part was also highly incorrect?

DR. LANG: Yes, it was.

MR. KENTRIDGE: It may have been that Mr. Biko would one day have said he had a cut, bruised, swollen lip, and he would have been called a liar?

DR. LANG: I see that now.

MR. KENTRIDGE: Isn't that why Colonel Goosen wanted the certificate?

DR. LANG: I don't think so.

Mr. Kentridge also asked Dr. Lang if he felt that Colonel Goosen had informed him of Mr. Biko's medical studies in order to imply that Mr. Biko was shamming. Dr. Lang replied: "This is a probability." Mr. Kentridge also asked why Dr. Lang had not asked Mr. Biko how his injuries had been sustained. Dr. Lang said he had assumed that they had been sustained while the police were trying to control Mr. Biko. He had also assumed that Colonel Goosen would have informed him if this were not the case, and he had not asked Mr. Biko while Colonel Goosen was out of the room because he "assumed he (Biko) would have told me himself."

MR. KENTRIDGE: Didn't the possibility of a head injury occur to you?

DR. LANG: Yes, immediately. The moment I saw the lip injury this was uppermost in my mind.

MR. KENTRIDGE: Why didn't you ask any questions about it?

DR. LANG: I can't answer that.

MR. KENTRIDGE: Colonel Goosen never said anything to you to suggest that he (Mr. Biko) had had a bump on his head?

DR. LANG: No.

He said no Security Police officer had ever mentioned the possibility. Dr. Lang agreed with Mr. Kentridge that his examination was to a certain extent dependent on the history of the patient given to him. If he had not been told a full and correct history he could well have been put off the track. Mr. Kentridge asked whether Dr. Lang ordered the leg irons not to be replaced due to the swelling on Mr. Biko's ankle. Dr. Lang replied he had not thought of it at the time but in retrospect would have recommended it.

Mr. Kentridge drew the attention of the court to the fact that after the medical examination Mr. Biko was left lying on his mat in the office in chains. Dr. Lang said he had examined Mr. Biko carefully and found nothing "emphatically" wrong with him. Mr. Kentridge asked why Dr. Lang had not ordered Mr. Biko to be kept in bed in view of the symptoms he had noticed. Dr. Lang said that he had told Colonel Goosen that if Mr. Biko's condition persisted he should be called again.

On the following day, September 8, Dr. Lang was again called by Colonel Goosen, who was, Dr. Lang said, very worried. He arrived to examine Mr. Biko with the chief district surgeon, Dr. Tucker. Dr. Lang said Mr. Biko was coherent. Mr. Kentridge said there were many witnesses who had said that after a certain period Mr. Biko was incoherent and that they could not make contact with him. Dr. Lang said Mr. Biko had replied clearly when asked his name. Mr. Kentridge said he had been instructed that questioning on that level was not an adequate test of the degree of consciousness or mental ability.

Mr. Kentridge noted that the fact that Mr. Biko was in chains had not been mentioned until Dr. Lang's fourth affidavit.

Dr. Lang said that on September 8 Mr. Biko was still lying on the mat chained by his foot. He could not remember whether Mr. Biko was handcuffed but he had not been told that Mr. Biko had been violent again. When asked if he was shocked by this, he replied: "I was rather surprised."

Before commencing the examination at 12.45 P.M., the doctors were told by Colonel Goosen that Mr. Biko had not passed urine for twenty-four hours. They found on examination that his blankets were wet with urine and that they were smelling. Nothing was done about this.

Dr. Lang said he and Dr. Tucker had given orders that Mr. Biko be removed to the Sydenham Prison hospital. Asked by Mr. Kentridge whether Mr. Biko might have spent some time under the wet blankets, Dr. Lang said "he might have." At the end of that examination Mr. Biko had asked for water because he was thirsty and had been given it by a member of the Security staff. There was no sign of dehydration about Mr. Biko; his tongue was moist, not dry.

During the examination on September 8, Mr. Biko had complained of vague pains in his head and back. Dr. Tucker said he also found a doubtful "possible extensor plantar reflex." This meant that when he was stroked on the sole of his foot, instead of his toes curling inwards, there was a sign that his big toe might be turning upwards. Dr. Lang and Dr. Tucker then said they wanted to take Mr. Biko to hospital for examination by a specialist.

MR. KENTRIDGE: At this stage did you think he was shamming?

DR. LANG: I couldn't understand why he had passed urine in the bed. My only conclusion was that he couldn't get up. I asked him and he couldn't give me a satisfactory answer.

MR. KENTRIDGE: He didn't give a good account of himself in that regard.

DR. LANG: No, not in that regard.

MR. KENTRIDGE: Do you still think of the possibility of his having a head injury?

DR. LANG: It was at the back of my mind.

MR. KENTRIDGE: It might have been at the back of your mind, but it was not in the forefront of your affidavit.

Asked what had been done when Mr. Biko complained of a pain in his head, Dr. Lang said he had been very vague about this.

At about 9.45 P.M. on September 8, a specialist physician, Dr. Hersch, was called in to see Mr. Biko in Dr. Lang's presence at Sydenham Prison hospital. Referring to an affidavit by Dr. Hersch on September 16, Mr. Kentridge asked Dr. Lang who gave him information on Mr. Biko's previous detention. Dr. Lang said Colonel Goosen had briefed him. Mr. Kentridge: "He dropped a rather heavy hint that this man may be shamming . . . and when Dr. Hersch started his examination he had his face firmly turned in a particular direction?" Dr. Lang agreed.

Dr. Lang said that on September 8 Dr. Hersch had found Mr. Biko suffering from echolalia, a condition where a patient repeats a word or part of a sentence addressed to him. He also displayed an extensor plantar reflex which was an indication of a lesion in the brain . . . (the rest of his statement was inaudible). Asked whether to sham an extensor plantar reflex was virtually impossible, Dr. Lang replied: "This is so."

Mr. Kentridge said at this stage the doctors faced the worry that there was something wrong in the brain and carried out a lumbar puncture. The results of this indicated a significant number of red blood cells, a sign of something wrong in the brain. Dr. Lang said this would have been so if the red blood cells had not been the result of a "bloody tap" – that is, blood drawn from a blood vessel, not from the spinal fluid.

He said the neurosurgeon, Mr. Keely, was consulted on September 7. Asked whether he was convinced at this stage that Mr. Biko was shamming, Dr. Lang said: "The whole picture presented such a bizarre appearance, I did not know what to think . . ."

Dr. Lang said it was Mr. Keely's opinion that all that was necessary was observation of Mr. Biko to see if there was any change in his condition. Dr. Lang wanted to send Mr. Biko back to the Walmer police cells from the Sydenham Prison since there was no trained staff at the prison. "The Security Police would not allow us to transfer him to a hospital. We had no option but to go along with them." After further questioning Dr. Lang said: "If he had been any other prisoner we would have sent him to a provincial hospital." Mr. Kentridge replied: "Of course you would."

MR. KENTRIDGE: You said an ordinary prisoner would have been sent to a provincial hospital?

DR. LANG: I was not a neurosurgeon, I had to make the best of the situation.

MR. KENTRIDGE: If Mr. Keely said close observation was necessary, he meant a hospital . . . you told him: "Sorry, no good, the Security Police want to keep him in a police cell and we have got to do the best we can."

DR. LANG: Yes.

Dr. Lang added that he also had the impression that there had been an improvement in Mr. Biko's condition, but that if he had had the free choice, he would have put Mr. Biko in hospital by September 10.

MR. KENTRIDGE: That's the Security Police, a law unto themselves.

DR. LANG: We are district surgeons. We are not with the Security Police.

MR. KENTRIDGE: You can't buck the Security Police. It's very difficult to do so. You haven't been in court for the last few days otherwise you would realize that.

(Adjournment)

Day Seven: Tuesday, November 22, 1977

When the inquest reconvened Dr. Lang was still in the stand. His cross-examination continued after Mr. Kentridge had asked the court whether Professor Proctor would be called to give evidence, since he understood that the dating of Mr. Biko's brain injury had been done by him. Mr. Prins said he would decide later.

Mr. Kentridge then referred Dr. Lang to the events of the afternoon of Saturday, September 10, when Mr. Biko was still in the hospital cell. According to his affidavit, Dr. Lang had told Mr. Biko he was to go back to the Walmer police cells.

MR. KENTRIDGE: How did he take the good news?

DR. LANG: He said: "Yes sir" – the way he normally addressed me.

MR. KENTRIDGE: According to affidavits of warders Shehab and Hamilton, you told Mr. Biko the tests had been negative.

DR. LANG: I did not discuss the tests with Mr. Biko, nor with the warders. They might have misunderstood me.

When asked again about Mr. Biko's head injury, Dr. Lang said he examined Mr. Biko's head very carefully on the first day.

MR. KENTRIDGE: It seems inconceivable that you didn't see the injury.

DR. LANG: I did not see it. I have no cause to hide the fact. I can offer no explanation. I examined his pupils and noticed a swelling on his upper lip but I saw no injury.

MR. KENTRIDGE: Isn't it perhaps the case that just as you omitted to mention in your report the chest injury and the lip injury you omitted the head injury?

DR. LANG: I saw the lip injury and the chest injury. I can assure you that the chest injury was not that obvious.

MR. KENTRIDGE: It is not always easy to make a precise diagnosis, particularly when the brain is involved. I am not suggesting that you as a general practitioner could have made a complete diagnosis but it does seem rather strange that neither you nor Dr. Tucker seemed willing to accept that you had a really sick man on your hands.

Dr. Lang answered that this was because of the bizarre picture Mr. Biko presented and the fact that he was apparently improving. It had seemed as if he was on the mend. "I had to rely on very inexperienced observers. I had no other choice," he said.

Mr. van Rooyen, for the police, then examined Dr. Lang, who repeated that Colonel Goosen had been worried about Mr. Biko's health and that he, Dr. Lang, had given him no cause for concern after the first visit.

MR. VAN ROOYEN: Colonel Goosen had been left with one conviction in mind: "My worry about his health is unfounded. This dropping of the veil is a form of malingering?"

DR. LANG: Correct.

MR. VAN ROOYEN: You had nothing to treat of any real substance. If Colonel Goosen had felt he would like to have continued his interrogation you would have had no complaint?

DR. LANG: Correct.

MR. VAN ROOYEN: On hindsight if you are now asked if your report was full and correct you have to say no?

DR. LANG: Correct.

MR. VAN ROOYEN: But on the day in question that was the correct report?

DR. LANG: Correct.

Mr. van Rooyen referred to the extensor plantar reflex. The previous day everything had been in order, he said. On the 8th, however, the position did not make Dr. Lang and his colleagues happy at all. Dr. Lang replied: "I could not tie it up."

Dr. Gordon of the University of Natal Medical School, one of the assessors, then intervened.

DR. GORDON: You can't sham a plantar reflex.

DR. LANG: We were not sure about it on the 8th. We were not sure if the toe went up or remained horizontal.

DR. GORDON: This was a critical question.

DR. LANG: We were worried about it. I think it was recorded as doubtful.

MR. VAN ROOYEN: At no stage did you even remotely suggest to Colonel Goosen that Mr. Biko needed treatment. On the contrary you made it quite clear to Colonel Goosen that you could not find anything organically wrong?

DR. LANG: Correct.

DR. GORDON: Where does diagnosis or treatment begin or end?

DR. LANG: (Reply inaudible.)

On the morning of the 7th, Dr. Lang said, he was alone for quite some time with Mr. Biko. Later he was again alone with Mr. Biko. Mr. Biko had had ample opportunity to complain to him about any assault but no such complaint was even hinted at, Dr. Lang said.

Mr. van Rooyen then referred to the examination at Sydenham Prison by Dr. Hersch and Dr. Lang, and referred to the fact that Colonel Goosen had given Dr. Hersch Mr. Biko's background. Dr. Lang said that Colonel Goosen had used words to the effect that Mr. Biko's behavior in previous detention had been similar to his present behavior.

MR. VAN ROOYEN: What you said must have warned Dr. Hersch that it was possible that this man was putting it on?

DR. LANG: Correct.

MR. VAN ROOYEN: Obviously, any reasonable specialist would have been on his guard?

DR. LANG: Yes.

Later, Mr. van Rooyen referred to the difference in Mr. Biko's condition between the afternoon of September 8 and the evening of September 8, when Mr. Biko was examined at 9.45 P.M. by Dr. Hersch. Dr. Hersch's report said that Mr. Biko had difficulty in turning over on the bed, but that Mr. Biko walked well, although with a left-side limp. Dr. Lang agreed that at midday on the same day he had the impression that Mr. Biko could not walk.

MR. VAN ROOYEN: Did you think that it could have had a psychological origin because on the night of the 7th he was walking reasonably well?

DR. LANG: Correct.

MR. VAN ROOYEN: And it produced rather a bizarre picture?

DR. LANG: Correct.

MR. VAN ROOYEN: Would it be fair to say that in regard to the possible plantar on the right and now the plantar on the left, would you have said that the picture was a bizarre one?

DR. LANG: Correct.

DR. GORDON: I can't understand his question.

MR. VAN ROOYEN: I want to put it to you that you thought it was impossible and bizarre?

DR. LANG: To remember what I thought then is now very difficult.

PROFESSOR GORDON: Why do you say bizarre when you have clear-cut evidence of a plantar?

DR. LANG: (Reply inaudible.)

MR. VAN ROOYEN: One thing is sure, that as of that night the discussions centered around the issue that there was quite a lot of shamming, but that a lumbar puncture should be performed the next morning?

DR. LANG: Yes.

MR. VAN ROOYEN: Is it that strange that Colonel Goosen should have had a clear impression that this man was shamming? After the lumbar puncture was done you would have expected him to have a headache?

DR. LANG: Yes.

MR. VAN ROOYEN: But he says he has no headache, no pain and he is comfortable?

DR. LANG: Correct.

DR. GORDON: Did you do an extensor test after the lumbar puncture?

DR. LANG: No, I did not. I did not want to disturb him too much.

Dealing with the events of the 9th, Dr. Lang said he discussed the lumbar puncture with Dr. Hersch. The results were largely negative, and the 9th went by with no further developments.

Mr. van Rooyen referred to the consultation which Dr. Lang had with Mr. Keely, a neurosurgeon. (Mr. Keely had been contacted on September 10, following a telephone discussion between Dr. Lang and Dr. Hersch concerning the fact that the cerebrospinal fluid obtained from the lumbar puncture on Mr. Biko was bloodstained. Dr. Hersch, Dr. Lang had said, felt that a neurosurgeon should be consulted and if necessary an X-ray of the skull obtained. Dr. Lang had said that Mr. Keely's response during a telephone conversation with him was that all that was necessary at that stage would be observation.) Mr. van Rooyen said that the ultimate result of the consultation by telephone was that there was no evidence of intracranial bleeding and cerebrospinal pressure and it was not necessary for a further special investigation. Dr. Lang said that Dr. Keely had said that it was not necessary "at that stage."

Dr. Lang also answered questions for Mr. Pickard, counsel for the doctors, and Mr. von Lieres. During these questions Dr. Lang said that Mr. Biko was the first person held under section 6 of the Terrorism Act that he had examined. He said there was no evidence of a "vicious assault" upon Mr. Biko. Asked whether Colonel Goosen would have allowed Mr. Biko to be hospitalized, Dr. Lang said it was a difficult question to answer as he got the impression that under no circumstances would Mr. Biko be allowed into hospital.

Mr. von Lieres said Dr. Lang's evidence suggested that he wished to send Mr. Biko to hospital for further observation. He asked Dr. Lang what the situation would have been if a definite diagnosis had been made. Dr. Lang said he believed that if he had told Colonel Goosen there was positive information that Mr. Biko was definitely ill, he would have been sent to the hospital.

The next witness was the chief district surgeon in Port Elizabeth, Dr. Benjamin Tucker. He answered many questions from Mr. Kentridge concerning his visit to Mr. Biko on September 8, when he accompanied Dr. Lang. When asked why he had not questioned Mr. Biko about abrasions to his wrist and lip, Dr. Tucker said that Mr. Biko had not volunteered any information. He had asked him whether he had any complaints and Mr. Biko had said he had a headache and a pain in the back.
MR. KENTRIDGE: You asked him one question and you got one answer. Was that the sum total of the questions?
DR. TUCKER: Yes.
MR. KENTRIDGE: On that basis you say in your affidavit: "He was alert but answered questions in an indistinct manner." That is a misleading statement.
DR. TUCKER: I am sorry.
MR. KENTRIDGE: It is not merely misleading, it is a plainly false statement.
DR. TUCKER: I cannot say that.
MR. KENTRIDGE: Well, I can. I will tell you why. He didn't answer questions. At most he answered one question. And secondly on the basis of that single

question and answer you had no right to say that mentally he was alert.

Dr. Tucker agreed that when Mr. Biko's reflexes were tested the upgoing big toe on the right side was not clear but may have indicated a neurological problem. Mr. Kentridge said that this sign implied that Mr. Biko was not a malingerer. "This is in the eye of the observer," said the doctor. At the end of the observation, Dr. Tucker said he did not think Mr. Biko was a malingerer. He did not tell Colonel Goosen that he thought Mr. Biko was shamming because he had a doubt. "I told him (Colonel Goosen) that I was unable to come to any conclusion and that I considered it advisable to consult a physician." Dr. Tucker said that he did not think he gave Colonel Goosen the impression that Mr. Biko was shamming.

When asked if he had thought of the possibility that Mr. Biko was suffering from a head injury, Dr. Tucker said that it had crossed his mind. He did not ask either Mr. Biko or Colonel Goosen about it. He said he thought the injury to the lip might have caused brain injury.

MR. KENTRIDGE: Dr. Tucker, if you thought the lip injury was possible evidence of a head injury, oughtn't you have gone into it further?

DR. TUCKER: From whom?

MR. KENTRIDGE: From Colonel Goosen?

DR. TUCKER: I don't think I can reply. There was this history of restraint and the injury could have come from that period.

MR. KENTRIDGE: Why did you not ask, as the obvious question, whether the man received a bump on the head?

DR. TUCKER: I did not ask it, and that is all I can say.

MR. PRINS: Did you ask Biko?

DR. TUCKER: No.

MR. KENTRIDGE: Was it not because you were reluctant to embarrass Goosen?

DR. TUCKER: No.

MR. KENTRIDGE: Either from reading about it or from your own experience, have you knowledge that the police assault people in custody?

DR. TUCKER: I have . . . (inaudible).

MR. KENTRIDGE: But on that occasion you did not ask?

DR. TUCKER: No, I did not. Where persons are brought to me for examination, my report is completed on a special form. This is all I am required to do.

MR. PRINS: Here we have a man with a swollen lip. Mention is made that he was involved in trouble and they had to restrain him. You were doing your tests, what were those tests?

DR. TUCKER: There was the history which I had to examine. The story was given to Dr. Lang . . . (inaudible).

MR. PRINS: You accepted as fact what Goosen told you?

DR. TUCKER: I may put it this way, if I am called to see a patient and he has a cut on his head, then I am interested in treating him and not in how he got the cut.

MR. PRINS: In your interest in treating the patient, is it not also essential and wise to know what caused it?

DR. TUCKER: There was the history that Biko had become hysterical and that he had to be restrained . . .

MR. PRINS: Why should it not have been caused by the brain injury?

DR. TUCKER: Dr. Lang said there were no signs of bruises around the head.

MR. KENTRIDGE: Let me start again. You are a professional man and you are not doing yourself justice. Are you not aware that sometimes there are cases of people assaulted in custody? Did you not think about it?

DR. TUCKER: No.

MR. KENTRIDGE: You say you had in mind the possibility of a head injury?

DR. TUCKER: Yes.

MR. KENTRIDGE: If someone said this man had bumped his head against the wall, would you have taken a different view?

DR. TUCKER: No.

MR. KENTRIDGE: If you see someone and you had the suspicion that he had some neurological damage and you knew he was in some sort of violent incident, would you not have asked whether he had received a blow on the head?

DR. TUCKER: (Reply inaudible.)

MR. KENTRIDGE: I am suggesting to you that the reason you did not ask was because you were dealing with the Security Police?

DR. TUCKER: No.

Mr. van Rooyen at this stage objected strongly to Mr. Kentridge's statement. Mr. Kentridge replied: "It is a question, not a statement," and continued to question the witness.

MR. KENTRIDGE: Don't you ask a question in that situation?

DR. TUCKER: I would say no, say no you don't.

There was a murmur from the packed court, and Mr. Prins called an adjournment for five minutes. After this he threatened to clear the courtroom if the laughter in the gallery did not stop. Mr. van Rooyen then objected formally to Mr. Kentridge's line of questioning. Mr. Kentridge, addressing the magistrate, said that it seemed that the objection was leveled at both him and Mr. Prins. He would attempt to phrase his questions as he had always phrased them.

Dr. Tucker then asked to rephrase his last reply. He said that questions asked by the district surgeon were not banned in the Security offices.

MR. KENTRIDGE: I don't suggest they are banned. I suggest that you personally did not ask the question.

DR. TUCKER: I can only object strongly. At all times I have always had all the cooperation necessary from the Security Police.

MR. KENTRIDGE: You used the word "cooperation."

DR. TUCKER: What cooperation? What does cooperation mean?

MR. KENTRIDGE: You used it.

DR. TUCKER: My meaning of the word is that when we require information and when we require things to be done, then they are done.

MR. KENTRIDGE: You deny that you have any inhibitions about asking them questions even if they embarrass them?

DR. TUCKER: Yes.

MR. KENTRIDGE: Why did you not ask whether Biko had got a bump on the head?

Dr. Tucker said nothing.

MR. KENTRIDGE: At no stage did Goosen say to you that this man had received a bump on his head?

DR. TUCKER: No.

MR. KENTRIDGE: Did anyone suggest to you that Biko had received a bump on the head?

DR. TUCKER: General Kleinhaus.

MR. KENTRIDGE: When?

DR. TUCKER: At the time of the interview.

MR. KENTRIDGE: That was the first time it was suggested to you?

DR. TUCKER: Also when I spoke to Professor Loubser, the chief state pathologist in Pretoria, on the following morning, probably the 13th . . .

MR. KENTRIDGE: When you last saw him (Biko) he was still on the same mat under a wet blanket with the same trousers on?

DR. TUCKER: Yes.

Dr. Tucker said he had given no orders in that regard.

MR. KENTRIDGE: Mr. Biko was examined by Dr. Hersch and you were told of his finding the following day.

DR. TUCKER: Yes. The following day.

Dr. Tucker said that he had known about the plantar reflex tests but had not known that red blood cells had been found in the cerebrospinal fluid.

Mr. Kentridge then referred to a statement in Dr. Tucker's affidavit that Dr. Lang had informed him that Dr. Hersch had examined Mr. Biko and could find nothing wrong except for a possible plantar reflex. "That was a very serious finding, was it not?" Dr. Tucker said it would have indicated a possible neurological defect. "I cannot express expert knowledge but it is a very serious sign of brain damage."

MR. KENTRIDGE: Did you get the results of the lumbar puncture?

DR. TUCKER: No.

MR. KENTRIDGE: Wasn't that of interest to you?

DR. TUCKER: The patient was Dr. Lang's.

(Adjournment)

Day Eight: Wednesday, November 23, 1977

The following day Mr. Kentridge questioned Dr. Tucker about his visit to Mr. Biko on September 11.

Dr. Tucker said Colonel Goosen had called him on the Sunday afternoon because he had been on duty and Colonel Goosen had said that he was unable to contact Dr. Lang. Dr. Tucker took the responsibility for medical decisions on that occasion, he said. He was called in because "evidently something had happened to Biko." Colonel Goosen told him that Mr. Biko had collapsed and had been found by Sergeant Paul van Vuuren. Dr. Tucker found that Mr. Biko was hyperventilating. Possible causes of this were hysteria, renal failure, bleeding of the brain, epileptic seizures, drowning or lung complaints.

MR. KENTRIDGE: You say the central nervous system showed no change from what was found at a previous examination?

DR. TUCKER: I did a rapid new examination.

MR. KENTRIDGE: How rapid?

DR. TUCKER: About five minutes.

MR. KENTRIDGE: Did you test for plantar reflex?

DR. TUCKER: No.

DR. GORDON: Surely of all the signs you go for the plantar reflex was the most important? The only positive thing up to that stage was the upgoing toe. Why did you not test that?

DR. TUCKER: I was going for signs of intracranial pressure. There was no paresis, no spasticity on either side.

DR. GORDON: Did you not consider the plantar reflex of great significance even in the absence of cerebral paresis?

DR. TUCKER: Yes.

Dr. Tucker said that Mr. Biko was "apathetic," but that "there was no localized sign to indicate to me that any further organic disease was present at the time." He recommended that Mr. Biko go to a hospital with trained staff. There was no trained staff at Sydenham prison hospital because the only male nurse was absent. A decision was taken to send the prisoner to Pretoria.

Dr. Tucker said that he knew that Mr. Biko was going to Pretoria in a motor vehicle and had not thought this inadvisable. He did not remonstrate about it. He had not known that Mr. Biko was going in a Land Rover but had been told that he was going in a Kombi. He knew that Mr. Biko was traveling without any medical attention because there was no male nurse available.

MR. KENTRIDGE: In your affidavit you said that as Mr. Biko's condition was satisfactory at that stage you did not consider that this would have any adverse effect. Did you consider his condition satisfactory?

DR. TUCKER: I did.

MR. KENTRIDGE: You were urgently called in on the Sunday afternoon and told that the man had collapsed. You found him still lying on the floor with froth at his mouth which was unexplained?

DR. TUCKER: Yes.

MR. KENTRIDGE: Similarly, he was hyperventilating but you did not know the cause?

DR. TUCKER: Yes.

MR. KENTRIDGE: You found his left arm somewhat weak?

DR. TUCKER: Yes.

MR. KENTRIDGE: You found him apathetic?

DR. TUCKER: Yes.

MR. KENTRIDGE: You knew that the physician who had examined him had found a plantar reflex?

DR. TUCKER: Yes.

MR. KENTRIDGE: Do you say that a man in that condition could be described as being in a satisfactory condition?

DR. TUCKER: There was a question in my mind about possible shamming, apart from the upgoing toe.

MR. PRINS: Was this question of shamming still in your mind overriding the other factors?

DR. TUCKER: As far as I was aware Dr. Lang had seen Mr. Biko and had not found anything materially wrong. I had seen him with a vague diagnosis. Dr. Hersch had seen him. Dr. Lang told me what Dr. Hersch had found. I had a very puzzling picture.

MR. KENTRIDGE: At the time when you advised Colonel Goosen that the man could go by road to Pretoria you knew that a lumbar puncture had been done but did not know the results?

DR. TUCKER: Yes.

MR. KENTRIDGE: I am going to submit that in that situation no honest doctor could have advised that Mr. Biko's condition was satisfactory.

DR. TUCKER: In the circumstances I thought it was.

Dr. Tucker said that he was later told by Dr. Lang that in the lumbar puncture nothing materially wrong had been found apart from the fact that microscopic red cells were found to be present. He knew that this might have more than one explanation, but it did not worry him because Dr. Lang had said that Mr. Biko had been eating and drinking and walking about.

DR. GORDON: When you heard that Mr. Biko was walking about was it conveyed to you that Dr. Lang himself had seen this?

DR. TUCKER: No, I'm afraid I can't say . . . honestly.

MR. KENTRIDGE: Let us assume that some holidaymakers from Pretoria had come to see you in Port Elizabeth about their child who had been acting in a bizarre way. The parents suspected that the child did not want to go back to school, but it showed a plantar reflex, was lying on the floor, had red cells in its spinal fluid, froth at the mouth, was hyperventilating and was weak in the left limbs. Would you have permitted his parents to drive 700 miles to Pretoria?

DR. TUCKER: The circumstances were different. I would have insisted that the child should go into hospital immediately. Here there was an uncertainty.

MR. KENTRIDGE: Shouldn't that have made you more careful rather than less careful? Isn't the only difference that in Biko's case Colonel Goosen insisted that he did not go into a hospital?

DR. TUCKER: I wouldn't say insisted. He was averse to the suggestion.

MR. KENTRIDGE: Why didn't you stand up for the interests of your patient?

DR. TUCKER: I don't know that in this particular situation one could override the decisions made by a responsible police officer.

DR. GORDON: Why didn't you say that unless Biko went to hospital you would wipe your hands of it?

DR. TUCKER: I did not think at that stage that Mr. Biko's condition would become so serious. There was still the question of a possible shamming.

MR. KENTRIDGE: Did you think the plantar reflex could be feigned?

DR. TUCKER: No.

MR. KENTRIDGE: Did you think a man could feign red blood cells in his cerebral spinal fluid?

DR. TUCKER: No.

MR. KENTRIDGE: In terms of the Hippocratic Oath are not the interests of your patients paramount?

DR. TUCKER: Yes.

MR. KENTRIDGE: But in this instance they were subordinated to the interests of Security?

DR. TUCKER: Yes.

MR. KENTRIDGE: The classic signs of brain damage are a deteriorating level of consciousness, an upgoing toe and blood in the cerebral spinal fluid.

MR. PRINS: In fairness I must point out that I have understood Dr. Tucker to say that when he examined Mr. Biko on the Sunday he had not been informed of the red cells in the fluid.

MR. KENTRIDGE: Yes, but he was told before Mr. Biko left for Pretoria.

Mr. Kentridge then referred to the photograph taken after Mr. Biko's death, showing a scab on his forehead. Mr. Kentridge said that, according to the pathologists, the injury on Mr. Biko's forehead was between four and eight days old, and must have been obviously visible to a doctor. Dr. Tucker said it must have been there but it was not visible. He said the only reason he could give for this was that it was colored in the same way as the prisoner's skin so that he could not distinguish it.

Answering questions from Mr. van Rooyen, Dr. Tucker said that when he examined Mr. Biko he was mentally alert and able to answer questions intelligibly. He had not complained of any assault or injury. He said that when he went to visit Mr. Biko at Walmer police cells on September 11, he understood that the prisoner had been discharged from the hospital because his condition was such that he could be put up at the police station. Dr. Lang informed him that after Mr. Biko had eaten and walked around, and after Dr. Keely, the neurosurgeon, had said that the lumbar puncture was negative, Mr. Biko had been transferred. Dr. Colin Hersch, the specialist physician who examined Mr. Biko after Dr. Lang and Dr. Tucker were puzzled by his symptoms, was then called. An affidavit by Dr. Hersch was handed to the court. It contained a medical report written by Dr. Hersch to Dr. Lang after Dr. Hersch's examination of Mr. Biko. The medical report was dated September 16 – four days after Mr. Biko's death. Answering questions from Mr. von Lieres, Dr. Hersch said the result of the lumbar puncture performed on Mr. Biko on September 9 left any conclusion on Mr. Biko's condition "wide open." The blood cells could have been due to a brain injury or a bloody tap – blood drawn from blood vessels, not from the spinal fluid. The ease with which a lumbar puncture was performed was a point against the possibility of a bloody tap. Notwithstanding the fact that he suspected damage to the brain, he did not mention this specifically in his medical report.

Mr. Kentridge then questioned Dr. Hersch, who said he had been phoned on September 8 by Dr. Lang and given the history of Mr. Biko. While in detention previously Mr. Biko had shown difficulty in talking and had dragged his left leg. Dr. Lang also mentioned the possibility of an upgoing toe on the right foot. Dr. Hersch said he suspected Mr. Biko was shamming.

Dr. Hersch later also gained the impression from Colonel Goosen that Mr. Biko might be shamming, although Colonel Goosen was keen for Dr. Hersch to rule out the possibility of a stroke. At no stage did Colonel Goosen mention the possibility that Mr. Biko might have had a bump on his head, although he did mention the episode where Mr. Biko allegedly threw a chair at an officer and had to be restrained.

Dr. Hersch also knew that Mr. Biko had been a medical student for four years. Dr. Hersch said he got the message that he was dealing with a man who might be feigning and that he was a dangerous man. He said that particularly in neurological cases a wrong history could prejudice the examination.

Dr. Hersch had never noticed the bruise on Mr. Biko's head or the scab that was apparent in the post-mortem photograph, "but in retrospect I have quite a clear picture of him standing with a whitish area over his left eye that I thought was dry saliva or sputum." He did not think he would have missed an abrasion had there been one.

When asked how he accounted for the fact that it was not seen, Dr. Hersch replied: "I really don't know. By the rest of the examination one could almost have expected it to be there. It fitted in with indications of brain injury that there should have been a lesion there." He said the upgoing toe on the left side was a significant sign . . . it showed a great likelihood of organic brain damage.

Asked whether it was possible to sham an upgoing toe, Dr. Hersch said he had never seen it in his professional career but that Dr. Marquard de Villiers, assisting the doctors' counsel, had managed to sham this reaction.

Dr. Hersch said he had not given Dr. Lang "the all-clear" after the investigation. He had explained to Colonel Goosen that there were positive findings of something wrong with the nervous system. "I don't remember the actual words. I made it clear there were positive findings."

Asked why Mr. Biko was not taken to a proper hospital, Dr. Hersch said: "This was not in our hands." There was no doubt that had he been a private patient he would have been hospitalized. Asked whether he would have allowed Mr. Biko to go to Pretoria in a Land Rover on four cell mats, Dr. Hersch said he would not have been unhappy if Mr. Biko's condition was the same as on examination. Answering a question from Mr. Kentridge, Dr. Hersch said he would never have allowed a patient to go 700 miles by road if he had collapsed and was in a semicoma.

Mr. Kentridge then drew the attention of the court to a form sent with Mr. Biko's spinal fluid to the Institute for Medical Research for testing. The name of the patient was made out as Stephen Njelo. Mr. Kentridge asked whether the false name had been filled in so the staff at the institute would not know the patient's real name. Dr. Hersch said he did not know who filled in the name on the form. It may have been an orderly at the Sydenham prison hospital – "I don't know who it was." Mr. Kentridge said he had tried to find out from the institute whether they had done tests on Mr. Biko's spinal fluid, and at first got a negative reply.

Mr. Kentridge also drew the attention of the court to a bed letter written by Dr. Lang on September 10 in which he said that he (Dr. Lang) and Dr. Hersch could find no pathology on Mr. Biko and that the lumbar puncture test was normal. Dr. Hersch admitted that they had found signs of pathology in the up-going toe and that there had been blood cells in the spinal fluid which could have pointed to brain injury. "It was compatible with brain damage as well as compatible with a normal lumbar puncture."

MR. KENTRIDGE: No doctor has the right to describe the lumbar puncture as normal?

DR. HERSCH: No.

Answering questions from Mr. van Rooyen, Dr. Hersch said he had been "worried" by Mr. Biko's condition but "not perturbed by the emergency of the situation." Mr. van Rooyen said that if Dr. Hersch had been really worried, he would have conveyed this to Colonel Goosen. Dr. Hersch replied that the situation was not then "immediately urgent."

MR. PRINS: The point is that you were not much worried?

DR. HERSCH: I was worried insofar as he was my client. A person who has positive neurological signs and a person who has abnormal cerebrofluid is worrying, but one is not worried that he is going to die. What was really within my mind was that the only person who could tell was a neurosurgeon. You can either watch him, treat him or do surgery.

MR. VAN ROOYEN: I want to say to you that nowhere in your report after you knew he had died did you say that you came to a definite conclusion that there was an organic condition?

DR. HERSCH: No, I did not, but one should have said it.

MR. VAN ROOYEN: You did not refer it to Mr. Keely but asked him whether further tests should be done?

DR. HERSCH: That is the same as referring it to him.

MR. VAN ROOYEN: I am afraid that I am mystified. You said that in your opinion there were signs of organic disease connected to the function of the brain?

DR. HERSCH: Yes.

MR. VAN ROOYEN: You did not say so in your report?

DR. HERSCH: Because I thought it was self-explanatory. It was not a good report.

MR. VAN ROOYEN: I submit your evidence is not good . . . that you were much less certain at the time of the examination.

(Reply inaudible.)

Mr. Prins asked Dr. Hersch what he had told Dr. Lang. Was it the same as he had written in his report? Dr. Hersch replied that he had mentioned four points on which he had based the diagnosis that Mr. Biko should be seen by a neuro-surgeon. Questioned about whether Dr. Lang had indicated that Mr. Biko was shamming before Dr. Hersch saw the prisoner, Dr. Hersch said that Dr. Lang had not mentioned shamming, only the facts.

(Adjournment)

Day Nine: Thursday, November 24, 1977

Mr. van Rooyen resumed his examination of Dr. Hersch. Dr. Hersch agreed that he did not go into the medical side of the matter with Colonel Goosen but had put it in very vague terms. Mr. van Rooyen said that when he read Dr. Hersch's report he could find no diagnosis, which implied that even by the time of the report there had been no diagnosis made. Dr. Hersch replied: "At the time I was convinced that there had been a head injury and brain damage. I can't argue with the fact that I did not convey this in my report."

After Dr. Hersch had been questioned about the medical details, Dr. Lang was recalled to the stand by Mr. von Lieres. Dr. Lang was shown a foolscap page and admitted it was from a bed letter in his handwriting which was signed in the prison hospital. Mr. von Lieres quoted from this page: "Examined by Dr. Hersch last night. Conscious. In possession of faculties. No pathology except with regard to reflex and apparent loss of sensation of lower limbs. No change of condition."

MR. KENTRIDGE: You were present when the plantar reflex was tested. You reported wrongly that it was tested on the right. It should have been on the left?

DR. LANG: Yes.

MR. KENTRIDGE: Yet you say in your bed letter that both Dr. Hersch and you could find no pathology. That was false?

DR. LANG: Yes.

MR. KENTRIDGE: And that the lumbar puncture was normal. That was false?

DR. LANG: No, it was incorrect.

MR. KENTRIDGE: It was false to say that no pathology could be found?

DR. LANG: I gave an incorrect statement in the bed letter. There was an omission of one word. It should have read gross pathology. This was the essence of what I told Mr. Biko. That there was no indication of gross pathology.

MR. KENTRIDGE: This was also false. A most significant sign of brain injury had been found.

DR. LANG: To my mind the upgoing toe was only one of a few.

MR. KENTRIDGE: I am going to suggest that it is perfectly clear that you made a false statement to Mr. Biko and in your bed letter, to get Mr. Biko back to the hands of the police as soon as possible.

DR. LANG: I deny that. It was an error on my part.

Mr. van Rooyen referred to Dr. Lang's affidavit in which he had said that he and Mr. Keely had agreed that Mr. Biko could be transferred to the custody of the Security Police and all that was necessary was observation. Dr. Lang agreed that he had advised Colonel Goosen of "this nonperturbing picture," and that he had told him that Mr. Biko could be moved provided there was no change in his condition.

DR. GORDON: You were off duty on the Sunday. You knew that he had been removed from the Sydenham prison hospital to the Walmer police cells. Am I right that on that day you would have been unable to carry out Mr. Keely's wish?

DR. LANG: I knew that he would be removed sometime during the morning. I intended seeing him in the afternoon, but I got a message from Dr. Tucker who said he had seen Mr. Biko.

DR. GORDON: It seems that your undertaking to keep Mr. Biko under observation was not carried out on this day. It was part of your undertaking that you would see him twice a day?

DR. LANG: This was my own decision. I gave no undertaking to Mr. Keely.

DR. GORDON: Carrying out your program of supervision you should have seen him on the Sunday. Why didn't you see him?

DR. LANG: I wasn't sure when he was being transferred.

DR. GORDON: Supervision in cases of head injury means more than seeing the patient twice a day. To my mind he should be seen at least hourly or half-hourly.

DR. LANG: That is correct when a patient is in a hospital. As a doctor I could not do this. I had nobody reliable to do it. I could not rely on a medical orderly who had a hundred-day course.

DR. GORDON: Could he have taken a pulse?

DR. LANG: Yes.

DR. GORDON: In your training as a doctor were you not told that when head injury cases are kept under observation the pulse should be taken at least hourly? On the Sunday Mr. Biko was deprived of observation in all respects?

There was no answer.

Dr. Lang was replaced on the stand by Brigadier Johan Coetzee, deputy head of the Security Police. Mr. Prins said he had received affidavits from Brigadier Coetzee and his chief, Brigadier C. F. Zietsman, and that he intended allowing them to give evidence.

Before Brigadier Coetzee could be questioned Mr. van Rooyen objected. He said that the whole issue started with the inadmissible handing in of newspaper statements with the intention to confront Colonel Goosen and attack his credibility. He had at that time lodged a sharp objection against the handing in of the document because there had been no evidence of prior inconsistent statements by Colonel Goosen. That objection was upheld, but Mr. Prins had indicated that he wished the brigadiers to be called.

Mr. van Rooyen said the problem was once again one of relevancy and admissibility. The court was putting the cart before the horse and was on the point of embarking on a process of leading evidence proving Colonel Goosen's credibility. This was not admissible.

Mr. Kentridge said it was absolutely correct for Mr. Prins to call for the brigadiers' evidence. Their evidence concerned not only prior inconsistent statements but went to the heart of what had happened in Port Elizabeth. Brigadier Zietsman had very properly disclosed a telex message he had received, and his affidavit disclosed many things contrary to what Colonel Goosen had said. He could understand that Mr. van Rooyen had to protect the interests of Colonel Goosen and Major Snyman because this evidence would destroy them to a large extent.

Eventually Mr. Prins said he would give his decision next day.

Professor Johann Loubser, chief state pathologist in Pretoria, then gave evidence on his post-mortem examination of Mr. Biko's body on September 13. Mr. Kentridge said he wanted to place on record that the Biko family had complete confidence in the thoroughness and integrity of Professor Loubser's examination. Before questioning Professor Loubser on medical details, Mr. Kentridge asked whether he had found any sign of dehydration in Mr. Biko's body. Professor Loubser had not.

Mr. Kentridge referred to a report submitted by Professor Neville Proctor, head of the department of pathology at the South African Institute of Medical Research. He said Professor Proctor had an international reputation as a neuro-pathologist, specializing in the pathology of the brain. In his report Professor Proctor concluded that Mr. Biko's brain showed several areas of damage, mainly features of hemorrhage and necrosis (death of tissue) and that the lesions were "clearly indicative of severe traumatic brain contusions and contusional necrosis." Professor Loubser agreed, saying the contusions (bruises) came from a "mechanical origin."

Mr. Kentridge asked whether Professor Loubser agreed that the contusions were between three and five days old at the outside. Professor Loubser said he and Professor W. Simson had judged the age of the contusions to be three to five days.

MR. KENTRIDGE: If one were to apply to the date of his death which was September 12, and taking five days back it would be September 7, and six days back would be September 6?

PROFESSOR LOUBSER: Such a period of time lapse could be applicable.

Mr. Kentridge said, summing up Professor Proctor's conclusions in less technical language, leaving aside secondary hemorrhage, that there were five distinct lesions in Mr. Biko's brain. Mr. Kentridge suggested that the infliction of these lesions would have required at least three, but probably four, blows to the head. He emphasized that his usage of the word blow meant the application of force to the head and not necessarily with a fist.

Referring to the first lesion, he said this was what had been called a contra-coup, meaning an injury on one side of the brain, caused by a blow on the other side of the head. The blow causing the injury is not inflicted on a place above the injury, but at another place distant from the injury. Professor Loubser said it was his considered opinion that the main lesion was caused by a blow on the left-hand side of the forehead. Professor Loubser said the actual situation of the skull and brain in relation to each other at the moment of impact was of the greatest importance. The force with which a person fell, for example, was not the prime determining factor in the extent of brain injury.

Mr. Kentridge summed up the picture given in court of Mr. Biko's behavior from the morning of September 7. He said Mr. Biko seemed to have drawn a veil down between himself and other people, his speech was incoherent and slurred, and he mumbled. He intermittently showed signs of weakness in the limbs, a possible ataxic gait, an extensor plantar reflex, symptoms of echolalia, weakness in his left arm and a slight limp. Red cells were found in his spinal fluid. Mr. Kentridge said taking this picture into account did this not sound as though Mr. Biko was suffering from a relatively serious brain injury? Professor Loubser replied: "The picture does not sound like a very grave injury. I find it perfectly agreeable with the pathological findings."

Mr. Kentridge said the neurological experts advising him had expressed the view that Mr. Biko's injury must have been followed by a period of unconsciousness of at least ten minutes, more likely fifteen to twenty minutes, and possibly up to one hour. Professor Loubser said he had no reason to disagree with this.

The questioning then turned to the visible injury on Mr. Biko's forehead. This injury consisted of a bruise, swelling and scab shown on a photograph before the court. Professor Loubser said that on examining the body he immediately observed the injury on Mr. Biko's forehead. He had no difficulty in seeing the wound.

The discussion then turned to the possible causes of the head injury. Mr. Kentridge asked Professor Loubser if it could be due to a fall. Professor Loubser said it could. Could it be due to a blow from a blunt object such as a rubber truncheon? Professor Loubser said he would have difficulty in explaining the size of the wound. The scab that appeared on the surface of Mr. Biko's head was the one aspect of the injury that could be compatible with a blow from a truncheon.

Mr. Kentridge then asked about the possibility of two or three blows having caused the injury. Professor Loubser said this theory seemed to be consistent only with the exterior of Mr. Biko's skin. Mr. Kentridge asked if the lesion might have been caused by a blow from a fist. Professor Loubser said that he could only agree with such a possibility in the abstract. Mr. Kentridge then said: "What about the fist of a man wearing a ring?" Professor Loubser replied that that was conceivable.

Returning to the possibility of the injury having been caused by a fall, Mr. Kentridge said that it would have had to be a fall that involved the left side of the forehead, including the cheekbone, but not the nose. Professor Loubser agreed. Mr. Kentridge then asked how someone could fall in this way and not involve the nose in the impact. Professor Loubser replied that it would have to be a fall on the left side of the face with the head turned toward the right.

Mr. Kentridge said that an epileptic could fall this way during a fit. Or someone who had been knocked unconscious might also fall in this way. What he found more difficult to believe was that a conscious man falling to the ground could sustain such an injury. Professor Loubser said this might be difficult. Mr. Kentridge said that if a man fell on his face or forehead there might be some reason to think that he could not use his hands to save himself. Professor Loubser agreed.

Mr. Kentridge then discussed the lip injury noticed on Mr. Biko. Professor Loubser said he could not tie the two lip injuries with the other head injuries. It seemed to him that the lip injuries were quite separate. He agreed with Mr. Kentridge that the cuts on the lip were more likely to have been caused by two blows than a fall.

Referring to the bruising of the rib area, Mr. Kentridge said these injuries showed that they were probably caused by a jab with a sharp object, for example a finger or a stick. Professor Loubser agreed, but added: "It wasn't a vicious jab, it was just a jab."

Professor Loubser said that he believed that the abrasions found on Mr. Biko's wrists and feet were caused by handcuffs and manacles. He said he had found a wound on Mr. Biko's left big toe, what appeared to have been a blister with a small hole in it caused by something like a "pin or needle." Asked what could have caused it, Professor Loubser said he believed it was a mechanical cause . . . "a bump or pressure at that point."

Mr. Kentridge then turned to the causes of contracoup head injuries. It was common, he said, that this type of injury was caused by rapid deceleration of a moving head. He pointed out that many head injuries suffered by boxers were of the contracoup type. Professor Loubser agreed that this type of injury was statistically the most important injury suffered by anyone who received a blow to the head in boxing.

It was agreed that the rate of motion of the head was not of vital significance. The important point was that the motion of the head was arrested suddenly. Professor Loubser said it was possible that if the head was in motion in a forward direction, and was arrested by a blow, the injury could have taken place. Mr. Kentridge asked if it could happen if a person was pushed against a wall by the scruff of his neck. Professor Loubser said that was possible.

Professor Loubser then drew the attention of the court to a children's program he had seen on television. In this program a police constable "in a compromising situation" had to get injuries on his body to convince the authorities that something had happened to him. "He bumped his head very hard against the wall of a house . . . It could have been something like this," Professor Loubser said.

(Adjournment)

Day Ten: Friday, November 24, 1977

At the start of proceedings, Mr. Kentridge referred to Professor Loubser's previous evidence, when he said that the brain injuries might have been caused by a man bumping his own head against a wall.

MR. KENTRIDGE: You are not advancing as a theory that this is what happened, are you?

PROFESSOR LOUBSER: I cannot put it forward as a probability, nor aside as a possibility.

MR. KENTRIDGE: Would that mean that such a man stood in front of a wall and dashed his head against it?

PROFESSOR LOUBSER: Yes, repeatedly.

MR. PRINS: A person in a struggle could bump his head against a wall and this could have been repeated?

PROFESSOR LOUBSER: Correct.

MR. KENTRIDGE: If someone else banged the head it would be easier to explain the acceleration?

PROFESSOR LOUBSER: I can conceive that a jack-knifing movement would be ample.

Professor Loubser said a fall from a chair would cause more lesions than a bump from a standing position. He had not in his experience found a similar lesion as a self-inflicted injury. "But there is always a first time," he said.

Mr. Kentridge then pointed out the contortions involved if Mr. Biko were to have tried this. One theory Professor Loubser put forward was that such an injury could be sustained by the person "lunging." He said. "He would have had to kick against the wall and with that movement to dive into the floor as a deliberate action."

Mr. Kentridge pointed out that if a man wanted to bang his head he could do it on the wall next to him. However, because of the position in which Mr. Biko was chained, it would have been on the opposite side of his head to where the injury actually occurred.

Mr. van Rooyen then began his examination. He said that his advice had been that one application of force to the forehead could have caused all five lesions. Professor Loubser agreed "on a broad basis."

Mr. van Rooyen then questioned Professor Loubser about whether Mr. Biko was unconscious during a particular incident. Professor Loubser could not say that Mr. Biko was definitely unconscious as a result of injuries sustained.

Mr. van Rooyen then referred to evidence given concerning an incident which occurred on the morning of September 7. At this time, he said, Mr. Biko allegedly went berserk, assaulted people and had to be restrained. No one had given evidence that during the incident Mr. Biko had hit his left forehead. However, Mr. van Rooyen described three specific occurrences as a result of which Mr. Biko's head could, possibly have been injured: (1) when Mr. Biko was forcibly pinned to the wall of an office in order to restrain him; (2) when Mr. Biko fell flat on the floor because the man holding him stepped back when Mr. Biko trod on his foot;

(3) when, following this, Mr. Biko was brought to the floor again as he was shackled with difficulty. Professor Loubser agreed that bruising of the type found could possibly have been caused by any one of these occurrences.

Referring to the fact that none of the people who saw Mr. Biko in life, except one, had admitted to seeing a wound on his forehead, Mr. van Rooyen asked if it were possible that the wound was not obvious. Professor Loubser said that he too, in doing post-mortems, had missed lesions because of the subjective factor. He said that he had been looking for lesions and that the lights in the dissection hall had been exceptionally good.

Mr. Kentridge rose later to say that it was virtually inconceivable that there would not have been an appreciable period of unconsciousness with the degree of brain damage under discussion. After some discussion, Professor Loubser said that he would have expected the injury to have been associated with unconsciousness but would not have been surprised if unconsciousness had not happened. He would have regarded unconsciousness as more than a 50 percent possibility.

MR. VAN ROOYEN: You cannot rule out the possibility that he was not unconscious?

PROFESSOR LOUBSER: Yes.

The next witness was Professor Neville Proctor, professor of anatomical pathology at the University of the Witwatersrand and head of the School of Pathology at the South African Institute of Medical Research. Mr. Kentridge asked him various technical questions about his findings on examining Mr. Biko's brain. During this questioning, the professor stated the conclusions he had come to as a result of this examination. He agreed with the view of the other pathologists that the main lesion in Mr. Biko's brain could be described as a contracoup injury. He said he thought it was extremely reasonable that the principal injury was on the left forehead.

In his opinion, all the lesions were not caused by a single blow. He believed there must have been at least three blows.

In response to Mr. Kentridge's description of Mr. Biko's behavior on the morning of September 7, Professor Proctor said that from that picture, given the nature and extent of Mr. Biko's injuries, he must have been unconscious. He said that Mr. Biko had suffered moderate to severe brain damage. In the case of a moderate injury, he estimated that ten to twenty minutes of unconsciousness was reasonable.

He said that the main lesion was in itself enough to cause death.

(Adjournment)

Day Eleven Monday, November 27, 1977

Professor Proctor was questioned by Mr. van Rooyen, Mr. Pickard and Mr. von Lieres.

Dr. Andries van Zyl, a Pretoria district surgeon who examined Mr. Biko on the day he died, then gave evidence. He read an affidavit that he had examined Mr. Biko at the Pretoria prison hospital at 3 P.M. on September 12. He had been told that Mr. Biko had refused to "partake of anything" for a week. Also that Mr. Biko had been examined by a doctor and a physician who could not find "any fault" with him.

Dr. van Zyl said he received no record from Port Elizabeth in connection with the patient. After examining Mr. Biko he diagnosed general weakness and dehydration as a result of his having had "no food or liquid" for seven days. Dr. van Zyl prescribed a drip and gave Mr. Biko a vitamin injection.

Mr. Kentridge asked Dr. van Zyl who had given him the history of Mr. Biko's alleged refusal to eat or drink for seven days. Dr. van Zyl said he learned this in a telephone conversation with a Sergeant Pretorius at the central prison hospital. As far as he could remember no one told him Mr. Biko's case was urgent. Asked by Mr. Kentridge whether Mr. Biko seemed seriously ill, Dr. van Zyl replied: "He was medically a sick, sick person . . . he was comatose."

Questioned by Mr. Pickard, Dr. van Zyl said that, before September 12, he had never been in the section where Mr. Biko was kept. Mr. von Lieres asked Dr. van Zyl whether the room in which Mr. Biko was kept was equipped satisfactorily. Dr. van Zyl said he had been taken to different wards, which looked like those in a hospital. Mr. Biko was in a private room.

Mr. Kentridge told the court he had available photographs of the room. "It looks as though the patient was lying on a mat on the floor, and not on the bed," he said. Studying the photographs, Dr. van Zyl said it appeared to be the correct place.

MR. KENTRIDGE: When you saw Mr. Biko, was he on mats on the floor?
DR. VAN ZYL: That is correct.

Dr. van Zyl left the stand, and there was some argument before the next witness, Dr. Gluckman, was called. Magistrate Prins eventually ruled that Dr. Gluckman, the pathologist for the Biko family, be called as a witness. He took the stand for the rest of the day, answering questions concerning the post-mortem examination of Mr. Biko.

(Adjournment)

Day Twelve: Tuesday, November 28, 1977

Dr. Gluckman continued to answer questions concerning the post-mortem. Professor Ian Simson, head of the Department of Pathological Anatomy at the University of Pretoria, then gave evidence. He had been present at the post-mortem examination of Mr. Biko and answered questions of a highly technical nature concerning the findings of the post-mortem.

Following this, the magistrate asked Mr. van Rooyen to argue further on whether the chief of the Security Police headquarters should be called to give evidence. Mr. van Rooyen said that in wishing to call the brigadiers, Mr.

Kentridge wanted to iron out discrepancies between statements before the court by Colonel Pieter Goosen, head of the Eastern Cape Security Police, and subsequent alleged statements by Mr. J. T. Kruger, the minister of police. There was no evidence of fabrication or contradiction between Colonel Goosen's affidavits and his evidence before the court. The discrepancy had arisen from hearsay statements allegedly made by the minister. This was inadmissible.

The magistrate then ruled that he had studied the statements of the two brigadiers and was satisfied that they, together with a telex message annexed to one of the statements, did not even suggest a previous inconsistent statement on the part of Colonel Goosen. Mr. van Rooyen's point was well taken.

The discussion then turned to whether affidavits by Dr. Reuben Plotkin, a specialist neurosurgeon, and Dr. Ronald K. Tucker, who advised counsel for the Biko family, should be admitted as evidence. Mr. Prins said he had read the affidavits and had to decide whether to call the doctors to give evidence.

Mr. van Rooyen objected to the submission of the affidavits as evidence. In terms of finding out the cause of death, or whether anyone was criminally responsible, the affidavits amounted to "irrelevant speculation." Mr. Pickard also opposed the submission of Dr. Plotkin and Dr. Tucker's affidavits, and Mr. Heath and Mr. von Lieres supported the arguments of Mr. van Rooyen and Mr. Pickard.

Mr. Kentridge said he believed the material in the affidavits would be of real value to the court in reaching a conclusion. By calling Dr. Plotkin and Dr. Tucker, the facts could be interpreted by two independent clinicians. The magistrate had three choices. He could either rule that there had been enough evidence on this subject and turn down the affidavits, or he could admit the affidavits without calling the witnesses to give evidence, or he could admit the affidavits and call the witnesses for cross-examination.

Mr. Prins said he would rule on the matter the following day.

(Adjournment)

Day Thirteen: Wednesday, November 29, 1977

Colonel Goosen made an unexpectedly early reappearance in the stand shortly after the day began. More expert medical evidence had been expected.

Mr. Kentridge questioned Colonel Goosen closely on discrepancies between his reports, by phone and telex, to the Security Police headquarters in Pretoria and statements made by the minister of police, Mr. Kruger, that Mr. Biko had threatened to go on a hunger strike. Brigadier Zietsman, head of the Security Police, had told Mr. Kentridge that at no stage did Colonel Goosen say Mr. Biko threatened a hunger strike. Colonel Goosen replied that Mr. Biko had never said so.

Mr. Kentridge continued that from the record of a telex and a phonecall to Brigadier Zietsman, it appeared as if Colonel Goosen had not said that Mr. Biko had verbally threatened a hunger strike. Brigadier Zietsman had also said so in a sworn statement. Could Colonel Goosen tell the court how Mr. Kruger had come to make the statement about the hunger strike threat? Colonel Goosen said that he could not comment on press statements. All reports to Security Police headquarters would be under his supervision, Colonel Goosen added.

MR. KENTRIDGE: We are left with the situation that the minister of police made more than one statement in public about Mr. Biko's detention which we in court have shown to be incorrect and misleading on the evidence and the matter is then left in the minister's lap as far as you are concerned?

COLONEL GOOSEN: I have no information, only my own opinion.

MR. KENTRIDGE: We can all form our own opinions, but we can't express them in court.

COLONEL GOOSEN: I reported and can't comment.

Mr. Kentridge then asked Colonel Goosen why he had sent Mr. Biko to Pretoria when the impression given in evidence was that the police thought Mr. Biko was shamming and there was no urgency. The telex said Mr. Biko was sent to Pretoria because the case had become urgent as Mr. Biko's condition had deteriorated since he was admitted to Walmer police cells when, at 9.30 A.M. on Sunday, September 11, he could still walk. Later, the telex said, Mr. Biko was in a semicoma. Mr. Kentridge said Colonel Goosen had never conceded this in his evidence to the court. Colonel Goosen replied that he had said Mr. Biko should be moved where there were better facilities, as soon as possible. Mr. Kentridge also asked whether Colonel Goosen had phoned Brigadier Zietsman and discussed where Mr. Biko should be sent. Colonel Goosen said he had.

MR. KENTRIDGE: You were worried about Mr. Biko, but thought he might be shamming?

COLONEL GOOSEN: That is correct.

MR. KENTRIDGE: Although he was in a semicoma?

COLONEL GOOSEN: I still thought there might be some shamming.

Mr. Kentridge said Colonel Goosen had made a negative reply when Brigadier Zietsman had asked how the investigation was progressing. Evidence to the court that Mr. Biko had promised to make a full statement but had withdrawn the offer was "a complete fabrication," Mr. Kentridge said. If Mr. Biko had admitted anything about the distribution of inflammatory pamphlets, Colonel Goosen would have told Brigadier Zietsman. Colonel Goosen replied that the phone coversation had been brief.

Warrant Officer Henry Fouche, one of the squad that allegedly guarded Mr. Biko on September 6 and September 7, then gave evidence. He read out an affidavit and a statement he had made to the investigating officer after Mr. Biko's death. Warrant Officer Fouche said he was on guard duty at the Security Police building in Port Elizabeth on the night of September 6 and on September 7. Mr. Biko was handcuffed to a grille in the interrogation room. He had looked into the interrogation room a couple of times, but did not speak to Mr. Biko. Asked by Mr. Kentridge whether Lieutenant W. Wilken, commander of the night squad, had spent any length of time with Mr. Biko in the interrogation room, Warrant Officer Fouche said he could not remember. It was possible that Lieutenant Wilken could have sat on a chair and looked at Mr. Biko for quite a while. He said that Lieutenant Wilken might have interrogated him for a while, but that the Lieutenant had not told him that Mr. Biko was willing to make a statement.

Later that night he had again heard voices from the interrogation room. Mr. Biko was talking, but they could not make out what he was saying. His speech was slurred.

In reply to further questions by Mr. Kentridge, Warrant Officer Fouche said he thought Mr. Biko was shamming.

Mr. Kentridge said he would submit to the court that Mr. Biko sustained his head injury between the evening of September 6 and the morning of September 7 and asked Warrant Officer Fouche whether he could explain how the injury was sustained. Warrant Officer Fouche said he had no idea.

Warrant Officer Fouche said he had helped to undress Mr. Biko and carry him to the Land Rover in which he was transferred from Port Elizabeth to the Pretoria prison. He said Mr. Biko did not give the impression of being in a coma. Asked by Dr. Gordon, why a man who was allegedly feigning illness should be transported to Pretoria so urgently at night, Warrant Officer Fouche said he had been informed that they were taking him to Pretoria for observation and not for specific medical treatment.

In reply to further questions, Warrant Officer Fouche said he had seen no injuries on Mr. Biko apart from the bruised upper lip. Neither had he seen or heard any violence in the interrogation room on the night of September 6.

The final witness was Warrant Officer Jacobus Beneke, the officer who was alleged to have been attacked by Mr. Biko during questioning on September 7. He told the court that Mr. Biko had made a confession concerning the distribution of pamphlets under interrogation on September 6. Mr. Kentridge asked him why he had not made mention of this in his affidavit handed in yesterday. He replied that he did not consider it important and did not think he was allowed to mention such matters.

Asked by Dr. Gordon if he had noticed whether Mr. Biko lost consciousness at anytime during or after the alleged scuffle on September 7, Warrant Officer Beneke replied that he had not been unconscious.

On December 1, Mr. Kentridge addressed the court with his argument.

He said that the duty of an inquest court was to establish the identity of the deceased and the date of his death, both of which had been clearly established. The court also had to establish the cause of death. There could be no doubt that it had been established that Mr. Biko had died of at least five brain lesions caused by the application of external force to his head, Mr. Kentridge said. The suggestion that he had been on a hunger strike and had suffered dehydration needed no serious consideration. He was submitting that the court should find that brain injuries were sustained and that the other symptoms were consequences of the brain injury.

The most important question which the court had to answer, however, was whether the death of Mr. Biko had been brought about by an act or omission amounting to an offense on the part of any person. The fact that the identity of the wrongdoer had not been disclosed did not mean that the court had to find that nobody was to blame. His submission was that a conclusion which could have the effect of exonerating everyone concerned was one which could not be considered on the evidence of the inquest.

Mr. Kentridge said his submission was that one or more members of the Security Police had been responsible for Mr. Biko's death and that the injury had been inflicted deliberately or negligently and without good cause. He was not submitting that Mr. Biko had been murdered. His submission was that Mr. Biko had been beaten and the person or persons who did this had not at the time cared whether serious injury had resulted or not.

He pointed out that the police had told the court how concerned they had been about Mr. Biko's condition and that Colonel Pieter Goosen, chief of the Eastern Cape Security Police, had said that he would have given his right arm for Mr. Biko's life. It was certain that they had not wanted him dead, but why was there this tremendous concern? he asked. His submission was that Colonel Goosen's main concern was to lead the doctors to believe that Mr. Biko was shamming.

The inquest was neither a criminal trial nor a private prosecution. The court had to attempt to ascertain if there was a prima facie case that some person known or unknown was responsible for the death of Mr. Biko. It did not have to come to a conclusion beyond reasonable doubt. The finding was, however, an important one in which Mr. Biko's family and other people had a substantial interest. The representatives of the Biko family had availed themselves of the opportunity to cross-examine witnesses, but although they had been permitted full scope in this examination, they had been subjected to a number of limitations in that they had no right to subpoena witnesses and that they would have liked to cross-examine more witnesses who had not been called. They also could not produce an eyewitness to the treatment which Mr. Biko received.

Mr. Kentridge said they had submitted police officers to extensive cross-examination in which they did not feel that they had been in any way hampered. There were not many countries in the world, even in the Western world, where officers of the Security Police would be permitted to appear in open court and be subjected to what amounted to a hostile cross-examination. "I think we have every right to be proud of that," he said.

He was submitting that, on the probabilities, Mr. Biko had been assaulted and that was how the brain lesion had been caused. The Security Police had denied the assault and had suggested that Mr. Biko's brain injury could have been caused in the incident on September 7 in which Mr. Biko was said to have been the aggressor. They did not persist in their suggestion of suicide.

The main issue was, therefore, whether one or other of the Security Police had assaulted Mr. Biko while he was in their custody. Counsel for the family had no direct evidence of this, but was submitting that the Security Police had closed their ranks and entered into a conspiracy of silence.

Mr. Kentridge pointed out that in some instances the circumstantial evidence could be far more cogent than direct evidence. He was suggesting that the circumstantial evidence which showed that one or more policemen assaulted Mr. Biko fell into five categories:

1 The time when the injuries were sustained. His submission would be that they were sustained between the evening of the 6th and 7.30 of the morning of the 7th.

2 The failure of the police officers to give a truthful explanation of the circumstances in which Mr. Biko received the injury. The fact that they concealed the truth and that some of them in court gave false evidence of what happened on the 7th.

3 The failure of the doctors to see what they should have noticed and the fact that they were drawn into the conspiracy of silence.

4 The medical evidence which showed that the scuffle as described could not have caused the injury.

5 With these factors should be considered the circumstantial evidence of how Mr. Biko was treated while in detention.

The evidence about his treatment was undisputed. When he was detained on August 18 he was in good health but he died twenty-six days later. The Security Police themselves admitted the treatment to which they had submitted Biko.

Mr. Kentridge said that he was submitting that the undisputed assault on Mr. Biko's dignity and the callous disregard of his human rights were highly relevant in assessing the evidence. He was kept in solitary confinement in the Walmer police cells and deprived even of the negligible rights he had as a Section 6 detainee. Mr. Kentridge referred to the warrant under which Mr. Biko was held and said the limited rights given to a detainee indicated that he could at least have a reasonable quantity of private clothing. Nobody other than a State official could have access to him and he could not receive any newspapers or food from outside, but otherwise privileges like exercise should have been allowed to him.

Instead Mr. Biko had been left naked, and he had had no proper washing facilities and no exercise. Mr. Biko had complained to a magistrate, but that was a dead letter.

Mr. Biko was then brought to the interrogation room and was put into handcuffs and leg irons. He remained shackled even after Colonel Goosen had suspected that he had a stroke, and remained shackled even after he was seen by Dr. Lang. He was shackled the whole day of the 7th, the whole night of the 7th and on the 8th. The Security Police had said that Mr. Biko had not made use of toilet facilities which were offered, but Mr. Biko was found in urine-wet trousers and on a wet mat. The doctor thought that Mr. Biko should be seen by a specialist physician, but even this did not help Mr. Biko much. He was simply left there.

In the Port Elizabeth prison Mr. Biko was shown some kindness by the warders but no channels of communication were open to report on his condition. On the morning of the 11th he was moved from hospital and placed in a cell. In fact this meant he was removed from a bed to a mat and again left naked. After a few hours he was found in a state of collapse on the floor. Doctors were called in and Mr. Biko had to go to a prison hospital 1200 kilometers away. He was transported in a Land Rover, lying naked in the back with nothing more than a bottle of water.

In Pretoria, although Mr. Biko had to be carried into prison, even there the Port Elizabeth Security Police tried to persuade officials that he could be shamming and could be on a hunger strike. According to Colonel Goosen there were outstanding medical facilities at the Pretoria prison. But for Mr. Biko these were a mat in a corner of a cell and the attendance of a newly qualified medical practitioner whose diagnosis was based on false information and whose treatment consisted of a drip and a vitamin injection.

At no time was the family notified.

"We end with Steve Biko dying a miserable and lonely death on a mat on a stone floor," he said.

Mr. Kentridge referred to Colonel Goosen's statement in the affidavit he made after Mr. Biko's death that everything had been done for the comfort of Biko. That was as cynical a statement as he had ever heard in a court of law.

He said that the concern of the doctors had to be judged in terms of their conduct rather than their profession. The importance of the doctors' evidence was that when the court had to consider the evidence of the Security Police it might find that the evidence was not acceptable in the light of evidence of Mr. Biko's treatment.

Mr. Kentridge then sketched the circumstantial picture of the reasons for Mr. Biko's death. Referring to the dating of the brain injury he said that it had been dated by Doctors Loubser, Gluckman and Simson as four to eight days old but probably five or six days old. Professor Proctor dated the injury at five to eight days before death. This evidence meant that the injury was suffered before the night of the 8th but not earlier than the 4th or the 5th.

Mr. Kentridge said that he was submitting that not only was there insufficient information, but false explanations were given by members of the Security Police of events of the 6th and 7th. The evidence of the night squad had been a bare denial that Mr. Biko had been assaulted. Mr. Biko had been either within sight or within hearing of these people at all times. Lieutenant Wilken and Warrant Officer Fouché told the court that they looked in on him from time to time from a nearby office. No explanation whatsoever was to be found in their evidence.

In the case of the day squad, the court did not have mere denials. They gave accounts of events alleged to have taken place. They told the story of aggression by Mr. Biko followed by a struggle after which Mr. Biko was pinned to the ground and manacled. According to them five strong men had been needed to overpower Mr. Biko. They said that in the course of the struggle Mr. Biko might have bumped his head against a wall but they could not explain Mr. Biko's injury. Not one of the members of the squad was prepared to say that they saw him striking his head against a wall. Not one of them was prepared to say that they saw the wound on Mr. Biko's left forehead. Not one of them said in his original affidavit that Mr. Biko might have bumped his head.

The whole object of the affidavit taken by General Kleinhaus had been to fix the attention of the members of the police force on the brain injuries. The failure to mention in the affidavits that he might have bumped his head during the scuffle led irresistibly to the inference that this did not happen and could not have happened.

Referring to the entry in the occurrence book, he said that the value of the entry had to be measured in the context of the whole evidence of Major Snyman (one of the interrogators). Major Snyman had stated as a fact in the occurrence book that Mr. Biko had fallen with his head against a wall and his body on the ground. When asked in court which part of Mr. Biko's head had hit the wall, Major Snyman said he had hit the back of his head against the wall. Major Snyman had given a remarkably muddled account of the scuffle. On his evidence, even if there had been this bump on the back of the head, this could not account for the injuries sustained. Mr. Kentridge asked the court to compare Major Snyman's description with the statement in the occurrence book, and said they were quite at odds.

Captain Siebert's evidence had been equally vague and unconvincing. He had told the court: "We fell against tables, chairs and on the ground," but did not say that Mr. Biko's head injury had been sustained on the 7th when Mr. Biko had to be restrained.

Warrant Officer Beneke contributed nothing to the explanation. Warrant Officer Marx attempted to give a more comprehensive account but did not say that Mr. Biko bumped his head against the wall. He finally conceded that he could not say that Mr. Biko had sustained any head injury in his presence.

It might be argued, notwithstanding the evidence that nobody saw Mr. Biko sustain an injury to his head, that in a confused struggle he might have sustained a bump without anybody seeing it. This was, however, entirely eliminated by the medical evidence on unconsciousness following an injury of this type. On the medical evidence it was virtually certain that Mr. Biko's brain injury must have resulted in a period of unconsciousness. He said this would not have been merely amnesia but Mr. Biko would not have been able to use his limbs. He would not concede that the unconsciousness could not have been noticed.

If they accepted that on the early morning of the 7th Mr. Biko did have this outburst, that he went berserk, that it took five men to pin him down and that even then he went on struggling in an irrational manner, it appeared from medical evidence that this violence could be symptomatic of a head injury which Mr. Biko had already received. Mr. Biko had been a strong man but not a superman. On a previous occasion, Major Hansen alone had brought Mr. Biko under control. One had the violence of a man who had had a brain injury. Then he had a relapse into supor and afterward the curve of unconsciousness went up again until Mr. Biko finally relapsed into coma.

When three of the leading pathologists of South Africa, and the leading neurophysician, said that in their opinions there must have been a period of unconsciousness, he had to submit that the court had to accept this as being so. The police account of the struggle completely excluded a period of unconsciousness, and it followed that in the case the injuries could not have been sustained during the struggle.

At some time during the night, or before 7 A.M., injuries were inflicted on Mr. Biko. The seriousness had no doubt not been realized at the time, but it had been thought necessary to call a doctor. It was then thought necessary to give an explanation which would make Mr. Biko the aggressor. Mr. Kentridge said the telex which Colonel Goosen had tried to conceal referred to injuries inflicted on Biko at 7 A.M. On the witness stand Colonel Goosen had said that this merely referred to the injury on Biko's lip. This could not be true. The vital point was that Mr. Biko's inability or refusal to speak had been directly related to the injury inflicted, because this telex stated "after the injury he refused to speak." Nobody could believe that a mere injury to a lip could account for a failure to react.

Dr. Lang had been induced to give a clean certificate which he had conceded to be incorrect. On the night of the 7th further alarming symptoms made further action necessary and the entry in the occurrence book was then made. The entry was significant because of the explanations given for it, which were contradictory and unacceptable. Mr. Kentridge submitted that none of the explanations about the late entry in the occurrence book were satisfactory and that the reason for the entry had been to lay a foundation to make Mr. Biko out as the aggressor.

The telex message connected Mr. Biko's refusal to speak with his injuries, but Colonel Goosen's affidavit did not. The telex had been intended only for the eyes of the Security Police. It said nothing of shamming, but the affidavit made the next day devoted a page to the theory of shamming.

Mr. Kentridge said that it was no wonder that Colonel Goosen denied the existence of any telex message. He read from the record Colonel Goosen's evidence denying that he had made any written report and saying that he had dealt with the matter only telephonically. There was nothing else in his generally unsatisfactory evidence which told against him so heavily. If Brigadier Zietsman had not very properly disclosed the telex, Colonel Goosen might have got away with this. He said that the part of the telex which dealt with the journey to Pretoria was as damaging to Colonel Goosen as the other part, because in that Colonel Goosen had said Mr. Biko had been in a semicoma.

The story of Mr. Biko's confession had hardly read true, he said. A great deal of effort had been made by the Security Police to portray Mr. Biko as a revolutionary and an urban terrorist and to show that his image as a man of peace had not been deserved. What finally told against the story of the confession was the telephonic conversation with Brigadier Zietsman. He had asked Colonel Goosen how far the investigation had progressed and Colonel Goosen had simply replied that Mr. Biko had asked for fifteen minutes and then would not co-operate. If Mr. Biko had made a confession Colonel Goosen would have mentioned this and not the fifteen minutes incident which, according to Lieutenant Wilken, was a trivial one.

Referring to the shamming, he said that the police had pressed this view on doctors and had maintained even in court that this had been their general belief at all times. This was demonstrably untrue.

Mr. Kentridge referred to the incident when Mr. Biko was found in the bath with his clothes on and said that although Colonel Goosen knew that Biko had died of a brain injury he had attempted to put forward the story that the bath incident was an attempt at suicide.

Warrant Officer Fouche said that even up to the last minute in Pretoria he thought that the man was probably shamming. But in the telex there was no mention of shamming, but a statement that Mr. Biko was in a semicoma.

Mr. Kentridge referred to "the unexplained mystery of the hunger strike." Shortly after Biko's death the minister of police issued a statement saying that Biko had threatened a hunger strike. It was clear from the evidence that he had not threatened a hunger strike. The question remained how such statements could be made at the highest level which were false and misleading. Why was nothing said of the scuffle, and why was it never corrected? The Security Police had not attempted to clear this up, and neither had the minister of police. Neither the minister nor any officer in Pretoria was likely to have invented this version, therefore it must have originated in Port Elizabeth. Dr. van Zyl, the last doctor to see Mr. Biko, admitted his diagnosis had been based on information that Mr. Biko's condition was the result of a hunger strike.

There were further indications that the police had something to hide. They gave instructions that no black persons should come into contact with Mr. Biko, gave a false name when sending the spinal fluid to the institute and concealed Mr. Biko's true name from Mr. Keely (the neurosurgeon) and possibly from Dr. Hersch. The only inference which could be drawn from the falsehoods was that of guilt.

Mr. Kentridge said that he regretted that it was necessary for him to deal with the Port Elizabeth doctors. "We owe it to the medical profession to say that their absolute integrity has led courts to place a great reliance on the district surgeon's findings." In this court, however, it seemed not only that no reliance could be put on the evidence of Doctors Lang and Tucker but that it joined with the Security Police in the conspiracy of silence.

He quoted from the judgment of Mr. Justice James, who ruled in August 1976 in the case of four members of the Security Police in Durban who were charged with culpable homicide for allegedly killing a detainee named Mdluli. The judge found that the injuries suffered by Mr. Mdluli were plainly sustained while he was in the custody of the Security Police. The court had acquitted the men, since it could not be found that they had specifically been responsible for the fatal injuries, but the distinction that had been drawn was important to the present proceedings. The court did not have to make a finding against particular policemen.

"Accordingly the verdict which we submit is the only one reasonably open to this court, is one finding that the death of Mr. Biko was due to a criminal assault upon him by one or more of the eight members of the Security Police in whose custody he was at Sanlam Building on September 6th and 7th, 1977.

"We submit this inquest has exposed grave irregularities and misconduct in the treatment of a single detainee. It has incidentally revealed the dangers to life and liberty involved in the system of holding detainees incommunicado.

"A firm and clear verdict may help to prevent further abuse of the system. In the light of further disquieting evidence for this court, we submit any verdict which can be seen as an exoneration of the Port Elizabeth Security Police will unfortunately be widely interpreted as a license to abuse helpless people with impunity."

Mr. van Rooyen told the court he found it difficult to know whether he should begin his summing up with the facts of evidence or with "the irresponsible fiction which has been delivered to Your Worship this morning." He said Mr. Kentridge had attempted to create a void by breaking down the positive evidence and then filling the void with allegations of assault.

"That means that without a pickle of evidence before Your Worship to show an unlawful assault, the way was clear to fill up the void with glorious imaginings. There is an element of fairytale here, just like Hans Christian Andersen, or more likely the Brothers Grimm."

Mr. van Rooyen said he had difficulty in understanding whether Mr. Kentridge accepted that there had been a fracas or not on September 7. Mr. Kentridge said early in his argument Mr. Biko was violent because of a prior brain injury, and therefore behaved as a man possessed or a man berserk. Whereas toward the end of his argument it was difficult to establish whether Mr. Kentridge accepted that there had been a fracas or not on September 7.

Mr. van Rooyen said it was very easy to say now that Mr. Biko was a dying man and yet he had been shackled, had been sent to Pretoria and had been shamming.

The cause of death had been determined by a unanimous finding by the pathologists, and an attempt had been made to change the findings by eliminating the sections saying that the injury was of a contracoup type and substituting some lesions of the coup type. This was obviously created to indicate that more blows than one were involved in Mr. Biko's injury, but this had now been abandoned.

He said the abandonment of the attempt to prove that more than one blow was involved certainly reflected on the credibility of witnesses who testified about this.

Referring to criticism of General Kleinhaus's investigation, Mr. van Rooyen said the general had started at the only logical point in attempting to find out where and when Mr. Biko had suffered this imprint abrasion and knew that if these questions were answered he would have solved the basic problem. He asked whether there was any reason for a cover-up and said it was "lovely to project a cover-up . . . sounding just like Agatha Christie." The Security Police had no reason to cover up the existence of Mr. Biko's head injury since they had not covered up the injury to his lip.

Mr. van Rooyen said the court faced two possibilities – the rather improbable and speculative idea that the injury was self-inflicted or, as he was submitting, that the injury was sustained during the fracas on the morning of September 7. Mr. van Rooyen said various witnesses had testified to this, including Captain Siebert and Warrant Officer Marx. He said the court could accept as fact that there had been a violent episode on September 7 and that this was initiated by Mr. Biko.

Evidence had been that Mr. Biko had been arrested with Mr. Peter Jones in Grahamstown in connection with the distribution of pamphlets on August 18. Police had not interrogated Mr. Biko after his arrest until September 5 since they were busy with Mr. Jones and other associates. When Mr. Biko was questioned, police had sufficient evidence to confront him, and he conceded authorship of some pamphlets after seeing the handwriting of his friends.

Mr. Prins asked Mr. van Rooyen about the police evidence not having referred at any stage to a state of unconsciousness in Mr. Biko after the fracas. Mr. van Rooyen asked whether medical opinion would be given such weight as to brand the police witnesses liars. He asked whether medical opinion meant that a certain course was applicable in all cases. "I submit it would be quite a clear travesty of justice to rely on medical opinion to call these witnesses liars." Mr. van Rooyen said he had received a concession by all the medical experts that there was at least a possibility that such an injury need not necessarily cause unconsciousness.

Mr. van Rooyen also dismissed the allegations that the doctors had entered into a conspiracy of silence with the Security Police. "Only if you want to clothe it with the dark garments of suspicion do you make this allegation," he said. At all times Colonel Goosen had heard that there was nothing materially wrong with Mr. Biko; he had believed that Mr. Biko would get the best treatment in Pretoria.

He also said that one could never say the hunger strike story was the basis for a cover-up because in the course of one week Mr. Biko had only eaten half a plate of food.

Mr. van Rooyen concluded that as far as the Security Police were concerned, in his submission, the court would not be able to find that they were involved in any act or omission which led to Mr. Biko's death, and which constituted an offense.

THE FINDING

The following day Magistrate Prins convened the inquest court to give his findings:

1 That "the deceased was Bantu Stephen Biko, a black man aged 30, that he died on September 12 and that cause of death was brain injury which led to renal failure and other complications."

2 That "the head injuries were probably sustained on September 7 in a scuffle in the Security Police offices in Port Elizabeth."

3 That "on the available evidence the death cannot be attributed to any act or omission amounting to a criminal offense on the part of any person."

The court rose. The Biko inquest was over.

6: THE INDICTMENT

SINCE THE STATE has not seen fit to indict anyone for the death of Steve
Biko, it becomes necessary to indict the State. By the State is meant, in this
instance, the minority regime that has ruled South Africa for thirty years,
with ever-increasing contempt for democratic values and with ever-
growing arrogance toward all who hold such values to be paramount. And
since the Nationalist Party government has consistently identified itself
with the State, has claimed that it represents the State, and has accused its
most zealous critics of being enemies of the State, let it now therefore be
regarded as the personification of the State for purposes of indictment.

This means that the Vorster government and all its supporters bear the
responsibility for what happened to Steve Biko. They bear this responsibility in varying degrees.

Judicial officers are supposed at all times to bear in mind the principles
of natural justice. Magistrate Prins had no moral right to outrage these
principles when he offered no word of censure against the horrifying
picture that emerged at the inquest. It is a picture of unbridled political
police power over life and death – a power which, condoned by the State,
descended to a level of brutality and callousness unmatched in any society
that still clings to at least some vestiges of legality.

At the very least, Colonel Goosen should have been indicted for culpable
homicide on two counts – for refusing hospitalization of a seriously ill
man and authorizing his land transport for more than a thousand kilometers while in that condition. His contention that illness was feigned
should have been branded publicly as a lie, since Goosen's own telex
message to Pretoria contradicted this contention.

Doctors Tucker, Hersch and Lang should have been similarly indicted, as well as cited summarily by the inquest court to the Medical Council for negligent treatment of a patient.

Those most obviously indictable, the direct agents of Steve Biko's death, can be narrowed down to ten Security Police officers – members of the interrogation team mentioned at the inquest – Colonel Goosen, Majors Snyman and Fischer, Captain Siebert, Warrant Officers Beneke, Marx, Coetzee and Fouche, Lieutenant Wilken and Sergeant Nieuwoudt. One or more of these men struck the fatal blows, and it is certain that most, if not all, of the others mentioned became accessories after the fact by concealing what really happened in the interrogation cell.

In all probability the blows were not meant to be fatal, but given the circumstances this does not affect the degree of guilt, because basic legal principle holds that a man is presumed to intend the reasonably possible consequences of his actions.

But precisely who struck the fatal blows is relatively unimportant. All these men mentioned so far are petty offenders in the scale of outrage. The real killer was the System – and all its representatives involved in this tragedy. Two members of the Nationalist cabinet are most responsible for the circumstances under which Steve Biko died – Police Minister J. T. Kruger and Premier B. J. Vorster.

More than anyone else, these two men created the conditions, the climate of opinion, the statutes and the state of mind of the Security Police which led to this particular killing.

The inquest reflected only a part of that state of mind. In any case, the inquest itself was irregular. The chief witness, the most important testifier, was not allowed to give evidence. Peter Jones, who could have given the most vital direct evidence, having been arrested and detained with Steve Biko and having no doubt experienced identical methods of "interrogation," couldn't give evidence because he was held incommunicado by the Security Police, and still is.

Secondly, there was no reasonable basis for the magistrate's refusal to permit Brigadier Zietsman to be called as a witness on the issue of credibility relating to Colonel Goosen or Minister Kruger. It was directly relevant to the inquest that Colonel Goosen's credibility be probed, yet this basic point was simply over-ruled by the magistrate.

Why, then, did Advocate Kentridge not withdraw from the proceedings, branding them a farce? Most probably because he knew from the start that they were a farce anyway, and that the most that can be hoped for from such State-protective inquests is an airing of at least some evidence of Security Police brutality.

But this indictment must be broadened, not only in regard to those whom it indicts but also in regard to those on whose behalf it is made. Steve Biko, after all, was only one of forty-five men who had died in detention in the hands of the South African Security Police. And Steve Biko was only one of more than twenty million South Africans whose lives have been made a trial and a torment by the evil of apartheid.

Because of who he was; because of his special stature – and because of the attendant circumstances, the death of Steve Biko symbolises the ultimate consequence of apartheid with all its implications. Just as Hitler's "Final Solution to the Jewish problem" was the ultimate consequence of earlier Nazi policy, so deaths such as those of Steve Biko are inevitably the appropriate result of the apartheid policy since its inception.

Having to wear a yellow armband and having to die in a gas-chamber at Auschwitz were but two links in the same chain of racism. These two links might have been at opposite ends of the chain – but the chain was the same. Having to carry a "pass" and having to die of assault in detention are similarly two links of the same chain.

If you feel impelled to enforce at all costs the wearing of armbands, you have to end up herding people into gas chambers. And if you feel impelled to enforce at all costs a separation of races, you have to end up killing people.

The death of Steve Biko requires a reaction of outrage to be shouted to the four corners of the earth. It has finally and incontrovertibly been established that the policy of apartheid is the most outrageous affront to all humanity that has ever been devised by collective decision since the dawn of procedural government.

The obscene laws which constitute apartheid are not crazed edicts issued by a dictator, nor the whims of a megalomanic monster, nor the one-man decisions of a fanatical ideologue. They are the result of polite caucus discussions by hundreds of delegates in sober suits, after full debate in party congresses. They are passed after three solemn readings in a parliament which opens every day's proceedings with a prayer to Jesus Christ.

There is a special horror in that fact.

This indictment will now seek to show that there is no valid apologia for those responsible; that they are culpable and indictable; that they are fit to stand trial.

Every year vast sums of South African taxpayers' money are spent financing embassies, missions, films, advertisements, symposia and lobbies to put what is referred to as "South Africa's" case. I will now put the case for their defense in the manner in which they present it to the world. And I will reply to each point of their case.

This case is based on the claim that white South Africans have a right to determine their own destiny in this country, on the grounds that their forebears arrived here at the same time as those of the black people. This is untrue, and is a politically motivated fabrication given currency only in South African history syllabuses. Besides, it is totally irrelevant. Even if it were relevant, it would be no justification for 15 percent of the population to assume unjust political domination of the 85 percent. But the historical point of arrival of whites in South Africa is not at issue. Not one significant black leader in South African history has ever disputed the right of white South Africans to stay in South Africa.

They say that they are a minority of the total population only because, unlike the white colonists of America and Australia, they did not commit genocide upon the blacks as was committed upon the American Indians and Aborigines. Genocide was in fact practiced to a certain extent upon the indigenous Khoi-san, but in any event a comparison of degrees of genocide upon indigenous people by white settlers in America and Australia generations ago is again not relevant to the moral and political issues here in this country today. Besides, the policy of apartheid has resulted in death for multitudes of blacks. While this may not validly be described as a calculated policy of genocide, it does not help to justify the results of apartheid.

A special claim is entered on behalf of Afrikaners as an African people – the first African Nationalists and the first to throw off the colonial yoke. It is said that the Afrikaners must defend what they have because they have nowhere else to go.

No black leader of any consequence denies that the Afrikaners are an African people with their own language and culture and as such have a place in this country. But this does not imply acceptance of the Nationalist assumption that such claims entitle the Nationalists to assume excessively more privileges or rights than other South Africans. As to the statement that they have "nowhere else to go" they are not special in that regard. They have no more and no less claim on any other area of the earth's surface than any other South African community, be it Xhosa, Zulu or English-speaking white. As well might a Welsh person claim that because Welsh people have "nowhere else to go," Welsh people have to subjugate, dominate and oppress English people and Scottish people in preserving control of all Britain for fear that Welsh culture may be submerged by the non-Welsh majority. It is a nonsensical argument, and its basic premise is not even true. Afrikaners who do not accept all the implications of living on the African continent and of accepting the reality of a black majority are no more prohibited than any other South Africans from emigrating to Argentina, Uruguay, Paraguay or anywhere else. If a minority can only preserve its culture by opressing the majority in a common country, that minority culture has no moral right to exist in that country.

The Nationalists regard all criticism of apartheid as a demand for "one-person-one-vote," which will inevitably mean black majority rule, a lowering of standards and vengeful actions against the white minority by the black rulers. They see this demand as communist-inspired, with the aim of securing the Cape sea route and all South Africa's valuable strategic minerals for the Eastern bloc.

The world community has tried for thirty years to persuade Nationalist Afrikanerdom to seek a realistic accommodation with the black majority in South Africa. For most of those thirty years there was no insistence on one-person-one-vote. And for generations not even the blacks insisted on it. Even recently some significant reforms away from racism, short of universal franchise, would have been welcomed by large numbers of blacks. But throughout this time Nationalism has refused to budge an inch from apartheid, using a one-person-one-vote alternative as an excuse. Today one-person-one-vote is only the least of the demands by blacks. They also want a significant redistribution of land and a fairer sharing of the wealth of the land.

Whether universal franchise in South Africa would inevitably lead to a lowering of standards is open to debate – a debate of interest only to whites – and so is the assumption that it would cause vengeful actions against the white minority by blacks. Again, these are not the most relevant considerations in the entire moral issue. It is not beyond the capabilities of delegates of goodwill, black or white, to negotiate a fair deal for all concerned with reasonable safeguards for the white minority. As to the Nationalist Government's claim to be a bastion for the West against communism, such a "bastion" is a disaster and an embarrassment to the West, and must be a source of relish to the East. The West has already lost considerable credibility in Africa because it has not been as hostile to the Pretoria regime as the East has been, regardless of whatever cynical motives the latter might have for such hostility. If the West does not oppose the apartheid regime more positively it will soon provoke the enmity of all of black Africa.

As to the Cape sea route, it is a medieval myth. There is no Cape sea route. There is a vast ocean between South Africa and Antarctica, and to call that a sea route is like calling the Atlantic a sea route. Where minerals are concerned, it is true that South Africa has these in abundance, but if the whole world can be blackmailed on that score then one day some extremely radical black successors to the Nationalist regime may well turn such blackmail to their own account, against nations whose short-term priorities were unwise on this score.

The Nationalists maintain that the ideal system for South Africa is "separate development" – the balkanization of the country into ethnic territories which become autonomous and fully independent nation-states protecting the identity of each ethnic group. Territorial apartheid, or "separate development," is a sham. Thirteen percent of the territory is allotted to 85 percent of the people, with that 13 percent of the territory fragmented among eight "ethnic groups." It is a transparent method of "divide and rule." It has no moral justification. There is more in common between, say, Zulu and Xhosa, culturally, linguistically, ethnically and politically, than between English-speaking and Afrikaans-speaking whites, who are regarded as one "ethnic unit" for political purposes. In May 1976, Transkei was granted "independence." Bophuthatswana's was granted on December 6, 1977. But so strong are the fiscal apron-strings securing these "Bantustans" to Pretoria that they literally could not afford to exercise full independence.

The main indictment against the Bantustans is that black South Africa has never been permitted to exercise a choice on the matter by vote or referendum. The Bantustans were ordained in Pretoria, by whites, and most blacks of real political consequence see the concept for what it is – an obvious attempt to avoid accommodating blacks politically and geographically.

The claim by the Nationalist Government that its motives are morally sound because the Afrikaner people are deeply committed to Christian principles is false. Their version of Christianity, which justifies apartheid, is rejected by leaders and theologians of all the major Christian sects – and the Nationalists know it. In fact, the Nationalist policy of apartheid can be said to contravene all ten of the Ten Commandments.

The First Commandment, "You shall have no other gods before me," is contravened by the essence of apartheid, which is to elevate the concept of racial purity above all other concepts including the Christian concept of "Do unto others as you would be done by" (and, incidentally, that same concept as enshrined in Judaism and Islam). In South Africa, ministers of religion who point this out are accused by the regime of "dragging religion into politics" and "meddling in matters beyond the preaching of the Gospel."

The Second Commandment, "You shall not take the name of God in vain," is contravened by frequent Nationalist claims that apartheid is God-ordained and is authorized in the Bible. Some Nationalists have even sought to justify apartheid by saying the Bible records that blacks, as the descendants of Ham, are condemned to be "hewers of wood and drawers of water" – the ready-made, perpetual servant class.

The Third Commandment, "Keep the Sabbath day holy," is surely contravened by legislation for separate church congregations under apartheid's "group areas" statutes, and the number of times Nationalist churchmen have used the Sabbath to preach race politics.

The Fourth Commandment, "Honor your father and your mother," is contravened by legislation for a migrant labor system which separates the mothers and fathers of millions and makes it a crime for a wife to join her husband, if he is black, and if he does not have special dispensation to be near a white urban area.

The Fifth Commandment, "You shall not kill," is contravened not only by the most obvious instances of political killing – such as in the case of Steve Biko and forty-four other detainees – but surely forbids also the killing of the spirit that is implicit in the degrading pass laws and population registration provisions necessitating racial classification.

The Sixth and Ninth Commandments, referring to adultery and coveting of one's neighbor's wife, are surely apposite to a migrant labor system which leads to the break-up of families and married couples. Black male workers are housed in "dormitories" and "hostels" in the urban areas far from their wives and families.

The Seventh and Tenth Commandments, forbidding theft and the coveting of the goods of others, are surely apposite to land confiscation for political purposes. Indian and Chinese businessmen, in particular, have suffered eviction from "white" business districts under "group areas" legislation.

And finally, the Commandment against "bearing false witness" is one of the mostly grossly contravened of all in South Africa by the Nationalist government. To imprison a person without charge, without evidence, without prosecution or trial of any kind and then to brand him by all manner of accusations, giving him no chance to defend himself, is surely bearing the most false witness possible against a human being. In Steve Biko's case false witness was borne against him even after his death, with attempts by Minister Kruger and his Security Police to smear his name by allegations of crimes they never confronted him with in public during his lifetime.

As recently as December 1977 Premier Vorster told an American television interviewer that no citizen is ever banned simply for opposing the government. Since I, for one, was banned for precisely that, I know Vorster's statement to be a lie.

To suggest that apartheid is not only unsanctioned by religious considerations but actually contravenes all ten of the Ten Commandments is not all. It is a general affront to all the major principles of religion known to man in that it is based on the total opposite of love. Love implies closeness, and a wish for unity. Enforced racial separation implies a rejection, a distancing-off of fellow humans who happen to have different skin pigmentation. The Nationalist claim to religious motivation is therefore a mockery of all religious values.

It is claimed that South Africa's blacks have a higher standard of living than blacks elsewhere in Africa; that foreign blacks stream into South Africa for employment; and that white enterprise has built South Africa up into the position of Africa's most modern industrial state, with impressive agricultural and mineral development.

South Africa happens to be the most richly endowed country in Africa with mineral, agricultural and natural wealth, a moderate climate and a more highly developed infrastructure bequeathed to it by the colonial power than was bequeathed to any other African state. What is of basic concern to blacks in South Africa is the position of blacks in South Africa vis-a-vis the white privileged people in South Africa. And the main argument is over civil rights in South Africa, not comparative standards of living elsewhere.

The same reply applies to Nationalist boasts that blacks come from neighboring territories to work in the South African mines. That is because the mines are where the minerals are, and the minerals are in South Africa. This is no answer to the question of why black South Africans are denied basic human rights.

The argument that whites built up South Africa and developed it into its present preeminence as a modern industrial state is also invalid, for not one single building or factory or house in South Africa was ever built without black labor – and cheap black labor, at that, in most cases. Nationalists often point out that whites pay most of the taxes in South Africa. This is a farcical claim, because Nationalists passed the legislation that prevented blacks from doing certain categories of skilled work, from receiving higher education in proper universities and from thus achieving the earning capacities of most whites, upon which tax assessment is based. To prevent people from being able to earn enough to pay high taxes, then to deny them rights because they don't pay high taxes, is the height of absurdity. For decades the entire social structure in South Africa has been designed to keep blacks politically and economically backward – and one of the Nationalist's main excuses for withholding equal rights from blacks is that they are politically and economically backward.

The claim that there are still enormous reserves of interracial good-will in South Africa is no longer true. Today most blacks have feelings toward most whites which vary from resentment to deep hatred. Unless the

Nationalists can be compelled, soon, to the negotiating table to discuss and implement significant concessions granting at least minimal democratic rights to blacks, there will inevitably be racial war in South Africa. Indeed, it has already begun. This crisis is in a most dangerous flash point which could touch off the most elemental partisanship on a continental scale. How can South Africa claim she is not a threat to world peace? How can the world dare decline to involve itself with the issues being disputed there?

It sounds reasonable to say that "South African problems should be solved by South Africans" with the obvious corollary that outsiders should not interfere; that the world should stand back and leave the conflict here to South Africa only. The world cannot afford that lunatic luxury. What is disputed here is not purely a South African issue – it is an issue which touches all people everywhere. It is the question of whether discrimination by law based on skin pigmentation is acceptable or not, and this question is the concern of every person everywhere because every person has some color of skin. Two-thirds of the people of the world are "colored" or, to use the insultingly arrogant phrase, "non-white." Therefore what is done to people of color here is a deep form of affront to people of color everywhere. And that it is done by whites here makes it the concern of whites everywhere.

It is the most contentious moral crisis in the world today, and those who refuse to interest or involve themselves in it are giving tacit approval to it. No human being of conscience can remain neutral in a moral crisis of conscience. Apartheid exists in defiance of this and this is why, today, it has now become a real threat to world peace.

As to the claim that South Africa has a free press, let the assurance be recorded here by at least one South African newspaper editor that whatever tenuous claims in this regard might have been valid before October 19, 1977, the validity of such claims expired beyond all doubt with the detention of Percy Qoboza, editor of *The World*, and with my own banning. Percy and I were punished and silenced without charge or trial, simply because of what our newspapers represented – the aspirations of black South Africans for a fair deal.

It is true that before that date some South African newspapers were able to publish the most trenchant criticisms of the Nationalist regime and of apartheid. Since that date this is no longer true. No South African editor can now be sure of what will happen to him if he annoys the authorities beyond a certain point – and that point is growing ever nearer the point of Nationalist preference. There were enough constraints upon editors before. We had to contend with more than twenty laws governing what could or could not be printed, and in recent years newspaper laws were passed which severely narrowed the boundaries within which we could attack apartheid. But we knew those boundaries. We knew how far we could go. However, on October 19, 1977, those boundaries were abolished, and the apartheid state took another giant step toward the enforcement of full conformity.

As to the commitment made three years ago in the United Nations by Ambassador Roelof Botha, that South Africa would move away from racial discrimination, this was a calculated piece of deception. What Botha meant was that apartheid would be abolished, but the discrimination would henceforth be based on "ethnic nationhood" rather than mere skin color. Laws would not discriminate against blacks, as such, but against Xhosa "nationals" of the Xhosa "nation" and Zulu "nationals" of the Zulu "nation" and so forth, all of whom happen to be black. This is why the new Nationalist catchword is "multi-nationalist" and the latest government line is to speak not of the races of South Africa but of the "nations" of South Africa.

While it is true that some token concessions in the field of sport and hotel admission took place in the last few years, these were of so grudging and minimal a nature and extent that they did not amount to significant reforms.

The Vorster government points with pride to the country's record of political stability and contrasts this with the instability of black-ruled states, citing with particular glee the tyrannical regimes of Amin and Bokassa, which do not have the South African tradition of impartial courts with their high caliber of judiciary. If political stability means long tenure of office, then Africa has rather a good record in this respect. Men like Kaunda, Nyerere, Kenyatta, Seretse Khama, Mobutu and others have led their states for more than a decade.

In these terms, Nationalist rule for thirty years is certainly evidence of "stability." But in South Africa's case it is the stability of entrenched authoritarianism, with voting dice loaded against even the acceptable white opposition since 1948, and with a mass of measures to bolster and buttress Nationalist rule. Yet in spite of these artificial aids, South African "stability" is a brittle illusion. The country could explode into total racial war at any time. One small incident could spark this off, and while the regime has in the past managed to contain uprisings in localized areas by rushing police reinforcements to these areas, it has never yet had to contend with a general uprising of blacks all over the country at once. It is purely a matter of time before this happens, unless the regime can be brought to its senses and to the negotiating table.

Additional pluses in the pro-Nationalist argument could be the great personal charm and courtesy of the Afrikaner people, the friendliness and hospitality of South African whites generally, and the sincere belief by the majority of whites that politically they are doing the right thing in the interests of all race groups. As a political journalist and editor, I have had many dealings with Nationalist cabinet ministers. These men are not monsters. Their basic instincts are to be liked and understood and this tends to make them friendly and outgoing. The personal charm of the Afrikaner, and indeed of all the people of South Africa, makes the tragic circumstances of the country all the more heartrending. That in the midst of so much scenic beauty, so much mineral wealth, and such excellent human material, there should be such hatred and tension only heightens the sense of tragedy.

The Nationalist government of South Africa believes that it represents the most advanced, the most civilized and the most developed country in Africa and that its long tradition of orderly government should be recognized by the world at large. It resents what it regards as the "double standards" applied by the world – for example in appearing to condemn apartheid more than the gross excesses of the Amin regime. It asks that it should be treated as the government of any African country is treated in international dealings, and that South Africa should be judged by the same standard as any other African country.

But Mr. Vorster's regime cannot have it both ways. Uganda has come into international disrepute only in comparatively recent times, since Amin's accession to power. But the Nationalist regime has been in power for thirty years. Under no less than four successive Nationalist premiers – Malan, Strijdom, Verwoerd, and Vorster – it has displayed a consistency of systematic repression that gives it a start of many years in the earning of international disrepute. The Ugandans know they are ruled by a maniac – but no Nationalist has ever claimed that Malan, Strijdom, Verwoerd or Vorster were maniacs. There are literally hundreds of apartheid laws which have been enacted since 1948, and they have been approved by many thousands of party delegates – none of them maniacs!

Apartheid is a carefully calculated, meticulously planned network of racist laws whose viciousness is equalled only by the deliberation of the process which gave birth to each one of them. The Vorster government should not boast of South Africa's long tradition of parliamentary law-making. The fact of that tradition does not mitigate apartheid; it condemns it all the more.

Nor should the fact of industrial development be cited as cause for higher esteem. This fact, too, diminishes any excuse for the policy of apartheid. The Nationalists inherited in 1948 one of the most richly endowed countries on the face of the earth, a country highly regarded internationally (its premier, Smuts, drafted the preamble to the Charter of the United Nations and played a leading role in the formation of the UN and in the Second World War put into the field against Hitler the largest volunteer army in the world.)

Nationalist Foreign Minister Botha appeals for support from Britain and America on the grounds that "we fought with you in World War Two" – a statement of crass hypocrisy since his Nationalist Party not only supported Hitler but opposed the Allied war effort of the South African Army to the hilt. Extreme members, like present Premier B. J. Vorster, actually held office in the subversive organization, the Ossewa Brandwag, which favored the cause of National Socialism against the principles of the western democracies.

Having taken over government of this richly-endowed internationally-honored state, the Nationalists have in thirty years plunged it into the position of an international outcast, a pariah, whose policies are deservedly loathed by the entire world community.

The Nationalist government then, must not wonder why it is hated not only by most people everywhere but also by most of its own citizens. Nor must it ask to be judged by the same standard as any other African State. Nor must it claim any special consideration for unmerited endowment not conferred on any other African State.

The Nationalist government asks for special consideration on the basis of its claim that "South Africa's problems are unique." But South Africa's "problems" are not unique. A multi-racial society, handled with goodwill and honesty, is not a problem.

South Africa has only one major "problem," and that is apartheid. And apartheid is certainly unique. It draws down upon itself the most uniquely unanimous censure of humanity in all recorded history.

In an already imperfect world, the Nationalists have achieved a degree of imperfection that stands out beyond any previous affront to human liberty.

This world has known tyranny before. The tyranny of the early militarists, such as Genghis Khan and Attila. The tyranny of Stalin's purges. The tyranny of Hitler, which was authoritarian, based on race and aimed at an oppressed minority.

And now the tyranny of apartheid – it is authoritarian, based on race, and aimed at a large majority.

Moreover, it persists three decades after mankind set its face resolutely against legislative racism and is promoted by a community which has had every educational and material advantage conceivable.

The Nationalists would reply that it is scandalous to equate the evils of apartheid in any way with the Hitler excesses under which millions of people were deliberately executed, and it is true that no Nationalist regime has ever been guilty of such premeditated physical murder on any scale. But they have committed spiritual murder, in a variety of refined ways, upon tens of millions of black South Africans since apartheid was codified in 1948.

They have waged brutal war on the human spirit against victims whose "crime" was to be born a certain skin color. The destruction of human potential in these thirty years, through discrimination in education, health services, employment laws, living conditions and environment, staggers the imagination.

One of the final claims made in its favor by the Nationalist government is that South Africa has a fair system of administration and justice and an independent judiciary. This claim, also, is no longer true. The Nationalists have finally destroyed the entire basis of the system of law inherited in 1948 from the Roman-Dutch legal tradition. All that is left is a tiny vestige of that once-proud legal tradition.

It is true that any South African citizen can still win a civil or criminal case – provided one has a great deal of money; one has the right judge and magistrate; and one is free to institute such proceedings. Today there are few independent judges or magistrates in South Africa where political cases are concerned. For example, most of the Transvaal Supreme Court judges are members of the Broederbond, Nationalism's elite inner circle of party elders. The State simply will not prosecute political wrongdoers if they are Nationalist supporters. Police investigation of such matters are perfunctory and token – certainly not designed to secure a prosecution and conviction. The result is that acts of right-wing terrorism against critics of the regime are tacitly, and sometimes explicitly, encouraged.

Several years ago students of the University of Cape Town held a peaceful protest on the steps of St. George's Cathedral against a government measure. Uniformed policemen formed up and charged them, assaulting them with batons and fists, and pursued some of them into the church to assault them there. Prime Minister Vorster's comment was that he was proud of "his police." "If they had acted any differently I would have been disappointed in them," he said publicly.

Police, magistrates, judges, prosecutors, few indeed are completely free to pursue objective standards of justice. Most judges in South Africa adhere to the belief that their function in regard to statute law is solely to interpret and apply it – which means in effect, in many cases, to implement apartheid regardless of the principles of justice.

Some statutes have removed the onus from the state of proving an accused person guilty. This legislation has also facilitated the bypassing of courts, giving a politician (the Minister of Justice and Police) the power to put people in jail or to ban them without any trial or judicial proceedings whatever. In all the thirty years of such legislation only one judge has spoken out in protest – Mr. Justice Kowie Marais, now a Progressive Federal Party Member of Parliament.

The question may be asked: how can such a regime, so hated by most of its citizens, have ruled for thirty years with every indication of steadily increasing power? The answer lies in the methods by which the Nationalist regime has consolidated its position since coming to power in 1948. Up until that year, Smuts's United Party was in power. Although that party had a record of racism, there were indications of a liberalizing general tendency within it. The speeches of Smuts's obvious heir-apparent, the brilliant Jan Hofmeyr, clearly indicated an intent to seek a fairer accommodation with blacks in the post-war years.

The Nationalists won a narrow victory by exploiting white fear of the Hofmeyr line, and by persuading enough white voters that their identity as a race group could only be protected by a Nationalist government applying what is called "apartheid" (separateness). Their win was by a slender margin of rural seats. In fact the overall vote-aggregate went against them, so that in respect of all votes registered they were a minority government.

Once in power they moved purposefully to entrench themselves. First they created six additional seats (all Nationalist) by creating six tiny constituencies of barely a couple of thousand voters each, for South West Africa, which had never previously been represented in the South African Parliament. Then they enlarged the Senate unconstitutionally, appointing dozens of party members as additional senators. This gave them a two-thirds majority of the upper and lower house combined, which meant they could amend the constitution. They did so in order to take the vote away from "coloured" voters whose votes were decisive in almost a dozen seats.

Then they passed bills removing from parliament even the white representatives of black and "coloured" voters. Then they redrew the boundaries of the voting districts to favor Nationalist constituencies, and loaded the rural (Nationalist) constituencies to such an extent that in future elections for Parliament a Nationalist vote was worth almost two anti-Nationalist votes.

The opposition challenged several of these measures in the courts, but the Nationalists overcame that by appointing their own judges to the highest court of appeal, which ruled parliamentary statutes to be irreversible. Before appointing their own judges to the appeal court, the Nationalists had passed a statute called the High Court of Parliament Act, which created the farcical situation whereby if the National Party's laws were ruled unconstitutional by the appeal court, parliament could convert itself into a higher court, with the party officials and members of the caucus sitting as judges.

The Nationalists then took over full control of radio broadcasting, and converted the state-run South African Broadcasting Corporation into a propaganda medium for the National Party. A daily program, "Survey of Current Affairs," relentlessly plugged the Nationalist line, and even news broadcasts were slanted to project the Nationalist interpretation through a combination of wording, emphasis or omission. News reflecting adversely on the regime was either left out of the bulletins entirely or "doctored" to give the party angle. The general impression promoted by South African radio was, and is, that to be anti-Nationalist is to be unpatriotic – "un-South African."

When television was introduced in early 1976 it soon became obvious that this was to be an even more powerful propaganda medium. In the months leading up to the 1977 general election, almost every telecast featured a Nationalist spokesman, usually in the guise of a cabinet minister, "explaining" some aspect of state policy or answering "questions" on which he was well-briefed beforehand, if he had not actually drafted them.

Opposition viewpoints were given only token projection, and black viewpoints virtually none at all.

School syllabuses were rewritten, school histories reshaped, and a different system of education for blacks, called "Bantu Education," was designed. It was designed, in the words of Dr. Verwoerd, to equip the "Bantu" for a set of expectations in keeping with the "Bantu role" in South Africa. It was, quite simply, education of an inferior grade designed to keep black aspirations sufficiently low for white political convenience. As blacks described it, it was "education for serfdom."

To strengthen Afrikaans "identity" and to keep Afrikaans youth from the liberalizing influences of English-speaking youth, all youth movements and service movements were duplicated. Afrikaners were encouraged to join not the Chamber of Commerce but the Sake Kamer; not Rotary or Round Table but Rapportryers; not Red Cross but Noodhulpliga; not the Boy Scouts but the Voortrekkers.

Legislation in Transvaal province compelled children of Afrikaans parentage to attend Afrikaans schools – the parents had no choice. Afrikaans universities received immense state grants and Afrikaans newspapers rich government printing contracts. Afrikaans trade and industry received similar state assistance, and Afrikaners were given all key posts in the Civil Service. Army, Navy and Air Force trainees were given lectures emphasizing the Nationalist view of politico-military issues and cadet programs in schools followed suit.

Today, therefore, white South Africa is largely a brain-washed society. Thirty years of Nationalist radio, military and school propaganda have done their work. Only a few English-language newspapers fight vigorously against this trend, but their wings are increasingly being clipped by threats of even stronger newspaper legislation and by intimidation such as the detention and banning of editors and reporters.

Among the whites, the voices of reason are steadily being choked into silence. There is a growing sense of conformity. University students, even on the English-language university campuses, are markedly more conservative then they were a decade ago.

The election result of November 30, 1977, illustrated all too clearly the almost complete success of decades of Nationalist propaganda as far as white South Africa is concerned. Only in a few metropolitan pockets are there still significant numbers of liberal white voters.

White South Africa is being placed on a war footing. Speeches by cabinet ministers and military chiefs, and even by many school principals and cadet masters, are all on the same theme: whites must prepare to fight "terrorism" and "communism." The enemy is seen to be everywhere – on the borders, within the borders, throughout South Africa, throughout the world, in the United Nations, in the rural areas, in the townships. The threat comes from the East. The threat comes from the West. The threat comes from the North. The threat is even anticipated from the South – which is all ocean until Antarctica.

The war psychosis rages. And the majority of the whites respond to it.

Inferior education, poverty and the successful silencing of radical black leaders as well as difficult general circumstances have made it virtually impossible for blacks to organize a significant, rational political response to Nationalist rule. One township of 180,000 blacks, Mdantsane, had for ten years exactly one telephone. Moreover, the townships, the black "universities," the schools and the rural areas are riddled with police informers. Any attempt to organize normal political resistance to apartheid's abnormalities is soon identified and stamped out.

That is why Steve Biko and his associates realized that for any meaningful black political response to evolve, short of violence, a political association of blacks would have to concentrate on an initial enlightening program to remove negative or inferiority complexes; operate within the law to survive; and appeal to black youth in the hope that the new generation would meet the challenge of apartheid more successfully than the old generation had.

The Nationalist government was right in seeing Steve Biko as a threat to apartheid, but it was tragically wrong in the method it chose in response to this threat. Wrong both for its own sake and for the sake of all whites and blacks in South Africa, because Steve Biko represented, in my opinion, the last hope for a peaceful accommodation to resolve the growing South African race crisis.

If the Nationalists had allowed Steve Biko to operate unfettered, within the bounds of normal law, apartheid could have been negotiated out of existence within five years for the benefit of all South Africans of every race. Not only the blacks, but the Afrikaner Nationalists themselves, could have been liberated from the crippling fears which imprison them within the laager they have erected.

In killing Steve Biko, and in condoning his killing, they have forced black resistance to apartheid into dark and violent channels. They have rendered it almost impossible to ensure that when apartheid goes it will be removed in an atmosphere of political and social stability in which all citizens could look to the future with confidence.

A new generation of blacks is rising. It looks back to the past and sees the fates of would-be negotiators – Luthuli dead in banishment, Mandela imprisoned, Sobukwe ill in restriction and Biko in his grave. And it looks ahead with no interest in negotiation.

So the situation in South Africa today is one in which whites and blacks are gearing themselves up for war, and for war on many fronts. The war on the borders will undoubtedly escalate further. Already news bulletins on South African television are carrying occasional items reminiscent of the early days of the Rhodesian war, announcing "large numbers of terrorists killed and two members of the South African Defense Force."

Inevitably internal unrest will break out again – possibly with more general nationwide effect than in the 1976 riots, which were mostly confined to Soweto and Cape Town.

The white military and police forces are well-equipped, and backed by a white civilian population almost unanimously in their support, and a civil service dominated by dedicated Nationalists. White South Africa can certainly hold out to preserve apartheid against such onslaughts.

For a time.

Ultimately, however, they are up against the inexorable laws of arithmetic. They are massively outnumbered by blacks within their own boundaries, and the younger leaders of the black population are growing increasingly militant. They know that history is on their side. They know that the entire African continent is on their side. They know that world opinion is on their side, and they hope to see such theoretical sympathy converted into meaningful sanctions and if necessary an effective internationally backed blockade.

The world hesitates at the moment to impose sanctions, which some claim would "drive the whites further into the laager," but the world will be brought to the realization that whites are already in the laager and need no strengthening of the will to fight.

For many years I have believed that all hopes for peace in South Africa lay in internal developments and pressures. In common with many white liberals I tried my hardest to apply those pressures, to bring both parties to the negotiating table and to spread throughout the country the idea that calm, reason and logic could be made to prevail. We white liberals tried to convert our fellow-whites. We tried to convert not only anti-Nationalists, but the Afrikaner Nationalists themselves, to the view that reconciliation in a non-racist society was the answer. At the same time we tried to maintain our links with black leaders and the black masses, so that polarization could be avoided.

In retrospect, given the driving force of Afrikaner Nationalism and its powerful appeal to white racial fears of a black majority, this was an impossible task we set ourselves. We probably realized it throughout, but would not admit it to ourselves, being reluctant to accept that our fellow-whites would never be converted through peaceful means to a higher, less selfish, vision of the human spirit.

Thinking back now over all the years, and of all the white liberal leaders who tried to persuade their fellow-whites to perceive the only peaceful solution – Alan Paton, Peter Brown, Nadine Gordimer and many others – it appears at first to have been all for nothing. I think back to all the editorials I myself have written; all the speeches made all over the country for all these years; literally millions of words aimed against apartheid; and have to conclude that it all amounts now to a lifetime of futility as far as concrete political results are concerned. Yet I am sure we would all do the same all over again in those circumstances, even with little hope, knowing that at that stage of our country's history these things had to be said and done, these gestures made, this vision upheld.

But now that role is over. Circumstances in South Africa are such that there is neither time nor hope for the conversion of most of the whites away from racism, through argument and debate internally, before the tidal wave of black anger breaks. In South Africa today, virtually all of the middlemen – the would-be conciliators between white and black – have been silenced by banning or detention.

While there are still voices of reason, like Helen Suzman and Alan Paton, they are not being heeded by most blacks or most whites of political consequence – the latter because they are blindly following the Vorster line and the former because they have abandoned hope of white compromise.

The Progressive Federal Party has some excellent individuals, and blacks obviously prefer them to the Nationalists, but blacks are increasingly becoming cynical about the PFP's rejection of sanctions as a weapon against apartheid. They see the PFP as a party-political apostle of capitalism which puts capital interest rates above black interests. In this way, the gray areas in South African political life are being washed away and the scene is increasingly being deep-etched in black and white.

The express train of white racism is now rushing at full speed on a collision course with the express train of black anger.

If the few concerned persons inside South Africa who reject apartheid can no longer do anything to avoid such a collision, what can a concerned world do to save the South Africans from themselves?

Before reply, this question warrants first an examination of the moral question – are national boundaries more sacred than serious issues of humanity? There can surely be little doubt that if the rest of the international community had been moved to "meddle" in a serious bid to divert Hitler from his evil course as early as the mid-1930s, millions of lives could have been saved and a world war avoided.

Instead, Hitler's excesses were met with tactful diplomatic words designed to preserve "dialogue." Clearly, there are times when the preservation of futile "dialogue" is counter-productive. When Hitler sent in his troops to occupy the Ruhr, they had orders that if a single French defender fired a shot they were to retreat across the border bridges and withdraw from the exercise. Not a shot was fired, and this "tactful" nonresponse brought the holocaust nearer.

It is my belief that there are no national boundaries when the welfare of the family of man is grossly assaulted.

If the world had spoken with one clear voice in defense of those Jews of Germany in the 1930s, there would have been no extermination camps – but only if those words had been backed up by deeds, and progressively by selective sanctions, and ultimately by total boycott reinforced by blockade if necessary.

The same applies to Uganda and South Africa or any other repressive regime, whether communist or fascist or socialist or capitalist or black or white. In the case of Uganda and South Africa the issues have been clearly and sharply defined for a long time, and the victims of authoritarian evil are easily identifiable – nothing is more identifiable than a majority!

And if a majority of a nation's citizens can clearly be perceived to be under serious persecution or oppression or discrimination, and to be vehemently objecting to this, how can their brothers in the international community fail to respond to their plight?

In such a case there is not only a right to "meddle" – there is a positive duty. But it is the precise form of intervention that has to be carefully considered.

In South Africa's case, for the sake of whites as well as blacks, Afrikaners as well as English-speaking, "coloureds" as well as "Indians," international intervention should be constructively positive. Given that no development within the country itself can avert violence and bloodshed, and that only external intervention can do so, it follows that such intervention should be constructive both in its method and in its intent.

That intent should be to achieve the goal of compelling all the real leaders of all the groups in South Africa to come to the negotiating table before their followers start killing each other on a large scale.

Ideally, the route to this goal of peace should be equally peaceful. But this goal cannot be attained with words alone. Words, international words of censure and condemnation, have been raining down on South Africa for thirty years, with virtually no effect.

Therefore, henceforth the mouths that utter these words must have teeth – teeth that can bite. And they must be prepared to bite. And they must bite if necessary. The only peaceful yet effective means of compelling the Pretoria regime to see reason and to meet in honest negotiation with the chosen leaders of the majority of their citizens is the employment of all the strongest pressures that can be brought to bear short of war.

There are many pressure points that can be applied in many fields, economic, diplomatic, strategic, financial and social. And they all add up to one word – ostracism. There has been a belief for many years that ostracism is a negative and destructive process, and this may well be so in certain contexts, but not where the Nationalist government is concerned.

Indeed, for many years I myself opposed the breaking of international links with South African associations – especially in the sphere of sport – until I was proved wrong by a young fellow-South African named Peter Hain, who organized anti-apartheid demonstrations in Britain. As recently as 1970 I pleaded for the retention of sporting ties with South Africa on the grounds that white South Africans could better be converted away from apartheid in sport by sporting friends abroad who built bridges of friendship through sports tours and were an educational influence. I argued, if South African sports people were ostracized this would drive them further away from reason and would confirm them in their prejudices in isolation.

Such links were preserved for many years, and the result was that apartheid persisted in South African sport. The white South Africans regarded the continuing tours from abroad as evidence that their approach was still acceptable in the world, that they were still approved of in spite of apartheid.

Then Peter Hain's campaigns, and those of other South African exiles like Dennis Brutus and Chris de Broglio, began to take effect and South African participants were increasingly ostracized from the Olympic Games, international cricket, and from some of the leading rugby countries. The result was marked. There was an immediate softening of apartheid in sport in South Africa, and although token integration of South African sport is still too minimal to be significant, the lesson is plain.

The same happened in the international monetary sphere. As soon as the gold price was pushed down by the Americans, the Pretoria regime grew more reasonable on a number of issues such as Rhodesia and South West Africa.

Opponents of international pressure often argue that such pressure will have adverse effects in South Africa; that it will drive the whites into the laager and make them more intransigent.

Not so. They are already in the laager. Mr. Vorster's recent election campaign was geared almost exclusively toward giving the world the message from white South Africa: "Do your worst!" There is really no alternative that the Vorster government has left the anti-apartheid world. He and his predecessors have proved that they regard "friendly advice" from abroad, unbacked by strong action, as weakness and condonation of their policies.

Has the time not come to take Mr. Vorster at his word?

For the sake of the majority of South Africans, that time has surely come. Indeed for the sake of the white minority as well, because the alternative, war, is in Vorster's own words "too ghastly to contemplate."

One of the most telling forms of ostracism of the Pretoria regime would be diplomatic ostracism – the closure of embassies, or at least the downgrading of diplomatic links to token status – and a much tougher policy on the granting of visas. The South African government has for years most improperly abused the right of withdrawing passports from its critics within its own population as a punishment. It should now be given its own medicine.

Predictable reaction to such proposals will be that they are too drastic, or "unrealistic," or against the interests of the world communities themselves in view of mutual trade consideration. Countries which adopt that attitude are taking a short-term view which could adversely affect their long-term interests vis-a-vis South Africa under a future black government. Above all, they are betraying a callous indifference to the present plight of black South Africans.

Apartheid is not simply a regrettable localized aberration of importance only to South Africa. It is a universal moral crisis and no nation can in conscience stand back and adopt a neutral or passive attitude to it. Apartheid is an affront to every single member of the family of mankind.

Apartheid is therefore a challenge to every citizen of every country on earth. It is a challenge that should be met with all the ingenuity and idealism of which all people of principle are capable.

If I could speak to every person on this globe, I would speak of my friend Steve Biko, who died naked on the floor of a prison cell after suffering torture and torment at the hands of men who represent an especially horrible form of evil – the evil of racism, which inflicts hatred and rejection upon its victims for being born with a dark skin. I would tell of how the society that bred such a system then exonerated his killers, condoned the laughter with which their superiors greeted the news of his death, and voted the man chiefly responsible for it back into office with an increased majority.

I would tell of how Steve Biko's death, although especially tragic for me, was by no means the first of its kind in South Africa, nor the last, and that it was but the most publicized, most heightened dramatization of the ultimate effect of unbridled apartheid.

Steve Biko's death could be regarded as a symbolic representation of the sufferings of all black South Africans under the apartheid system. His death was physical. Most of the deaths caused by apartheid are spiritual. There are countless deaths of morale and hope and self-esteem.

For many of his fellow-citizens, Steve Biko ended such deaths of morale. He shattered many of the psychological bonds that used to shackle young blacks in South Africa. In terms of the spiritual self-esteem of young blacks in South Africa, particularly, he was a breaker of chains.

Perhaps that, far more than any other, was the reason why the System killed him.

In concluding this Indictment, in calling for his killers to be brought to justice, I feel I must seek to imagine how he would want this to be done. It is probable that he would not want them simply to be identified as James Kruger and his Security officers who happened to be stationed in the city of Port Elizabeth during the month of September 1977. It is probable that he would regard his real killers as all the people who support the Nationalist Government of South Africa and its policy of apartheid.

It is also probable that he would not want them punished in a retributive or vengeful sense, but rather compelled for their own sake to perceive the enormity of their crime against his people. In other words, ideally, to be brought to justice by being brought to their senses and thereby enabled to enter into the inheritance of a fullness of life for themselves and for their children in the kind of South Africa he foresaw and worked to bring into being.

This indictment, having listed the evils of the apartheid system as charges against the accused protagonists of that system, having listed also and replied to each of their arguments in mitigation as expounded by their own leaders, must end with a call to all who accept its conclusions for purposes of effective prosecution.

Help to finish the work of Steve Biko. Help to smash the remaining links of the chains he broke, and let the sound of this work echo around the world so that chains may be broken wherever they hold in bondage the bodies and minds of men.

INDEX

B
B

Biko, Bantu Stephen

Withdrawn

2 19
3
8 7

79-79

DATE DUE		
MAR 5 1981		
MAR 2 0 1981		
MAR 1 5 1984		